The Educational Philosophy
of Martin Buber

SARA F. YOSELOFF MEMORIAL PUBLICATIONS
In Judaism and Jewish Affairs

This volume is one in a series established in memory
of Sara F. Yoseloff,
who devoted her life to the making of books.

The Educational Philosophy of Martin Buber

Adir Cohen

Rutherford ● Madison ● Teaneck
Fairleigh Dickinson University Press
London and Toronto ● Associated University Presses

© 1983 by Associated University Presses, Inc.

Associated University Presses, Inc.
4 Cornwall Drive
East Brunswick, N.J. 08816

Associated University Presses Ltd
27 Chancery Lane
London WC2A INF, England

Associated University Presses
2133 Royal Windsor Drive
Unit 1
Mississauga, Ontario, L5J 1K5, Canada

Library of Congress Cataloging in Publication Data

Cohen, Adir.
    The educational philosophy of Martin Buber.

    Bibliography: p.
    Includes index.
    1. Buber, Martin, 1878–1965.   2. Education—Philosophy.
I. Title.
LB775.B7493C62   1983   370'.1   81-68084
ISBN 0-8386-3098-7

Printed in the United States of America

Contents

Acknowledgments

Thanks are due to the editors of the following publications for permission to republish essays, some of which appear here in their original form, and others of which have been revised and elaborated before inclusion in this book.

Chapter 1 appeared as "Martin Buber and Changes in Modern Education" in *Oxford Review of Education,* vol. 5, no. 1, 1979.

Chapter 2 appeared as "The Question of Values and Value Education in the Philosophy of Martin Buber" in *Teachers College Record,* vol. 80, no. 4, 1979.

Chapter 3 appeared as "Society and Social Education in the Philosophy of Martin Buber" in *Educational Studies,* vol. 10, no. 4, 1980.

Chapter 8 appeared as "Aesthetics and Aesthetic Education in Martin Buber's Thought" in *The Journal of Aesthetic Education,* vol. 14, no. 1, 1980.

Introduction

Martin Buber's mind ranged wide and inclined him no less to creative and practical activity than to theoretical speculation. His restless intellect left its mark on an impressive variety of disciplines. Anthropological philosophy and theology, sociology, and Zionism all fell within his scope. Buber was as much occupied with the problems of government as he was with the study of culture. His contributions to biblical scholarship have deepened our appreciation of the Hebrew Scriptures. His investigation of Hasidism has added significantly to our understanding of that movement and has revived our interest in Hasidic narrative. Our pleasure in the arts of literature and drama has been enriched by his explorations of aesthetic experience. And finally, with regard to the subject matter of this book, we owe a novel concept of the educator to Buber's philosophy of education.

Each of the fields to which Buber contributed is stamped by the impress of his remarkable personality and bears the unique seal of his philosophy of man. Everything Buber wrote and did was a call to dialogue demanding of each of us receptive and profound personal engagement in the quest for our existential confirmation in the existence of our fellow man. Both the man and his work challenge us to assume responsibility and enact the relation of *I-Thou* with mankind, the world, and the Absolute.

At a time when scholars and scientists confine themselves to ever narrowing fields of specialization, Buber deviates from the accepted pattern in the learned world. His exceptional scope has inspired more anxiety than admiration among the technocrats of learning, and his audacious encroachments on so many of their terrains have opened Buber up to the charge of having dissipated his intellectual energies and courted superficiality. However, Buber's sweep deserves better than to be thought of as stemming from the prodigal use of his mental powers; it derives from the response of an integrated personality to dialogic encounter. Having all of his life hearkened to the call addressed to him by the Thou in man, society, and the universe, Buber could hardly have confined his thoughts to a modest compass. Moreover, fragmented and professionalized learning was a source of deep anxiety to Buber and represented for him scholarship set spiritually adrift: such atomized expertise seemed to him to deprive mankind and society of their spiritual core and to lead to their eventual enslavement to purely mechanical laws. Buber was convinced that authentic existence must be achieved through obedience to the will of the Spirit, whose command can be rightly understood only if we interpret it always with reference to the constant flux of actual circumstance.

It would, however, be a mistake to assume that Buber underrated the importance of rigorous scholarship or that he rejected the ways of science. He merely refused to regard these as the ultimate values and exclusive tools of learning. His attitude in this regard is illustrated by his remarks to Ben-Zion Dinur concerning the use of documents in teaching history: "The whole basis of my doubts is my well-founded fear that our exaggerated use of documentary sources may involve a concession by which we forfeit *man* in the interest of *things;* this concession is far more inclusive than might appear at first sight. . . . We should take care, especially at this time, to refrain from taking any action which is not directed at man; for *things* seem more important to their *makers*—sometimes even without their knowing or sensing this to be the case."[1]

Buber points out that the primary meaning of the word *yeda* or "knowledge" in Hebrew, as distinct from that of the words for knowledge in European languages, has to do with contact and relation. From the perspective of Jewish linguistic tradition, therefore, knowledge is achieved by intimate involvement with its object rather than by detached observation. This, at any rate, was Buber's mode of knowing. His relationship with all the disciplines upon which his scholarship touched was direct and unmediated, and he thought of each discipline as serving the interests of dialogic encounter with the Absolute Thou.

Whether Buber put his mind to the Bible or Hasidism, sociology or philosophy, art or political theory, his attitude remained unchanged. The Scriptures and Hasidic literature, for example, were to Buber more than historical documents: they were abidingly vital sources of wisdom, there to be drawn on by his contemporaries for practical guidance in coping with the severe spiritual trials they are experiencing in the present. Buber's approach to scholarship does contain a potential threat to the rules that are inherent in all learned disciplines and that order the conduct of the professional scholar toward his material. Yet however much Buber's personal vision may distort historical actuality and put into question his reliability as a scholar, his approach—especially to the materials of the Bible, Hasidism, and Israeli history—extends the spiritual significance of events, grants them immediacy, and helps us to perceive them from a wholly new perspective.

The scholarly and scientific bases of Buber's assumptions should nevertheless be treated with caution. It would indeed be difficult to deny the legitimacy of much of the criticism that has been leveled at Buber's scholarship. And Buber's theories on education have enjoyed no special immunity from attack. In discussing the various facets of Buber's philosophy of education I have made a conscious effort to give Buber's critics a fair chance to state their opinions. I have given special prominence to the criticisms of Gershom Scholem on Buber's interpretation of Hasidism, of Yehezkel Kaufmann on Buber's approach to the Bible, of Nathan Rotenstreich on the concept of *I-Thou,* of Karl Frankenstein on Buber's philosophy of dialogue and concept of psychology, and of Raphael Seligmann on Buber's attitudes toward political and national questions.[2] Buber's positions in respect of the last issues are still a subject of bitter controversy and continue to vex many political Zionists and Israeli national leaders. Buber's ideas on religion are no less a cause of controversy and to this day they draw fire from religious circles, whose views I have also made an effort to include.

It is undeniable that under the influence of his own philosophy Buber injected a spiritual content into the materials he was studying. In the interests of objective scholarship we could hardly do less than to bring him to account for the errors he committed because of his philosophical bias. Yet this bias (if we must call it such), however much we may attribute to it Buber's failings as a scholar, is an expression of a philosophy remarkable for its consistency and for the persuasive manner in which it selects and orders the elements of our experience. But to the educator, the most salient distinction of Buber's philosophy is its relevance to education today. For it points our way to the kind of education we should hope to see established: education no longer dedicated only to the transmission of information and the development of intellectual faculties but intent on fostering true dialogue.

Buber's approach to scholarship is too inclusive to be judged by the highly circumscribed standards of the precise disciplines. His Hasidic studies serve as a case in point. As we review the development of Buber's attitude toward the subject in the works that were written by him over a period exceeding forty years, we can observe his growing conviction that the real purpose of studying Hasidism cannot be fulfilled by the accumulation of historical data concerning the movement or by the aesthetic reshaping of its literature. As much as his published works may satisfy such interests, Buber's ultimate intention in studying Hasidism aimed rather higher: to reclaim the essential truth possessed by Hasidism in the days of its youthful vigor for his contemporaries, and thereby to restore to them their relation to the Absolute. The same principle governed Buber's attitude toward Judaism, Jewish nationalism, and Zionism. At no point in the half-century during which he contemplated the history and intellectual traditions of Judaism did Buber treat it as a subject for detached study. In all of his books, essays, oral communications, and addresses on Jewish subjects Buber was consistent in representing Judaism as a teaching that, throughout its long history, managed to preserve its essential nature unimpaired, while accommodating its outward form to the personalities of its exponents and the conditions of the moment.

This attitude of giving science and objective scholarship their due without submitting to their domination was also taken by Buber toward education and teaching. Buber believed that education has to be soundly anchored in science and to keep pace with its findings. He insisted, however, that education must also preserve its autonomy if it is to be a spiritual force of any consequence. And to fulfill that purpose education must become the medium through which the claims made on mankind by the times and by life itself—claims science largely neglects—make themselves heard.

Man, in communion with other men and God, was the central article of Buber's philosophy. In his life, too, Buber's commitment to humanity was complete. In a small volume of intimate recollections called *Pegishot (Encounters)* Buber tells us that had he in his youth been given a choice between people and books for his sole companions he would have favored the company of books. But as he matured his outlook underwent a change; in his adult years his attitude toward literature became one of admiration rather than love, whereas people seemed to him worthy of love rather than admiration: "When I emerged from my mother's womb I knew nothing of books, and then I found that I should die for want of them, even when another person's hand was in mine. But now when I shut the door of my study to give myself up to a book, I do so only because I need merely re-open the door in order for man to look in on me again."[3]

In his philosophy of education Buber tried to embrace the whole complex of man's relationship with his fellowman and with society, with creation, and with God. The task he sets for the educator is to teach the pupil to make a covenant with the world. Buber conceives of education as a process by which the pupil is made aware of the existence of a person on whom he can depend and whose confidence he can gain. The pupil begins his tutelage bemused by the world's complexity, unsettled by its disunity, frightened by its enormities, and his confidence in it shattered by its unreliability. He then comes to know that his teacher takes part in his life and acknowledges his unique humanity. The trust that the pupil acquires in this way for his teacher becomes a model for his trust in the world as well. For the pupil will learn to extend the confidence he has bestowed on his teacher to others who earn his trust and, eventually, to the world as well. The communion of pupil and teacher thus serves more than its own ends: in it the universal communion based on the relation of *I-Thou* is nurtured and fortified.

Buber did not think of himself as a professional teacher or educationalist. Ernst Simon recalls that when Buber was offered a chair in pedagogy by the Hebrew University he turned down the appointment on the grounds that he was more interested in the practical side of education than in its theoretical aspects.[4] It is a fact that Buber founded no educational movement, proposed no educational methodology, and expounded no theoretical precepts to which a teacher could resort for guidance in his work. Buber held that education must remain in constant and immediate touch with reality that is experienced by pupils. "Whatever is remote from the reality experienced by us and has no bearing on it, either directly or indirectly, can have no place in the [school] curriculum," Buber wrote, "and all of the subjects therein contained must be studied in such a way that the conclusions about our reality derived from them should result from the pupils' own mental exertions; for they must be taught to think for themselves."[5] Buber believed that only an education nourished by reality can guide man to assume the responsibility which the acts of realization and choice entail.

Just as Buber had refused a university chair in education so he declined the offer of the minister of Culture and Education in Israel, Ben-Zion Dinur, to take charge of the State Council of Culture in order to coordinate the Ministry's programs for adults. In justifying his decision Buber explained to Dinur:

> The whole enterprise of education [can be summarized in the Psalmist's words:] *Out of the depths have I cried out to thee*. We must arouse a man's thirst for culture, arouse the *de profundis* yearning of an individual to know and to think. This is the only sphere in which I have been active, in which I have tried to be effective. As for cultural activity on behalf of the *general* public, I am in favor of it only if such an enterprise arises out of a situation of "And one cried out to another, and said [Is. 6:3]"; individuals should come first, before the generality.[6]

What Buber was conveying to Dinur was not his opposition to civic cultural activities as such, but to the idea of its being imposed by a superior authority—particularly if that authority happened to be the state. The only public culture that Buber could have accepted would have been one based on the free association of individuals.

We have observed that Buber had no inclination to be a theoretician of education and offered no pedagogic system. Nevertheless his writings abound with matter from which the educator can profit. Singly, each of his works can be read as a self-contained lesson in education; taken together, they constitute a philosophical framework that is sufficiently liberal in scope to accommodate as many approaches to education as may foster accessibility, commit themselves to the world, and embrace the visions of the spirit. The generous latitude of Buber's educational philosophy arises from his conviction that education cannot be subject to a fixed and immutable system of principles. He maintained that throughout recorded history, educational principles have been confined to particular civilizations, societies, and communities and created by them at given moments in their histories. And although he allowed that education may have at times been structured, Buber could acknowledge no educational order to be autonomously valid and universally binding. For Buber the significant fact about such systems of education was that in their particular manifestations they represented a choice made within the real world and were determined and put into effect by the personality of the educator. "The educator musters the constructive energies of the world," he explains. "By himself and within his own person, being replete with the world, he makes distinctions, confirms the valid and rejects the invalid. Moreover these constructive energies are eternal and irrefrangible: they are one with the world of communion intent on addressing God."[7]

Thus, Buber consciously refrained from devising a rigorous and exhaustive doctrine of education. "As for me," he confesses in *Gog and Magog*, "I offer no doctrine. I do no more than direct attention to reality. And anyone who expects a doctrine other than direction of this kind from me will inevitably be disappointed."[8] Buber's principal object was, therefore, not to instruct us in any explicit way but only to suggest a "direction" for us to follow, to clear a path to enlightenment.

Similarly, Buber did not let himself be drawn into making dogmatic assertions about the goals of education. These, he believed, could not be defined in words but had to be realized in action: the goals of education have, in other words, to be determined by the educator who is responsible for carrying them out. In Buber's view the ultimate goal of achieving genuine human perfection and fulfillment is, however, contingent on man's accessibility to the call; on his conscious receptivity to the *I-Thou* relation; above all, on his turning to God:

> When all other goals fail man, there emerges humanity's one true goal, which is directed towards the creating Spirit, towards the Spirit of God moving upon the face of the water. Here then is man's true *autonomy*— the fruit of the freedom which no longer betrays and alienates but is *responsible*. Man, God's creature, who gives shape to Creation and transmutes it, cannot himself create. But he can—every man can—open his own heart and the hearts of others to the work of Creation. And he can call upon the Creator to *redeem and perfect his image* [my italics].[9]

In determining the plan of this book I took my cue from Buber. Accordingly, I kept in mind that all of his works embody a "direction," the consciousness of which attended me constantly as I considered the principal aspects of Buber's philosophy from the point of view of education.

The first chapter of this book is devoted to Buber's overall view of education, which I present in connection with his response to the changes that education has undergone during the modern period. In this chapter Buber's conception of education is set against the predominating modern educational trends, originating in the theories of a long line of thinkers that includes Pestalozzi, Dilthey, Spranger, Dewey, Kerschensteiner, Bergson, Ruskin, and Gaudig. The confrontation between the ideas of Buber and those of the pioneers of modern concepts of education sets into relief Buber's pedagogic convictions on such subjects as freedom and discipline, individualism, propaganda, creativity, the teacher's role, teacher-pupil relationships, the principles of "inclusion," "eros," and "relation," the education of character, the concept of the "great character," and the place of existentialism in education.

I next consider the subject of values and ethics. In chapter 2 the problem of value education is discussed in connection with Buber's philosophy. Buber believed that the judgments and decisions we make in respect of values are bound up with our dialogical relation to other human beings, to the world, and to God. Personal responsibility occupies a central position in Buber's philosophy of values, and he therefore refrained from laying down a code of precepts to be applied to specific situations involving moral choice. For it was the circumstances in which we are called upon to make a choice that Buber regarded to be the point of departure for the formulation of values. Hence Buber calls on us to rescue the idea of responsibility from the professional province to which it has been long confined, and to bring down to earth the commandment that hovers in space beyond man's reach: to make it part once more of actual existence. True responsibility—Buber proposes—begins when there is true response.

Chapter 3 is devoted to Buber's social thought and to his ideas concerning social education. Buber greatly hoped that a future generation might be educated to authentic social consciousness and will. He regarded social education to be a force that could one day bring about a revolution from within society against political power, whose coercive influence, he believed, distorted social existence and prevented it from becoming manifest in an authentic form. Education is a potent instrument, the proper employment of which society—in whose hands it largely remains to this day—is lamentably ignorant. The goals of social education conceived by Buber are diametrically opposed to the social persuasion aimed at by political propaganda. In discussing Buber's notions of social education I have addressed myself to the following problems: Of what nature is the process by which society is formed? What place do the individual and the public have in the social scheme? Of what nature is the sphere of the "interhuman"? What is true "community"? What role are we to assign to social education and what has its function been in efforts to bring about social renewal?

Chapter 4 has for its subject what must surely be accounted the crowning achievement of Martin Buber's thought: his philosophy of religion and his concept of religious education. In this chapter I consider the problem of the attenuation in modern times of man's *I-Thou* relation with God, and of the decline in faith signaled by the proclamation of the death of God. In examining Buber's views on the revival of man's relation with God, I focus especially on Buber's thesis that religious faith is determined by the experience of God's immanence rather than by any manifestation of divinity in a personal guise. Buber did not regard knowledge about God's nature to be a prerequisite for devotion to Him; he rightly points out that there are many authentically religious persons who can speak *to* God without being able to speak *about* Him. Buber's dictum, "The Unknown God—if we only dare live for His sake, seek Him out, address Him—He is the true subject of religion," defines Buber's concept of the nature of religious education.[50]

Chapters 5 and 6 are linked by the theme of national historical memory. As conceived of by Buber, the historical recollection of a people is dynamic, acquiring ever larger scope whenever it is handed down from one generation to the next and each time the fate of a nation takes a new course. Buber was careful to distinguish it from historical consciousness, by which objective events are chronicled and whose sequence describes the history of a people. Consciousness of history is possessed by all national groups and is expressed in all languages; historical memory, on the other hand, gives expression to the significant relationships a people has with events in its history. In chapter 5, I take up Buber's notion of historical memory in connection with his idea of biblical humanism. Buber regarded the Old Testament and the Hebrew language to be the two sources of Jewish historical memory. Buber traced the roots of Jewish humanism to the Hebrew Bible, whose language and literature seemed to him to contain the purest representation of human nature. He conceived the idea of biblical humanism in order to extract from the language of the Hebrew Bible the basic components that go into making up the human personality.

In chapter 6 I turn to Buber's concept of Hasidism and consider the relevance of his ideas on Hasidism to modern education. In his studies of Hasidism, Buber reveals to us the existence of a rich and complex tradition of education which has very real and immediate application to the experiences and needs of the present. Buber concentrated on the features of Hasidism that could appeal to the contemporary mind. He selected from the materials of Hasidic tradition those aspects that have a bearing on modern life and on which contemporary man can draw in order to cope with the problems confronting him. The religious existential choice that emerges from Buber's Hasidic studies offers us a key to the renewal of our dialogue with the young, and therefore goes a long way toward helping us resolve the problem of religious education today.

Any discussion of Jewish education would be incomplete, to say the least, if it fails to take account of the pertinency of Arab-Jewish relations. Buber regarded the question of the relations between Jews and Arabs to be especially germane when he came to deal with Jewish education. I, therefore, saw fit to follow my examination of the subjects of Judaism and Jewish education in Buber's philosophy with an account in chapter 7 of his attitude toward the responsibility of Jewish education to Israeli Arabs. Buber believed that the moral problems that have arisen in the encounter between Jews and Arabs must exist at the heart of Jewish education, and are indeed inextricably part of the Zionist educational enterprise to the extent that if Jewish education chose to ignore them it would become involved in a willful contradiction of its very purpose and nature.

Aesthetic experience and education are in a province wholly different from the one to which the subjects of the preceding chapters belong. There is in fact no extensive study by Buber on aesthetics, but the corpus of his writings—especially that part of it devoted to religion and anthropological philosophy—abounds in insights concerning creativity in the arts, the nature of the work of art, the quality of the experience of the arts, and the function and place of aesthetic education. In chapter 8, I have arranged in what I hope is a coherent order Buber's scattered references to these subjects and tried to describe the main drift of Buber's thoughts on aesthetics and the arts in education.

The final chapter of this book is reserved for a discussion of Buber's very substantial work on behalf of adult education. By his insistence that the principal object of teaching adults should be to foster in them the spirit of action and to make them the agents of their own learning, Buber shows his affinity for the ideas of Bernhard Bolzano, Nikolai Grundtvig, and Kristen Kold. The theories of these men serves as the background for my examination of Buber's approach to adult education. I also discuss at length Buber's work in the field of adult Jewish education, in which he was engaged both intellectually and practically: first in Germany, during the period of the Nazi rise to power, when he became actively involved in the education of Jewish adults—and later in Israel, where he worked vigorously for the cause of popular education and the training of teachers for adults. Buber conceived of adult education as progressing simultaneously along three routes: from the receptivity achieved in dialogue to self-education; from the enactment of the relation of *I-Thou* with another person to the consummation of that relation with the Absolute; and from the solitary and unique "self" to a merging of national traditions with the universal heritage of the human spirit.

Throughout this book I have sought to demonstrate that in his philosophy of education Buber attempted to apply the principles of his anthropological philosophy to the concrete realities of teaching and learning. And although Buber's philosophy of education offers no pedagogic model to which the teacher can refer in his day-to-day work, it performs an estimable service for the contemporary educator by suggesting the ways in which education may be extricated from its current predicament.

The preparation of this book entailed not only the task of closely studying all of Martin Buber's books, essays, speeches, and notes but also having to sift through his thousands of letters. In addition to having examined this daunting collection of Buber's own writings and addresses, I also read extensively in the vast body of literature that has been published on Buber. The bibliography appended at the end of this book includes those works that were most useful to me and of which I made constant use in the course of my writing.

This book has meant more to me than the opportunity it provides to bring before the public the fruits of my research. Writing it was not only the consummation of my investigations into a significant if neglected aspect of

Buber's thought but also an expression of a deep personal awareness of the task that Buber's philosophy sets the educator. I have tried both to present an objective account of Buber's philosophy of education and, insofar as my small influence may have effect, to advance the cause of dialogue in our times. While I was engaged in the practical work of sorting, collating, and analyzing the materials that are contained in this volume, I sought consciously to catch the sounds of Buber's voice emanating from his writings and to become earnestly engaged in *I-Thou* relation with them. If this book succeeds in drawing the reader into a similar encounter with Buber's thought and arouses in him a wish to enact the dialogue urged by Buber, I shall consider my labors to have been amply rewarded.

I bring these introductory remarks to a close with Buber's exhortation from his essay "Biblical Humanism"; his words seem to me an apt motto for this book and to offer us consolation and wise counsel in these troubled times:

> This night of terror, these emergent voids, this peril of annihilation—seek no refuge from them in the universe of Logos or Perfect Form. Hold your ground—Attend the Voice calling out of the turmoil—Give ear! This terrible world is God's: it summons you. As a man of God, stand fast in the trial it makes of you![11]

I have to thank many people whose assistance and inspiration made it possible for me to write this book, but I owe a very special debt of gratitude to my teacher, the late Samuel Hugo Bergmann. This outstanding educator and scholar, who was all of his life engaged in a discourse with the world of the spirit and who speaks to us still through the medium of his books, first opened the portals of philosophy to me as to countless others; it was under his inspiring tutelage that I and so many of my contemporaries were introduced to Buber's philosophy of dialogue.

Many thanks to Ted Gorelik, scholar and man of letters who worked with me on the translation of this book from the Hebrew manuscript.

My thanks are due as well to all of the students who have attended my seminars in the philosophy of education at the University of Haifa since 1972. For in undertaking to participate in our common enterprise of studying Buber's philosophy of education they have become in a real sense the coauthors of this volume.

And last, my thanks to those most dear to me—to my wife, Bilhah, and to my children, Ariel, Telalit, Amaziah, and Hila, to whom I shall be grateful always for the years we have spent together in mutual dialogue, and for having awakened me to the experience of communion in small, which I would like to think is a foretaste and model of the universal communion of man we all await.

NOTES

1. Ben-Zion Dinur, "Shalosh pegishot im Buber" [Three encounters with Buber], *Molad*, [New Man] 1 (xxiv), ḥoveret 2 (1967) 234.

2. Gershom Scholem, "Perusho shel Martin Buber laḥasidut" [Martin Buber's interpretation of Hasidism], *Amot 2, ḥoveret 8 (1964): 82–83; Yehezkel Kaufmann, "Torat ha-noviim" [The doctrine of the prophets]* Moznaiim 15 (1943): 155–59, 234–43; Nathan Rotenstreich, "Maḥ-shavato ha-dialogit shel Buber" [Buber's dialogic thought], in *Sugiot be-filosofia* [Problems in Philosophy] (Tel Aviv: Devir, 1961), pp. 299–343: Karl Frankenstein, "Ata va-lo-ani, le torat ha-du-siaḥ shel Buber" [Thou and not-I: A contribution to Buber's philosophy of dialogue], *Shdemot*, ḥoveret 36 (1970): 113–23: Raphael Seligmann, "Matspen ra" [Bad conscience], *Moz-naiim* 2 ḥoveret 4 (1934): 605–613.

3. Martin Buber, *Pegishot: zikhronot* [Encounters: recollections] (Jerusalem: Mosad Bialik, 1965), p. lx.

4. Ernst Simon, "Martin Buber, the Educator," in *The Philosophy of Martin Buber*, ed. Paul Arthur Schilpp and Maurice Friedman, (London: Cambridge University Press, 1967), p. 543.

5. Martin Buber, "hinukh mevugarim" Adult education], in *Teuda ve-yiud* [Mission and purpose] 2 (Jerusalem: Ha-Sifria ha-Tsionit, 1961), 411.

6. Dinur, "Shlosha pegishot," p. 235.

7. Martin Buber, "Al ha-maaseh ha-hinukhi" [On education] in *Be-sod siah: Al ha-adam ve-amidato nokhah ha-havaya* [Dialogue: On man and his encounter with existence] (Jerusalem: Mosad Bialik, 1964), p. 259.

8. Martin Buber, *Gog V-Magog* [Gog and Magog] (Jerusalem: Sifrei Tarshish, 1944).

9. Buber, "Al ha-maaseh ha-ḥinukhi," p. 261.

10. Martin Buber, "Dat u-filosofia" [Religion and philosophy] in *Pnei-adam: Beḥinot be-antropologia filosofit* [The face of man: Studies in anthropological philosophy] (Jerusalem: Mosad Bialik, 1962), p. 239.

11. Martin Buber,"Humaniut ivrit"]Jewish humanism], in *Darko shel Mikra]The Way of the Bible]* (Jerusalem: Mosad Bialik, 1964).

The Educational Philosophy
of Martin Buber

1

Martin Buber and Changes
in Modern Education

Martin Buber was invited to deliver the inaugural lecture of the Third International Educational Conference, which took place in Heidelberg in 1925. For its topic, the conference had chosen "The Development of the Creative Powers in the Child." The subject accorded well with the new educational mood sweeping Germany after the First World War, and was a characteristic choice of theme for the movement that aspired in those years to reconstruct pedagogic theory and practice. The idea embodied in the subject of the conference and notions of a similar stamp, such as "creativity" and "freedom," were key concepts of this movement, which arose in protest against the "old" education; to counter the officially endorsed conception of education, the movement proposed a "new" and progressive pedagogy that was founded on the principle of freedom.

In the aftermath of the far-reaching changes in Germany's political, social, and economic structure during the nineteenth century and the beginning of the twentieth, winds of change began to stir in the educational climate of the country, and pedagogic thinking took a new course. The growth of productive capacity had raised the living standard and created a shorter working day; the increase in leisure time confronted education with a new challenge. The continuous trend toward urbanization, too, opened new vistas to education. City dwellers—especially those belonging to the middle class—were more receptive than were the inhabitants of the countryside to new ideas in education.

As humanitarian aspirations gathered momentum in the closing decades of the last century and at the beginning of the twentieth century, so did the demand to extend fundamental privileges to disfranchised and economically exploited groups in society. Children, for example, constituted one such group, and the incidence of child labor during this period was in continuous decline. In Germany, the creation of an industrial organization and the advances made in the techniques of production brought about the economic and technological progress which in great measure determined the readiness to forego the employment of minors and canceled the advantages of training young apprentices. Henceforth, as children were increasingly exempt from having to assume an economic role, the phase of childhood was prolonged.

Formerly childhood was regarded to be little more than a necessary stage of development best gotten through quickly, and, when viewed from a pedagogical perspective, was thought of primarily as a preparation for adult life. Childhood now came to be understood as part of life's cycle, of which it was a phase estimable in its own right and worthy of being prolonged and nurtured for its own sake.

Women made up another disfranchised group of the period, and made a significant contribution to the humanitarian trends of the time by their struggle for equality. The growing contribution being made by women to social and economic life helped to widen the educational opportunities that were available to girls.

The momentous changes in the class structure of Europe and the radical transformation that took place in its culture and economy undermined the binding authority of ideas and values whose universal dominion had until then remained unchallenged. There followed a period in which the past was reviewed and the future probed: both cultural traditions and pedagogic conventions were reexamined. That warder of conventions, traditional education, which was dedicated to the principle of the transmission of values sanctified by past generations, came under attack by the advocates of innovation and change. Fierce criticism was leveled at the old education, in which the values of the past, textbooks and teaching programs were given priority, while the child was made to serve as a mere passive object, a receptive vessel for storing the articles of the teacher's creed. A number of theorists made a case for considering the child's individuality, and demanded that the scales of education be tipped in favor of the condition of childhood per se as it is experienced by the child himself. As a consequence, human experience and action came to be more highly esteemed, while the personality as an active agent became a major consideration in the thoughts of educationists.

The German philosopher Wilhelm Dilthey (1833–1911), who occupied chairs in philosophy at Basel, Kehl, Breslau, and Berlin, had considerable influence on theorists in the fields of psychology and education. Dilthey made existence as it is immediately perceived and life as experienced firsthand cardinal issues in his philosophy. He laid particular stress on the unique nature of the humanities and insisted on their independence from the natural sciences. Dilthey rejected the trend in philosophy that sought to fetter the humanities in the shackles of a preconceived system, and urged the cause of the free spirit acting on history. Dilthey argued that history must be perceived as a vital unfolding of the creative human spirit, whose evolution reveals to us the supreme importance of singular and unrepeated manifestations; this perception of history can be arrived at through individual experience and by the faculty of emphathic understanding.[1]

Eduard Spranger (born 1882), who was much influenced by Dilthey's teachings and heir to his master's philosophy of culture, stressed the autonomous value of the individual. Spranger's investigation of what he called *Lebensformen* or "life-forms" provided the basis of his own philosophy of culture. He assigned particular importance to the role of psychology, which he conceived of as a science whose function is to discover the principles informing objective intelligence.[2] Spranger defined the soul as the comprehensive idea embracing all actions, experiences, and responses emanating from the self; he defined education as the process by which the objective revelations of culture are first assimilated and then infused into the pupil's existential molds and his subjective patterns of action. Put another way—the release of the formative potentialities of the values of culture is conditioned by private being and personal action.

By the second decade of the twentieth century, the educational philosophy of John Dewey (1859–1952) had already become known in Germany and had influenced a number of educationists in that country. Dewey argued that thinking was not in itself a goal but the means by which the problems of the present are understood and resolved. In Dewey's view, the concrete problems inherent in reality are the only serious spur to the workings of the mind, whereas mental activity, in its turn, determines human behavior: experience whose sphere is perpetually enlarged by experimentation prepares us to know our changing world, to understand its structure, and to predict its future shape; consciousness is the process by which action is exercised within the concrete realm of existence, which is ever changing and ever amenable to being changed; thought aims at the continuous enhancement of life. Thus, the purpose of education is the reconstruction of experience so that it may be constantly adjusted to the changing environment. Education— Dewey is at pains to point out— is not a preparation for life, but life itself; it is the context of existence and men's personal experience of the world.[3]

While American Pragmatism was being introduced to Germany, the philosophy of Henri Bergson (1859–1941) began to exert an influence as well. Bergson conceived of life as an autonomous spiritual process and an act of creation; life, in other words, means unlimited freedom and unending creativity. Bergson cites artistic creativy as an example of the personal creation characteristic of the whole of existence; the nature of action participates in the nature of reality as a whole. According to Bergson, the multiplicity of forms in which reality manifests itself is inescapable, for action and creation generate this diversity. The work of art is stamped by the character of individuality and the qualitative character of reality reflects its creative nature. Life is never grasped except by the faculty of inward experience; in this way we perceive life not as a causal necessity but as inner freedom—not as a static and material "being" but as an emergent and creative "becoming."

The influence of the adherents of art education in German educational theory at this time was considerable. Art educationists were arguing the importance of creativity and of unimpeded freedom of action; they favored granting the child freedom of expression, and advocated the sympathetic estimation of experience and the nurture of the imagination and feelings. The ideas of John Ruskin (1819–1900) concerning the place of the arts in the life of man and their significance to society and education gained wide currency. Ruskin's concept of art was not confined to masterpieces; in his view, every man is able to experience the joys of creation and find satisfaction in the making of art. The implication that Ruskin drew from this for education was that art is a creative and plastic activity that is accessible to every child. Creative activity, Ruskin argued, liberates the child's potentialities and develops his inherent gifts. Ruskin proposed, moreover, that art education contributes to the creation of a desirable human type—to wit, the man in whom spirit, intelligence, and action exist in a state of equilibrium, and whose personality is a harmonious blend of the principles of visual sensibility, abstract knowledge, and creative activity. In his book *Elements of Drawing* (1857), Ruskin anticipated by many years the ideas of modern education by calling attention to the pedagogic potentialities contained in art. He advocates in this work that the artistic experience of children should be neither inhibited nor regimented until they reach the age of twelve or fourteen: until then, free play should be given to the child's experience of art; at no time should the child's paintings be corrected and under no circumstances should he be taught the established rules of drawing and coloring—rather, every occasion should be sought to praise the child's efforts when they reveal care, veracity, and original expression.[4]

In Germany, Alfred Litvak reveals an intellectual kinship with Ruskin. From 1900 on, Litvak, who was primarily active in the field of art education, conducted symposia for teachers at the art museum in Hamburg. The main intention of these meetings was to promote the idea of the central role that art could assume in the life of mankind in general and in the classroom in particular. Litvak was able to found teachers' art associations that created various professional committees active on the behalf of education through the visual arts, literature, music, and manual labor. This artistic and creative trend gained a large following in Germany at the time.

While Litvak was active in Hamburg, Georg Kerschensteiner (1859–1932) held the posts of adviser to schools and director of education in Munich. Kerschensteiner's writings and activities had an enormous impact on German education; he is considered to be the originator of the idea of the *Arbeitsschule,* where his theories of education were put into practice. In 1908 Kerschensteiner became familiar with Dewey's educational philosophy, but by then his own attitudes—much influenced by the doctrines of Kant, Pestalozzi, Dilthey, and Spanger—had already taken definite shape in his mind. Kerschensteiner insisted that education must adapt itself to the child's natural development, and that it should concentrate the child's mental faculties on action in the sphere of tangible reality. He believed that education towards a trade or profession ought to be in its initial stages highly diversified and constantly adjusted to the changing interests of the child as he grows older. Education, in Kerschensteiner's opinion, must be made to correspond to the individual nature of the pupil, whose grasp of values changes at each stage of his development.

Kerschensteiner, following Spranger's lead, defined education as the act of channeling a person toward a particular "life-form" that corresponds to his inner nature; by means of this act a person's individuality crystallizes while becoming integrated with a system of values. Thus, education attends primarily to the development of a child's interests, which unfold in stages as, first, the child outgrows the phase of the instincual gratification of his needs, and then, becoming conscious of his own self, begins to make the distinction between the goals which he sets for himself and the means of achieving them, and finally perceives the identity between the structure of his own personality and the pattern of the values which he is acquiring. The child's interests from the point of view of education are distinguished by the qualities of spontaneity, objectivity, emotionality, and singlemindedness.

Kerschensteiner believed that the classroom can have no share in the formation of character unless it grants the pupil freedom, so that the formation of character becomes a personal achievement. He insisted, moreover, that schools must abandon the outworn contemplative ideal of education, and instead concentrate on cultivating the virtues of action and independent creativity. Kerschensteiner had the conviction that once these principles were adopted, the traditional educational institution would give way to the *Arbeitsschule,* dedicated to performance, creativity, and professional training.

This book cannot hope to give an exhaustive account of the work of the many educationists who contributed to the theory and practice of education in the early twentieth century. The list of prominent personalities is too long and the scope of this chapter too narrow for justice to be done even in the cases of the most outstanding educators and theorists. However, before abandoning the subject, at least passing mention should be made of Hugo Gaudig (1861–1923) and Berthold Otto (1859–1937). Gaudig took the position that the primary task of education is to develop the whole range of the psychological potentialities in the child's possession in order to form his character. He argued that a more significant role in education should be given to emotions, to independent activity, and to self-expression; he suggested that the pupil, rather than being confined to a receptive role, should become an active agent, whereas the teacher should abandon his active role for a passive one. Berthold Otto thought that education should be motivated chiefly by the child's preoccupations, his experience of the world, and the fields in which he exhibits special interests; at the same time education should extend opportunities to the child for independent activity and personal expression.

The new educational ambience created by these pioneer theorists and educators resulted in radical changes in the field of education in Germany and throughout Europe in the years preceding the Heidelberg conference. The emphasis of education shifted to the individual child, who was now conceived of as a unique human being possessing his own gifts, inclinations, and requirements. On the other hand, the pedagogy that constrained the child to conform to conventional patterns and encouraged uniformity by blurring the contours of each child's personality fell into disrepute. Rather, it was urged that education should provide the ideal conditions for the child's development and encourage the child to give independent, original, and creative expression to his latent potentialities. While philosophers taught that the life processes and the vitality of phenomena were the first principles of judgment and that man was a free agent able to make actual his creative and vital potentialities—educators promoted the ideas of the "active person-ality" and "creativity."

Keeping this setting in mind we readily grasp the significance of the theme of the educational conference at Heidelberg. We can easily imagine the agitation of the audience on hearing Martin Buber begin his address with the statement:

"The development of the creative powers in the child" is the subject of this conference. As I come before you to introduce it I must not conceal from you for a single moment the fact that of the nine words in which it is expressed only the last three raise no question for me.[5]

Despite the apparent tenor of these words, Buber did not intend to say that he denied the existence of the great potentialities that are latent in every child and await discovery and development by education. Rather, he wished to point out that the concept of "the development of creative powers" neither adds to our understanding of the task of education nor exhausts the subject.

Buber reminds us of two aspects of the child's nature that we are prone to forget: first, that each child is born with the impress of history stamped upon it by the heritage of past generations; second, that each child is the potential begetter of unborn generations, has an indisputable portion in the act of Creation itself, and is a latent source of renewal. Hence, Buber argues that the problem faced by education concerns the means by which this power to generate the new can itself be renewed.

Buber turns his attention to the disciples of Ruskin's art-educational creed, who regarded art as the consummate expression of the faculty of fabricating objects (called the "originative instinct" by Buber), which is shared in varying degrees by all men. To the adherents of this school of thought, it is in the nature of an ethical mission to base the education of the whole person on the development of the autonomous and natural activity flowing from this power. Buber speaks at length about man's drive to make objects, and about the opportunities of which education can avail itself in order to release this instinct so that it can become actual. But after examining the subject with care, Buber concludes that the decisive significance of the work of education is found not in the release of a particular drive but in the forces that encounter it. For, as Buber puts the case: "There are two forms, indispensable for the building of true human life, to which the originative instinct, left to itself, does not lead: to sharing in an undertaking and to entering into mutuality."[6] Thus, while admitting that the creative undertaking of an individual is important, Buber assigns first place to the shared enterprise fostered by a man's acting in partnership with other men.

Man, the maker of things, is a solitary creature, Buber insists. Although himself free and the master of his own enterprise, man nevertheless exists in a condition of unrelieved isolation from which even the understanding and enthusiastic acclaim of a vast public cannot release him. "Only if someone grasps his hand not as a "creator" but as a fellow creature lost in the world, to be his comrade or friend or lover beyond the arts, does he have an awareness and a share of mutuality."[7]

Buber does not deny the advantages that art educationists and the advocates of creativity in education adduce on behalf of learning by fabricating objects and making art. He admits that a child learns much from the making of things which he would not learn otherwise. Nevertheless, Buber argues that art education cannot foster one essential ingredient of existence—namely, the relationship arising from partnership, in which "Thou" is addressed to the world. Buber warns that a pedagogy whose only goal is to foster creativity and the making of objects may impose upon mankind a condition of painful isolation. Whereas the artist, whose creative act flows from within, can learn about the objective nature of the world by seeing it from the perspective of his art, he cannot grasp the world as subject. Buber repeatedly emphasizes: "What teaches us the saying of *Thou* is not the originative instinct but the instinct for communion."[8]

In his philosophy, Buber attaches special importance to our need for "realization" in our relationship with the world. By "realization" or *Vergegenwärtigung,* Buber means the act of imagination by which a man concretely "pictures" what another man is sensing, feeling, or thinking at that very moment. What is thus imagined is perceived not as a subject separate from the other person but as an integral part of his reality and life process. This "mental image" contains something of the nature of that which is being imagined. The experience can be compared to genuinely shared grief that is not merely routine solicitude, but a *felt* participation in the particular sorrow experienced by the other person.

The need of realization requires that the world appears to us under the guise of another person who is present and reaching out toward us, while seeking his confirmation in ourselves as we seek ours in him. Buber contends that the self, although lodged in the depths of being, cannot thrive in a one-way relationship of a man with himself but only in the mutuality of his relationship with another person. For the self to flourish, it must be realized by another's self while at the same time the other person is conscious of this realization, which is mutually declared to be taking place.[9]

Buber's belief in the need for mutual realization leads him to conclude that the release of creative potentialities can merely serve as a preliminary to education. Buber has no doubt that it is desirable to give the pupil the opportunity to express his creative powers; the spontaneity of youth ought to be encouraged rather than repressed. But while admitting that this approach makes art education possible, Buber argues that it is not principally at issue when we consider education as a whole, and he expresses serious doubts that the nurturing of the creative instinct will advance the cause of education.

Buber passes harsh judgment on the authoritative teacher, who dominated traditional education and who perceived his task as the mere transmission of information in the form of maxims, laws, and principles that the child was required to receive and to learn by rote. Under these conditions, the child was reduced to being a receptacle of subject matter whose nature was determined by adult values, which the child was expected to accept and to which he was expected to conform.

For all of Buber's animadversions on the subject of the authoritative teacher, the representative type of the modern educator does not escape Buber's censure. The teacher of the "new" education neither imposes a conventional system of values nor acts as the plenipotentiary of society or its authorities. He is conceived of as an acolyte of the normal and spontaneous development of the child: his principal task is to help the child help himself, to show the way to his pupils, but under no circumstances to offer them ready-made solutions. Buber, for his part, is unable to conceive of such a teacher in the role of an altogether uncommitted bystander. He cannot accept that aspect of the doctrine of the new education which prohibits the teacher from making demands on the pupil, and limits the teacher's role to guiding the pupil to sources of information and to methods of approach only when the pupil is moved to request guidance. Buber believes that the teacher should adopt the role of critical guide and directing spirit. He argues that in no way can such an approach be regarded as coercive; although the teacher's role is founded on the principle of freedom, his function also expresses a point of view and an orientation. So, for example, when a teacher of drawing places a broom-twig in a jug on a table and asks his pupils to represent the subject, although he may have imposed no rules on his pupils and established no limits to their creative impulses, nevertheless the teacher's role has not been exhausted by the mere act of having offered the subject to his class. Here Buber elucidates:

> Now the delicate, almost imperceptible and yet important influence begins—that of criticism and instruction. The children encounter a scale of

values that, however individualistic it may be, is quite unambiguous. The more unacademic this scale of values, and the more individualistic this knowledge, the more deeply do the children experience the encounter.[10]

Buber asserts that authoritative education, which gives priority to laws and maxims, which puts the child's expressive faculties under restraint and narrowly circumscribes the fields which he may study, which confines education to a single direction that it allows to be correct—can only bring the child to a state of resignation or drive him into rebellion. By contrast, a pedagogy gives scope to the child's personal experience and encourages him to develop by means of experimentation and self-expression, while it retains its capacity to criticize and direct, will inspire the child to respect his guide. In Buber's words: "This almost imperceptible, most delicate approach, the raising of a finger, perhaps, or a questioning glance, is the other half of what happens in education."[11]

Buber is as much opposed to the new pedagogy's idea of "absolute freedom" untempered by guidance or response as he is to traditional education's coercive discipline, from which freedom is altogether absent. In Buber's view, modern education's doctrine of developing the child's potentialities from within is inadequate. He therefore rejects the idea that the original and directing force of education should be the child's requirements and preoccupations, and that the educational process must adapt itself to the child's potentialities, needs and, even, his passing whims. Buber cautions against exchanging traditional education's "symbol of the funnel" for the new education's "symbol of the pump."

Buber agrees that the powers of the child, the limits of his educability, and his inborn gifts should all be taken into account by the educator. However, these are not the be-all and end-all of education. The whole of education cannot be founded on the child's inner powers, for they do not determine the nature of the adult. Buber argues that were it indeed possible to analyze the soul of a newborn child, we would find that its faculties are no more than capacities to apprehend the world and its appearance. It is the world at large that engenders man in the particular; for it is the world as both nature and society which "educates" the individual. The primary question to which education must address itself here concerns which aspects of the world will penetrate the consciousness of the child who has been made receptive to the stimuli of his environment. For in Buber's definition, education "means *a selection by man of the effective world:* it means to give decisive effective power to a selection of the world which is concentrated and made manifest in the educator."[12]

Buber assigns a role of great significance to the educator. The relationship between pupil and teacher in education is defined by purpose, according to Buber. There was a time, he notes, when the master craftsman lived in close communion with his assistants and apprentices, who, having been made sharers in their master's labors, learned no less from his spiritual musings than from his oral instruction and his practice of the craft; they would learn without being conscious of the fact, and even when the intention of actual study did not exist. But times have changed: the intimate fellowship between master, journeyman, and apprentice has dissolved, and educational activity has had to take on a conscious purpose. Buber nevertheless maintains that the master must continue to serve as a model for the teacher in our own day. He stresses, however, that the teacher should not confuse the influence of the world flowing from the presence of his whole being with direct personal interference; for the teacher's interference can only impair the educational process and will incur the rebellion of his pupils.

For many theorists and disciples of modern education the word *freedom* has taken on the character of a magical incantation: it has been invoked to represent a vast spectrum of ideas ranging from total permissiveness to self-discipline. A. S. Neill is one of the prominent adherents of the doctrine of freedom in education. Neill makes a special point of the significant difference between freedom, which is desirable, and permissiveness, which is the reverse of freedom. According to Neill, permissiveness leads to anarchy, which is freedom's antithesis, whereas self-restraint and self-control are the true derivatives of freedom. Neill argues that self-restraint should not be identified with the Victorian ideal of the repression of drives and the cultivation of the virtues; it should rather be associated with such ethical notions as the consideration of others and respect of their rights. Neill's operating terms are self-control and self-direction; he defines self-direction as the right of the child to live in freedom and without interference from external authority in matters concerning his body and mind. Freedom is necessary, Neill believes, because only when the child is free can he mature in a way that is natural to him. In Neill's opinion, we must grant the child his right to be self-centered and to pursue his interests throughout the period of his childhood; moreover, when the concerns of the individual child come into conflict with his social interests, priority should be given to the child's personal inclinations.[13]

As we have already seen, Buber concluded that the release of potentialities is only a preliminary to education and not its substance. Buber proposes that the concept of freedom should be submitted to rigorous examination. Although he concedes that freedom is the rock upon which authentic existence is founded, Buber contends that freedom cannot be identified with life itself. This premise applies to both the "inner" freedom, which is the freedom of choice, and the "outer" freedom, which exists in the absence of restraint and compulsion. Thus Buber proclaims to his audience:

> As the higher freedom, the soul's freedom of decision, signifies perhaps our highest moments but not a fraction of our substance, so the lower freedom, the freedom of development, signifies our capacity for growth

but by no means our growth itself. This latter freedom is charged with importance as the actuality from which the work of education begins, but as its fundamental task it becomes absurd.[14]

We are being urged, therefore, not to confuse the conception of freedom as the source and precondition of education with the perception of freedom as the goal toward which educational principles should tend.

Buber elucidates the meaning of freedom according to his own lights. His conception of freedom differs from the popular view, which treats freedom as the reverse of compulsion. According to Buber, it is communion and not freedom which is the opposite of compulsion; for whereas compulsion is a negative reality, communion is a positive reality. In Buber's words:

> Compulsion in education means disunion, it means humiliation and rebelliousness. Communion in education is just communion, it means being opened up and drawn in. Freedom in education is the possibility of communion; it cannot be dispensed with and it cannot be made use of in itself; without it nothing succeeds, but neither does anything succeed by means of it: it is the run before the jump, the tuning of the violin, the confirmation of that primal and mighty potentiality which it cannot even begin to actualize.[15]

In our own period, when the bonds of tradition are disintegrating, the tendency toward freedom has become exaggerated. Buber observes that contemporaries are unaware that freedom is neither a doctrine nor a program, but only a domain of possibilities. Man's abandonment of tradition has meant his assumption of a responsibility that is altogether private rather than one which is shared by many generations. To the extent that a man can subscribe to a doctrine, law, or tradition, he is able to devolve responsibility to them. When, however, such opportunities are wanting, man is still not free of responsibility. Rather, the contrary is the case. When man is unable to pass on his responsibility to an authority, he must perforce assume a burden of responsibility all the more onerous for its being personal: for his responsibility is that of a man towards himself.

Buber cannot conceive of the possibility of freedom without responsibility; responsibility invests freedom with both content and direction. The root meaning of responsibility (Latin *respondere*) contains the idea of response; therefore, the man who is "responsive" to the situation that he confronts may be described as responsible. Buber, who conceives of life as dialogue, argues that whenever we make an utterance, we ourselves become the object of a summons. For the most part we are inattentive to the call. However, when the summons reaches us and we respond, the possibility of human existence is restored to the world. Hence, responsibility is to be deduced from freedom; the faculty of response from responsibility; and human vitality from the faculty of response.

In Buber's opinion, the new pedagogy errs when it regards freedom to be the preeminent principle of education. For man—as Buber perceives him— is responsible to himself, to his neighbor and to reality; he possesses the ability to choose and to actualize. Neither the release from responsibility nor the exclusive concentration on the self and the forces that create the self can ever lead to actualization and the authentic existence of man with man. Thus Buber asserts: ". . . the decisive influence is to be ascribed not to the release of an instinct but to the forces which meet the released instinct, namely, the educative forces."[16] What is important to education is not freedom lacking direction, but communion having both a direction and purpose.

Here Buber is being faithful to his concept of ethics and ethical education. His definition of good and evil brings the subject into sharper focus. Buber rejects the polarization of good and evil, for in his view they do not constitute "polarized directions or forces," and their meaning becomes clear when we recognize that "they are not equal in their natures."[17] Buber defines evil as the absence of either direction or orientation. According to this definition, evil is bound up with the existential situation of man and with man's nature. Buber asserts that the human personality is sensible to the existential category of the possible and that this sensibility is revealed in no creature other than man. Among all living beings man alone perpetually exists in a situation where "the possible perpetually surrounds the real."[18] The alternatives which beckon to man are legion, and, so long as he refrains from choosing among them, he remains caught in a "maelstrom eddying in upon itself and without direction."[19] The man who is trapped in the maelstrom and exists without choosing tends toward evil by having exchanged undirected possibility for undirected reality. On the other hand, whoever discovers direction turns toward the good: insofar as the soul can attain unity it will come to know direction and will recognize its mission to pursue direction; only then does the soul begin either to do good or to act on behalf of the good.

Man is charged with having to distinguish between and to choose among the possibilities which his concrete environment offers to him. But man is obliged as well to distinguish and choose among alternatives by knowing his own distinctive qualities and by being conscious of his personal goal; from among the available possibilties, a man can therefore choose those which are appropriate to his ends. Buber believes that the one-time creation of human life was a creation not for the mere sake of existence itself but for the filfilment of the purpose of existence. In Buber's view, this purpose has a personal character and represents the realization of the intention in an infinite variety of shapes and guises.[20]

The dual objective of choosing among the possibilities offered by the environment and choosing within the soul can be realized by man, because among the creatures of the world only man is able to assume an attitude of detachment toward both his environment and himself. Man's capacity of detachment toward himself is of a degree that allows him to make of himself a separate entity that he can investigate objectively, and which he can consciously judge, approve, and censure as well.[21] Not only can man understand objects and situations but he can also understand this understanding.[22] Man's choosing is no single and unrepeated act: at every hour man confronts the need to choose.

Hence—Buber believes—evil is an evasion of direction: it is the avoidance of orienting the soul so that it can assume responsibility. Good is choice: it is acceptance, through response, of direction. "Man," Buber asserts, "is neither good nor bad; his chief quality is that he is both good and bad."[23] He alternates between situations of choice and absence of choice, Buber observes. However, only when the soul has attained wholeness can we make a choice; for it is only then that we can reply to the situation confronting us, and only then that our response emerges from our private selves. This choice engages "all the potentialities of the soul, and, whatever direction the soul may incline towards or intend to pursue, it must immerse itself in choice when any situation of choice confronts it; for otherwise there will only be a stuttering, a semblance of a reply, a substitute for response."[24] Buber's argument here leads to the conclusion that the "new" educationists' position respecting the pupil's freedom recalls the case they make for the release of instinct: in both instances direction is lacking—which is to say that both incline in the direction of evil, as it is defined by Buber.

In this connection, one of the central principles of Buber's educational doctrine comes into play—that of encounter, which is the focus of the process of education. Buber contends that the child is an active partner in the process by which his creativity is transformed, and that the agency of that transformation is the child's "originative instinct."[25] This instinct is primary and spontaneous; although it can direct the child either to create things or destroy them, it tends rather toward the making of things than aimless action. The encounter leading to "communion" between pupil and educator is meant to guide, direct, and support the child's potentialities, of which the instinct of creation is one of the most important. By virtue of this encounter, the reality with which the pupil grapples is made vital and actual, and those of its aspects that were abstract prior to the encounter become concrete and immediate.

As we have seen, Buber argues that the total environment educates the child. The difference between the influence of nature and society on the child, and the influence of the educator is in the intention underlying the educator's activity. Buber maintains that the aspiration to change another person is out of keeping with the teacher's vocation. The teacher's task is not to impose the "correctness" of his views or his personal truths on his pupils, but to implant and nurture in them what he believes to be correct, desirable, and true, and to do so by exerting his personal influence while appearing to his pupils in a guise which suits his own nature; for it is proper that the teacher's beliefs should ultimately come to rest in another person's being.[26]

The "old" education emphasizes the materials of study and assigns an exaggerated importance to the role of the educator; the "new" education stresses the role of the child;[27] whereas Buber gives equal weight to both the child and the teacher, while at the same time attaching great importance to the teacher's role.

Buber rejects the idea of the traditional pedagogue, who appears under the guise of the "man with a will to power"; the old teacher was an incarnation of values sanctified by the overwhelming forces generated by tradition. If we conceive the teacher to be the world's representative in the classroom, then the traditional teacher was the apostle of the historical world, who interpreted his mission as one in which he either imposed the values of the world on the consciousness of the child or drew the child's consciousness toward the values of the world.

In the modern era, the authority of our heritage is in decline and the spell of conventions has lost its hold over us. As a consequence, the modern teacher can no longer assume the role of the representative of tradition; when he appears before his pupil he does so in his capacity as a private person. In this confrontation between the teacher as individual and his pupil, the "Eros" principle makes its appearance. It is against the erotic principle that Buber now sounds the alarm; for Eros means the desire to take pleasure in man, and so cannot be tolerated by education. "Eros is choice," Buber declares, "choice made from inclination. This is precisely what education is not. The man who is loving in Eros chooses the beloved. The modern educator finds his pupil there before him. From his unerotic situation the *greatness* of the modern educator is to be seen—and most clearly when he is a teacher."

Hence, Buber defines education as a responsibility entrusted to the educator over the domain of life. Moreover, the teacher does not wield his responsibility in order to impose himself on life; neither is his responsibility an instrument of his will to rule; nor, again, is it an extension of his erotic inclination. The educational situation requires the striking of a delicate balance between dedication and detachment, between intimacy and distance. The problem with which Buber now grapples concerns the manner in which this equilibrium can be achieved and the means by which the educator can assimilate the essence of education. Buber suggests that these may be accomplished by means of the elemental experience from which education begins and which Buber calls "experiencing the other side."[28] Buber explains that once a man has this experience, he will in each of his future encounters experience a two-fold emotional response: his sense of himself and his feeling for "the other side." Buber illustrates his meaning with an example:

A man caresses a woman, who lets herself be caressed. Then let us assume that he feels the contact from two sides—with the palm of his hand still, and also with the woman's skin. The twofold nature of the gesture, as one that takes place between two persons, thrills through the depths of enjoyment in his heart and stirs it.[29]

This kind of experience makes of the other person someone who is abidingly present; from the moment this takes place, subjectivity can no longer be the exclusive ingredient in the relationship. Buber calls what has taken place "inclusiveness," which he warns us is not to be confused with "empathy." Empathy—Buber tells us— means a man's getting out of his own skin, so to speak, and entering by means of his feelings into the dynamic structure and essence of an object; in the process he comes to understand the object's form by the perception he has of his own muscular structure. Empathy is therefore an act of self-annulment and self-omission. In-clusiveness, by contrast, is an extension of the self: it is the fulfilment of the situation in which we partake; the simultaneous perception of the two poles of the experience; the complete presence in a shared reality. Buber discerns three constituent elements in inclusiveness:

. . . first, a relation, of no matter what kind, between two persons, second, an event experienced by them in common, in which at least one of them actively participates, and, third, the fact that this one person, without forfeiting anything of the felt reality of this activity, at the same time lives through the common event from the standpoint of the other.[30]

The concept of inclusiveness introduces us to a new and important impli-cation of Buber's philosophy of *I-Thou*. Buber asks if mutuality is an abiding aspect in the relationship between one man and his fellow; if total mutuality can be permanently maintained; if indeed it ought to be maintained at all times. In his philosophy of *I-Thou*, Buber concentrates on the mutual turn-ing toward one another by two autonomous persons; Buber suggests that there are classes of relationship and some circumstances in which limits are set on mutuality. "There exist I-Thou relationships," Buber asserts, "which by their nature cannot be allowed to become wholly mutual, for otherwise they would be deprived of their distinctive character."[31] Examples of such limits to mutuality are furnished by the relationships between doctor and patient, and between teacher and pupil. Buber defines the situations in which the *I-Thou* relationship must be restricted as those areas of action that are characterized by a relationship wherein "conscious purpose is at work which is directed by one man towards another."[32]

The relationships between teacher and pupil, and doctor and patient are, as it were, ordained never to attain complete mutuality: for in such cases complete mutuality can lead to one side's domination of the other, and the other's dependency; or, at best, to friendship and mutual acceptance. Buber defines the pedagogic situation as one of bipolarity in which the teacher and education occupy opposite extremes, so that the teacher can be sensible to and conscious of his personal influence and the effect of his teaching, and do so from both his own perspective and that of his pupil.

What of the source of "inclusiveness"?—is the nature of inclusiveness framed in the world of the *Other,* or does its character take shape in the relationship of the *I-Thou?* Buber defines inclusiveness as "the experience of knowing that the self is aware of the other side."[33] If such is the case, then inclusiveness is in the domain of cognition and experience which appertain to the *Other.* But then, inclusiveness requires that the *presence* of the sharers in the experience of inclusion be characterized by complete and perdurable realization; its transactions, moreover, are unaccompanied by any outward signs that it is taking place. Hence, the teacher's act of inclusion embraces both the realization and the perception of the pupil's whole personality, which is connected with the relationship of the *I-Thou;* equally, the teacher's inclusive act is a reflection of his awareness and recognition of the student, and these emanate from the domain of the *Other.*

Buber discerns three archetypes of the dialogical relation. The first model describes a relationship based on an abstract although mutual experience of inclusiveness; in this experience of our fellowman, we assume our spirituality with reluctance and give voice to our thoughts out of the fullness of our personal essence and existence. The other two models of relation flow from an inclusion of this full reality. The relation of education is based on the experience of tangible although one-sided inclusiveness.

Buber believes that education is the transference of a selection of the world to the pupil through the medium of the teacher; he therefore warns of the risk that the educator may make his selection and exercize his influence not through the medium of the student's reality, but through himself alone and the concept which he has created for himself of the pupil, thereby making of education an arbitrary act. To illustrate the danger, Buber cites the example of Pestalozzi's teaching method. Indeed, when we examine Pestalozzi's concept of education, his pedagogic approach and his teaching method, they reveal Buber's criticism to be justified.

Pestalozzi put the child at the center of education. He maintained that education must consider each and every child individually; that all existing rules of pedagogy which are aimed at children as a group rather than at a particular child pervert education and injure the child. Since education, in the opinion of Pestalozzi, is entirely a matter of the development of the inner potentialities of human nature, it can only play the midwife to nature and be a ministering guide to emergent natural forces. Pestalozzi viewed the independent development of the child's powers as the sole natural process that concerns the education of man. However, to bring about the consummation of man's intellectual, moral, and physical potentialities, the child has need of the assistance of the teacher and his art. Moreover, the craft of pedagogy must be subject to the straightforward ways of nature. Teaching, then, according to Pestalozzi, is no more than the encouragement of the pupil to help himself. But the moment Pestalozzi put his theory into practice, his initially uncomplicated approach began to take on an increasingly arbitrary character: rather than begin with the reality of the pupil, Pestalozzi made himself and education, as something whose nature is self-determined, his point of departure. Pestalozzi insisted that the child must learn according to nature's way: by experience; by becoming aware of reality; by observing his environment; by direct contact with his society. By his concern of "natural" learning, Pestalozzi does not mean that education should be left to nature, from which the child learns at random through his altogether haphazard contact with it; his real intention is a system which would regulate the child's assimilation of ideas which the child learns from nature. When, however, Pestalozzi came to implement his ideas, he was trapped by the dangerous notion of basing the whole of teaching on merely three elementary pedagogic principles: number, form, and word. Thus, Pestalozzi's method abdicates its claims to being natural: it leaves room for neither the child's inner development nor his immediate perception of the external world. Instead we are faced by a mere reflection in the mirror of a contrived triad of principles remote from both nature and the child. In this way Pestalozzi subjugated all of teaching and the faculty of observation itself to the three spare precepts constituting his personal theory of cognition.[34]

Buber points out that the contradiction contained in Pestalozzi's approach and the doctrines of those who take a similar line arises from the stifling of the act of inclusion. Buber tells us that a man called upon to exert his influence on the being of those receptive to it must perceive this act from the other side; he must, as it were, face himself as if standing on the side opposite, exist within the other's soul. This other soul is no abstract entity, no mere idea in the mind, but is the soul itself, the very actuality of another person who is a partner in the shared labor of teaching and learning.[35]

However—Buber adds—it is the teacher solely, and never the pupil, who experiences the other side as something felt and known. While the pupil's learning will be cognizable to the teacher, his teaching cannot become known to the pupil. The teacher is present at both extremes of the shared experience; the pupil only at one. For the moment the pupil is able to sense and know the teacher's work, the pedagogical relationship will either crumble or be transformed into a relationship of friendship experienced reciprocally. Friendship is the third model of the dialogic relation: and although friendship shares with the educative experience the quality of being actual and tangible, it is unlike education because it is two-sided, whereas education is exclusively one-sided.

The teacher and his pupil respond to each other's presence as to a unique essence that is concrete and actual; they realize one another, but in a way that is unaffected by mutual inclusion, which is a transaction belonging to a different sphere of experience. As we have remarked earlier, mutual inclusion would destroy the educative relation. By contrast, mutual realization and the perception by two persons of one another as a presence sustain the educative relation because they lay the foundations of the pupil's confidence in the teacher.

A distinction should be drawn between the pupil's trust of his teacher—which is based both on the preservation of his personal being and on the maintenance of the mutuality of realization—and the trust which is total and is conferred on the "Demonic Thou." The "Demonic Thou" is often embodied in the type of the leader of which Napoleon is an historical example: he is attached solely to his own interest; he is untouched by the relation of the *I* to the *Thou,* and altogether free of the realization of the *Thou.* All about him is the *Other,* constituting the sphere of his interest; reciprocity has no part in the relationship with the Demonic Thou, to whom no man can be *Thou.*

> All are set afire by his flame, while he himself stands in a flame that burns cold; in the thousands, threads of relationship stretch towards him, yet not even one thread stretches from him; he has no portion in any reality, whereas boundless and innumerable are the realities which have a portion in him.[36]

This, then, is the peril in store for education which is void of the mutuality of realization.

Hence, the educative relation is composed of both the mutuality of realization and the one-sidedness of inclusion. Mutuality makes possible the relationship of education, because it makes the pupil trusting and accessible. One-sidedness sustains the educative relation, because it preserves the distance between participants. Finally, distance assures the continuance of one-sided inclusion, and so prevents the destruction of the educative relation and its conversion into the relation of friendship. It is this simultaneous duality of distance and intimacy that informs the nature of the teacher's relation to his pupil.

These relations are the context in which the teacher discovers his pupils: he comes to know both what they lack and what they have need of; he also gains a deeper understanding of his own limitations, which determine what he can and cannot do for his pupils. The sense of responsibility which the teacher thus acquires toward the soul entrusted to him opens the way to self-education. The world's potentialities, which the pupil needs in order to shape his existence, are collected by the teacher to be stored in the pupil's breast. In gathering the creative forces of the world, the educator also teaches himself to be their instrument.

Buber takes strong issue with Georg Kerschensteiner, one of the most influential figures in the modern educational movement in Germany. Buber concentrates his attack on the theory of the education of character proposed by Kerschensteiner in his well-known work, *The Concept of Education and Character.*[37] While stressing that education worthy of its name is the education of character, Buber reminds us that we would do well not to exaggerate the importance of the part of the educator in shaping character; in this aspect of pedagogy more than any other the educator must keep in mind the limits set on influence that is consciously exerted.

Georg Kerschensteiner distinguishes between two catagories of character, which he calls "character in the most general sense" and "ethical character." By his first category, Kerschensteiner means the attitude a man adopts to his environment; it is, in Kerschensteiner's words, "That abiding disposition of the spirit according to which each and every transaction of the will is unambiguously determined by principles or laws that endure within that spirit."[38] Kerschensteiner's second distinction, that of the ethical character, concerns the attitude which in implementing values prefers those whose claim is absolute to all others. In response to Kerschensteiner's distinction concerning the ethical character, Buber argues that were we to accept it, then we should face a problem of such gravity in respect of the education of character in our age as to make the very possibility of such education an unlikely prospect.

Buber attempts to elucidate the meaning of the "values whose claim is absolute" to which Kerschensteiner attaches so much importance. It is clear to Buber that Kerschensteiner is not speaking here of the subjective claim made by the man who is acting. Nonetheless, one of the most conspicuous trends in our period has in fact been the denial of the reality of universal values and norms whose claim is absolute. Buber argues that this denial is not merely aimed at the sanctioning of norms by religion—as is sometimes believed—but at the nature of the norms themselves and their whole claim to absolute validity; at their demand to dominate man by virtue of their nature and to impose their dictates on all of mankind. As a result, the very ground for the creation of what Kerschensteiner calls "ethical character" is continually shrinking. Today, there no longer exists a suspreme authority of idea, faith, or spirit: its place has been usurped by collectives, each of which lays claim to sovereign dominion over those who have become its bondmen. Hence, the man for whom there exist no values, whose claims are of an absolute and universal validity, cannot be educated to adopt "the attitude which in implementing values prefers those whose claim is absolute to all others." Only someone who in fact wishes to adopt a significant ethical posture can be so educated. Therefore, the method of the education of character must be shifted from the domain of the individual's relation to that of his private self. The personality must be saved from the collective; but to reestablish our personal contact with the absolute, we must first reestablish our human nature.

Kerschensteiner introduces the concept of the "personality" into his discussion of the education of character. The essential nature of the autonomous personality—Kerschensteiner believes—is always self-formation independently willed by the personality. Character is self-discipline and voluntary acceptance of laws that are created within the person himself by the lessons he draws from his inward experience and introspection; and this holds whether the laws are first received by him and then accepted in their entirety for his very own, or whether they have been consciously enacted by him alone. So long as the organization of values takes shape as an autonomous and conscious enterprise, and so long as it does so in accordance with the laws governing the conscious mind of the individual person, we may legitimately speak of an autonomous or free personality that has a moral dimension.

Buber refuses to accept the personality described by Kerschensteiner as being free. The personality in Kerschensteiner's system, Buber tells us, is one that has merely acquired the habit of self-control: the discipline which is imposed from the outside is by degrees transformed into self-discipline. Hence, the underlying basis of the definition of character proposed by Kerschensteiner is merely an arrangement for achieving self-control through the accumulation of laws, and so is really no more than a system of habits. Buber does not belittle either the utility of beneficial laws or the virtuous habits acquired by the personality. But, as Buber remarks: "the determination of his own goal, the autonomous concept of character (which is his main concern), can be comprehended by him—even if rarely—only on the very highest plane of his activity, high above all laws and habits."[39]

Buber's criticism of John Dewey's theory of human nature described in Dewey's book *Human Nature and Conduct*[40], resembles his objections to Kerschensteiner's doctrine of character. In his book, Dewey stresses the centrality of habits in behavior. Dewey's thesis is that character is the integration of habits; without the continuous engagement of the whole range of habits in every act, the personality as a whole would remain unintegrated and there would exist only a series of discrete responses to separate situations. In Dewey's book, habits are the foundation of his philosophy of ethics, his definition of character, and his analysis of human psychology.[41] Buber rejects Dewey's approach as he does Kerschensteiner's.

As an alternative to the ideas of Kerschensteiner and Dewey, Buber offers the concept of the "great character," which is constituted by his distinctive nature to act with his entire being in order to respond as an active agent to each situation according to its unique demands. In this way the education of character does not become merely a method of administrating culture, order, and law in the hope that civilization and the rule of law may eventually be internalized by the pupil and inwardly enacted by him.

It is not Buber's intention to imply that the great character stands outside of norms, but only that the decrees of genuine norms can never become a set of rigid precepts for him, and that his obedience to them can never take on the character of routine habit. The decrees of norms do not operate on the level of his consciousness, but take place at the deepest layer of his being, for it is there that they are stored and there that they await their summons each time a situation requires their enactment. Here we are at the heart of

Buber's disagreement with Kerschensteiner. For Kerschensteiner, as well, argues that the consciousness of unity exists at the core of the personality, and that both the consciousness of the will to achieve unity and the consciousness of the direction toward which this will strives are at the core of the ethical personality. Thus, the ethical personality strives to achieve a comprehensive knowledge of its whole nature in all its aspects; it tends to enlarge so far as possible its capacity to assume values, while at the same time it restrains its will respecting its faculty and potentiality of action, because it is aware of the need of self-restraint in the formation of personality.[42] In Kerschensteiner's view, the decree of a norm is an integral part of the personality's consciousness: intention, action directed toward a goal, and the self-imposed limits set by the personality in consideration of laws are all active principles. The case of Buber's "great character" is different. In the great character, the decree of a norm emanates from the inmost layer of his nature, and it is called into being by the situation that demands its enactment, even when he himself had no previous knowledge of the form that the decree would take.

Having dedicated so much space to Buber's criticism of the attitudes of the adherents of the new education, we ought now to consider those views and trends in modern education to which Buber subscribed. Buber was in particular sympathy with the insistence of modern education that coercion, indoctrination, propaganda, and preaching be cast out of the classroom.

Buber raises his view in protest against the concept, still very much in evidence, according to which the primary concerns of education are, first, knowledge, which is *transmitted* by the teacher and with which the pupil is *imbued*—and, second, values, which are *inculcated* in the pupil and in whose image the pupil is *formed*. Similarly, Buber rejects the view that the individual is not to be defined merely as a member of his society, but as one whose personality is the product of his social existence, and that the vocation of the pupil is to conform to the patterns of conduct accepted by the society in which he expects to live. Thus Buber rejects the position of Durkheim, who defines education as the influence exerted by adults on those as yet unprepared to take an active role in society; the aim of education, Durkheim maintains, is to awaken and develop the intellectual and moral attitudes in the child which are required by both the society and the particular environment in which the child will take his place when he matures.[43]

Buber recoils from the methods by which some educators hope to influence their charges by imposing on them opinions and patterns of behavior in a way designed to make them believe that the spiritual result stems from their own ideas, whose emergence was merely encouraged by the teacher's influence. Buber cautions against disguised indoctrination and propaganda, which are the real intention of this method. He is unequivocally opposed to the propagandistic approach to education, because it is blind to the unique nature of the other person and is exclusively concerned with its own immediate goals; the propagandist not only regards men as objects with whom he can never develop a relationship, but he even takes pains to deny them their very substance and autonomy.

Buber maintains that the propagandist has no interest in the humanity of those whom he wishes to influence. He is concerned with the other's personal qualities so that they may be used in order to dominate the other person. Not only in the traditional but even in the modern school—where vestiges of traditional education are still preserved—propaganda and indoctrination continue to exert their influence. To this day the school pursues the aim of leveling mankind in order to ensure that the individual should conform to a uniform pattern of social behavior and to the ideals put forward by society's leadership; this is the reason—Buber holds—that so much of pedagogy and teaching is given to indoctrination, preaching, and compulsion.[44]

In contrast to the propagandist, the educator as conceived by Buber exists in a universe constituted by discrete individuals to whose needs he ministers. The educator recognizes each of the individuals whom he serves to be a unique being whose presence in the world occurs no more than once: a living creature who is a subject for guidance toward a form of existence which is particular to himself and which is fulfilled by himself alone. The educator perceives every man as one who exists in a process in which the potential is becoming actual, and he interprets his own role to be one of encouraging potentialities to emerge.

> The educator cannot wish to impose himself, for he believes in the activity of potentiality becoming actual—that is to say, he believes that submerged in each man is the potentiality of probity which exists as something personal, unrecurring and unique; he is entitled to impose himself in no other way than that of the educator, and as such he is entitled, obliged indeed, to reveal and nurture probity.[45]

The educator believes in man; therefore he believes in the possibility of educating men and in men's own capacity to arrive at a unique form of existence. The teacher's task of assisting in the process of maturation is made possible by encounter.

For this reason Buber shrinks from the idea of structured education imposing a pattern on the pupil that has been fixed either by tradition or by a system of socially acceptable values. Buber rejects, for example, the opinion of Yehezkel Kaufmann, who maintains:

> In its essence, the task of education is *authoritative*. Its aim is always the *conquest* of the soul of the pupil by the spirit which is born by the educator; without this conquest education cannot function at all . . ., and so far as the pupil is concerned, he always remains a pupil, and ever remains the heir and offspring, even if he ends by casting away his inheritance or changing it to suit his inclinations.[46]

Kaufmann considers the principal task of education to be one of the advancement of the formation of the personality in the spirit of the values that have taken shape within a particular culture. The individual, Kaufmann observes, has to assume the burden of both the human values and the objective spirit which a specific culture has given rise to. According to Kaufmann:

> The objective spirit, actualized in civilisation, perceives the conquest of the soul of individuals as the fulfilment of its absolute privilege. It makes of them *civilised human beings* without consulting them. It endows them with its own established values, and commands them: by these shall ye live all the days of your civilized lives.[47]

Buber does not accept the validity of a received doctrine of values. He argues that a good teacher can demonstrate a value orientation to his students, but the very nature of his calling denies him, under any circumstance, the right to dictate an established value-doctrine meant to be adopted by his contemporaries. Rather, each of his pupils must discover the values for himself by mustering all of the potentialities of his personality in his quest for values. Although Buber keeps aloof from any rigid doctrine of binding values, and notwithstanding his insistence on personal decision in the domain of values, he nevertheless does not regard himself to be exempt from having to offer values to his pupils and suggesting alternatives; from introducing his pupils to the idea of value, from submitting values to careful scrutiny, and, finally, from presenting to his pupils examples of personal choice. Buber is a strong believer in the young, and wishes only to acquaint them with the possibilities and to elucidate for them the varieties of relationship, while allowing the young to choose for themselves.

Like many adherents of modern education, Buber rejects the idea that knowledge should be given priority in the classroom. Traditional education has laid down that there exists a set of subjects which men must master and which the school is therefore required to transmit; such knowledge being essential, it must be inculcated in such a way as to be acquired by the pupil and willingly accepted by him. To achieve this end, the pupil must be tested in order to assure that knowledge has not only been received but retained as well. Buber counters the assumptions of traditional learning by arguing that the mere quantification of disparate items of knowledge cannot be regarded as learning unless they become a part of an organic spiritual unity, which cannot be achieved solely through the acquisition of subject matter. What is important to education is not the accumulation of knowledge by rote learning, but constructive criticism, the direct experience and the personal integration of the discrete data that have been received; not information which has been collected and memorized but information which after having been considered and weighed has been converted into "active knowledge" that operates as an integral part of personal conduct. Buber's recoil from the concept of education as a hoarding of passive information that remains unintegrated in a significant context recalls the position of Alfred North Whitehead, when he warned against the "inert ideas" that the conscious mind assimilates without actually putting them to use, submitting them to examination or arranging them in new combinations. Whitehead explains that the failure of educational institutions is the result of the sheer weight of inert ideas which they have shouldered. Inert ideas—Whitehead claims—not only yield no benefits but do harm. He remarks that intelligent, mature women who have had no formal education are at times the most cultured group in society for the very reason that they have been spared the dreadful burden of inert ideas. Every intellectual revolution that has ever raised mankind to greatness, Whitehead asserts, has also brought with it an emotional protest against inert ideas.[48]

Buber holds that rather than impressing a vast array of facts on the student's memory, we must educate him in such a way that his knowledge—that is, the whole complex of his information—becomes an organic part of his existence. Hence Buber opposes the widespread idea that teaching is in the main a purely intellectual activity with which other factors can only interfere.

Buber's attitude has a number of implications for the teacher's position in the educational process. Buber conceives "relation" to be the basis of education. He does not intend this term to represent an intellectual relationship between teacher and pupil in which a developed mind exerts its influence on one that is still immature. Rather, relation is the affinity of one soul to another. Buber does not take for his model the representative of the world of knowledge and ideas, or the spokesman of society, whose vocation is to form, communicate, transmit, and inculate; the teacher, in Buber's view, does not address himself *ex cathedra* to those seated at his feet. Rather, Buber believes that the act of education is a genuine reciprocity: an exchange taking place between an adult spirit and spirits in the process of being formed. This is not a transaction in which pupils address their questions from below and the teacher replies from on high; indeed, it does not in any way involve questions and answers being issued from both sides. Buber advocates a genuine, shared, and reciprocal dialogue which, although managed and arranged by the teacher, is at the same time uninhibitedly and directly entered into by the teacher with the whole of his personality.

Some students of Buber who have attempted to translate his educational philosophy into a practical program of education either had made mistaken assumptions that have distorted the nature of Buber's point of view or have strayed into making a simplistic interpretation of his doctrine as a set of directives to be applied to the didactic situation. These directives are formulated in such a way as to contradict Buber's whole philosophy. Howard Rosenblat's suggestion of putting Buber's concepts at the service of education is a case in point.[49] Although Rosenblat grasps the tenor and the principles of Buber's concepts of the *I-Thou* relation and of dialogue, he does not seem to be aware that in his discussions of the examiniation and evaluation of pupils, and of the teacher's *obligation* to enter into dialogue with his pupils, he has left Buber's formulations intact but has done violence to their spirit. The nature of the "relation" between the teacher and his pupil is such that the dialogic situation is not subject to dictates, nor to the laying-down of rules, nor to the establishment of a rigid framework. Nevertheless, John Schudder proposes a "Buber model for teaching" that joins freedom and authority.[50] Schudder believes that an interpretation of Buber's philosophy of dialogue can provide the basis for a teaching model in which freedom and discipline are combined, and which would go a long way toward solving the intellectual and moral perplexity of our age. He maintains that especially in our own times, when traditional principles are being shattered—in an age of great confusion concerning values, widespread doubt, and difficult reassessments—a Buber-based model might allow the teacher (who is conceived of as an expert by his pupils) to demonstrate his relation to truth by his genuine authority, while making no coercive demands on his pupils to accept his relationship with the truth. In this way, the pupils can develop their own individuality in a situation in which they respond to the teacher while he himself maintains a dialogue with the world of knowledge and science. The dialogic situation, in which mutuality of realization and inclusion that is both tangible and one-sided exist, is one of authority and freedom, which are the conditions of true democracy as well. Although Schudder is correct to view authoritative guidance and the freedom of the individual as a part of Buber's concept of education, he has moved a considerable distance from their original intention when he incorporated them into a model for teaching. The pith and marrow of Buber's philosophy is in the dialogic encounter with the reader, the pupil, and the *Thou*—and any attempt to congeal these into representative models is a violation of Buber's thought. No two encounters are alike: no dialogic situation can be repeated or reenacted. It is impossible to base an educational model on Buber's philosophy, since the encounter between teacher and pupil is newly enacted each time it takes place.

It might be said that Schudder's own encounter with the philosophy of Martin Buber was confined to the *I-Other* relation. Thus, he devotes much of his essay to a teaching model and very little to education itself, although teaching and education are at the core of Buber's thought. Before everything else, Buber's concept of education is concerned with the influence of the teacher's being on that of his pupils. This influence exists in every transaction that takes place between them: during classroom time and during recesses; when they speak and when they refrain from talking. The most important condition imposed by education is the true and actual presence of the educator in both spirit and body. Buber maintains that in true dialogue the appeal to the interlocutor is sincere. Each speaker addresses his partner with the knowledge that the latter is a private person. What takes place is inclusion; and this act is not exhausted by the mere fact that the speaker apprehends the person whom he is realizing, but he must also acquire his fellow as a partner in dialogue and confirm all that depends on his confirmation. This confirmation is not consent, but an affirmation of the pupil in his capacity as a human being.[51] We should remember that Buber does not attach great important to teaching per se. For it is not teaching that in his view educates, but the educator. Buber recognizes the urgency and indispensability of acquiring knowledge, but he considers its influence on a person's character to be only partial, affecting only one or another of his faculties. The teaching that concentrates merely on the inculcation of knowledge and the nurturing of habits is an incomplete activity and much the easier goal, because it makes no demand on the teacher that he be present with his whole being. The teacher's passivity toward his pupil's being will not necessarily cause him to fail in inculcating the knowledge he has to teach; the acquisition of information and the communication of new data rarely meet with opposition. When, however, pupils feel that the educator wishes to influence their character, "some of them who possess more than the average substance of real and independent character will rebel."[52] Only the teacher's complete presence and his sincere, genuine, confident, and responsible relation to the pupil will gain access to the pupil's trust, and so permit the teacher to exert his influence on the pupil's personality. As Buber puts the case:

> The educator need not be a moral genius in order to educate men of character; but he must be a vital man who expresses his being directly to his fellow men. His vitality is imparted with greater force and purity *especially when he has absolutely no wish to influence them* [my italics].[53]

However, none of this can take place within the framework of a model for teaching. Schudder's mistake arises from his excessive concern with the surface of Buber's philosophy and his failure to penetrate to its dialogic core.[54]

Buber sympathizes with some of the fundamental assumptions of existential education but also takes issue with a number of its principles. Unreligious existentialism represented in the philosophy of Sartre holds that there exist no *a priori* ethical models either in the form of divine commandments or arising from an objective cause external to the body and personality of man. According to this view, the absolute moral or religious values by which man would plan his existence are an illusion. Reality recognizes no essence prior to human existence. The absence of an external paradigmatic and purposive cause in life bestows on man a sense of freedom and independence from the authority of factors external to him. Hence, man is freeborn.

The choice he makes concerning his life and reality originates in him alone. Each of man's deeds is proof of a choice that is unencumbered by a preexistènt model. Activity is a demonstration of man's existential consciousness and marks the continuous process by which he exercises his options. "Accordingly," Sartre asserts, "the primary goal of Existentialism is to awaken in man the sense of that which he is, and to make him assume full responsibility for his own existence."[55] As we have seen, Buber's concept of freedom is very different from the idea of freedom as independence; hence Buber's conception of responsibility differs from the one presented by Sartre.

Buber's grasp of the relation of the *Other* and of the problem of values is poles apart from Sartre's. Sartre stresses separate existence; his heroes live solitary lives. For Buber, existence is principally the enactment of communion. The self is transformed into an autonomous essence in the very process in which the relationship with the other person unfolds, when the self is confirmed by another person.[56]

The educational existentialists who adhere to Sartre's ideas hold that the intellectual attitudes adopted by men toward situations are many and varied. However, what is decisive in the existentialist knowledge of the world is the priority of the consciousness of existence (I exist, therefore I am). Martin Green claims that the thinking individual does not ask what he can know but how he can know; he does not stand outside the world which he perceives as an object of substance, but seeks first of all to know the way in which the world is revealed to his senses as an actual and living entity. Not all knowledge is grasped as something immediately comprehensible, as something given by experience. However, in order not to distort his relationship with the world, the individual who knows how to begin with the consciousness of his own being must also recognize that he is situated in the midst of life.[57] Buber takes issue with the whole idea of making the self and self-consciousness a point of departure. In Buber's view, without the *Other,* the *I* is an impossibility.

Existentialist education is based on a subjective and individualistic bias that tends entirely toward the self. Existentialist educators argue that the tendency toward individuation present in man brings him to self-consciousness. Hence, a distinction is drawn by existentialists between the self and the world. Buber rejects both this distinction and the subjective tendencies of existentialist thought. Instead, he proposes that genuine existence can only develop within the communion which takes place in the relationship of a man and his fellow man. Man is not discharged from personal responsibility merely by sharing in the pursuit of a common goal; nor is this pursuit-in-common the principal aspect of communion. Communion requires that in the course of this pursuit the affinity between man and man, which flows from the *I* to the *Thou,* should take place at all times. "Communion is only found where communion takes place. Collectivity is based on the organised annihilation of the personality, communion—on the exaltation and encouragement of the personality within the context of the dialogue between man and man."[58]

The educational philosophy of Buber is the consummation of his thought on the subject of education. A pedagogical model, designed to be imitated, cannot be based on Buber's philosophy. Nevertheless, Buber's philosophy confronts modern education with a challenge and makes a genuine contribution by suggesting some solutions to the perplexity of education in our times.

NOTES

1. For a thoroughgoing account of Dilthey's approach, see H. A. Hodges, *Wilhelm Dilthey: An Introduction* (New York: 1944).

2. See especially Eduard Spranger's works: *Lebensformen* (1914); *Kultur and Erziehung* (1919); *Psychologie des Fugendalters* (1924); *Volk, Staat, Erzeihung* (1932).

3. The following studies comparing the philosophies of Martin Buber and John Dewey are of particular interest: James Mullins, "The Problem of the Individual in the Philosophies of Dewey and Buber." *Educational Theory* 17: (1967): 76–82; Paul E. Pfuetze, "Martin Buber and American Pragmatism," in *The Philosophy of Martin Buber,* edited by Paul Arthur Schilpp and Maurice Friedman, (London: Cambridge University Press, 1967) pp. 511–42.

4. On Ruskin's special contribution to education through art, and on the application of Ruskin's ideas by Ebenezer Cooke, consult: Herbert Read, *Education through Art,* (London: Faber & Faber, 1943) pp. 167–68.

5. Martin Buber, "Education" in *Between Man and Man,* trans. Ronald Gregor Smith (New York: Macmillan, 1948), p. 83.

6. Ibid., p. 87.

7. Ibid.

8. Ibid., p. 88.

9. For a more detailed discussion of the subject, see my article "Sheelat harakhim ve-ha-hinukh le-arakhim be-mishnato shel M. Buber" [The question of values and value education in the philosophy of Martin Buber], *Ha-hinukh,* (Tishri, 1976), pp. 32–54.

10. Buber, *Education,* p. 88.

11. Ibid., p. 89.

12. Ibid.

13. A. S. Neill, *Summerhill: A Radical Approach to Child Rearing* (New York: Hart Publishing Company, 1960).

14. Buber, "Education," pp. 90–91.

15. Ibid., p. 90.

16. Ibid., p. 86.

17. Martin Buber, "Tmunot shel tov va-ra" [Images of good and evil], in *Pnei adam: Behinot be-antropologia filosofit, [The Face of man: Studies in anthropological philosophy]* (Jerusalem; Mosad Bialik, 1962), p. 346.

18. Ibid., p. 363.

19. Ibid., p. 364.

20. Ibid., p. 374.

21. Martin Buber, "Ashma vi-rgashot ashma" [Guilt and guilt feelings], ibid., p. 202.

22. Martin Buber, "Rahak ve-zika" [Distance and relation], ibid., p. 117.

23. Martin Buber, "Ha-sheela she-ha-yahid nishal" [The question asked of the individual], in: *Be-sod siah: al ha-adam ve-amidato nokhah ha-havaya, [Dialogue: One man and his encounter with existence]* (Jerusalem: Mosad Bialik, 1964), p. 204.

24. Buber, "Tmunot shel tov va-ra," p. 375.

25. Buber, "Education," p. 85.

26. Buber, "Rahak ve-zika, p. 128.

27. Buber, "Education," p. 94.

28. Ibid., p. 96.

29. Ibid.

30. Ibid., p. 97.

31 Martin Buber, "Aharit davar la-sefer ani-ata," [Epilogue to the book of I-Thou], in *Be-sod-siah,* p. 99

32. Ibid., p. 101.

33. Ibid., p. 97.

34. See my book *Pestalozzi: Ha-ish ve-darko ba-hinukh* [Pestalozzi: The man and his career in education] (Jerusalem: 'Shealim', 'sifria pedagogit le-madrikhim, ha-makhalaka le-inyanei ha-noar ve-he-haluts shel ha-histadrut ha-tsionit, 1963).

35. Buber, "Education," p. 100.

36. Martin Buber, Ani ve-ata [I and Thou], in *Be-sod siah,* p. 53.

37. Georg Kerschensteiner *Theorie der Bildung* (Leipzig; B. G. Teubner, 1926).

38. Ibid.

39. Martin Buber, "Al hinukh ha-ofi" [On education of character], in *Teuda ve-yiud* [Mission and purpose], vol. 1: *Maamarim al inyanei ha-yahadut* [Essays on Judaism] (Jerusalem: Hotsaat ha-sifria ha-tsionit al-yedei hanhalat ha-histadrut ha-tsionit, 1965), p. 373.

40. John Dewey, *Human Nature and Conduct,* pp. 1–89 (New York: Henry Holt, 1922). See especially the first part, which treats the problem of habits as social functions, habits and will, character and behavior, custom and behavior, custom and ethics, habit and social psychology.

41. For an analysis of Dewey's conception of psychology and his philosophy of ethics, see: W. Gordon Allport, "Individual and social psychology in the philosophy of Dewey," in P. A. Schilpp, ed. *The Philosophy of Dewey,* (New York: Tudor Publishing Co., 1955), pp. 265–90; Henry W. Stuart, *Dewey's Ethical Theory,* ibid., pp. 293–333.

42. Kerschensteiner, *Theorie der Bildung.*

43. E. Durkheim, *Education and Sociology,* (Glencoe, Ill.: The Free Press, 1956), pp. 70–71.

44. Martin Buber, "Yesodot shel ha-ben-enosh" [Principles of the [relationship] between man and man], in *Be-sod siah,* p. 227.

45. Ibid., p. 228.

46. Yehezkel Kaufmann, "Nefesh va-ruah ba-hinukh" [Soul and spirit in education", in H. Y. Roth, ed. *Al ha-hinukh ha-tikhoni be-erets-israel,* [On high school education in Palestine] (Jerusalem,1939), pp. 245–274.

47. Ibid.

48. Alfred North Whitehead, *The Aims of Education* (New York: Macmillan, 1929).

49. Howard S. Rosenblat, Martin Buber's Concepts Applied to Education," *The Educational Forum,* (1971): 215–18.

50. John R. Schudder, "Freedom with Authority: A Buber Model for Teaching," *Educational Theory,* (1968): 133–42.

51. See Buber's discussion in Sikha ka-havayata" [Dialogue as experience], in *Yesodotav shel ha-ben-enosh",* p. 230.

52. *Buber, Al hinukh ha-ofi,* p. 367.

53. Ibid.

54. For severe criticisms of Schudder's Buber model, see: Edward David Kiner, "Some Problems in a Buber Model for Teaching," *Educational Theory* (1969): 396–403; Haim Gordon, "Would Martin Buber Endorse the Buber Model?" *Educational Theory,* (1973): 215–23. Kiner

and Gordon also discuss Schudder's errors of interpretation of a number of Buber's educational concepts.

55. Jean-Paul Sartre, *L'existentialisme est un humanisme* (Paris: Nagel, 1946).

56. On this subject, see: Theodore Dreyfus, "Behinot ba-zika ha-ani-zulat lefi Mordekhai Martin Buber ve-Jean-Paul Sartre" [Aspects of the I-Thou relation according to Martin Buber and Jean-Paul Sartre], *Bar-Ilan,* Sefer ha-shana lemadaei ha-ruah shel universitat Bar-Ilan, 12 (Yearbook of the Humanities of Bar-Ilan University, 1974): 243–53.

57. M. Green, ed. *Existential Encounters for Teachers,* (New York: Random House, 1967), p. 66.

58. Martin Buber, *Netivot be-utopia,* [Paths in utopia] (Tel-Aviv: Am Oved, 1947), p. 137.

2
The Question of Values and Value Education

Martin Buber examines this difficult question of values in the light of the attempts made by philosophy in the course of the history of thought to understand the role of the absolute and the relative in the domain of values. Thus, Buber conceives Plato's theory of Ideas to be a protest against the imposition of relativism on all values—a supreme effort by speculative thought in antiquity to restore the relationship between the moral and the absolute. As opposed to the world of physical objects, Plato establishes a world of pure forms, remote and beyond the reach of defilement, to serve as a primary image. He then charges man with the task of actualizing within his own self the absoluteness of the Ideas. The objective imitation of the Ideas by material things unfolds within the sphere of the subjective, by whose means it reaches out to embrace the totality of spiritual activity that is in the image of the Idea. Buber elucidates Plato's conception by stressing the fact that value is recognized at the moment that it is revealed to an individual who is determined with his whole being to become that which he was intended to be. Such knowledge cannot be taught except by awakening the personality's essential being to its affinity with that which thrusts beyond mere existence.

Buber confronts Plato's approach to the problem with the attempt of the Jews at the outset of their history to join the fundamental differentiation between good and evil to the Absolute. In this regard, Buber remarks:

Law and justice, the sanctioning of virtue and the suppression of wickedness, are not to be conceived of here as embodied in a heavenly polity which serves as a model to the community of men. The determining agent is not the cosmic order, but rather its Master, the Lord of heaven and earth—He who has commanded men, the creatures of His handiwork, to separate good from evil in their own souls, just as He in creating the world divided the light from the darkness.[1]

Buber observes that we are accustomed to perceive the relationship of Judaism to ethics and values as a mere reflection in a mirror created by divine commandment attended by the threat of retribution. He makes the point, however, that the prior assumption of the connection between morality and religious faith constitutes the fundamental conception that man, in being created by God, was also vested by Him in an autonomy which has remained inviolate ever since. In the dialogue between man and the Creator—which in Buber's view is the very essence of existence—man participates in unlimited freedom and in full possession of the capacity to initiate. It is in this way that choice, consummated by man inwardly within his own soul, is established.

By contrast, we have been witness in the last two centuries to a severe and ongoing crisis in the attempt to mediate between the ethical and the absolute. This crisis is revealed in the doctrines of various schools of philosophy in which relativism is made to dominate values. In this connection, Buber observes: "Such a philosophy, which adds the mirror of biology to that of sociology and psychology—just as Sophism had done at one time—enjoins us to expose and denounce the world of the spirit as a cluster of deceptions, delusions, ideologies and sublimations."[2] Thus, Marx locates all religious, ethical, political, and philosophical ideas in a historical process whose meaning can only be perceived in the changing means of production, and in the conflicts arising therefrom. The values and morality of every period are the ideal expression of the conditions in which the ruling classes exist; so long as class warfare continues, every distinction between good and evil is no more than a function of the class conflict and all norms of existence are merely the expression of the governing authority and the means by which it imposes its will. And what has been said concerning the changing content of morality may be said of moral judgments as well.

Nietzsche too conceives of the historical doctrines of ethics as instruments in the struggle for power between the rulers and the ruled. He maintains that values and the transformation of values stand in direct relationship to the increase in the power of those who determine the values. Nietzsche points out that the modern period is an age of the decline of the moral interpretation of the world, and as a result has arrived at nihilism. This nihilism will be checked when there will arise out of man himself an alternative to the existing race in the shape of a "superman" who is destined to become the criterion of the new values. Upon this concept, Nietzsche establishes the biological system of values wherein the "good-and-evil" scale is substituted by the "strong-weak" scale. In response to Nietzsche, Buber remarks: "In contrast to the doctrine of Ideas, that of the Superman is no doctrine at all, and in contrast to the scale of values determined by the Ideas, the strong-weak values scale is in no way a scale of values."[3]

Every attempt in our technological age to examine the subject of values must address itself to the relativity of values and the diminishing consensus respecting fundamental social norms. In addition, modern philosophy superimposes upon these factors the declining authority of traditional standards and the pluralism of values, which is at the source of the conflict between divergent social, political, cultural, and religious goals, and which underlies the expanding tolerance of democratic societies toward individualized styles of existence. Leo Tolstoy was preeminent in his day among those who challenged the prerogative invoked by traditional education to inculcate absolute values. Indeed, Tolstoy discarded the very concept of "education" and replaced it with the idea of "culture." Tolstoy conceived culture to be a reservoir accumulating heterogeneous values that survive and coexist because they continue to suit man's contemporary needs and are the point of departure for man's pursuit of newer and better modes of life. Tolstoy repudiates the existence of an ultimate goal for mankind; his system excludes rigid and immutable value criteria. He asks us to abandon the external values of tradition, which are more often than not degenerate manifestations serving the immoral purposes of our physical inclinations as adults. Instead, Tolstoy enjoins us to liberate the individual human spirit, possessed of its own unique purpose, by assisting it toward self-development.[4]

More recently, Jean-Paul Sartre has argued that no ethical model exists under the guise of either divine edict or an objective cause existing, so to speak, outside the body and personality of man. The absolute values furnished by either tradition or religion, in accordance with which man would lay out the course of his existence, are illusory. For reality knows no essence prior to the existence of man. The very absence of a paradigmatic and purposive cause endows man with a consciousness of personal liberty and his independence from authority external to himself. Man, Sartre holds, is freeborn. The choices man makes concerning his life and reality are actions that he alone initiates. Each of his deeds attests to the existence of choice unencumbered by preexistent models. Action itself demonstrates man's existential consciousness, which is the ongoing process by which he exercises his options. "Accordingly, the primary goal of Existentialism," Sartre asserts, "is to awaken in man the sense of that which he is, and to make him assume full responsibility for his own existence."[5]

In Sartre's universe man is solitary. Forlorn in a hostile world, he constitutes a challenge unto himself alone from which comes his sense of spiritual orphanhood. Modernism in Western literature has characteristically given ample expression to this concept. From the perspective of Sartre's heroes, the *other* represents a relentless menace. "Hell is other people" is the way Sartre expresses the idea in his play *No Exit*. An impassable barrier exists between a man and his fellows. "Because of the other," the self asserts, "I am denied my assigned place in my own world." The subjective entities remain absolutely separate, and "conflict is the original meaning of existence for the sake of others."[6] Here we have the source of the profound revulsion that accompanies the growing perception of the "other" in Sartre's *Nausea*.[7] However, the extreme of despair brought on by unmitigated solitude and life emptied of content is reached by Sartre in *The Age of Reason*.[8] In this novel Sartre's hero, Mathieu, is looking for an abortionist for Marcelle, who is pregnant with Mathieu's unwanted child. Mathieu meets Sarah, who has herself undergone an abortion. Sarah, trying to dissuade Mathieu, asks: "Don't you see what you intend to do?" To which Mathieu replies: "And when children are brought into the world, does anyone understand what he intends to do?" Sartre then has Mathieu add: "A baby—self-consciousness once more, a tiny unsteady point of light moving round and round, strive as you may you can never escape."

Although Buber is committed to existentialism, his grasp of the problem of values and the nature of the "other" is radically different from Sartre's. Sartre stresses existence in isolation; his heroes recognize only discrete *existences*. But for Buber, existence is in its essence an "existence-with." The self is transformed into an autonomous entity by the process in which it binds itself to the "other"; according to Buber, the I is confirmed in the "other."

Buber too raises the issue of personal consciousness. He repudiates all certitude that does not derive from the sincerity of personal consciousness. He insists that man stands in the presence of being and while doing so replies to the great questions of existence. The *I-Thou* relationship is located, as it were, in the zone between the *I* and the *Thou*. This relationship is one of genuine mutuality; it is neither reasoned nor analytical, but a dynamic movement of the *I* toward the not-*I*. The encounter of the *I* and *Thou* is a reciprocal act not to be achieved one-sidedly, for the relationship preexists those who participate in it.

Buber's philosophy of values is founded on religious faith and on the relationship between the *I* with the *Absolute Thou*. Buber defines religion as the bond of the human personality with the absolute at the moment that the personality immerses itself completely in this relationship. Buber argues that the man who aspires to make distinctions and to exercise choice within his own soul cannot rely on his inner being alone to provide him with a choice that is appropriate to his value system. Rather, the options of a value system issue forth only from man's personal relationship to the absolute. It would be proper to stress here the fact of the essentially personal relationship, rather than the criteria bequeathed by religious tradition. For as Buber says: "Even when the individual has acquired a criterion derived from religious tradition, such a criterion must return to the hearth of the essential truth of his personal relationship to the absolute, there to be reforged in order to achieve authentic validity."[9]

Maurice Friedman in his analysis of Buber's philosophy of dialogue and the *I-Thou* concept remarks that this philosophy is as important to Buber's theory of ethics as it is to his religious doctrine. Friedman asks whether Buber's philosophy of dialogue and the *I-Thou* relationship might not of themselves constitute an autonomous ethics based on Buber's "anthropology," without necessarily being connected to the relationship between man and God.[10] And indeed when Buber addresses himself to man's preferences, to man's acceptance or repudiation of the conduct and actions that are subject to his choice in accordance with whether or not they possess a particular value—Buber makes the claim that "the criterion by which such distinctions and choices are habitually made may be either traditional or illuminated and revealed independently to a particular personality: the main thing is that the flame of critical evaluation—whose beginning is to illuminate and whose end is to scorch and purify—should each time blaze anew from out of the depths of the soul."[11] Choice depends on *authentic being*. In Buber's religious philosophy authentic being inheres in the relationship between man and God, and in his anthropological philosophy it exists in the relationship between man and man. However, a more profound analysis of the subject reveals that we are not faced here by two separate doctrines of value, one religious and the other anthropological, but rather by their coalescence into a single doctrine. Following Buber, Friedman demonstrates that man meets with the *Eternal I* in his encounter with the *Human I;* for the essential value choice, realized and made concrete in the relationship of man to the world, opens the way to God.

In his essay "Images of Good and Evil" ("Tmunoth shel tov va-ra") Buber sets out to prove that there exists only a single tendency for sincere human choice. In the reality of being, the vast variety of human choices are merely variations of a unique choice that is continually realized in only one direction; and this direction can only be conceived of as the path leading to God. This holds true so long as man designates by the name of God not a mere projection of his own personality, but only his Maker, the creator of man's unique essence, which cannot be derived from the material world. Man's singularity is a paradigm or exemplar that has been placed in his care so that he may perfect it in action. Buber argues that the significance of an exclusive and one-time creation of human existence is not a creation for the sake of existence itself, but for the fulfillment of the purpose of being—a purpose whose particular manifestations are realized under an infinite variety of guises.[12]

In Buber's view, the source of every ethos is revelation, whether or not such revelation is consciously known or faithfully obeyed. Revelation is not conceived by Buber as a supernatural manifestation; nor need it be heralded by portentous thunders and lightnings on the mount amid the awful splendors of the wilderness. Revelation is eternal; among the infinity of its signs, there is no thing so small that it cannot serve for a token. What becomes known to us through revelation is not the pure essence of God unconnected with our existence, but God's relationship to us and our relationship to Him. Buber claims that we know of no revelation other than the one which is created in the encounter of the divine and the human—an encounter in which man takes an active part.

Because revelation is a meeting between the divine and the human, the possibility of distinguishing between them becomes the severe trial on account of which we risk the terror and dread that accompanies us in the act of choosing and in life. However, in accepting this course we establish an approach that is at once believing and critical. For we are thus enjoined by a difficult personal choice, taken in fear and in dread, to distinguish the godly from the human, both of which are contained in all genuine authority. Clearly, such a view must regard the congealment of this encounter by the dogmas of established religion to be no better than a mere deception. Buber argues that the historical religions tend to become a goal unto themselves and to put themselves in place of God. Thus, Buber exhorts established religions "to walk humbly with God and His will. Each must recognize that it represents but one of the ways by which God's word is made manifest in man."[13]

Buber defined his journey through the realm of values as a passage along a "narrow ridge." By this Buber meant that he does not cling to the broad plains of a comprehensive system embracing fixed, immutable, and absolute laws, but chooses instead to follow his own rocky path between gulfs which, though it lacks the security of declared religion, is marked by the certainty of what remains unexpressed and uncommunicated.[14] Maurice Friedman opens his book on Buber with a chapter devoted to the journey on the narrow ridge, and remarks that no expression could more perfectly describe the quality and meaning of Buber's life.[15] When applied to the situation of value choice, the phrase is indeed wonderfully appropriate. Man must risk by making a choice. For otherwise, by responding mechanically, he faces the peril of forfeiting his humanity.[16] Yet man has no way of knowing whether he has made the right choice in his journey along the precipitous path. No certitude exists in the realm of choice, only chance. The risk of making a decision is no surety for attaining truth. However, it is only by choosing that man is led to where the breath of life can be felt.[17] Such choice is never easy or secure, and we are constrained to choose according to the circumstances and the profundities of the situation to which we are subject.[18]

Buber indignantly rejects Marvin Fox's criticism that his views would imply that he does not believe that moral principles can have universal validity. In reply, Buber dismisses Fox's assertion by remarking that he has no doubt about the validity of the commandment "Honor thy father and thy mother." Buber adds, however, that no man can know in every circumstance and in every situation how the word *honor* is to be interpreted. Man learns the meaning of eternal values only by experiencing choice in his own life.[19]

Another argument of Fox's raises issues whose implications for education we dare not ignore, despite Buber's rejoinder and persistent adherence to his position. Fox asks what our attitude should be toward a man who commits a crime in the sincere belief that he is obeying the call of God. Buber responds that the situation described by Fox is absurd. For such a man is clearly mad and imagines himself to be God.[20] A sane man, Buber argues, can believe that he is fulfilling God's call only when he acts out of total dedication and with all his heart and soul.[21] Buber's reply not only confronts the educator with the potentialities latent in personal choice, but reveals the perils of significant personal choice as well. In this regard, we must take into account a man's maturity, the extent to which his humanity has developed to make him equal to the task of exercising choice, and, finally, we must calculate the chances of his slipping from the "narrow ridge" into the abyss.

A better understanding of the anthropological basis of Buber's concept of values would be gained by reexamining his doctrine of dialogue. According to Buber, our being cannot achieve fulfillment on its own, but must do so through the medium of the contact of man with man—through the mutual affinity between the *I* and the *Thou*. Buber contends that neither *I* nor the *Thous* exists apart: only the *I and Thou* relationship exists, which precedes both the *I* and the *Thou*. Man is transfigured into the authentic *I* by realizing the *Thou* relationship—by entering into a relationship with his fellow man that is direct and unmediated. Similarly, neither the *I* nor the *It* exists apart: only the *I and It* relationship exists, which is technical in nature and re- served for routine affairs and the achievement of practical ends. In the *I and It* relationship, the other person participates in the guise of the *It*. In Buber's words, "The primal utterance of *I-Thou* can only be made by a man with his whole being," whereas "The primal utterance of *I-It* can never be made by a man with his whole being."[22] In other words, the *I*—inherent in man from the very beginning—is realized and made manifest by way of encounter, and by the establishment of a bond of affinity with the *Thou*. However, this vital and direct relationship risks losing its place to the *I-It* relationship, from which the bond is missing, and which transforms the outside world into an object to be comprehended by rational categories merely. In Buber's view, it is the destiny of each *I* to become an *It;* for the genuine relationship of the *I-Thou* requires a bond of exceptional strength, tending easily to slacken and be loosed. By contrast, the *It* of merely routine social intercourse makes trifling demands, and as a consequence we flee from the importunate *Thou* to the less severely demanding relationship of the *I-It*.

Both the humane and the human, Buber asserts, come into being during true encounters. Each man has the need to confirm the existence of his fellow through the personal presence of each in authentic encounters. But a requirement that is even more fundamental to mankind is each man's need to know the truth, with which he grapples inwardly and which he finally grasps when it is revealed under another guise and to another man, whose differing relationship to the essence of that truth is shaped by the uniqueness of his particular nature.

Buber stresses that the achievement of deep inwardness by the self cannot come through the relationship of a man to himself, but only be means of his relationship to another. Put another way, the deepening of the self's inwardness occurs through the mutuality of "realization" or *Vergegenwärtigung**— by a man's *realizing* another self while the other is conscious of this realization, which is simultaneously and mutually declared to be taking place. Buber maintains that man wishes to have his presence confirmed by his fellowman and to be strengthened by the proximity of his fellowman.

Man's value choices are ineluctably bound to his dialogic relationships with his fellow man, with the world, and with God. Hence, in Buber's philosophy of values, *responsibility* has a vital role. As a consequence, Buber does not offer us a system of values that can be applied to specific cases. To the contrary: he makes the situation itself his point of departure. Buber believes that the idea of responsibility must be salvaged from the ancient domain of professional ethics—from the commandment hovering out of reach in space—and returned to earth where life is being lived. True responsibility exists only where there is true response.[23]

From this notion it follows that all received values—such as the Decalogue's Thou shalt not kill, steal, commit adultery, bear false witness, and so on—are the product of *I-Thou* relationships. Such values do not exist solely as rigid precepts codified in a book of laws, but constitute, rather, an essential choice made by man within the *I-Thou* complex of his relationships.

The *I-Thou* principle, which occupies the center of Buber's system, at times overshadows the category of the *We*. Too few students of Buber pay sufficient heed to the place of the *We* in Buber's philosophy. Although the dialogue is always transacted between the *I* and the *Thou*, Buber—following the lead of Heraclitus—remarks: "A man cannot make his whole need known in its primary significance, except that he say "We," and utter it neither lightheartedly nor insolently, but say it in truth."[24] Buber's *We* stands in absolute opposition to what Kierkegaard called "the crowd."

In Buber's own words, "The true *We*, as it is in its objective existence, may be recognized by the fact that each of its parts when examined reveals dwelling at its side—either actually or potentially—the essential bond between one person and the next, between the *I* and *Thou*."[25] The lifegiving principle of the *We* is speech, the shared discourse that begins in the exchange of the spoken word.

The *We* of which Buber speaks is not a collective, nor a group, nor any multitude that may be construed as an object. This *We* comes into being wherever a man reveals himself to his fellows in such a way that he is

---

*By *Vergegenwärtigung* Buber means the act of imagination by which a man concretely "pictures" what another man is sensing, feeling, or thinking at that very moment. What is thus imagined is not perceived as a subject separate from the other person, but as an integral part of his reality and life process. This "mental image" contains something of the nature of that which is being imagined. The experience can be compared to genuinely shared grief that is not merely routine solicitude, but a *felt* participation in the particulat sorrow experienced by the other person.

perceived as he really is—wherever a man transmits to his fellow man his own particular experience in such a way that it penetrates the core of the other's experience of the world and consummates the other inwardly. As is the case with the *I,* Buber's *We,* as an active principle, is not likely to be couched in the grammatical third person. However, the *We* lacks the permanence and continuity of the *I.* Buber observes that by virtue of its existing at the source of the whole history of man's thought and deeds, this *We* bodies forth, time and again, as a palpable presence, only to vanish repeatedly. This *We* may become manifest in the group, but is just as likely to blaze into life outside of collective existence.

According to Buber, man has always framed his thoughts in his capacity as *I,* and in the capacity of *I* man set his ideas in his heaven; but when man has acted in his capacity as *We,* he has planted his ideas at the very essence of being. The flight from a shared universe to the world of private stock-taking—which is perceived to be true being—is an escape from the existential claim made on the human personality that it be confirmed and validated in the *We.*

In his analysis of the character of the typical man of our times, Buber concludes that modern man's flight from the responsibility of personal existence has become polarized in a special way. A man who has no wish to bear the responsibility of validating his existence either escapes to the all-embracing collectivity, which frees him from his onus, or locks himself in the preserve of his private self, which is accountable to none but itself. "In our own age," Buber declares, "when the true meaning of all speech is hemmed in by fraud and deceit, when the first intention of the eye's glance is choked by suspicion, everything vitally depends on our recovering the purity of language and the innocence of the experience of *We.*"[26]

In replying to his critics,[27] Buber concedes to their charge that he neither recognizes a traditional creed of received values nor offers his own doctrine of values or ethics. But Buber adds that this fact is essential to his philosophical conception as a whole and pervades his educational consciousness. Any attempt to propose a binding system of values would necessarily strike at and annihilate the very core of his outlook on the world. Buber cites Hugo Bergmann, who formulates the pedagogic problem in his study "Buber and Mysticism" ("Buber ve-ha-mistica") in the following way: "Men ask their teachers to show them the way to mystical experience. They ask: 'Well then, what are we to do? How do we learn to accomplish this deed in the wholeness of our being inclining towards God? How shall we be taught to charge the act with the potency of intent?' "[28] Buber, while stressing that he is totally opposed to this kind of question, shifts its focus from the sphere of mysticism to the problem of providing the pupil with guidance in the domain of values. Buber is aware of the perplexity of a generation that is in search of binding values which would map out the proper path for it to follow. He insists, however, that a good teacher will do no more than to show the direction to his students. For the very nature of his calling enjoins a teacher from ever dictating to his students a fixed doctrine of values for them or their generation to adopt. Each of his pupils must discover the values for himself by summoning the full potential of his personality in his quest.

At most, the educator may indicate the way, suggest possibilities—but no more. Buber asserts that he has never offered in the past—indeed never will offer—a consummated doctrine of values: a text of principles which his students can consult when they confront a situation of having to make a choice, and from which they can crib the answers to the problems they face. Buber rejects out of hand the possibility that there can exist universal values which are valid for every man.

Buber argues that questions like "Why educate?" and "To what purpose?" could only be answered by those generations who acknowledged the universal validity of ideal images based on such ethical types as the Christian, the Gentleman, and the Citizen. When answering, these generations could point to luminous ideal images suspended in the heavens above. But in our times, when the whole structure of exemplary images lies in ruins, when no single image can break through the formal shell that confines it, only the image of God abides.[29]

For Buber, God alone is the source of all our ethical values. Only when man comes into contact with God's immortal power is he able to discover eternal values. Here, Buber lays special stress on the concept of *discovery*. Many cannot create values; however, he does have the capacity to discover values. "A man can receive values as a guide in life only if he discovers them, but not if he invents them," Buber declares.[30]

Discovery is closely connected with the meeting of man and God, with the encounter of hearkening and response. In our present world, we tend for the most part to be deaf to the summons. But when the call does reach us, and we in turn reply—then human existence, despite its defects, is made possible once again. The summons is always there; what is important to man is his readiness to heed the call. Man, by hearkening and responding, comes face to face with God and, in so doing, discovers values.

Divine revelation is no other than this coming face to face, this hearkening and response. However, revelation does not impose values on man. While God is the source of all values, He neither dictates them to man nor fixes the confines within which man is constrained to act.[31] The chief thing is for man himself to choose and decide.

Although Buber makes the divine indispensable to absolute values, he does not advocate heteronomy. Buber is no adherent of moral legislation from without. For lying at the very heart of Buber's conception are the acts of hearkening and response: mutuality, in other words. Indeed, the whole significance of mutuality resides in the fact that it does not seek to impose itself, but asks only to be taken hold of. Buber observes that mutuality merely offers us something to grasp, but does not give us the perception itself. The act of discovery must be entirely our own, so that it may disclose what has been given to us to reveal, what is designated to be discovered to each of us individually. Thus Buber announces: "In the Lord's theonomy shalt thou seek thy law, and true revelation shall reveal thee to thyself."[32]

Especially noteworthy in connection with this subject is Buber's response to the problem posed in the title of his article "What Is to Be with the Ten Commandments?" ("Ma yehe al aseret ha-dibrot?").[33] Here Buber is faced by a system of decrees claiming universal validity, and in a manner consistent with his approach, Buber lays stress on the oral nature of the Decalogue as discourse.* In Buber's view, the Ten Commandments are not an impersonal code in which the laws of the community at large are recorded in language purged of personal pronouns. The Commandments are expressed in the idiom of the *I* and *Thou*. The Decalogue opens with the "I" of *I am the Lord thy God* and is directly spoken into the ear of the auditor, who is addressed as "Thou." God does not address the hearer coercively. The words are proclaimed, and man is free to choose whether to attend the call directed at the *Thou* or to retreat from the summons.

Society, which is attentive to its needs and well-being, has an interest in seeing the Commandments obeyed, but it is not prepared to cede their maintenance to individual whim by making their acceptance or rejection a matter of personal choice. For this reason, society translates the Commandments from the sphere of faith to that of ethics and values, from the idiom of the spoken word to the language of coercive law; from here the road leads to juridical action and to the clear reckoning of punishment. Buber grants that the actions taken by society are legitimate, but argues that they have nothing to do with the essential nature of the Decalogue, nor with the existence of mankind, nor with the situation where the speaker and the spoken-to stand facing one another.

As to the question of what to do concerning the Ten Commandments, Buber answers that we must come closer to their real essence as speech. Thus, Buber exhorts us earnestly "to draw near them, not to the chapter and verse, nor even to the tables of stone on which they were engraved by the finger of God when He spoke them, but to their nature as spoken utterance [ela el ha-dibriyut ha-dvura]."[34]

Buber deals with the question of whether education should aim at the creation of a definite characterological type based on models embodying notions of value. He rejects the approach of Alexander Dushkin,[35] who proposes a model based on the synthesis of five historical Jewish types: the

---

*Buber's meaning is conveyed with greater immediacy to the speaker of Hebrew, to whom the Ten Commandments are known as the "Ten Utterances" or *asseet ha-dibrot*. *Dibrot*, meaning "utterances" or "words," is derived from the same root as the verb *daber*, "to speak."

Talmid ḥakham (the traditional religious scholar); the *ḥasid* (follower of the Hasidic movement); the *maskil* (intellectual of the Jewish Enlightenment); the Zionist; and the *ḥaluts* (early pioneer settler in Israel). Buber does not believe that education should aim at the creation of such a synthesis. Moreover such syntheses hardly exist, according to Buber, and even when they do, he insists that they cannot be made up of more than two such types that have merged by virtue of a profound intimacy that has been achieved during close collaboration. Historically, classical types have not been brought into being by pedagogic intention; they are created either as a personal expression of the conditions of an autonomous culture or as a personal response to the demands of historical circumstances. The historical circumstances of the early period of settlement in Israel gave rise to a genuinely new type in the figure of the *ḥaluts*. Although it is impossible to create new types pedagogically, it is possible to educate according to the example set by a new type that has emerged in a given historical setting. Moreover, when such a type appears as a contemporary of the educator, the teacher's pedagogic opportunities become more richly varied. New and still pliant, this type is receptive to the teacher's efforts to give it greater scope and depth; it is possible to influence the type itself, to make actual in it what is latent, to compensate for the deficiencies caused in the type by the situation from which it emerged. However, even the *ḥaluts* cannot serve as an ideal model because of his unsound and unintegrated relationship to tradition. This defect is made all the more acute by his dogmatic atheism, which prevents him from recognizing the difference between living faith and decadent varieties of religious belief.[36]

In place of a method based on exemplary patterns to be imitated, Buber proposes three pedagogic approaches by which values may be taught without having to confront an established dogmatic creed with another dogma that has been newly devised.

Buber's first proposal is for the teacher and pupils together to read the great spiritual documents of Jewish history from the Bible to Hasidic literature. By this approach, the students will not only come to understand the subject but will absorb from their readings something that is immediately relevant to them. Buber shows himself here to be close to the neohumanist educators. Although his approach is more profound and is charged with a religious and national purpose that is uncharacteristic of the neohumanists, they, too, put great stress on education based on the great works of the human spirit in order to deepen man's consciousness of ethics and values.[37]

Buber's second method leads the student by way of science to the limits beyond that human knowledge cannot reach—to that very question which marks the boundaries of reason and is accessible only to the soul's silent prayer. In the third approach, the teacher must exemplify and act out all that he has to teach; for what man is in truth remains a mystery that eludes interpretation.

Of far greater importance to Buber than the pedagogic use of representative types are the examples set by the teacher himself: the teacher's projection of his own personality, the intimacy he achieves with his pupils, and the dialogic relationship that he forms with them. The path toward genuine value education is opened to the student by the example of the teacher's own life, by the awareness of the personal choices made by him, and by heeding the teacher's speech and his silence.

In the past, the teacher exemplified the morality of secure values. He was the representative of the historical world, of what existed prior to education's coming into being. The teacher's conception of his task was to implant the values of the historical world in the minds of his pupils, or—in the best of cases—to attract the consciousness of the child toward the values. The authority of the educator flowed from the magical powers contained in cultural heritage. Now that such authority is continually losing its hold, the teacher can no longer appear before his pupils as a representative of tradition, but merely as a private person. From this time forward, the teacher is duty-bound to assume the full burden of responsibility for his authority over those who have been placed in his hands, and whom he must influence and guide, without, however, imposing his own personality on them. In order to bestow value perspectives on his pupils, the educator must dedicate himself chiefly to teaching his pupils to refine their newly acquired experiences and to submit these experiences to independent analysis. The pupils, in their turn, must discover the essence of their existence and arrive at abiding values independently. The student who becomes aware of the mystery lodged in the unity of inwardness learns to respect the mystery in all of its guises. Whoever comes to venerate this mystery in all of its manifest forms grasps the eternal as well. Thus, Buber proclaims: "Whoever looks and hearkens from within unity will also behold and hear again what has always been there to be seen and heard. The educator who assists man to find his unity, and returns man to himself, helps to set him once more before the face of God."[38] Buber believed that if the student learns to be sincere and forthright with himself, if he recognizes his inward unity—if, in other words, he seeks eternal values honestly—only then will he succeed in discovering values. It is by way of the *I* that we attain abiding values.

In contrast to those who speak of value education and pedagogic instruction, Buber maintains that it is the teacher rather than any instructional aspect that is important to education. The good teacher educates both by speaking and by keeping silent, during teaching hours and during recesses; he educates by the fact of his very own existence and by his intimacy with his students. The heart of education is discourse; the dialogue of query and reply in which both sides ask and both sides answer; the dialogue of the joint study by teacher and pupil of man, nature, art, and society; the dialogue of true friendship, in which the intervals of silence are no less dialogic than spoken discourse.[39]

Buber argues that education to be worthy of its name must be education of character. But he also observes that undue importance ought not to be assigned to the role of the teacher in the formation of character. Moreover, in this pedagogic sphere more than in any other, it is important for the educator to keep in mind the limitations of influence that is consciously exerted. In this regard, Buber turns his attention to the opinion of Georg Kerschensteiner, who in his well-known study *The Concept of Education and Character*[40] distinguishes between character in its most general sense— or the perception that a man has of his human surroundings—and *ethical character*—defined as the position taken with respect to action when those values whose claims are absolute are preferred to all other values. Buber makes the point that were we to accept Kerschensteiner's distinction concerning the "ethical character," we should confront a problem of such severe implications for the education of character in our times that serious doubt would be cast on the whole enterprise.

Buber attempts to elucidate the meaning of the "values whose claim is absolute" advocated by Kerschensteiner. It is clear that Kerschensteiner is not referring to the subjective claim made by the man who acts; the notion of the absolute claim can only refer to the universal values that the man of ethical character recognizes and acknowledges. However, the most conspicuous tendency in our period is precisely the denial of the reality of universal values and norms whose claims are absolute. Buber notes that this trend is directed not merely at the sanctioning of norms by religion but against the nature of the norms themselves and their claim to absolute validity—against their demand to hold sway over man by virtue of their nature and to impose their authority on all of humankind. As a consequence, the ground for the creation of what Kerschensteiner calls "moral character" is continually shrinking. Today, there no longer exists a supreme authority of idea, faith, or spirit: its place has been taken by collectives, each of which lays claim to sovereign dominion over those who have become its slaves. As Buber remarks: "People who have lost their independence to such an extent by their veneration of the collective Moloch cannot be redeemed from their perdition by the invocation of the absolute, for its throne has been usurped by Moloch."[41]

The path to the education of character originates in the relationship of the individual to his inner being. Buber urges that the true essence of the private self must be rescued from the maw of the collective. He argues that in order to personally reexperience the absolute we must start by rediscovering our human nature. "The retention of the alertness to pain and to pleasure is the first task of anyone who grieves at the eclipse of eternity; this is also the first task of the true teacher in our times."[42]

Buber introduces the concept of the *great character* to the discussion. He describes the "great character" as one who is not to be conceived of as a system of rules nor, again, as a system of habits, but as one who is distinguished by his ability to act with his whole being. The great character's particular virtue is his ability to respond to every situation that makes demands on him, and to do so in a way that accords with its unique nature.

> I call that person a great character who, out of deep readiness to assume the responsibility for his whole existence, responds with the totality of his actions and attitudes to the demands imposed on him by the situation; in this manner is revealed, together with the sum of his actions and attitudes, the unity of his being—a being which willingly accepts responsibility. Because his being is unity—the unity of the willing acceptance of responsibility—his active life, as well, merges with that unity. And we should add, perhaps, that the very situations to which he has responded, and for which he was responsible, bestow on him the unity of moral destiny, a unity which remains inexpressible."[43]

Buber does not mean to say that the great character stands outside of norms. He contends, rather, that the behest of true norm never assumes the guise of rigid rule and that its fulfillment never becomes routine habit. The command of genuine norm does not act as part of the great character's consciousness, but exerts its influence on the substratum of his essential self where it is kept in latent reserve until such time as it is concretely revealed to him by a situation demanding obedience to its call.

Although Buber keeps aloof from all rigid and binding value doctrines and upholds, instead, the principle of personally determined choice, he does not consider himself to be exempt from the task of bringing the values to the attention of his students: from introducing his students to the concept of value itself, from proposing alternatives, from submitting these to critical examination, from enumerating specific examples of personal choice. Buber is confident in the discernment of the young. He asks only to lay before them the possible modes of conduct and to elucidate their nature; the choice itself he leaves to youth.

Buber prefaced his 1918 lecture "Zion and Youth" ("Tsion ve-ha-noar") with the statement "The eternal hope of human felicity is youth, upon which mankind chances time after time, and which time after time mankind forfeits."[44] Youth possesses the momentum of action: it is animated by revolutionary enthusiasm for renewal and quickened by yearnings for the absolute; it is dedicated to ideals to the point of self-sacrifice; it is prepared to rebel, to force every obstacle, and to bring about change. But at the very moment youth undertakes its great enterprise, its young spirit is overpowered by the trivial goals appointed for it by society; and so, swept up by selfish instincts, by the temptation of pride and by the lust for fame, youth deserts its ideals. Society gets the better of the young by making it clear that the rebel's aspiration to be free of the cult of expediency will deprive him of the benefits of social success and make him an outcast. The young, dreading nonconformity and isolation, yield and accept the yoke of deceit, under which they spiritlessly plod within the furrows plowed in society's soil.

Buber believes that there exist moments of crisis in history when youth rebels against the inertia that society imposes on it. He contends that our own period is experiencing just such a crisis which summons youth to free itself from society's "vain apparatus" of coercion. The young are summoned to dare an impossible deed: to lengthen the hour of their youth—as Joshua lengthened the day of battle when he made the sun stand still upon Gibeon to complete his victory over the Amorites—and by doing so bring on the hour of change.

Yet Buber is aware that the summons goes unheeded. In his important essay on the subject of value education, "The Preconceptions of Youth" ("Deotav ha-kdumot shel ha-noar"),[45] Buber examines some of the reasons that prevent the call from being heard. He especially concentrates on the danger posed by preconceptions, which interpose themselves between man and the world. Preconceptions are opinions acquired in advance of experience, upon which alone an opinion should be formed. The opinions that men form on the basis of the experiences in their own lives frequently impede them from acquiring fresh experiences that would generate new conceptions. Buber proposes that even the young—despite their hunger for experience—resist the acquisition of new experiences. He notes that the young first adopt their attitudes in a rush of enthusiasm, and then, having chosen their position, they cleave to their opinion and preserve it from all change. For this very reason, the young are unwilling to compare their preconceived notions with new experiences that are essentially different from those they have already acquired. "They have no desire to acquire experiences which may subvert that which was seized upon in a moment of zeal; they desire no experience other than that which endorses their having taken a stand."[46]

Buber is not opposed to zeal; indeed, he is convinced that it is a matter of great importance for men to take a stand and zealously persist in it. Nevertheless, men must remain receptive to the world; they must see what is available to be observed, experience what is given to them to experience, and integrate each of their experiences in such a way that they may inform men's undertakings. Receptivity of the spirit is precious; by its virtue men's perception of the world is continually deepened and increasingly made to approach reality.

Buber lays great stress on the vital principle that is inherent in personal responsibility. He maintains that true community among men can only be realized in the achievement of mutual responsibility. The profound social crisis of our times cannot be prevailed against unless the individual commits himself in total earnestness to a position of personal responsibility toward the situation. It is from having to make such a commitment that our contemporaries retreat into the collective. Membership in the collective exempts the individual from having to assume personal responsibility. One need make the decision to join the collective but once in order to be delivered from the cares of responsibility. From that time forward the individual relies on the will and objectives of the collective and need not ask himself repeatedly if the means which the collective selects to achieve its ends are proper or if the ends for which society exists have been preserved.

Buber makes an essential distinction between the collective and the *community*.* The collective, he argues, is not a true bond, not a nexus by which men are bound one to another, but a "bundle" of discrete individuals existing side by side from which the vital connection between one man and another is missing. In the collective, the relationship between members exists only to the degree required for the achievement of a joint undertaking; responsibility in the collective is jointly held and exists for the sake of a joint enterprise. In this way, the collective relieves its members of personal reponsibility. By contrast, community is founded on the relationship of man with man. Here too members share the pursuit of a common goal; but this is neither the chief aspect of community nor does it exempt the individual from having to take personal responsibility. At every juncture in the shared journey, the members are drawn to each other by the flow of sympathetic affinity from the *I* to the *Thou*. Thus, Buber remarks: "Community is found only where communion flourishes. The collective is based on the systematic annihilation of the personality—community on the exaltation and the encouragement of the personality while the objective of the cohesion of man to man is being pursued."[47] This exaltation of the personality is closely bound up with the total assumption of personal responsibility.

Buber does not repudiate the idea of enlistment in a group, a party, or a movement, so long as these are in the nature of "communities." Nor does Buber believe that a movement need necessarily serve its members as a refuge from the claims of responsibility. Indeed, to be engaged lovingly and with passionate militancy in the life of a group can be a meritorious and desirable thing. A member's duty, however, is to support all that is good and just in the movement, without falling under the spell of its slogans. Buber says of the member: "In the battle waged externally he must defend the rightful demand of the movement, and in the battle waged within he must oppose all illegitimate interpretations and uses of this demand—and he must do both these things with every fiber of his responsible being."[48]

Only when the participation in a movement is of such a nature that the freedom of individual members is preseved can the responsibility of the

---

*The term that Buber employs here, and which is usually translated as "community," is a word of Aramaic origin meaning "fellowship" in both of its senses: a collective noun signifying "a close association," and the state of attachment, companionship, or friendship. The latter aspect is revealed in the proverb quoted in the Talmud: *O ḥavruta o mituta*—literally, "Either fellowship or death." The proverb is traditionally taken to mean, "Rather death than solitude!" *ḥavruta* is diametrically opposed to solitude, and conveys the notion of the emotional ties achieved among members of an intimate community.

individual be brought into play. In Buber's view, freedom and responsibility go hand in hand: when freedom makes its appearance in society it has the need of a corresponding sense of responsibility, while the sense of responsibility requires as a precondition to its achievement the existence of freedom. The important pedagogic conclusion to be drawn here is that: a man learns to be responsible only by living in an atmosphere of freedom in which he is required to take action of his own responsibility.

Buber's understanding of the meaning of freedom differs from the widely held conception of it as the reverse of compulsion. It is communion rather than freedom that is, in Buber's view, the contrary of compulsion. Compulsion is a negative reality; communion is a positive reality. Freedom is possibility. As Buber asserts:

> Compulsion in education is abasement and rebelliousness; communion in education is the heart's receptiveness and the mind's union. Freedom in education is the potential capacity to enact communion; it cannot be relinquished and cannot of itself be made use of; without it nothing succeeds, nor does anything succeed by means of it; it is the leap before the race is joined, the tuning of the violin. Freedom is the token of confirmation for that mighty and primeval power which it cannot even begin to set into motion.[49]

Now that the bonds of tradition have been attenuated, the trend toward freedom is continually being impeded. Our contemporaries fail to perceive that freedom is neither a doctrine nor a program, but only a realm of potentialities. Man's disengagement from the bonds of his heritage has meant, in effect, that he has assumed a responsibility that is entirely personal and which has replaced his participation in the responsibility of past generations. Hence, a life lived in freedom is one on which personal responsibility weighs onerously. To the extent that a man is able to follow a doctrine, law, or tradition, he can place responsibility in their charge. However, when this possibility is denied him, man is not freed from responsibility; rather, his responsibility becomes all the more great, since he is unable to find an authoritative sanction for it. In this way, responsibility comes to mean man's responsibility to himself.

It is the teacher's task to inspire his students with the courage to assume the burden of their own lives. The teacher must quicken his students' craving for the personal unity upon which the unity of mankind is founded. Neither the belief in this unity nor the ambition to bring it into being can be regarded in any way as a return to individualism; instead, they are a stride taken beyond the dualistic limits defined by individualism and collectivism.

Buber calls our attention to the loss of immediacy in the relationships between men in the modern world. The young of the current generation have no faith in the possibility of unmediated human ties. The first symptom of this attitude is recognized in youth's protest against the sentimentalization of life; young people are embarrassed by the expression of feelings for fear that it will be construed as sentimentality. Yet, while this protest is being made, the entire complex of interpersonal relationships has been impaired. The undisguised immediacy of interpersonal transactions has vanished from human relationships and been replaced by the unmitigated matter-of-factness of advantage. The commitment to pragmatic advantage has engendered suspicion, which has brought, in its turn, estrangement rather than intimacy. Men grow secretive in the presence of their fellows, conceal their feelings, weigh, and calculate so that unmediated initimacy gives way to the relationship mediated by the principle of utility. Buber argues that it makes no significant difference whether this pragmatism and utilitarianism by which one man takes the measure of another is aimed at social rather than private advantage. A man's neighbor is not a mere cell in the body politic or a cog in a piece of machinery that has been designed for a specific purpose—nor does he exist for the sake of the party's objectives; rather, he is a living person. Life is enriched by the directness and profundity of real intimacy; in the absence of such intimacy, life is made arid and deteriorates.

Buber takes strong exception to the widely accepted notion that a group is to be appraised on the basis of its objectives and achievements, while no significance is assigned to what is taking place within the group beyond the contribution of such activity to the efficient conduct of the group's affairs. Such a view ignores the autonomous value of the group itself and of the individuals who compose it; it fails to grasp the importance of the direct relationships that exist within the group. This shallow approach leads to what Buber designates as the "idle prattle" about the sacrifice of personal being and the renunciation of self-realization. Buber contends that wealth, property, authority, influence, even life itself may all be relinquished, but being can never be sacrificed. Nor is it possible to renounce the directness and the authenticity of the relationship between members of society. A renunciation of this kind is, in truth, the surrender of humanity and true fulfillment. The organic life of a society cannot prosper unless it is allowed to develop in every place and between each and every member of the group.

The grave crisis of our era is characterized, in part, by the disruption of the immediacy of relationships, by the adversity that overwhelms the sincere discourse of direct and open communication, by the widening gulf between men, and by the rancor of suspicion that has come to pervade the whole range of human intercourse. Rather than credit a man's speech in its own right, we immediately demand to know his underlying reasons, the unconscious motives that lurk behind his words, the personal or party interests that he seeks.

Buber believes that if we succeed in establishing the directness of the relationships between men—if we defeat suspicion and master the deep-seated distrust felt by men toward their fellow men and by parties toward their rivals—then we shall have brought about a momentous change and greatly mitigated the crisis to which our age is subject.

In examining the problem of youth's preconceptions and perplexity, Buber discovers the common denominator of the young in most countries today in their disbelief and distrust in spirit. This lack of faith in the spirit is certainly understandable: what mankind has experienced in the past fifty years hardly testifies either to the victory of the spirit or to man's redemption by the spirit. Buber makes no attempt to blur the fact of the failure of the spirit in our age. He admits to the spirit's betrayal of our times. The spirit has sequestered itself in a remote sphere of lofty ideas that revolves in a closed orbit; it has disavowed its essential mission, and has become alienated from the very role by which it is legitimatized—namely, its readiness to confront reality and exert its influence upon material existence. Even worse, the spirit has become a toady to falsehood and iniquity, a cat's paw of the rule of brutality.

The failure of the spirit in our age has not entirely annulled its value and potential. By way of analogy, Buber likens the spirit to the king in the folktale who was cast into the desert and whose throne was usurped by a demon who appeared to the world in the king's guise. But a devil, whatever his shape, remains a devil. Men rebelled against this demon-king without imagining, however, that he was a false king and that no true king could possibly behave as this demon did. And so, the subjects never thought to look for the true king who was lost in the wilderness. Such is the spirit's case: the complaints raised against the spirit are not directed at true spirit, but against an imagined and false one; the conclusion that we are asked to draw is not to repudiate spirit, but to seek authentic spirit.

In cautioning against the preconception of the young that disallows the reality of absolute truth, Buber sounds the alert against the doctrine of the relativity of truth. This doctrine proclaims that no actual truth exists for man, but that all truths are contingent on the social circumstances from which they derive. Every man is subject to a profusion of external and internal conditioning circumstances, and it is these that determine what man believes to be the truth and what he designates as such. Although Buber does not deny the fact of men's dependence on the conditions of their social class, he argues that men's nature is not identical with this dependence. In a number of respects, the boundaries of human nature extend beyond the limits set by man's conditioning circumstances. There exists in man's soul an element that is original to him and personal, and not merely the consequence of society's influence. This aspect of man's soul sometimes strikes out toward absolute and unconditioned truth. Even at such times, man cannot free himself from his dependency on the conditions that determine his fate. Yet, for all that, a change does occur; some small particle of independence imbeds itself in the matrix of man's contingent existence.

Buber remonstrates against the alienation of our era from this fundamental fact of our existence. Because of our skepticism concerning the possibility of absolute truth, we impose the principle of utility on the concept of truth, which in turn acquires a relative character. Rather than pursue absolute truth, we bestow the title of truth on whatever serves our own best advantage.

Buber asks whether it is in our power to acquire truth. He does not pretend that the absolute is within one's grasp and there for the taking but he does believe that the quest for truth and the belief in truth's existence have the effect of producing in man's soul the proper relationship toward truth. This relationship is created by man's breaching the confines of his conditioning, not in order to escape from it—something which he can never accomplish—but in order to experience, even in a small way, the condition of noncontingency. The sense of being free from conditioning quickens man's relationship to truth. The soul, in aspiring to truth, takes on authenticity. But whoever believes that all truths are relative and that only what is advantageous is true is likely to alienate truth from himself and to become himself totally estranged from truth.

Buber alerts us to the dangers of the modern period's pragmatic approach, which brings in its wake the denial of both the value and the reality of the concept of truth, a denial founded on a utilitarian base. He dismisses the attempt—itself nothing more than a delusion—to oppose the hypothesis of man's conditioned status with an axiomatic doctrine that upholds man's unconditioned nature. Man must understand the conditioned nature of his thought and, with this understanding for his starting point, he must also bring about the cohesion of the whole of his essential nature that apprehends being. Only in this manner can man forestall the disaster that lies in wait for him. For as Buber remarks: "The functionalization which dominates the concept of truth threatens to undermine the essence of the human spirit, which is once again deprived of its status when it loses its faith in truth."[50]

We have had occasion to remark on Buber's anxiety concerning the great danger posed in the modern period by the granting of priority to collectivism. This collectivism appropriates to itself the full responsibility that the individual ought to assume. The collective takes on the character of an existential first principle to which man is made a corollary and is thus deprived of his personal accountability. In this way an important value is undermined: the value of personal response. In the dialogue between the generations, the multitude cannot take the place of the individual. When such a perversion occurs, truth is exposed to the imminent threat of destruction. As Buber points out, man only discovers truth when he fulfills its claims; human truth entails the responsibility of the individual. In contrast, the collective, which dominates modern times, proclaims the principle of response to group interest—either real or imagined—to be demonstrable and irrefutable truth, against which the individual is powerless either to press the claims of a truth known to himself or to act in the light of his own judgment.

Buber discerns in the appearance of the "man-without-truth" one of the outstanding symptoms of the crisis of our times. By the man-without-truth, Buber has in mind something far worse than the mere liar, the deliberate perverter of truth. Buber defines the type of the man-without-truth as one who has no belief in truth—who rejects the very existence of a truth in whose light his whole being is weighed, examined, and judged; the man-without-truth replaces the concept of truth with truth's perversions in the shape of utility and profit, which are made manifest in the corrupt ideals of the "good" of the party, of the institution, of the state, and of the government. To counter this notion of truth, Buber advocates the restoration of biblical truth, by which he means that which is trustworthy and abiding—that which stands fast and does so not merely as something we apprehend and acknowledge but as something we enact and bring into being.

Among the preconceptions of youth, Buber includes the prejudice against history. The young like to imagine that the world begins in the present and that it originates in themselves alone—as if the labors of past generations are altogether unworthy and wicked, whereas the task of the young will be accomplished in a different and better way. There is merit, even beauty, in the young's faith in their own resources and in their bias in favor of the future and against the past; there is also great daring, without which the young would be unable to act. Yet, if a man shuts himself off altogether from the past and becomes impervious to his heritage, he faces the terrible risk of disaffection from the world and of spiritual desolation. This sealing off of oneself from the heritage of the past obstructs the influence of eternal values, which have molded reality and shaped the younger generation itself. In Buber's conception, every new generation is but a fresh link in a great chain and must bind itself to its predecessors. He makes the point that if man strives to achieve a goal, it is not enough for him to know merely where he is heading, but he must know from where he comes. Therefore, the vocation of education is to give access to the history of the nation and to the inchoate creative vigor in the life of the people.

Buber repeatedly calls our attention to the existence of a great crisis in our age, one that was clearly revealed for the first time in the early 1930s. This crisis did not simply bring about the collapse of an economic and social system but shook the very foundations of man's being. In a time of great crisis, the examination of the present and the recent past is an inadequate basis for pitting oneself against the shock of upheaval. The mission of education in these troubled times is to consider the stage in history reached by man and to compare it with the beginnings of man's historical journey—to understand both man's accomplishments and failings, and to do so from a profound historical perspective and by the exertion of every effort to master the nature of the problems that beset the present without underestimating their severity.

Buber's philosophy of values and his views on value education are founded on true personal consciousness, on response, on dialogue, on the relationships with the "Absolute Thou," and, lastly, on the realization of discourse directed toward the individual and enacted under the conditions of genuine being.

NOTES

1. Mordekhai-Martin Buber, "Likui ha-or ha-elohi" [The eclipse of the divine light], in *Pnei adam: Behinot be-antropologia filosofit* [The face of man: Studies in anthropological philosophy] (Jerusalem: Mosad Bialik, 1962), p. 304.

2. Ibid., p. 306.

3. Ibid., p. 310.

4. See my article, "Mishnato ha-ḥinukhit shel Tolstoy" [Tolstoy's doctrine of education], *Iyunim be-ḥinukh,* (Studies in education) ḥoveret 1 (Iyyar, 1937); 26–37.

5. Jean-Paul Sartre, *L'existentialisme est un humanisme* (Paris: Nagel, 1946).

6. Jean-Paul Sartre, *Being and Nothingness,* trans. Hazel Barnes (London: Methuen, 1957).

7. Jean-Paul Sartre, *La nausée* (Paris: Gallimard, 1938); and Lloyd Alexander, *The Diary of Antoine Roquentin,* trans. John Lehman (London: John Lehman, 1949).

8. Jean-Paul Sartre, *The Age of Reason,* trans. Eric Sutton (London: Hamish Hamilton, 1947).

9. Buber, "Likui ha-or ha-elohi," p. 299.

10. Maurice S. Friedman, "The Bases of Buber's Ethics," in *The Philosophy of Martin Buber,* ed. Paul A. Schilpp and Maurice Friedman, *The Library of Living Philosophers* (London: Cambridge University Press, 1967), p. 171.

11. Buber, "Likui ha-or ha-elohi," p. 296.

12. Mordekhai-Martin Buber, "Tmunot shel tov va-rah" [Images of good and evil], in *Pnei adam,* p. 37.

13. Ibid., pp. 8–9.

14. Martin Buber, *Between Man and Man,* trans. R. G. Smith (London: Routledge and Kegan Paul, 1947), p. 184.

15. Maurice S. Friedman, *Martin Buber: The Life of Dialogue* (London: Routledge and Kegan Paul, 1955), p. 3.

16. See Marvin Fox's critical comments in his article, "Some Problems in Buber's Moral Philosophy," in *The Philosophy of Martin Buber,* p. 71.

17. Buber, *Between Man and Man,* p. 17.

18. Ibid., p. 69.

19. Martin Buber, "Replies to My Critics," in *The Philosophy of Martin Buber,* p. 720.

20. Ibid., p. 162.

21. Ibid., p. 720.

22. See the article of Samuel-Hugo Bergmann, "Ha-filosofia ha-dialogit shel M. M. Buber" [The dialogic philosophy of Martin Buber], in *Ha-filosofia ha-dialogit mi-Kierkegaard ad Buber* (The Dialogic philosophy from Kierkegaard to Buber) (Jerusalem: Mosad Bialik, 1973), pp. 246–69.

23. Buber, *Between Man and Man,* p. 16.

24. Mordekhai-Martin Buber, *Raui le-yelekh akhar ha-meshutaf* [Dedicated to him who would pursue the communal], in *Pnei adam*, p. 171.

25. Ibid.

26. Ibid., p. 174.

27. Buber, "Replies to My Critics," p. 717.

28. Samuel-Hugo Bergmann, "Buber ve-ha-mistika," *Iyun* 9, (Study) hoveret 1 (Tebet, 1958): 9.

29. Mordekhai-Martin Buber, "Al ha-maaseh ha-hinukhi" [On the act of education], in *Besod siah: al ha-adam ve-amidato nokhah ha-havaya* [Dialogue on man confronting existence] (Jerusalem: Mosad Bialik, 1964), p. 261.

30. Buber, *Between Man and Man*, p. 107.

31. Martin Buber, *Israel and the World* (New York: Schocken Books, 1963), p. 138.

32. Buber, "Likui ha-or ha-elohi," p. 299.

33. Mordekhai-Martin Buber, "Ma yehe al aseret ha-dibrot (What will happen to the Ten Commandents) in *Teuda ve-yiud*, [Mission and purpose] vol. 1: *Maamarim al inyanei ha-yahadut* [Essays on Judaism] (Jerusalem: Ha-Sifria ha-Tsionit, 1965), pp. 154–156.

34. Ibid., p. 156.

35. Alexander-Mordekhai Dushkin, "hinukh ha-ofi u-mahalkhei ha-horaah" [The education of character and the processes of education], in *Al ha-hinukh ha-tikhoni ha-ivri be-Erets-Israel* [On the Hebrew secondary school in Eretz-Israel] (Jerusalem, 1939), pp. 84–115.

36. See also Tsvi Kurzweil, "Buber u-veayot ha-arakhim" [Buber and the problems of value], *Keshet*, (Rainbow) hoveret 65 (1975);

37. Richard Livingston, *Education for a World Adrift* (London: Cambridge University Press 1941).

38. Mordekhai-Martin Buber, "Al hinukh ha-ofi" [On the education of character], in *Teuda ve-yiud*, vol. 2: *Am ve-olam: maamarim al inyanei ha-shaah* (The nation and the world: essays on recent questions). (Jerusalem: Ha-Sifria ha-Tsionit, 1965), p. 377.

39. On this subject see my article, "hinukh mevugarim be-mishnato shel Mordekhai M. Buber" [Adult education in the doctrine of Martin Buber], soon to be published in the volume honoring A. I. Katz, president of Dropsie College.

40. Georg Kerschensteiner, *Theorie der Bildung* (Leipzig: B. G. Teubner, 1926).

41. Buber, "Al hinukh ha-ofi," p. 371.

42. Ibid., p. 372.

43. Ibid., p. 374.

44. Mordekhai-Martin Buber, "Tsion ve-ha-noar," in *Teuda ve-yiud*, vol. 2, p. 215.

45. Mordekhai-Martin Buber, "Deotav ha-kdumot shel ha-noar," ibid., pp. 378–86.

46. Ibid., p. 378.

47. Mordekhai-Martin Buber, *Netivot be-utopia* [Paths in Utopia] (Tel Aviv: Am Oved, 1947), p. 131.

48. Buber, "Deotav ha-kdumot shel ha-noar," p. 382.

49. Buber, "Al ha-maaseh ha-hinukhi," p. 247.

50. Mordekhai-Martin Buber, "Le-matsava shel ha-filosofia" [On the situation of philosophy], in *Olelot* [Gleanings] (Jerusalem: Masad Bialik, 1966), p. 10.

3
Society and Social Education

Martin Buber had a profound belief in the power of education ultimately to bring about a revolution from within society against political force and the concentration of authority, which he conceived of as agents that distort the true nature of the human community. Buber's hopes for social revolution were animated by his faith in the possibility of educating an entire generation to authentic social consciousness and to a real sense of political purpose. According to Buber, education is a powerful instrument over which society continues even in our own day to exert its considerable control, but of whose uses society remains ignorant. Buber thought of social education as the antithesis of propaganda, which he regarded with passionate aversion and to which his own philosophy of education was altogether opposed. For propaganda ignores the individuality of those to whom it is addressed and is dedicated solely to the realization of its immediate goal. The propagandist, because he conceives of men as objects, will never enter into relation with them. Rather, he does everything in his power to deprive men of their personality and autonomy: he imposes himself on those whom he wishes to persuade while he takes no genuine interest in their humanity. Indeed, the propagandist concerns himself with the personal traits of another human being only to make use of those traits in order to augment his control and enhance his influence over his fellow man.

Buber points out that the intention of the propaganda of political parties and the state is to instill the public with a ready-made purpose which the public believes to have been generated in its own mind and to represent its own will. On the other hand, social education—according to Buber—is concerned with inspiring and nurturing spontaneity in human association. The achievement of such an end presupposes the development of the private self and of personal modes of thought. For the goal of education to be fulfilled, Buber tells us, "it is necessary to eliminate the total politicization of education which is dominant throughout the world; for there exists no real civic education other than education which aspires to the realization of society."[1]

Buber's discussion of the problems of society and social education focuses on a number of questions: What—he asks—is the nature of the realization of society? What are the roles of the individual and the community in the social scheme? What is the nature of the sphere of the interhuman? What is true communion? By what means can the great crisis of our times be resolved? What place does social education occupy and what role does it play in the efforts to achieve social renewal.

Buber utterly rejects the ideas of Max Stirner (1806–1856), who began his career as a disciple of German post-Kantian radical idealism and ended by adopting a philosophy of absolute solipsism. In his book, *Der Einzige und sein Eigenthum* ("The Ego and his Own"), published in 1845, Stirner based the life of man on the principle of the egoism of the individual. In Stirner's system, each individual exists unto himself to a degree that denies the existence of society except as an association of egocentric selves. In Stirner's view, the only reality in either the physical world or the world of ideas is the ego, and the supreme, even the sole value is the individual. In this way Stirner disallows all ideals that concern society, the state, God, and the spirit. Stirner did not regard truth to represent a value; rather, he recognized only the self-contained ego to be the truth. By asserting the ego to be a self-sufficient entity that allows no other within its domain, Stirner was able to dispose of the problem of the significant relation between the individual self and other selves. The only significant relationship of which Stirner's system admits is that of the individual to himself. In Buber's judgment, Stirner's philosophy is an early manifestation of the tendency of our times to intellectually repudiate the reality of responsibility and truth.

Like Stirner, Sören Kierkegaard (1813–1855) made the individual the core of his philosophy. But whereas Stirner thought of the individual as being engaged in a discourse with himself alone, Kierkegaard conceived of the individual as existing in an ongoing dialogue with God. The essence of man is rooted in man's relation to the Deity—so argued Kierkegaard—and man therefore realizes his being when he bases the whole of his existence on his alert receptivity to God's will. Kierkegaard contended that whoever wishes to realize himself must also free himself from the influence of his environment and must respond with his whole being to the call of God, who speaks to him at every moment of his existence.

Kierkegaard warned of the threat posed to civilization by a triumphant collective, to which the individual, by seeking refuge within the crowd rather than living autonomously and responsibly, may one day relinquish his personal responsibility. Responding, therefore, to the peril he perceived in the collective, Kierkegaard created the category of the "Single One." Kierkegaard's category is religious, for it is to the Single One, to the solitary individual standing alone, that God's call is made. To illustrate the situation of the Single One, Kierkegaard cites the example of the bitter test undergone by Abraham in the Book of Genesis, when he was called upon to sacrifice Isaac and could seek no man's counsel, but was obliged to stand alone with God and to respond with his whole being to the voice that spoke to him.[2] Buber interprets Kierkegaard's category of the Single One to refer not to man as a subject nor a mere general concept but to palpable uniqueness. Nor does the Single One signify the existing individual, but stands, rather, for the person who is finding himself. Kierkegaard insists that only as an individual, as one who yearns for singularity, can one walk with God. Elucidating Kierkegaard's idea, Buber remarks: "To fulfill the first condition of religiosity is to be a solitary man. And therefore the Single One is a category through which must pass—from a religious point of view—time, history and the age."[3]

Thus, Stirner and Kierkegaard differ widely in their perceptions of the problem of the individual. In Stirner's view, each person unto himself is *the* individual. Kierkegaard, on the other hand, believed that all men have the potentiality, are obliged indeed to be singular, and require only to be made individual.

Buber takes a position on the subject of the individual that is radically opposed to Stirner's by arguing that the personality of a man is bound to the society into which he is born. But Buber also maintains that whereas it is a man's duty to acknowledge the society to which he belongs and to be conscious of the solemnity of his connection in his dealings with it, he must never allow himself to become its bondman. For he must be aware, too, that to be truly a member of society means to be sensible of the limits to one's belonging and to know that they can never be permanently defined and fixed. A man who lives by his responsibility can act socially, even politically, only if his conduct is rooted in his own being—in other words, only if his responsibility is the outcome of his attitude of response.

Although he shares Kierkegaard's perception of the threat posed by society to the individual seeking self-realization, Buber rejects the radicalism of Kierkegaard's demand to uproot man from the natural soil of his instincts and social environment. Buber is as aware as Kierkegaard that the personal and existential choice of a man who lives within a community is being constantly jeopardized by the very existence of collective choices taken by the group. Buber warns against joining a group when an individual's choice is annulled by his association from the start, so that he is required thenceforth to act in conformity with the group's behavior. In such cases, the group assumes the individual's political responsibility, leaving the individual with the sense of being released from his liability. Rather, Buber argues that while associating with a group, a person must remain faithful with the whole of his being—which includes his social existence—to God. Such loyalty may move an individual to oppose a tactical decision by his group or, in doing battle on behalf of humane principle, to form or strengthen an opposing faction within the group.

Buber acknowledges the urgency of the problem of determining what is morally right in a particular instance. Buber answers the question of how we can know what is just, by proposing that no group can discover justice unless its members actually devote themselves to discovering the right, and—having acquired such knowledge—they also bend their efforts toward making justice known to their fellows. Here Buber confronts a second and no less urgent problem that is raised by his answer to the first, namely: How can anyone, even after having devoted himself to knowing what is right, be certain of discovering it? Although Buber admits that there can be no certainty of discovering justice, he insists that there exists a possibility of the discovery being made. Thus he tells us, "There exists one prospect alone: boldness does not guarantee truth, but only conveys us to the domain of truth—and it is boldness alone which can accomplish this."[4]

Stirner asserted, "True is what is mine." The collective makes the same claim, though in collective terms, by declaring, "True is what is ours." Buber, on the other hand, is committed to the preservation of the human. He is convinced of humanity's need for uncollectivized individuals and un-politicized truth; for the authentic responsibility of the individual in his historical context. Buber interprets such responsibility to mean the individual's readiness to confront the whole of being which is within his ken, and to do so by assuming responsibility for existence of which the public that constitutes his society is an integral part. Buber regards the first step toward the establishment of the responsibility of which he speaks to be the elimination of the illusory choice represented by individualism and collectivism that preoccupies the modern mind. Buber asks us to consider as an alternative to these false options a third and, in his view, authentic choice.

Buber argues that the validity of individualism is confined to only an aspect of the whole man, whereas collectivism accounts for man only as a part of a larger entity, so that neither comprehends the totality of man. "Individualism," he observes, "perceives man only in his relation to himself; collectivism perceives man not at all, but is aware only of society. The former distorts the image of man, the latter covers it up and conceals it."[5]

In Buber's view, both individualism and collectivism in their modern form arise from the same human situation, and the difference between them is merely a matter of the stage to which this condition of mankind has developed. The human condition referred to by Buber is that of cosmic and social homelessness, of man's sense of himself as one abandoned by nature and solitary in the human world. The spirit's first response to becoming conscious of this condition is modern individualism; its second response—modern collectivism. By choosing individualism a man defiantly consents to his condition; for the very reason of his being abandoned by nature, he isolates himself within the solitariness of his own personality and accepts his condition of abandonment because through it he becomes an individual. Indeed, not only does he accede to his solitariness, but he becomes immoderate in his praise of it.

The response of collectivism comes—according to Buber—after the response of individualism has met with failure. Wishing to escape his isolation, man now immerses himself in the multitude of a group. For its part, the collective claims to provide him with total security. By joining the collective the individual merges his own will with the general will and relinquishes his personal responsibility for a life that has become inordinately complicated to the group, which has the ability to impose order on life's complexities. Buber maintains that the security provided in this way by the collective is largely deceptive. For the individual in the collective does not exist as man with man, and therefore remains unredeemed from his isolation. The crowd claims the individual for its own, while at the same time it diminishes the significance of the connection between man and man. Buber observes that in the collective, "The vitality of that tender aspect of personal essence yearning for connection with other beings is continuously sapped and its sensibilities increasingly dulled in every way."[6] Man's sense of isolation does not disappear in the collective; it is only repressed. But in the depths of his soul, man's solitariness increases until it is cruelly revealed when the illusion of his security evaporates. For Buber, modern collectivism represents "the last barrier that man has raised against his encounter with himself."[7]

The authentic alternative proposed by Buber is the "between," in which man neither segregates himself within his own self nor immerses himself in the collective. Buber believes man's encounter with himself to be possible only when it is an encounter of individual man with his fellow man. When the individual recognizes another in the wholeness of that one's otherness as a personality, as a human being, and in consequence of that recognition reaches out to him, only then does he breach the barriers of his isolation.

Underlying the whole of Buber's thought is his idea that the essential fact of man's existence is found neither in man's existing for himself nor in society's existing for itself, but in man's existing with man. According to Buber, "The pre-eminent and clearest distinction of man's universe resides, first and foremost, in the fact that within it there takes place something between one being and his fellow which in all of nature has no parallel. Language is nothing else but a symbol and an instrument in man's hands, and all the achievements of the spirit were stirred into existence and brought into the world by his hand. Man is made man by himself."[8] The "sphere of the between" is Buber's designation for the common ground which is shared by two human beings who exist in relation with one another, and which extends beyond the domains of the individuality of each. He regards this sphere to be the primary category of human reality, even though it can never be made wholly manifest and is realized only in varying degrees. The mere establishment alone of the concept of "intermediacy" will not—in Buber's view—gain us any advantage unless we also refrain from situating the relation of man with man either in the soul of man or in the world at large, but situate it in fact and actually *between* them.[9]

Buber explains that whereas the dialogical situation can only be grasped ontologically and existentially, it cannot be grasped from within personal existence. Nor can it be grasped through the existences of two individuals, but must be grasped from what exists between and transcends them. "From beyond the subjective, the objective looks out on the narrow ridge upon which *I* and *Thou* meet: there is the realm of the between."[10]

In Buber's philosophy, the doctrine of *I-Thou* tends so to dominate that it overshadows his concept of *We*,[11] which as a consequence has failed to attract sufficient attention from Buber scholars. Although Buber holds that dialogue always arises only between *I* and *Thou,* he follows Heraclitus in stating, "A man cannot make himself fully known to the logos in its original meaning unless he utter We, and say it neither frivolously nor insolently but in truth."[12] Buber accepts Heraclitus' belief that individuals, even in the state of sleep, when each is immersed within his own condition of individuality, act on and influence the activity of the world. He adds, however, that men build the human cosmos in concert while they deal with one another in the world and assist one another through the power of the logos to perceive the world as universal order.

Buber therefore takes strong exception to the mescaline-induced intoxications that are enthusiastically described by Aldous Huxley. Huxley is preoccupied with the individual's longing to turn inward, whereas Buber considers mescaline intoxication to be a state that, rather than being conducive to an individual's free participation in a common existence, causes him instead to enter into a private and closed realm of which he becomes a part for a short time only. In Buber's opinion, "The chemical freedom of which Huxley speaks is not only freedom from the inconsequential self entangled by its own efforts to satisfy its needs, but is also freedom from the participating personality engaged in a partnership with the logos and the cosmos— freedom from the summons, often the cause of great discomfort, to persevere as a personality."[13]

Buber is opposed to Huxley's advocacy of liberation from an environment that may be repugnant to us. He holds, rather, that man is entitled to master his condition and his environment in all of its manifestations and in any way that he wills. Man, according to Buber, is entitled to take his place in his environment and to change it, but he neither can nor is it worthy of him to shrink from the claims of his situation and withdraw into a condition of utter nullity.

The concept of *We* as it is applied by Buber is opposite in every way to what Kierkegaard designated as the "crowd." Thus, Buber tells us, "The authentic *We,* as it objectively exists, can be recognized by the fact that when we examine any one of its parts we discover lodged inside, either actually or potentially, an essential relationship between one personality and another, between *I* and *Thou.*"[14] For Buber, the animating principle of *We* is speech: the shared colloquy that begins when one man addresses another.

By *We* Buber does not mean the collective, nor the group, nor any multitude that can be represented as an object. This *We* can exist in any circumstance in which a man has revealed to his fellow something of the world in such a way that it is thenceforth truly grasped by the other, when he has conveyed his own experience so that it has penetrated the complex formed by the other's experiences and the other becomes, as it were, inwardly consummated. Although this *We* is as unlikely as the *I* to be an active concept expressed in the grammatical third person, it does not possess the same degree of permanence and continuity as the *I*. Buber notes that the *We* is the active principle that underlies the whole history of the spirit and action. Time and again it becomes actual and present, and time and again it wanes and is no more. The *We* can become actual within a group or it can kindle outside of group existence.

Buber points out that only those who can truthfully say "Thou" to one another are capable of saying "We" to one another. The *We* does not depend in any primary way on the mutual relation to which *I* and *Thou* are subject; it is the result of factual relation. Among all of the social forms in which the *We* can be observed, the *community* is nearest to an actualization of the *We*. Nevertheless, the *We* and the community are not identical; for *We* is the realm of mutual relation, which approximates more closely the actual realm of human reality.

Buber contends that though man has always framed his thoughts as *I*, and in that capacity has set his ideas in his heaven, it is in his capacity of *We* that he has established his ideas at the center of his existence. Man's flight from the cosmos of mutuality to the sphere of the private is an escape from the existential summons to the personality to confirm and validate itself in the *We*.

Buber assigns a principal role to dialogue in the system of relationships between men. However, the dialogue to which Buber refers is not the kind that is usually designated as such. Buber holds that in general the conversation of men, even if they seem to address one another, in fact consists of words emitted into the empty space of an imaginary realm. Buber finds an illustration of the usual kind of colloquy between men in Chekhov's *The Cherry Orchard*, in which there appears a family whose members talk only about their own particular concerns rather than converse with one another. This "dialogue of the deaf," in which the responses of those being addressed bear no relation to what is being said by their interlocutors, is the characteristic pattern of dialogue in Chekhov's plays and short stories. When they are asked to listen, Chekhov's characters are too immersed in their own affairs to be able to respond to the other person and to realize him by including him in real dialogue. Chekhov has thus revealed the roots of man's isolation and wretchedness. For the spiritual meanness of man's life does not stem from the order of his universe but from his own imperviousness to his environment and from his lack of accessibility to his fellow man.

Buber observes that whereas Chekhov treats the spiritual imperviousness represented in *The Cherry Orchard* as an adversity that man experiences when he is locked within his own being, Sartre makes of it a life principle. Sartre considers the barriers between those engaged in conversation to be permanently unbreachable, for each man is in possession solely of his own self, with which he is exclusively preoccupied. In the world of Sartre's heroes, the other person represents a constant threat—an idea expressed in *No Exit* by the statement, "Hell is other people." In *La Nausée,* the profound revulsion that accompanies the perception of the other person is brought on by the impassable obstacle between one man and another by which subjective individuals are kept apart.

Rather than regard the development of man's inward being as eventuating from his relation to himself as does Sartre, Buber conceives of the growth of the inward self as a product of one man's relation to another: that is, of the mutuality of realization, wherein one man realizes another's selfhood and the other is conscious of this realization, which is at the same time reciprocally announced. Buber tells us that man wishes to be confirmed in his existence by the actuality of the other and to confront the actuality of the other by his own presence. "The soul of man needs confirmation," Buber declares,

> because man qua man is in need of confirmation. An animal requires no confirmation, for it exists simply because it exists and is never disturbed by doubt. This is not the situation of man however: he is sent out from nature's kingdom of the species into the hazards of the single category; from birth he is encompassed by chaos, and keeps his lonely and fearful watch for existence to give him its sign of affirmation, which can only come from the soul of man to the soul of man. It is men who nourish one another with the manna of being.[15]

The importance of the dialogical relation of the self with another self derives from this need of man for confirmation. Buber regards the precondition of actual dialogue to be a situation in which each of the interlocutors addresses himself to a particular "other" as he really is and acknowledges him as a human being. Such acknowledgement, however, does not mean agreement with the ideas of another, for dialogue can take place even when two men are at odds in their views. What acknowledgment does require is that mutuality be established between the speakers.

In examining the situation of total acknowledgment of one's fellow man, Buber speaks of "knowing a man in one's heart." He explains that knowledge of this kind means sensibility to the wholeness of another as a personality that is joined to the unity of spirit: "It means to sense the dynamic center, which lays claim to all of a man's manifestations, to the actions and conduct of a man which are stamped by the singularity of his outlook."[16] To know a man with the heart's knowledge is impossible if that man is treated as an object which is observed as something separate from oneself. It can only be achieved if one enters into a simple relation with a person and "if he is made actual to [the self]. Therefore the self designates the heart's knowledge— understood in this special sense—as *personal realization.*"[17]

Buber discerns one of the harshest manifestations of the crises experienced by man and society in moderen times in man's relation to language and dialogue. It has always been in the nature of war that it breaks out whenever men are no longer able to converse with one another. Buber maintains that modern man has disposed of trust, which is the precondition of dialogue, so that man is constantly imperiled by hot and cold wars. Buber's thoughts on the subject seem still to be pertinent in the contemporary world: "The disputations of the representatives of states which reach us through the medium of broadcasts are in no aspect similar to human colloquy: they do not speak with one another but to a faceless crowd. Even the assemblies and conferences which are convened in the name of concord among nations lack the one element which alone can raise bargaining to the level of true dialogue: the directness of call and response between men which is free from any alien motive or design."[18]

In Buber's analysis, the absence of true dialogue is no more than a tangible instance of men's general reluctance or inability to speak with one another directly because of their lack of trust in their fellows and their knowledge that their fellow men, too, withhold trust. This want of confidence in existence and man is for Buber the sign of an ailing instinct for life. He is convinced, however, that the malady can be healed and contends that the obligation to initiate dialogue rests on the shoulders of men in every nation who now participate in the struggle against the antihuman. It is these men who must engage each other in unconditional dialogue while, conscious of the differences among them, they are also prepared together to meet the needs of the hour.

Buber dwells repeatedly and at length on the severe crisis experienced in modern times whose symptoms first became discernible in the 1930s. A subject that is of especial concern to Buber is the role which education has to play in the resolution of the crisis. In Buber's view, the crisis is not merely one of conflicting economic and social systems, but a crisis that strikes at the very roots of man's existence. Buber observes that despite man's control of both the elements and his own world and his belief in his sovereignty over the natural and human universe, his exalted state is, in fact, tenuous and unreal.

Buber argues that technology, having acquired an autonomy bestowed on it by man, now threatens to overwhelm and enslave its maker. Machines—he warns—are asserting their power over humanity: "The worker today is becoming more and more an organic appendage of the machine, which with mounting cruelty makes the pattern of his life one of increasing wretchedness."[19] The machine, having freed itself from man's domination, possesses the character of a natural force, whereas man, "has yet to learn the mystic name by which to bind the monster he has formed with his hands and thus deprive it of its power."[20] The harsh picture drawn by Buber of the extraordinary power exerted by the machine in "abnormal" periods of civil strife and wars among nations has been since substantiated to such an extent that we in our own times must fear for a future in which periods of war will be accounted normal, and peace will be regarded merely a lull in which to prepare for further war.

Buber does not advocate that humanity retreat to preindustrial civilization; he urges instead that technology revert to mankind's control. In his article on Gandhi, Buber writes that the Western world cannot, and indeed need not, relinquish the benefits of its industrial technology, and that the Orient is unable to cut itself off from the technology of the West.[21] For Buber, the problem facing man is not how to prevent the proliferation of machinery and bring a halt to technological advancement, but how to harness technology in his service while man is himself conscious of both his goal and the path by which it can be reached.

In his analysis of the changes that have taken place under the influence of technology, Buber maintains that the danger faced by man because of his altered relationship to technology can also be understood in psychological terms. Rather than the machine being an extension of the hand of man as was the craftsman's tool, it is man who has become a prehensile extension of the machine. As a result—Buber asserts—man is losing his feeling for work, his sense, that is, of his personal and intimate connection with the objects he produces. Moreover, the prodigious activity that machinery displays both in the magnitude of its productive potentiality and in its limitless capacity for destruction in war has caused man to lose his "sense of proportion," which is defined by Buber as "man's capacity to make what he wills and produces dependent on his own nature and his true relationship with his environment."[22] Buber stresses that so long as man is constrained to live in this way, the good in mankind will, despite man's intentions, be lost to him.

Buber's dismay over the effects of the supremacy of the machine is equalled by his concern over man's loss of individuality when he is absorbed in the collective, which blurs the contours of his personality. Buber notes that in the confusion and turmoil which mark modern life and which can be concealed by efficient economic and political organization alone—and then only with difficulty—man seeks security by binding himself to the collective. Man feels himself to be increasingly dependent on large collectives, which he perceives as the sole agent likely to come to his assistance, and, therefore, relinquishes to them his personal responsibility. Hence, rather than aspiring to autonomy, man now wishes only to obey, and so suffers the loss of his most cherished asset—the relationship of man to man. As a consequence, "Autonomous associations lose their value, personal relations dry up, the soul itself hires out to a clerk in the power of the state or a party. Man is transformed from a living member of the social body into a cog on the wheel of the apparatus of the collective. He is about to lose, together with his sense of work and proportion, his sense of communion."[23]

Buber takes anxious note of the dangers that derive from the priority given to collectivism. He perceives collectivism as a force that deprives the individual of full responsibility. In Buber's view, the collective becomes the sole progenitor and man its mere issue, so that man is deprived of personal response. It is in this way that the very value of response is lost. Buber denies that in the dialogue between generations the group can take the place of the individual. When such a distortion occurs truth disintegrates. Buber argues that man actually discovers the truth only when he enacts it. Buber regards human truth to be dependent on the responsibility of an individual. By contrast, moderen collectivism proclaims group interests—whether actual or imagined—to be demonstrable truth that no individual may rightfully oppose with either a claim in behalf of a truth known to himself or his own judgment.

Buber is fully aware of the importance of the power wielded by the economic, technological, and political institutions of society. He recognizes these institutions to be agencies that man has created in order to organize efficiently his social life. Nevertheless, Buber argues that the forces of economy, technology, and the state are intended ultimately to serve the needs of the spirit—to make possible, in other words, the conditions for man's self-realization. Buber is concerned, therefore, with discovering the limits that must be set on the organizational and political principle to prevent it from overwhelming and, finally, destroying the different structures contained by society. When—Buber asks—does the centralized state exceed its own sphere and invade the domain reserved for authentic mutuality between men? At which point do social institutions cease to serve human society and, disburdened, hurtle themselves forward by their own momentum toward ever more foolish and senseless achievements in organizational efficiency?

Buber makes a fundamental distinction between the collective and the community. The collective, he argues, is not a true bond, not a nexus by which men are bound to one another, but a "bundle" of discrete individuals existing side by side from which the vital connection between one man and another is missing. In the collective, the relationships between members are merely external and exist only in the degree required for the advancement of a joint undertaking. Responsibility in a collective is general and exists for the sake and in the name of a joint enterprise. In this way, the collective relieves its members of personal responsibility. By contrast, community is based on the relationship of man with man. Here, too, members share in the pursuit of a common goal. Yet this is not the principal concern of community, nor does this exempt the individual from having to assume personal responsibility. At every juncture in the shared journey the members of the community are drawn each to each, and a sympathetic affinity flows from *I* to *Thou*. In distinguishing between community and the collective, Buber observes: "Community does not exist except where communion flourishes. The collective is based on the systematic annihilation of the personality, community— on the exaltation and strengthening of the personality while the goal of the cohesion of individuals is being pursued."[24] This exaltation of the personality is closely bound up with the individual assuming total personal responsibility.

Buber questions the legitimacy of the approach taken by Marxism, which under the influence of its monistic prejudice suppresses the human by narrowly defining man as a social animal, without crediting him with even a trace of individuality. As Buber puts it, "Mankind can be converted into a monistic system only by relinquishing total reality, only by erasing the traces of the fingerprints of the absolute."[25] Buber maintains that man is not dependent entirely on the society in which he lives; he also has a real and autonomous spiritual basis, "the gift of the absolute, which has entered into the relative and exists there."[26] This aspect of man's existence is ignored by Marxism. Marx saw the basis of human existence in the conditions of production, and Marxism therefore proposes to achieve man's self-realization through an organizational and institutional transformation of the system of production. Buber, for his part, cannot believe that such change offers any prospect of genuine social renewal.

Buber takes issue with the widespread tendency to judge a society on the basis of its goals and achievements, and to give weight to what takes place within a society only insofar as it contributes to the efficient operation of the group. This attitude represents a failure to appreciate the value of the group for its own sake, the autonomous value of the individuals who compose the group, and the importance of the relationships taking place within the group. Buber condemns such an approach as a simpleminded renunciation of self-realization and nothing short of a sacrifice of being. Wealth, property, power, and influence, even life, may all be relinquished, but being must never be sacrificed—Buber insists. Nor is it possible to renounce the directness and authenticity of the relationship between the members of a society. Such a renunciation amounts to a surrender of the human and of authentic social fulfillment. The organic life of society cannot prosper except if it is allowed to develop in every place and between all members of the group. "Were even the innermost possession—personal love itself—introduced into the apparatus and made subordinate to it, the soul of the group would, despite itself, lose its vitality and expire."[27]

Buber explains that true social spirit does not exist where men only collaborate in order to achieve a goal. Joint ventures of this kind do not create community. Real social spirit takes place when the community struggles to realize its own social reality. It is this struggle that decides the fate of the future, which contains within it the indispensable beginnings from which the hoped-for transformation of the social and political order is likely to grow.

Far from rejecting association with a social or political group, Buber regards groups as necessary, even primary, conditions of a healthy social organism. However, his acceptance of groups is conditional on their having the quality of community. Nor does Buber believe that an association with a group or even a party need be an escape from the claims of responsibility. Buber is convinced of the importance of being engaged lovingly and with passionate militancy in the life of a group. Once having joined, however, the member must align himself squarely on the side of justice within the group and avoid falling under the spell of its slogans: "In the struggle waged externally he must defend the rightful demand of his party, in the struggle waged within he must oppose the illegitimate interpretations and uses of this demand—and he must do both with every fiber of his responsible being."[28]

Only when a group preserves the freedom of its individual members will participation in the group allow the responsibility of the individual to come into play. Freedom and responsibility go hand in hand in Buber's view. Whenever freedom becomes actual in a society it must be met with a corresponding sense of responsibility, whereas the sense of responsibility requires as a precondition to its achievement the existence of freedom. Buber's concept of interdependence of freedom and responsibility leads him to the pedagogic conclusion that a man learns to be personally responsible when he lives in an atmosphere of freedom, for only then is he obliged to behave responsibly.

Buber continually stresses that the mere fact of human beings living in society and sharing their experiences and responses is no indication of the existence in society of personal affinity among them. Often, the leadership of a group prefers to thrust aside the principle of personal relation in favor of the collective principle in its pure state. Generally the members of the group acquiesce to the will of its leaders in order to feel themselves to be more secure. But whereas the collective may free the individual from his feeling of isolation, his sense of abandonment, and his fear of the world, it also ousts from society the interhuman basis of life mutually experienced.

In Buber's philosophy, social groups do not exist in their own right but are based principally on the nature of those fundamental existential human relations that are constituted by the mutuality and realization of the transactions between men. Only the experience of such relations, when they are undistorted by external constraints, can create the forms by which society is realized, to wit—the authentic communities without which an organic social structure is impossible to achieve.

Buber calls our attention to a distinction made by the German economist and sociologist Max Weber (1864–1920), whose writings established the theoretical basis for the methodology of modern social science. Weber distinguished between a "society" and a "community," regarding the former as an association based on common *interests* and the latter as an association based on shared *feelings*. Not wholly satisfied by Weber's formulation of the difference between society and community, Buber observes: "Usually I have reservations about any attempt, either in theory or in practice, to base objective reality on feelings. Objective reality is the reality of being and, therefore, must be based on an antecedent which does not exist entirely in the soul but encompasses all of those who exist within it. Emotion is not itself sufficient to determine community."[29] Buber illustrates his reservations concerning Weber's thesis by citing the example of affiliations that, though formed by men with strong feelings about the need to change the social order by revolution, do not thereby become communities. Buber's choice of example here really seems not to apply to Weber's intention in speaking of shared feelings, for Weber is concerned about an interhuman complex of emotions that are shared *among* people, whereas Buber has chosen an example in which revolutionary sentiments create a partnership based on a *common interest,* which is the overthrow of a social order.

Rather than follow Weber in distinguishing between associations based on interests or on feelings, Buber differentiates between associations based on interests and on life. Buber calls an association of interests a "society" or "public," and an association based on life a "community" or "partnership." In speaking of "life," Buber means day-to-day life and the will to live communally; only when this will becomes more than mere intention, but is realized in fact as part of existence, does authentic community come into being.

Buber draws a distinction between the *social* and the *interhuman.* He is obviously familiar with the concepts of those sociologists who hold that society is the creation of human relationships and exists through them. The doctrine of relationship is the basis, after all, of sociology. Some sociologists assign especial importance to the reciprocal human transactions that make up the complex of relationships in society among its members. According to this approach to social science, society is principally shaped by simple but nevertheless real human relationships that are not clearly defined in any formal way nor necessarily connected with the system of hierarchical distribution of power. Yet there is more to Buber's concept than is contained in this approach. Buber points out that "relationship" can be understood in two ways. The elementary relationship experienced by, say, members of the same profession is not what concerns him. The class of relationship that does concern Buber has to do with the sphere of the interhuman —defined by Buber as only those real events taking place between persons which are mutual and of which the indispensable condition is that they are jointly engaged in by both partners. "The sphere of the interhuman," Buber explains, "is the sphere of one person confronting his fellow, and I term the process by which the one whom we confront is understood—'dialogue.' "[30] It would therefore be incorrect to understand interhuman perceptions as spiritual, and so to adopt Weber's position regarding associations based on feelings. Buber is talking about authentic dialogue, whose interhuman significance is that men reveal themselves to one another as they are in essence. What is important here is not that one man reveals all of his thoughts to another, but that he allows the sharer of his self-revelation to participate in his personal being.

A sharp controversy arose between Buber and the Jewish philosopher Hermann Cohen over the latter's article "Religion and Zionism," in which the author proposed that the idea of the state is the essence of mortality on earth.[31] Whereas Cohen had in this way subordinated spirit to the state, Buber countered that it is the state which is subordinate to spirit. The dispute between the philosophers was an occasion for Buber to introduce a socioeducational principle that is as characteristic as it is central to his attitude. Buber readily concedes that a citizen must acknowledge his duties to the state, fulfilling them strictly and responsibly. However, should the state diminish that stature of humanity, he must recognize the superiority of the claim made on his loyalties by his duty to rebuke the state and confront it with the true image of mankind. Humanity, Buber insists, takes precedence over the state.

Buber regards state and nation to be categories apart and opposes any attempt to treat them as the selfsame thing. The state, he observes, imposes itself on the nation and proclaims itself to be the nation's embodiment, with the result that the nation's character is falsified. Buber is convinced that it is the nation that embodies the spirit and morality; for the nation serves the idea of itself as both subject and incarnation of the idea rather than as a means by which it proliferates. The nation is thought of by Buber as a dialogue between those who belong to it and the spirit.

Buber concludes that any attempt to resolve the modern crisis by means of new institutions and social reforms must prove inadequate, since these methods "of themselves cannot assure success so long as no strong new spiritual attitude is established."[32] The ideas of the positivist French philosopher August Comte (1798–1857)—who had been a disciple of utopian socialist Saint-Simon and had served as his secretary—strike a sympathetic chord in Buber, who quotes the following passage from one of Comte's letters: "All of the bargaining about the ordering of institutions seem to me ridiculous so long as no new *spiritual* organization of society comes about or, at any event, we make no honest progress."[33] Like Comte, Buber is persuaded that only spiritual change has a reasonable chance of delivering mankind from its crisis.

Buber senses a readiness in the times for spiritual change. "The spirit has recognized the social crisis to be its own and has assumed the task of overcoming it by spiritual transformation,"[34] he notes, and expresses the belief that the transformation will take place when authentic community is reestablished. In surveying the spiritual condition of contemporary man, Buber is impressed by the intense longing of many in the West for community, especially among those who have been forced out of their crumbling niches in society and, alone, in the midst of social turmoil, sense their isolation to be absolute. However this craving—Buber maintains—cannot be satisfied by the modern state, which is incapable of providing the sense of fellowship demanded of community.

Buber reminds those who would seek social change that the spirit is not a part of social reality but is, rather, more like its associate and partner in dialogue; its purpose is to learn from social reality what it already contains and then to teach it what ought to be. Since our crisis in not merely social but spiritual as well, the spirit can only achieve its ends by acquiring a new social vision. "With the acquisition of a new social vision," Buber asserts, "the spirit would also acquire a new and essential relationship with which to encounter reality without being absorbed by it; it would acquire a new dialogical relationship having the potentiality of cleansing and purifying it."[35]

Buber suggests that sociology take on an educational role in addition to its traditional one as a science. He anticipates the objection of social scientists that education and politics are outside of the scope of their field by urging that they are under an obligation to educate men sociologically to live the common life.

Buber takes a critical view of the assertion of Jewish sociologist Siegfried Landshout that social science is an expression of "the Copernican revolution in public consciousness, whereby mankind's decisive hopes shifted from the life of the individual to the organizations and regimes of communal existence."[36] In such a case—Buber counters—the spirit, rather than engaging reality in dialogue, becomes the mere medium through which reality proclaims itself and, thereby, loses sight of its main purpose; whereas, "if the spirit continues as a partner in dialogue of reality, it will know that it must aspire to self-improvement and change, without which even reformed regimes will become vacuous, sterile and corrupt."[37]

The crucial question that the social thinker must ask himself continually—Buber points out—is, How can the spirit influence the process of change in social reality? In coming to grips with the question, Buber examines the contrasting attitudes of the philosopher Plato and the prophet Isaiah.

Plato believed in the reality of the spirit, in its right to govern, and in its power to cleanse and purify a state that has grown corrupt. Socrates was condemned to death by the Athenian Republic for having persisted in the face of its opposition in educating men to live authentic civic existences, and in this respect Plato saw himself as Socrates' disciple. In Plato's view mankind's redemption requires that philosophers be rulers and rulers philosophers.

Buber follows Plato's lead in asserting the doctrine that the perfected soul recalls a prior vision of perfection. According to Plato's theory, a man's spirit has already perceived the Form of Justice in the world of Ideas before his birth, and as his spirit develops in its earthly existence it remembers this Idea of the Good. Moreover, the spirit does not restrict itself to merely knowing justice or proclaiming it to others, but also seeks to realize it in the world of man through the just state. The just state, according to Buber, "is the spirit's truth and is received by reality from the spirit; it is spirit that makes truth a concern of reality."[38]

Neither the modern usage of the term *philosophy* nor its older sense as "love of wisdom" adequately conveys the meaning of Plato's idea of the rule of philosophers. Plato describes the spirit of philosophy as a longing of the soul for union with reality. He argues that the motive force impelling men toward knowledge is the same as the one that urges them to become one with the nature of being, and that the issue of this union is truth, which relieves the sufferings of the soul. Thus, Plato speaks of the philosopher

> "as one born to strive towards reality, who cannot linger among that multiplicity of things which men believe to be real, but holds on his way with a passion that will not faint or fail until he has laid hold on the essential nature of each thing with that part of his soul which can apprehend reality because of its affinity therewith; and when he has by that means approached real being and entered into union with it, the offspring of this marriage is intelligence and truth; so that at last, having found knowledge and true life and nourishment, he is at rest from his travail."[39]

Plato considers that the philosopher, by his union with the divine and the perfection of its order, approaches becoming divine and perfect, and he becomes the spirit's embodiment contemplating reality when he recognizes truth to belong to the domain of the spirit. However, the spirit has never been able to make its contribution to reality, and the doctrine of Plato remains unrealized either politically or socially.

The prophecies of Isaiah furnish Buber with a contrast to Plato's philosophical visions. The Hebrew prophet, unlike Plato, does not regard the spirit to be the property of a person. For Isaiah the spirit, rather than being an object, is an occurrence that descends upon man from on high. Nor does Isaiah share the Platonic belief that a "man of the spirit" is especially suited to govern. The nature of the prophet as exemplified by Isaiah is to be without power and to confront those who wield it as an instrument of state by enlightening them about their personal responsibility for their actions.[40] The absence in the prophet of any ambition to rule accounts for the unique "sociological" character of his role. Whereas the philosopher is distinguished by his knowing the form of the just state that he wishes to actualize, the prophet is the bearer of a message rather than of an idea. The prophet's function is not to establish institutions but to proclaim their duties with his rebukes and demands; these are directed at each man individually and make clear to all that a true nation is a vast fellowship ruled by impartial and uncoercive justice. According to Buber's exegesis of Isaiah, "The transformation of the spirit into something real and tangible will act as a lodestone on that part of mankind which has despaired of spirit—this is Isaiah's teaching. When the Lord's mountain is established on the foundations of the reality of the true life of fellowship, then only will all nations flow unto it in actual fact to learn peace."[41]

Although Isaiah was no more successful in his lifework than was Plato, Buber regards the prophet's lack of success to be of a different kind than Plato's, and submits as evidence of this difference the fact of Jewish survival. Buber attributes the continued existence of the Jews to men of Isaiah's cast, who believed in God's word and stood by their faith while living within social and political reality. Isaiah's failure concerns his own time and not the future of his people. "His testimony is in the custody of the people, who preserve it as something meant to exist at another time, in other conditions and under another guise. No prophet's spirit grants to its own time what it intends to give, but stores it away in the inwardness of the people; and it lives in the people's heart in the form of men's desire to enact truth."[42]

Buber continues to contrast the roles of the prophet and the philosopher by noting that the prophet does not claim to know a general, abstract, and timeless truth. Whenever the prophet fulfills a mission he does so with regard to a particular historical moment, rather than offer—as does Plato—a utopian vision of perfection that is equally valid for all men in all times and in all places. "In order to enact and realize truth," Buber tells us, "the prophet has need for a topos—for a particular location, for this place and this people; for his mission requires this people to begin the work of realization, that is of becoming an authentic nation, a people of fellowship by whose reality he can, as it were, call on all peoples to join together in a nation of peoples, in a nation of mankind and of true humanity."[43]

Buber regards the social thinker to be a philosopher rather than a prophet, a teacher rather than one charged with a mission. Only when the social thinker perceives that his role is to change social reality and when his vision meets expectations of change will the social thinker become a prophet and properly assume the prophet's role as one who rebukes and demands. Buber is aware that the crisis of our times has yet to awaken men's response to the spirit's voice. Our vocation, therefore, is to educate: to teach and prepare mankind for the future; to elucidate and distill ideas; to revivify man's knowledge of society from within.

Buber takes a highly critical view of modern socialism, which he believes threatens to destroy authentic community. Buber observes that modern socialism attempts to surmount the problem of the atomization and structural breakdown of contemporary existence by granting to the state absolute powers to regulate and manage both economic activities and social processes. In Buber's opinion this tendency of socialism must inevitably lead to the destruction of whatever remnants survive of our autonomous organic will. In his assessment of modern socialism, Buber shares the pessimism expressed by Max Weber concerning the chances for socialism to develop

while preserving the political and social liberties of the individual. In justifying his doubts concerning socialism, Weber cites the evidence of the tendencies of socialism toward centralism and the increasingly bureaucratized
control exerted over mankind by the devices and machinery of the state.[44]

Although Buber is willing to grant that the aims of modern socialism may
lift the curse of social atomization, he also fears that it will put an end to the
blessings of spontaneous communion, whose continuing if rare survival it
views as a threat. Buber regards this to be the inevitable result of a historical
ideology. For although modern socialist ideology is dedicated to a reconstruction of society on the basis of the rule of justice, it is also capable of
converting this law of the spirit into an omnipotent instrument of total transformation and must, thereby, destroy freedom. "Should the socialist state
come to dominate completely," Buber predicts, "it would become a supreme
master whose rule would be totally disinterested and whose domain would
extend no toleration to the exploitation of man by man, nor to the degradation of man—who was created to be a goal unto himself—to the rank of a
means to an end, but it would equally deny sanctuary to community."[45] The
community that existed in the past in villages, households, guilds, and fraternities no longer survives as a general social condition but only as a private
occurrence taking place as part of the system of relationships within groups
and associations that are incapable of holding their own in the face of the
absolute power of a socialist state.

The problem of whether historical development has led to the decline of
community or to its revival has profound significance for social education.
Buber is optimistic about the prospect for achieving a new organic social
unity. Although Buber admits that we cannot reinstate the social patterns of
the past, he believes that we can pave the way for a new social form that
would contain the conscious seed of reborn community.

As an alternative to modern socialism—seen by Buber as the consequence
of the ideological exacerbations created by the vast upheavals of our social
development—Buber puts forward the idea of *religious socialism,* which he
calls, "the instrument and herald of a great religious development."[46] Buber
believes there is a new movement in the making, latent as yet and revealing
itself only to the most penetrating scrutiny, but containing the seeds of
rebellion against the overweening lust for power to which our era is prone:
"A movement which is based on the priority of the spirit, itself the expression of man's longing for God and borne forward by the hope of humanity
joined to a true community representing a revelation of divinity (an expression unsuspected by God himself)—a hope which by its nature can never be
transformed into the lust for power without annulling itself, but to the contrary, of which no manifestation is possible without the inward power to
rouse soul to an affinity with one another and to self-sacrifice for one
another."[47] Whereas modern socialism believes it can bring about a fundamental change in human relationships by establishing new institutions to

replace existing ones, religious socialism attaches no importance to the creation of institutions and seeks, instead, to change the face of the actual life of
human beings with one another. These living relationships do not take place
within the state but within a community—"at the vital locus of communion,
understood in its functional, emotional and spiritual sense."[48] Buber reminds
us that such communities had once existed in the countryside, cities guilds,
fraternities, and religious societies. However, having first been sapped of
their vitality by the modern state they finally gave way. Buber compares
contemporary society to an organism whose cells are moribund and whose
gradual demise is being presided over by an apparatus that disguises itself as
an organic structure. But although Buber is ready to grant that the apparatus
can be highly efficient, he also notes that for all of its well-oiled efficiency it
contains no spiritual promise and cannot breathe life into the organic units
that make up real social existence.

The social and educational goal to which Buber aspired is the reanimation
of the organic tissue of society, the restoration of vitality to its living cells—
the liberation of mankind, in other words, to exist in communion. Buber
asks for community in all of its forms to be imbued by a new reality that is
based on relationships between men characterized by greater immediacy
and greater justice, so that the union of many such communities can give rise
to a single true and vital community. Buber argues that the state can never
become a living organism unless it becomes a union of such smaller communities: "A great aggregate of individuals cannot be called a community
unless it is composed of small living groups—of strong cells of unmediated
partnership, of units among which mutual relationship is as direct and essential as the relationship of the individual human members within each of
them—and these groups join together in the same direct and essential manner as individuals do when they join each group."[49]

Buber calls for the revival of communities such as local councils, craft
associations, fraternities, and religious congregations within which public
life would acquire the character of partnership. "Only here," he insists, "can
the inherent affinities of the communality of old be revived under a new
guise: communal land, communal work, communal life, communal faith—
the four principles of affinity that are comparable to those four kinds of
communality."[50] For the revival of community to take place however, communities must be granted true autonomy, scope for the full vigor of their will
to operate within their natural sphere. Yet if the contemporary state is
unwilling to extend such wide scope to the activities of groups, the socialist
state can hardly be expected to tolerate communal autonomy and relinquish
its centralism in favor of the organic principle.

Buber observes that autonomy cannot be made to order but is the outcome of the development and self-determination of a community which is
created from the union of small authentic associations. For this process to
unfold, men must forgo some of their personal advantages and privileges for

the sake of their groups. Buber thinks it essential for men to be wholly dedicated to their associations and to participate in building these as if they were their homes: "Men must be made aware that this small and modest creation does not rank lower than the vast and majestic state but can acquire importance even in excess of that possessed by the state—that direct participation in intimate communal assemblies requires spiritual strength in no smaller degree than is called for by participation in any parliament."[51]

Buber laments the fact that modern society has abolished community. Those of our contemporaries who participate in public life do so without forming any real association. He illustrates the situation of public figures by the example of ideologists who labor greatly to give their concept legal shape while they feel no inner necessity to endow their idea with a vital form. So for example, justice is for them something to be achieved rather than something that can and must begin by being actively realized in life. Their tendency, moreover, to speak magniloquently on the need for social and moral change while taking no action furnishes Buber with still another symptom of the absence among political thinkers of any real sense association. Buber observes that despite the rhetorical passion with which intellectuals join the struggle for changing human relationships, their own relationships with one another are so rarely in evidence and so indirect, and their awareness of this contradiction is so nearly nonexistent, that their ideas and schemes can exert no influence whatever on society. Buber insists that the authenticity of a person's political being is tested and enhanced only in his own natural and unpolitical sphere. This is the soil from which the efficient force that acts on society draws its sustenance. In this regard Buber calls to witness, "The effulgent doctrine of Hasidism, which holds that the things existing in a man's environment were given to him only so that he may redeem them; he is allowed to make his environment more perfect and say: There is no shorter path to the redemption of the world. No community which has to do with life is lost, and there exist no other principles on whose basis the community of mankind can be built."[52]

It should be remembered that Buber is not contemptuous of the aspirations of socialist thinkers who work for social change and for the establishment of a new social order. He acknowledges the need for far-reaching changes in the structure of society—for correcting the severe distortions of class structure, for improving the forms and distribution of labor, for bettering the security of both society at large and the civil liberties of the individual. Yet none of these changes, though in themselves vital and advantageous, can assure the existence of community. People who live together and maintain just institutions that adhere to the rule of law do not, by this fact alone, live in a community. Buber is at pains to point out that within this very complex of institutions which are perfectly adapted to the ideals of social justice, "it may well be that community alone will find no place it can call its own. Community cannot be built among those who have themselves undergone no change, and institutions on their own are powerless to transform people who have not been prepared for community into such as are ready for it."[53]

Students of Buber's social philosophy have asked whether Buber's personal ideology should be classed among the sociopolitical doctrines of utopian socialism or those of anarchism.[54] That Buber was neither a utopian nor an anarchist can be amply demonstrated.

Buber made extensive studies of a great variety of theories of social organization, including the doctrines of Proudhon, Kropotkin, and Landawer, as well as those of Marx and Lenin.[55] Buber undertook his investigations not only in the capacity of social historian but also in order to make a personal systematic contribution to social theory.

Buber exhibits considerable interest in many aspects of the thought of Peter Kropotkin (1842–1921), although he shared Kropotkin's views only to a degree and with some reservation. Kropotkin advocated the cause of total individualism, whose evolution he conceived of as taking place in conjunction with the development of voluntary association in groups. He thought of voluntary association as being applicable in all circumstances and as answering to every purpose. For Kropotkin such voluntary associations contained within them the principles of their own perpetuation, and could at any time assume whatever shape was required by the various and manifold ambitions of all of their members. He believed that popular social and political spontaneity must be given the fullest possible scope for development. Kropotkin recognized that such social organization must inevitably be frustrated under bureaucratic government, and that to survive it needs to create for itself an independent and local existence in the form of small neighborhood communities of a popular kind, whose government would be conducted on the basis of self-rule as a "forum" rather than adopt the pattern of a representative parliament.

In assessing Kropotkin's ideas, Buber notes that the Russian anarchist is more concerned with the organization of the state than with the ways in which the state is ruled. "The anarchism of Kropotkin," he observes, "as that of Proudhon is actually *acratia;* not an absence of authority but an absence of control."[56] For a definition of anarchism, Buber turns to the utopian socialist Pierre Proudhon (1809–1865), who characterizes anarchy as "a form of authority or legislation whose principle of rule is that policing agencies, the instruments of providing incentive and assuring submission, bureaucracy, taxation and the like be so reduced that they appear only in the simplest forms."[57] Proudhon's view of anarchism could just as easily have been expressed by Kropotkin.

Although Kropotkin regarded it as axiomatic that a fundamental change in the general social order cannot take place without revolution, he was conscious that the tragedy consisted of the reversal of the original noble intentions of its most devoted and sincere advocates. Nevertheless Kropotkin was convinced that educational activity could influence revolutionary movements and so prevent revolution from imposing a centralism as bad and even worse than its predecessor. Buber takes up Kropotkin on this point by arguing that the fundamental fact of revolution is that it is a liberating force rather than a creative one. As Buber puts it: "In respect of social creation, the moment of revolution is one of birth rather than of begetting—if, that is, it is preceded by a begetting."[58]

Buber is in greater sympathy with the attitude of Gustav Landawer (1870–1919), who did not consider the state as something to be destroyed by revolution. He regarded the state as constituting a relationship between men, as the medium by which men express their mutual need of one another. Landawer argued that the state may be done away with only by the creation of another system of human relationships.

Landawer elucidates a principle that was left unexplored by Kropotkin. Landawer notes that for political revolution to serve the interests of socialist revolution, three conditions must be met: (1) the revolutionaries must free the land in order to create community and establish the union of groups; (2) once the land has been freed, the characteristics of community should be determined by institutions of administrative economy on whose basis such an alliance would be formed; and, (3) the preparation of such an alliance of communities should be pursued according to the *spirit* of true community. No previous socialist thinker reveals himself to be as aware as Landawer of the importance and value of spirit to the creation of a new social order.

Buber was no utopian. One of the conspicuous characteristics of social utopianism is its tendency to plan society according to a vision of a perfect social order. Buber, however, does not offer such a program, nor does he reveal even an inclination to do so. Utopian philosophers devise perfect communal forms of existence that are organized according to a rational plan. Most varieties of social utopianism share a confidence that systematic analysis of social orders and rational planning can bring about a better form of social organization. Although Buber's vision of authentic community contains many utopian elements, he is not interested in an abstract principle contained in a perfected program that is to be realized at some future time. Buber is concerned with the means by which his vision can be realized in the immediate present—with the limits of realization, with the boundaries that define what is required at a particular time and in a particular place because it can be achieved then and there. Buber is opposed to programs whose shape has been perfectly and finally determined. In referring to Landawer's philosophy, Buber remarks: "Socialism cannot be something absolute. Socialism is the creation of human community to the degree and in the form that can be willed and accomplished at a specific time and under given conditions. Anything which is made actual faces the threat of becoming congealed; whatever pulses with life today can become encased in an impenetrable shell that will prevent any leap to greater heights."[59] Buber refuses to contemplate any new program, or campaign of relentless change, or the establishment of institutions having unlimited power. Instead he speaks of reassessment and ongoing change through the spirit as the fundamental law that should govern our lives. This, Buber contends, is the process by which true community can be realized here and now rather than any program designed for a distant future that is detached from time and place. That Buber's socialism is more "topian" than than "u-topian" can be judged from his following observations: "The utopia which is a game of technical fantasies can now only exist in the novel, usually of the light variety; and that form of utopia which proffers a plan of building an advanced society becomes a system, and within it—within that socialist utopia—there has emerged the full force of dispossessed messianism."[60] But on the other hand, he continues, "We must build, in the spirit of utter non-romanticism and as people who are truly alive now, real community from the recalcitrant material of our own time."[61]

Buber resists satisfying our curiosity concerning the guise that will be assumed by community based on direct human relationships. He is altogether disinclined to lay out a precise program for the future for fear that it would impose limits on the potential development of such a society. Buber believes that community will be determined dialectically. The only part Buber foresees that our age will play in this process is the fulfillment of its unmediated tasks, which would themselves constitute a transitional stage in the creation of new spiritual and social conditions for future generations. Avraham Klein is correct in warning us against confusing Buber's actual position with that of the advocates of evolutionary gradualism. For the philosophy of Buber—because of its distinctively Jewish character and its strong connections with messianism—also assumes a sudden leap in development to be possible. The formation of early Christian sects represents for Buber a leap of this kind, just as the emergence of Hasidic communities does in the history of Judaism. Buber observes that Hasidim, who attach themselves to a rabbi of exceptional sanctity, and particularly those who make up his immediate entourage or are in regular contact with him, form a community of exceptional dynamism. The followers of a Hasidic rabbi derive their enlightenment from his answers to the questions they submit to him. By his commentaries and fables the Hasidic rabbi is able to lift his followers from the profane world of their daily concerns to the heights of incandescent religious devotion and faith. In his evocation of the relationship between the Hasidic rabbi (or *zsadik*) and his congregation, Buber describes how "The zsadik, through prayer and the Torah, becomes one with [his congregation], and he prays from within it not merely as one who speaks for it but as its vital center, within which is joined the communal zeal; and it is through his power that this zeal mounts as it merges with his own soul's zeal. . . . The congregation is a field of force for his speech, a field of force within which words cause the spirit to reveal itself in ever expanding concentric waves."[62]

The Hasidic congregation deserves our attention because it incorporates a number of Buber's principal ideas concerning community. Hasidic groups do not aim at detaching themselves from the outside world in order to preserve some secret creed. They are associations formed by autonomous individuals who live their lives in communion with a rabbi who acts as both leader and teacher. The members of the congregation are joined in an enthusiastic union that can only exist close to the kindling source provided by the person of their *Zaddik*. A charming fable illustrating the emergence of the Hasidic congregation and the significance of the *Zaddik's* role is offered in the conversation between Rabbi Bunam and Rabbi Isaac Parischa, called the "Yud," which Buber records in his book *Gog and Magog.*[63]

Another leap of the kind Buber is concerned with was realized in the kibbutz, or pioneer agricultural communes established in Israel.

Buber attached great importance to every form of communal settlement, and most especially to the kibbutz. He entitled his essay on the subject of the kibbutz "An Experiment That Did Not Fail." In this study Buber represents the kibbutz as one of the most important attempts at social revival and renewal of community to have taken place in recent history. Although he does voice some criticisms of the kibbutz enterprise, Buber is nevertheless convinced that in the kibbutz we are witnessing an authentic development that is well worth being fostered. Buber's definition of the kibbutz as an "experiment that did not fail" is not a symptom of his reservations concerning the kibbutz idea but an indication, rather, of his great admiration for it: "I have said that I see in this daring undertaking by the Jewish people a model of non-failure. I do not feel it possible to say, 'a model of success.' For it to become such, much remains to be done. Yet this is the way and this the pace—with retreats and disappointments and ever renewed audacity—by which true revolutions are achieved in the world of man."[64]

The communal movement is regarded by Buber to be the essence and goal of society's self-renewal, of the revival of spiritual communion in new forms, and of the union of groups into one community. These were the motivations behind the attempts in Europe and America to establish agrarian settlements on communist and cooperative models. Generally these experiments proved to be unsuccessful. Some of them failed after enjoying only a brief existence, some adopted capitalistic patterns, whereas others were merely isolated, social acts. The only undertaking of this kind that can be regarded as having been in any way successful is the Jewish communal land-settlement movement in Israel.

For Buber the importance of this social experiment derives from the fact that it was a natural consequence of the search for a communal pattern of existence that was suitable to the needs of groups of men in pursuit of a new way of life. The communal movement in Israel never lost its original character as a quest for new social forms, nor was its development arrested because of complacency born of success. The thriving health of the kibbutz movement is amply demonstrated by the ongoing establishment of new communal settlements throughout the country that derive from the same root-urge of social creativity. Israel's land-settlement movement obeys Buber's dictum that "even community must never become a principle; it must fulfill its obligations not in respect of a concept but of a situation. The realization of the idea of partnership—as is the case with the realization of all ideas—does not occur once and for all, nor is it valid for all time, but takes place on each occasion as a response of the moment to the demand of the moment."[65] It has been the great virtue of the cooperative movement in Israel to be alert and responsive to its own problems. The movement has shown itself to be prepared to confront its problems and to struggle in order to surmount them; it has created the means and institutions by which to achieve an understanding of its own nature and purpose.

Buber regards the land-settlement movement in Israel as having enjoyed from its inception the particular advantage of being a response to a situation rather than the creation of a doctrine: "In the establishment of the group it was not ideology but action that led the way."[66] The movement's ideology was not conceived in the aftermath of action in order to provide accomplished facts with a rationale. Demands of the moment were met with reasoned argument and analysis, so that ideology remained pliant and could accommodate itself to fresh needs as they arose. In the history of the land-settlement movement, ideas never congealed into ready-made programs: they nourished an ideal without inspiring the pen; they established priorities without creating models.

Buber warns us of the dangers we court by submitting communal partnership to the purposes of ideology: "For the sake of the *raison d'être* of the idea of partnership and community we must build a hedge around it in order to prevent it from being contaminated by sentimentality, hyperbole or delusion. And if we find it intolerable that defective social or political forms which are altogether foreign to authentic and spontaneous communal life should be called a "partnership" (within which and for whose sake we can and must live), then we have no less a need of rejecting absolutely the invariable form assumed by those complacent associations which, under the influence of the kind of festive or sentimental situation uniquely characteristic of fraternal communion, masquerade as community."[67] Buber's remarks remain pertinent, particularly to the kibbutz, which although it no longer faces an external threat to its existence faces an internal threat of becoming a "complacent association" in which communal life will lose the quality of community.

That this social experiment unfolded against the background of the historical situation of the Jewish people is a fact of paramount importance to Buber. He represents the communal movement in Israel as a national *inner revolution* that resulted from the nation's response to an external crisis. According to Buber the historical circumstance of the Jews led to the creation of a pioneering elite, and the life form that best answered the needs of this elite was the cooperative settlement. It was through this form of social organization that the Jewish concept of nationhood could be impregnated by the social ideals of the elite.

Buber attached great importance to the educational and social role of such an elite. He writes at length concerning the significance of an elect group to social renascence. On this subject Buber's ideas have much in common with those of the Zionist thinker A. D. Gordon. It was Gordon's contention that an elite corps exerts its influence on other members of a group not by its words or intentions but by its very existence, in much the same way as nature influences mankind.[68] Taking up Gordon's notion, Buber stresses that this elite is not made up of "men of the spirit" (by which he means "intellectuals") in the sense that the expression is normally applied, "but men of a spirit which has immersed itself so completely in life that we no longer discern it as spirit."[69] Buber's ideas concerning an elite group that educates by its own example will doubtless continue to influence social-educational theory. The fostering of an elite corps that by its living example projects its influence outward toward the periphery is the precondition of social renewal in our times.[70]

Buber points out that the pioneering movement in Israel has always existed in relationship to the process of national reconstruction, so that it is prevented by its very nature from regarding itself as self-sufficient and autonomous; for it to perceive itself as such would be tantamount to an act of self-annihilation. The cooperative village—in Buber's analysis—has acted not only as a lodestone of a society in the making by attracting adherents of the idea of social regeneration but has also educated those who have joined it in the ways of community. Even more—it has had a formative influence on surrounding society.

It is Buber's belief that the whole purpose of social education in Zionism is the creation of just such an ever-expanding nucleus of elite that serves as an example to society. In his discussion of this elite nucleus Buber ranges beyond its specific manifestation in the cooperative village. He observes that in every settlement there exists a similar nucleus whose adherents can be described as surrounding it in three concentric circles representing three degrees of their relationship to the vital core: an inner circle of those whose commitment is spiritual and inward, a second circle consisting of those whose sympathies are merely intellectual, and a periphery made up of the indifferent. All of these groups are subject to varying intensities of influence from the center, which acts on them not in any intentional or preconceived way but existentially and by the example of its actual being.

Buber notes that the members of this nucleus in communal settlements tend to impose severe demands both on themselves and on their associates and submit their achievements and undertaking to the strictest scrutiny and appraisal. Buber regards their critical self-appraisal to be the principal factor underlying the continuing development of this social enterprise: "They repeatedly measure the actual—the child of a given moment—against the potentiality which they carry within their visionary soul. There are even moments when the whole group stops short, as it were, and asks itself: 'Where do we stand? What have we achieved? Have we deviated from the right path?' "[71] The importance of self-appraisal consists of its being a product of constructive reasoning rather than of example. Buber cites the statement made by Yaakov Rabinovich in 1925 as having particular relevance to the land-settlement movement in Israel:

> The aspiration for exalted and just forms of existence is not a longing for the absolute—which can never be achieved—but for life which is immediate and soon to be realized. And to the extent that man can limit the scope of exploitation and can labor independently he has a solution. But neither should we tend to the opposite extreme. The forms have not yet crystallized and free choice does not yet exist. People pass from one form to another and everything is in flux. So let man not boast of his perfection. Let us not grow overwise! We shall allow work and suffering to find their way.[72]

Notwithstanding his admiration of the settlement movement in Israel, Buber does not refrain from calling attention to the problems of survival they face. Buber's first concern is with the chances that exist for the movement to perpetuate its original character—a problem that has acquired increasing relevance in modern times. Has the pioneering elite remained faithful to its social role or has it abandoned its role in favor of a relationship purely with itself, he asks? Is the elite capable of the self-realization and self-renewal required of it in order to fulfill its social role? To Buber it seems at times as if the kibbutz elite is in the process of abandoning its open and outgoing character and tending instead toward self-involvement and exclusiveness. Even capitalistic tendencies have come into play in the kibbutz's relationship with the rest of Israeli society. Buber argues that the problem of preserving the elite may resist a solution because of the elite's inability to realize two critical objectives: (1) to influence the young generation of the kibbutz to continue the undertaking in a way that is proper, and (2) to establish centers where by selection and education the old generation could create a spiritual progeny capable of synthesizing principles which have proved themselves to be valid, rejecting others, and achieving a balance between old principles and new ones. Buber believes that because of the kibbutz elite's failure to carry out either of these aims, the whole social experiment in communal living is being jeopardized.

It is the nature of the relationships between members of the community that is the inner resource of the kibbutz. Here, too, Buber discovers the kibbutz to be beset by difficulties, particularly by the problem of psychological isolation that plagues all of society today. Buber was persuaded that cooperative settlements are under an obligation to extend their pioneering work to the domain of personal relationships, and that they must be characterized by the broadest possible spiritual receptivity. "The social questions concerning the inner nature of a particular group are actually a single question concerning the authenticity of that group and one, therefore, of the group's inner strength and inner existence," Buber notes.[73] In Buber's estimation the kibbutz has yet to find its way to true community based on realization and mutuality.

The changes wrought in Israeli society by immigration has confronted the experiment in communal settlement with still another set of intractable problems. Mass immigration to Israel since the War of Independence has created a large segment of the population which is inaccessible to the influence of the kibbutz. It has also introduced external influences into the kibbutz, whose educational value has been diminished as a result.

Excessive politicization has had a divisive effect on kibbutzim. Formerly a kibbutz member could truthfully say, "We are a community and not a party." A fundamental change has taken place since, and conditions have become increasingly unfavorable for the achievement of unity.

Buber's analysis of the kibbutz leads him to conclude that the kibbutz is confronted by four principal tasks: First, the amalgamation of kibbutz units by renouncing politicization and tearing down the barriers which kibbutzim have erected among themselves; second, the preservation of their role as an educating elite which exerts its influence on Israeli society as a whole; third, the maintenance of their receptivity and their character as true communities; and fourth, the creation of an authentic elite that would serve not itself but society as a whole—one which could fulfill and renew itself by educating its own young and by training a spiritual succession to carry on its work.

The conditions that Buber regards to be necessary for the establishment of social partnership and true community can be summarized under the following headings:

Mutuality. Buber defines the interhuman sphere as one of "man in the presence of and with his fellow man." To participate in such a situation is to exist in mutuality.

Realization. By this concept Buber means the concrete form of imagination by which one man pictures in his own mind the sentiments, feelings, and thoughts of another, not as a subject distinct from the reality of his fellow man but as part of the vital process of that person's being. This "mental image" is accompanied by something belonging to the nature of what is being imagined. When realization is taking place each person wishes to have his existence confirmed and his presence sustained by the presence of the other.

Partnership. Community becomes actual through active and cooperative participation in a common undertaking and cannot take place unless this condition is fulfilled. Such partnership is the soul of communal existence.

Land. The precondition of authentic communal existence is for land to be handed over in its entirety to cooperative control rather than to private ownership. Buber considers land to be the life-giving principle of a life of partnership.

Independent Labor. The inner imperative of independent labor is the shared basis of communion. In modern times we have experienced a loss of the sense of any real relationship with work and have made no effort to reestablish it. Social renewal depends on the creation of a new relationship with work. For Buber, labor represents man's covenant with the land, a covenant that awaits being renewed.

Communal Life. People who live together experience the sense of being bound up with one another. Communal life exists not only by virtue of one's readiness to help a neighbor in need but by one's apprehending another person's nature and being, and in this way satisfying a need of which he is himself unaware—the need to experience the serene warmth of brotherly feeling. Even when members of a community are denied the possibility of knowing one another (as is inevitable in very large communities) communal existence can still take place so long as the members remain accessible to one another and establish direct relationships. Buber is aware that the state of community cannot be maintained permanently and without abatement. He regards it as essential, however, that the potentiality of community be permanent and unimpaired by prejudices and reservations.

A Center. Community can only occur when the members of a group experience a relationship with the center and when this relationship is superior to all other relationships. Although the primacy of this center can only be acknowledged if it is receptive to the absolute, the center is authentic only to the degree that it bears the stamp and impress of the physical world.

Organic Community. Communal life is realized as organic community when unmediated relationships between man and man become actual. The individual cells that compose the organic tissue of society have such forms as neighborhood communities, cooperative societies, and fraternal organizations, all of which are characterized by direct relationships between men in which the divine principle is manifest and by which the whole acquires permanence.

The Public. The public—in the sense that the word is used by Buber—is the partnership of organic communities: the association of small social groups whose relationships are based on the same unmediated inwardness which characterizes the relationships within each separate community.

Representation and Leadership. Buber believes that political representation will be as necessary to the new type of society as it is to contemporary society, but that it will have an altogether different character. Rather than being merely apparent and determined by the votes of an amorphous electorate, representation will be made up of working members of various communities. Moreover the connections between representatives and their constituencies would exist not through abstract generalities contained in the programs of political parties but through cooperative action and shared experience.

Humanity. Buber defines humanity as the association of all of the formal guises assumed by society that are joined on the basis of a similar principle of unmediated relationship.

Spirit. The spirit's task is to educate and prepare mankind for the future and, when change does take place, to keep watch over justice so that the newly constituted social forms and institutions do not dominate the life force striving for betterment. The spirit's role is to act the part of a true prophet pointing the way to renewal. It sustains the social forces that assure the constant improvement and renewal of the forms of society.[74]

God. Dominating the whole and constituting the goal of all achievements—even of those who are not religious in the conventional sense of the word—is the nameless God. "God does not hover over His creation as He did over the universe when it was without form and void. He embraces it," Buber asserts. "He is the infinite *I*, the one who transmutes every *Other*, every arbitrary object, into his *Thou*. The individual is in harmony with God when he humanely embraces that part of the universe which he apprehends as did God divinely embrace the whole of his creation. He sustains the image of God the moment he says Thou with the whole of his being to all of humanity around him, and to the full extent of his powers to utter it personally."[75]

The revival of authentic community and the renewal of our confidence in humanity and in existence requires that education be directed at men's hearts. This goal is not confined to education alone but must be the conscious aim of all of our activities. Buber urges that if we wish to make the life of man more humane we must create affinity among men. He believes that such affinity could be more easily achieved were men to live in actual proximity. According to Buber, physical conditions should be so arranged as to encourage intimacy and to facilitate human colloquy. He, therefore, calls on architects to assist in the revival of dialogue: "We must demand from those who are masters of the art of building that they, too, know how to build for the sake of human intimacy such environments as would invite encounter and such centers as would determine encounter."[76] Social education is an invitation to human encounter; it is a preparation for maintaining dialogue, an instrument that assists men toward becoming accessible to one another, to nature, and to God.

NOTES

1. Martin Buber, "Ben hevra li-mdina" [Between society and state], : behinot be-antropologia filosofit [The face of man: studies in anthropological philosophy] (Jerusalem: Mosad Bialik, 1962). p. 39.

2. Sören Kierkegaard, Fear and Trembling and the Sickness unto Death, trans. by Walter Lowrie (New York: Doubleday & Co., 1954).

3. Martin Buber, "Ha-sheela she-ha-yahid nishal" [The quesion to the single one], in Be-sod siah: Al ha-adam ve-amidato nokhah ha-havaya [Dialogue: On Man confronting existence] (Jerusalem: Mosad Bialik, 1963), p. 158.

4. Ibid., p. 195.

5. Buber, "Beayat ha-adam" [The problem of man], in Pnei adam, p. 107.

6. Ibid., p. 109.

7. Ibid.

8. Ibid., p. 101.

9. On this subject, see: Ronald Gregor Smith, "Martin Buber's View of the Interhuman," The Jewish Journal of Sociology, 8 (London: 1966): 64–80.

10. Buber, "Beayat ha-adam," p. 112.

11. Ibid., p. 113.

12. Buber, "Raui le-yelekh aharei ha-meshutaf" [For the one who pursues the mutual], in Pnei adam, p. 171.

13. Ibid., p. 164.

14. Ibid., p. 171.

15. "Raak ve-zika" [Distance and relation], in Pnei adam, p. 131.

16. Buber, "Yesodot shel ha-ben-enoshi" [Principles of the interhuman], in Be-sod siah, p. 224.

17. Ibid.

18. Martin Buber, "Ha-siha ha-amitit ve-efsharuyot ha-shalom" [True dialogue and the chances of peace], in Olelot [Gleanings] (Jerusalem: Mosad Bialik, 1966), pp. 26–27.

19. Martin Buber, "Al ha-mashber ha-gadol" [The great crisis], in Teuda ve-yiud [Purpose and mission], vol. 1 (Jerusalem: Ha-Sifria ha-Tsionit, 1961), pp. 76–77.

20. Buber, "Beayat ha-adam," p. 55.

21. Martin Buber, Pointing the Way: Collected Essays, trans. Maurice S. Friedman (London: Routledge and Kegan Paul), p. 138.

22. Buber, "Al ha-mashber ha-gadol," p. 77.

23. Ibid., p. 79.

24. Martin Buber, "Al ha-havruta" [Community], in Netivot be-utopia [Paths in utopia] (Tel Aviv: Am Oved, 1947), p. 131.

25. Martin Buber, *Ha-ruah ve-ha-metsiyut* [Spirit and reality] (Tel Aviv: Mahbarot le-Sifrut, 1952), p. 48.

26. Ibid.

27. Martin Buber, "Deotav ha-kdumot shel ha-noar," in *Teuda ve-yiud,* Vol. 2, p. 383.

28. *Ibid.,* p. 382.

29. Buber, "Al ha-havruta," p. 137.

30. Martin Buber, "Yesodotav shel ha-ben-enoshi" [The principles of the interhuman], in *Be-sod siah,* p. 216.

31. Hermann Cohen, "Religion und Zionismus," *Juedische Schriften,* (May–June, 1916): 319–327.

32. Buber, *Ha-ruah ve-ha-metsiyut,* p. 4.

33. As quoted by Buber in "Tviat ha-ruah ve-ha-metsiyut ha-historit" [The claim of the spirit and historical reality" in *Teuda ve-yiud,* , 2, 49.

34. Buber, *Ha-ruah ve-ha-metsiyut,* p. 4.

35. Buber, "Tviat ha-ruah ve-ha-metsiyut ha-historit," p. 50.

36. Ibid.

37. Ibid., p. 51.

38. Ibid., p. 56.

39. Plato, *The Republic,* trans. Francis MacDonald Cornford (New York and London: Oxford University Press, 1960), p. 197.

40. For a discussion of this subject see Buber's essay, "Ha-shaah ha-teopolitit" [The theopolitical moment], in *Torat ha-neviim* [The doctrine of the Prophets], 2d rev. ed. (Tel Aviv: Mosad Bialik, 1950), pp. 117–42.

41. Buber, "Tviat ha-ruah ve-ha-metsiyut ha-historit," p. 59.

42. Ibid.

43. Ibid., p. 60.

44. See Max Weber's essays contained in *Gesammelte politische Schriften* (1921) [Collected political Essays], and *Gesammelte Aufsaetze zur Soziologie* (1924) [Collected Sociological Essays].

45. Buber, "Al ha-havruta," p. 132.

46. Ibid.

47. Ibid., p. 133.

48. Ibid.

49. Ibid., p. 134.

50. Ibid., p. 135.

51. Ibid., p. 136.

52. Ibid.

53. Ibid., p. 138.

54. for an examination of Buber's social philosophy, see: Alexander s. Kohanski, "Martin Buber's Restructuring of Society into a State of Anocracy," *Jewish Social Studies* 34 (1972): 42–57.

55. See Buber's book dedicated to social problems, *Netivot be-utopia.*

56. *Buber, "Kropotkin," in Netivot be-utopia,* p. 47.

57. Ibid.

58. Ibid., p. 48.

59. Buber, "Landawer," in *Netivot be-utopia,* p. 58.

60. Buber, "Ha-yesod ha-utopi ba-sotsialism" [The Utopian basis of socialism,] ibid., p. 16.

61. Ibid., p. 22.

62. Martin Buber, *Or ha-ganuz* [The hidden light] (Jerusalem and Tel Aviv: Schocken Books, 1968), p. 18.

63. Martin Buber, *Gog-u-Magog* [Gog and Magog] (Jerusalem: Sifrei Tarshish, 1944), pp. 97–98.

64. Buber, "Nisayon she-lo nikhshal," [An experiment which did not fail] in *Netivot be-utopia*, p. 126.

65. Buber, *Hearot la-rayon ha-kibutsi* [Observations on the idea of the kibbutz], ibid., p. 140.

66. Buber, *Nisayon she-lo nikhshal*, p. 121.

67. Buber, *Hearot la-rayon ha-kibutsi*, p. 140.

68. Aharon David Gordon, *Mikhtavim u-reshimot* [Letters and notes] (Jerusalem: Ha-Sifria ha-Tsionit, 1957), pp. 158–63.

69. Buber, "Hithadshut haiei am" [Renascence of national life], in *Netivot be-utopia*, p. 171.

70. On this subject see the chapter entitled "Hinukh leumi ve-hinukh tsioni be-mishnato shel Buber" [National education and Zionist education in Buber's philosophy] in my book, *Mishnato ha-hinukhi shel Martin Buber* [Martin Buber on education] (Tel Aviv: Yahdav, 1976), pp. 241–75. On the subject of the elite in Buber's writings, see: Ernst Simon, "Martin Buber—The Educator," in *The Philosophy of Martin Buber*, ed. P. A. Schilpp and M. Friedman (London: Cambridge University Press, 1967), pp. 542–76. Simon applies the term *elite* in the spirit of Buber by using it in connection with the concept of an "elite of service" in his discussion of secondary education in Israel found in the collection of essays published on the subject in high school education entitled, *Beayot beit-ha-sefer ha-tikhoni* (Jerusalem; 1953), pp. 53–65, 169–71.

71. Buber, "Hithadshut haiei am," p. 178.

72. Ibid., pp. 178–79.

73. Buber, "Nisayon she-lo nikhshal," p. 123.

74. Buber, "Derekh ha-kodesh" [The holy way], in *Teuda ve-yiud* 1, 114–16.

75. Buber, "Ha-sheela she-ha-yahid nishal," p. 176.

76. Buber, "Yahadut u-sviva" [Union and environment], in *Olelot*, p. 34.

4
Religion and Religious Education

Martin Buber evolved his religious philosophy in response to the view of religion that predominated among thinkers at the close of the last century, who were inclined to regard religious belief as merely one of many manifestations of purely human activity, of a kind with other products of mankind's civilized industry. Those in the late nineteenth century who adhered to a historical point of view, especially the historical materialists, tended to interpret religion—as indeed they did all of the forms taken by man's spiritual life—in terms of history, philosophy, sociology, psychology, and like objective categories. Accordingly, religion was thought of as having come into being because of alterations in the material conditions of human existence, the evolution of culture, and changes in man's attitude toward the world.

In short, religion was regarded as being immanent in man—a position that Buber implacably opposed. He argued that God was not a metaphysical idea, nor an ethical ideal, nor any other man-created projection upon the world. All of these are posterior to religious actuality, to the encounter between God and man, to God's advent. And those who limit their idea of God to the concept of an immanency in man have in mind something other than God.

In criticizing the prevalent philosophical attitudes to religion, Buber faulted philosophers for having assumed that the basis of religion is intellectual, whereas in fact it is not wholly accessible to reason. Further, no matter how confident we may be in our powers of reasoning, if we attempt to deal with the subject of religion without possessing the faculty of communion with God, we shall be able to deal only with the problem of whether we can acquire knowledge of God's *reality;* and because this question cannot be empirically resolved, logically consistent argument must compel us to conclude that the reality of God is unknowable. "Now religious teaching," Buber insisted,

"insofar as it is concerned with consciousness at all, does not understand this to mean the relation of a thinking subject to the object of his impartial reflection, but the concrete mutuality of contact taking place between active being and active being, and existing within nature's plenitude. And it understands religious faith to mean an immersion in such mutuality: a communion with Being—with that existence which cannot be shown,

113

verified or proved but nevertheless does become known to a person through his communion with it, and from which the meaning of existence as a whole derives."[1]

Buber was also critical of the mystics, who, in order to rescue religious experience from relativism and to put it out of the range of rationalist analysis, distinguished between the concrete reality of everyday life, which they professed to despise, and "superior reality," experienced through mystic union with God. Buber believed that by regarding the religious as a special category of experience, mysticism had misconceived the nature of religion. At issue, he insisted, is not religious experience as such but the whole of a person's life lived by him in response to God's summons. Encounter with God impends always and everywhere, and takes place by way of life so that a truly religious life is realized by someone not in his self-annulment before God but through his living encounter and relation with God. In his essay on Hasidism's founder, the Baal-Shem-Tov, Buber spelled out the meaning of religiosity in this sense: "The world is no illusion from which a man must turn away in order to attain true reality, but is tangible reality between God and man by which mutuality is proclaimed. . . . The world is God's creating Word to man, and man responds to the Word by his works. It is destined to be redeemed by the meeting of the deed of God and the deed of man."[2]

Buber's dispute with mysticism had to do with his wish to shift the grounds of religious experience from a monological relation, entailing the believer's self-renunciation and personal eclipse in God, to a relation of dialogue with God, whereby man takes an active part in the work of redeeming the world. Buber maintained that life becomes real in the degree that men meet in dialogical I-Thou encounter and engage in discourse with the world, and that it is this relation which opens men's path to God. Buber's rejection of mysticism took place early in his career, when he was put off by mysticism's insistence that the world made available to man through his sensations should be set aside to clear the way for man's supersensible and unfleshly faculties to penetrate to God's being. He was attached to this, the temporal world, whose actuality he wished to see magnified and exalted, and was convinced that the reality of that part of the universe which makes up our concrete existence is made more glorious as our experience and realization of it takes scope. The degree of this reality was functionally determined for Buber by the intensity with which it was experienced and realized.

It was Buber's contention that philosophy always sets out by disregarding man's concrete situation, whereas religion takes for its point of departure the reality of the "fear of God." The term "fear of God" (yirat-elohim in Hebrew) was used by Buber to express something more complex than conventional piety or simple reverent awe of God; it denoted the whole complex of feelings that overwhelms a person when life becomes for him enigmatic and dreadful because all of his certitudes have been undermined by the unknowable and essential mystery of existence. But through it he can also return to a routine reality that has become hallowed as a place which he must share with that mystery, and he becomes dedicated to and bent upon the concrete circumstances of his existence. Hence, authentic manifestations of religiosity all have a personal aspect that is expressed in a tangible situation in which the personality, *qua* personality, takes part.

Buber took to task those schools of philosophy that tried to preserve the idea of divinity as the principle of religion while stripping the concept of God of its concreteness and thereby denying the actuality of our relation with Him. Buber cites the example of Immanuel Kant, who believed that the concept of God is a postulate of our practical and ethical intelligence and that we know nothing about him on the basis of pure reason. The conclusion to which Kant finally was led by this position is contained in a passage quoted by Buber from the notes Kant kept in his last years: "God is not an external substance but an ethical relation existing only within ourselves."[3] Kant bestowed on mankind a metaphysical status that serves as a criterion for the individual—a point of view that Buber would not accept, explaining "I am constitutionally incapable of viewing myself as the original source of this yea-naysaying, as sole guarantor of such perfect certitude, when this affirmation and rejection is in no way mine to pronounce and I am no more than attuned to it in spirit. Encounter with that primal Word, with the One who uttered yea-nay from the first of time, cannot be substituted by any encounter with the self nor exchanged for it."[4]

But modern philosophy was not content merely to do away with God's actuality by grounding Him in an ethical principle. If Kant had shifted the focus of civilization from God to man without questioning the concept of the divine, Hegel made Spirit—the entity we call God—accessible only to reason and not to the total man living a tangible existence. Buber noted that although in the Hegelian system the Absolute (the intelligence of the universe: i.e., *God*) makes use of all that is and occurs in nature and history, including man, in order to realize itself and attain consummate self-consciousness, it neither exists in an actual and direct relationship with man nor favors man with the grace of a relation to itself. Therefore, what Hegel and his followers termed "God" is hardly God who appears to men in their moments of despair and wonder.

Martin Heidegger, taking as his starting point Nietzsche's mordant pronouncement "God is dead," interpreted it to mean that man had plucked the idea of God out of objective existence and implanted it in subjective immanence. The death of God meant for Heidegger the end of the supersensible world, which was in any case man-made. Heidegger conceived of man as individual and substituted the idea of God with that of "Being" which is finite, historical, and indwelling in man as his immanent core. Man was barred from knowledge of absolute being, he concluded, and the modern period was, therefore, marked by God's absence. Responding to Heidegger's thesis that the supersensible world has been superseded, Buber asserted that the Living God, who appears to men when they summon Him, can no more be made to occupy the supersensible world than be made to tenant the world of sense as an object of subjective cognition.

Jean-Paul Sartre took Friedrich Nietzsche at his word, and to drive Nietzsche's apothegm home Sartre declared: "He is dead, He spoke to us and is silent now; we touch nothing but His corpse,"[5]—a statement from whose gruesome finality Buber recoiled in disgust. Yet if he rejected Sartre's death-of-God views, Buber took seriously Sartre's idea of God's silence. Buber agreed with Sartre that in the past men may have heard God, whose voice has since been stilled; however, he concludes from this that the Living God is not only God who makes himself manifest but also God who keeps himself hidden. Sartre, having interpreted God's silence merely to be a sign of His absence, insisted on our need to put God out of our minds, to liberate ourselves from Him and to achieve for ourselves the freedom of creation that we used to assign solely to Him. "There exists no world other than the human world, the world of human subjectivity," he wrote.[6] On the other hand, Buber suggested that when God and man fall silent mutually, something has occurred not in human subjectivity but within existence itself. So, rather than offer facile and extraneous explanations having to do with God's death in order to explain the event, man would do better to face up to the silence as it is, "and existentially direct his consciousness towards another event, towards a new transformation in being, towards the sound of resurgent speech reverberating between Heaven and earth."[7] Sartre took God's silence as a sign of His having departed, but he failed to consider the part played in this silence by man's own spiritual imperviousness and deficient hearing.

The *I-Thou* principle was conceived by Buber as all-embracing, even in respect of the relation between man and God, which is a dialogical relation reciprocally enacted by both. When man enacts the relation of *I-Thou,* his object, whatever its nature—plant or animal, and certainly man—becomes for him a medium in which the divine is made manifest. This idea, which is so pervasive in Buber's thinking, echoes the Hasidic doctrine that in establishing a relationship with any object, man can ascend to a relation with God. Hasidism sought to do away with the distinctions between the sacred and profane by teaching the hallowing of every secular act in the reverent performance of it. It taught the doctrine of the redemption of divine "sparks"— those spoor-embers of God's effulgence that are lodged in all things living and inanimate—by raising them and causing them to rejoin their supernatural source. Moreover it did so, as Buber points out, without lapsing by way of pantheism into a repudiation of values or disavowal of the mutuality of communion between the human and divine. In Buber's terms, Hasidism conceived of an *I-Thou* continuum spanning earth and Heaven and undiminished in its actuality even to the very threshold of Eternity and beyond.

Buber regarded the *I-Thou* relation with the world to be the portal to communion with God as Absolute Thou. The human Thou takes on substance in all of man's relations, but achieves a consummate state only in its relation with the Eternal Thou, which alone is exempt from being transformed into an "Other." In Buber's religious philosophy, history is a dialogue between the Creator and mankind wherein man is an active partner, responding to God's call by actions that are at one with the call's spirit. In concrete reality, no moment, place, or event exists that is unmarked by the influence of God's speech with His creatures.

Men have called the Eternal Thou by different names, Buber observed, but as they came in the course of time to think of the Eternal Thou as of an Other, they began to speak of it as they would of a third person, and these names degenerated into a mode of indirect address. However, the name by which the Eternal Thou is called is of no significance and serves its purpose so long as man invokes it in order to speak *to* God and not *of* Him, calls on Him, and intends Him solely. In considering the nature of such authentic religious feeling, Buber goes so far as to argue that even a person who actually believes himself to be repudiating God, if in doing so he addresses with his whole being the Thou in his own life, a Thou which will not be diminished by any other Thou, also calls on God.

Apropos of the word "God," Buber tells of a conversation he once had with an elderly and gentle intellectual who, on hearing Buber talk of God, vehemently observed: "What word in human speech has been so abused, so soiled, so loathed as this word! All the innocent blood spilt because of it casts a pall over its radiance. All the iniquity it was compelled to help shield has blotted it out. Sometimes, when I hear the Most High being called God I think it blasphemy."[8] Buber conceded that this word, fraught with greater meaning than any other, had long been corrupted and discredited. But it was precisely because the word had been abused for so long in history that he felt himself unable to renounce it: "For generations man have rolled the burden of their wretched lives' yearnings onto this word and pressed it down into the earth; so that now it is covered over with dust and has everyone's ideal heaped upon it. For generations men of every religious persuasion have rent this word into tatters, killed and died because of it; and the marks of all their fingers and the blood of all are upon it. Where shall I find its equal to designate the Almighty!"[9] Men have murdered in God's name. They have committed untold crimes for the sake of monsters whom they have conjured in their imaginations. But this dark sorcery is also a manifestation of men's religious yearnings. It represents men's calling on God out of their isolation and it is a sign of their having ceased to speak of God as "He" and begun to call out to God as "Thou" and to rediscover Him. "We cannot wash the word

'God' clean," Buber wrote, "nor can we mend it; but we can raise it from the ground and, soiled as it is and tattered, bear it aloft until it hovers high as a miracle over times of great dread."[10]

Buber observed that when an individual has experienced disappointment in his relationship with all personal Thous, which have become for him mere Others, his frustrated Thou-sense wishes to abandon these mutable Thous and transcend them in order to discover a private and eternal Thou. Having, however, made this choice, he faces a number of deceptive alternatives. Anyone renouncing life in order to seek God will not find Him. By seclusion, withdrawal from the world, mortification of the flesh—in short, by any immersion wholly within the self—we lose all chance of true encounter with God. But each event involving relation becomes a small window through which we can glimpse the Absolute. Nevertheless, God cannot be inferred from a mere thing; He cannot be, as it were, extrapolated from either nature or the universe, anymore than He can emerge from within the subject. He is actuality that faces us, and can only be called out to but never be expressed.

When Buber considered the question of whether an individual may gain access to God by isolating himself, and of whether his immersion in the self and his self-communion may evolve into a communion with the divine mystery, he distinguished between two kinds of isolation. There is an isolation that comes from having renounced relationships with things which are based on knowledge and use of them: in this case seclusion may be a preparation for establishing a relation of communion. But there is also an isolation which ends in the absence of any relationship whatever with the external world, and this kind cannot lead to encounter with God. When our isolation is reclusion, a refuge to which we retire in order to enjoy the pleasures of egocentric communion rather than an occasion for self-examination preparing us to meet the future, then we become involved in "a betrayal of Spirit and in its transformation into mere spirituality."[11]

Buber emphasized repeatedly that whoever speaks to God without speaking to men misdirects his words. This is the lesson we are asked to draw from a parable of Buber's own invention: A man was so inspired with love of God that he renounced all property and human connections and set out in quest of God. His journey took him into a great wasteland, through which he wandered until he reached the gates of the Mystery. And the man cried out at the gates, "I have proclaimed Thy fame to mortal men and they heeded not. And now I have come to Thee that Thou mayst hearken unto my speech and answer me." And the man was thrust away, and a voice answered from within, saying: "There is none here that will give ear to thee. I have planted Mine hearing in the unheedingness of mortal men."[12]

Following a line of reasoning that is personal to him, Buber concluded that men can only perceive complete relation as duality. In man's relation to the Absolute, he senses at one and the same time both the condition of being created and Creation: "You always know in your heart that more than anything you have need of God. Yet aren't you also aware that God, in all His infinitude, has need of you as well? . . . the world is no game played by God: it is divine destiny. And one of the divine mysteries is that the world exists, that man exists, that man's personality exists, that you and I exist."[13] Creation, according to Buber, takes place within us and we take part in it; we encounter one another in the Creator and place ourselves at His service as helpers and companions.

This relationship seemed to Buber to be born in prayer and in the ritual of offerings that is described in the Old Testament. A worshiper praying to God is convinced that he is actually affecting God. And this feeling is strongest in the worshiper when he prays without seeking personal gain, when his prayer is of the kind represented in Judaism by the Confessional Prayer said on the eve of the Day of Atonement. The same may be said of ritual offering, although this represents a practice belonging to a primitive stage of religious belief. In the Bible, the bringer of burnt offerings places his savory meats on the altar in the belief that God longs to breathe in their fragrant smells. But the bringer of offerings also senses profoundly that he is important to God, that he participates with God, that God has need of him.

Buber drew a distinction between magic and the practice of prayer and the rite of offering. Magic aspires to produce its effects without entering into relation; it sets its forces into motion in a spiritual vacuum. But prayer and sacrifice are a species of the relation of communion; they are the occasions of our standing before God, the deeds of the piety of mutuality. Prayer was conceived by Buber as the speech a man pours out before God. However, to be realized in its complete sense, prayer must primarily express—whatever immediate purpose the suppliant may have had in mind—the worshiper's earnest desire for a revelation of divine presence and to experience that presence dialogically. "The sole precondition of true prayer," Buber believed, "is for a person to be wholly prepared for this presence; to bend the whole of his being, his unreserved spontaneity, towards it."[14]

Still, Buber could not accept the idea that a religious person's total involvement with God somehow exempts him from having to become involved in the world and its creatures. He argued that we cannot compartmentalize our lives, reserving one part of our existence for authentic relation with God and another for *I-Thou* relation with the world; praying to God on the one hand and making use of the world on the other. Anyone who sees the world as something that exists in order to be made use of must have the same attitude toward God. Such a person projects his prayers into a void and can truly be called *God-less:* "It is he who is without God, and not the 'unbeliever' who calls out to the Nameless One from the darkness of the soul's night and from the yearnings of the body's vessel."[15]

On this point Buber's differences with Kierkegaard are especially marked. Kierkegaard viewed the relation of the individual—the "Single One"— wholly from the perspective of profound inward solitude in which a person's relationship with his fellow man and the world has no place. Taking issue, Buber emphasized the importance of the temporal world to the individual person as his own legitimate Thou and his bridge to the Divine Thou.

Kierkegaard thought that the relation to God was man's sole relation, or rather the relation that gives rise to all other relations. God's voice comes to a person existing as someone solitary and singular, so that man stands alone in God's presence. Nothing could have been further from Buber's conception. In taking Kierkegaard to task, Buber suggested that Kierkegaard's doctrine of religious solitude may owe something to its author's own personality and private life. Couching his criticism in most graphic terms, Buber noted with asperity: "Kierkegaard treats us as would a schizophrenic intent on drawing the beloved Single One into his own world as though it were the true world. Only that world is not real."[16] In *Fear and Trembling,* Kierkegaard even makes the claim that the renunciation of worldly existence, although the highest form that piety can take, may also be the height of egoism. The Single One, he argued, corresponds to or "replicates" the image of God by becoming singular. And although God is no egoist, His is Infinite Ego.[17] Buber countered Kierkegaard by arguing: "The Single One corresponds to God when he humanly embraces the part of the world available to him in the way that God divinely embraces His creation. He sustains God's image when he says "Thou" with his whole being to fellow beings living in his presence and does so to the limits of his ability to say it personally."[18]

What "asset"—Buber asks—accrues to a person once he has experienced encounter with the Absolute? He answers that the encounter bestows on an individual a "Presence" which takes the form of new spiritual potency. This Presence is described by Buber as having three aspects. First, it represents true mutuality, realized in full and embracing the whole spectrum of communion: the relation of both "being received" and "binding oneself to"— without, however, being able to describe the nature of that to which he is being bound. This binding does not ease a person's life but actually makes it more burdensome, charges it with significance. Second, it confirms for us the fact of life's significance in such a way that the whole question of life's meaning ceases to exist for us. For that meaning becomes a certitude even though it cannot be defined or put into words. Third, it confers on us a relation with God that does not belong to another mode of existence but to this, *our life* and *our world.*

Once we have responded to God's call and established a relationship of mutuality with Him, we are no longer the persons we were prior to our encounter. We are enriched, we acquire new creative capacities, and we must relinquish the hope of redemption taking place in any way other than by our own creative influence upon the concrete world. Yet even though we approach God by our enactment of dialogue with the Absolute, we come no nearer to deciphering the secret of existence. For the nature of dialogical encounter with God is not of a kind that enables us to communicate the wisdom we gain in it to other persons by precepts that tell them what they must know, do, and fulfill. "We can do no less than set out and enact," Buber wrote; "and even if this is not a duty imposed on us—we can, we are under a compulsion to."[19] Buber believed that man should not set himself the task of puzzling out the riddle of the universe. Neither man nor his existence is at the center of human concerns, but the world and its creatures that encompass man and in which he acts in keeping with the spirit of God's summons to him.

Buber stressed that the Eternal Thou cannot be transmuted into an Other. For by its nature the Eternal Thou cannot be measured nor can its limits be determined; it cannot be apprehended as a sum of quantifiable traits, located either within the world or outside it, acquired as a possession, comprehended by thought. Yet we persist in our desire to turn it into an Other, to objectify it as a thing. This tendency is manifest in the conceptions of the articles of religious faiths and in the practices sanctioned by religious traditions.

The tendency was traced by Buber to man's deep-seated yearning to experience continuity that is unlimited by time and space: to his desire to take hold to divinity and be held by it unceasingly. And because Presence alone cannot gratify man's wish for continuity, man ends by making God a *subject* of religious belief. Man's dialogical encounter with the Absolute is really the meeting of a single person with God. So that it is only in the capacity of a particular human being that man can set out in quest of the Deity and encounter Him. But this one-to-one relation does not endure, and so fails to satisfy man. Men aspire to immediate transcendence—to instantaneous theophany, an incarnation by which the community of faithful becomes one with God. The result is that God becomes the subject of a cult ritual that gradually replaces Him.

Pure relation, Buber proposed, is formed and maintained in the sphere of time and space only when it is actualized as the whole substance of life. By no show of ceremony will we fulfill our obligation to God unless we repeatedly "realize" Him. Encounter with God does not take place just so that we may have dealings with the Deity. God's every advent is a mission undertaken by Him to humanity and to the world. Therefore, those among us who style ourselves religious, but who confine ourselves to having transactions with God rather than realizing Him in the world, really believe in God only as Other and address Him as Other.

Religious dogma seemed to Buber to repress the dialogical forces emanating from the concrete circumstances of human existence, and so to obscure revelation. There seemed to him to be no more effective means of screening the face of God from men than the fully articulated creeds of established religions.

We know of no other form of God's advent, Buber insisted, than encounter between the divine and human in which man takes direct part.

Hence even oral or written traditions that may have arisen from true advent and revelation cannot be taken by us, in the form they have been handed down to us, as actually being God's word or the record of His regulation. For we have, after all, no way of establishing with certainty and for all time which elements in these traditions have a divine origin and which are merely man-made.[20]

For although the source of all religions is revelation, no religion represents absolute truth but only human truth; the relation, that is, of a particular group of men, as a group, to the Absolute. Only a religion that does not aim at itself but at God in particular leads to God, whereas all established religions, because they are intent on maintaining themselves, put a distance between man and God. Worse than any form of unbelief is the idea that religion is a *commodity,* either serving the practical needs of a person or being advantageous to the life of a people. This is mere pretense of realism; pernicious fiction masquerading as fact. The complete reality of man with God, with the world, and with his fellow man is the encounter of man and God within the world. We do not serve God with mere spirit—Buber reminds us—but with the whole of the reality of both nature and essence. Authentic piety aims to stop being religion and to become life. And until man realizes such true religion he is condemned to the diaspora of the established faiths. Nevertheless, Buber held out the hope of redemption, when men will be released from their separate spiritual captivities to rejoin one another and together share God's world.

Buber believed that in every period we can discern the signs of an ongoing conflict taking place within religion itself, between the religious principle and principles of a nonreligious nature. Metaphysics, gnosis, magic, and politics press in from all sides and insinuate themselves into the perpetually self-renewing stream of religious life; and as they try to replace religion, they make use of myth and ritual, although these had originally been solely created as a language for expressing religious relation. Buber characterized this conflict as "a struggle in defense of existential concreteness as the unshakeable ground of the meeting between the human and divine."[21]

The idea that religion concerns only one aspect of life, and that life's other aspects are independent of religion and obey laws of their own, was unacceptable to Buber. For to restrict the relation of religion to a narrow sphere, and to put vast reaches of human existence under the authority of the group, the party, or the state is to set limits on the influence of the divine and to confine the dominion of God within a pale.

There is no manual of conduct for realizing the relation of faith; no practical guide in which we can read the obligations imposed on us by a particular situation taking place at a certain moment in time. Whatever God demands of us is intended by Him to exist in relation to us at the very moment the demand is being made. Neither God's summons nor our answer can be found between the covers of a book. For God's call requires a response that is realized in the choice made by us, individually, out of our personal consciousness of what we must do or refrain from doing, and by our assuming personal responsibility toward our moment. That responsibility, Buber urged, must never be handed over by us to our group, which is in all events not empowered to relieve us of it. And anyone, no matter of what rank or authority, who offers us a ready-made answer that tempts us away from attending to God's summons is doing the Devil's work.

Yet Buber was far from denying the value of the group. The community was thought by him to be no less than the force field of human relation. And although every person can himself experience divine revelation, it is only in the *I-Thou* relation of individuals with one another that the divine is fully revealed. Hence society is the true sphere within which God's call is actualized. Buber had stressed that man individually confronts God and must disencumber himself of those characteristics he took over from humanity at large. But Buber also insisted that each person is a product of human society, and, therefore, belongs to it and must regard himself to be responsible for its welfare. Nevertheless, Buber saw that the very existence of group decisions acted as a constant threat to personal existential choice. The choices of an individual are validly arrived at so long as they are made within the same existential stratum in which he becomes conscious of an event as being God's word to him. But once the individual turns over his right of choice to a group, so that it should decide in his behalf, he also relinquishes his privilege to God's response. For as Buber would have it, God will not respond to his prayer.

The importance to Buber of the group is evident as well from his criticism of Kierkegaard's idea that man's encounter with the divine is a meeting between the solitary individual and God. Buber argued that the encounter of man with God could only result from man's significant relation to the world and his community. God does not wish man to approach Him in solitude, Buber said. In bypassing the world, man can enact only a superficial relation with God, whereas God's intention is for man to commit himself to God completely. But for a society with its traditions and religious faith to fulfill its part in man's encounter with the Deity, it must be open and constantly renewing itself; it has to be capable of preserving historical memory, but without arresting the process of recollecting the past by fixing it in the form of laws that circumscribe existence and put man's living encounter with God and the world under constraint.

The story of the revolt of Korah the Levite against Moses and Aaron, told in the Book of Numbers, provided Buber with material on which to elaborate his ideas on the balance that must be struck between personal and received revelation. Buber took for his text Numbers 16:3, in which Korah and his party air their grievances:

> And they gathered themselves together against Moses and against Aaron, and said unto them, Ye take too much upon you, seeing all the congregation are holy, every one of them, and the Lord is among them: wherefore then lift ye up yourselves above the congregation of the Lord?

In his exegesis of the verse, Buber interprets the Kohrahic argument to be that the entire nation is sacred because God exists within it as a whole; and if the people as a whole are sacred there is no justification for instituting laws that govern their lives nor any reason for having an official legislator such as Moses. Since all men have a share in holiness, Moses can have no precedence over them in sanctity. They have no need of an intermediary between themselves and God, for each person has access to the Lord, whose commandments he can receive directly. The revolt of Korah and his followers is, therefore, represented by them as a rebellion against the rule of one man, who leads his people in the name of God, and himself decides for them what they may or may not do.[22]

Now the revolt of Korah might have been justified—Buber thought—had it been inspired by fear of the law's becoming inflexible; were it undertaken in response to the danger that laws and judgments would stifle the spirit and establish patterns of coercion which were alien to the spirit of God. The conclusion which Korah should have reached, therefore, was that there exists a need to ensure perpetual renewal by remaining receptive to the call of God, whose voice was not heard only once on the Mount and stilled, but addresses man continually, each day and every hour. "At that hour, religions must hearken with all their might to what God demands, and in the light of His revelation they must resolve the problems of the moment which confront them, doing so within the contradiction that exists between God's will and the present, concrete reality of the world."[23] But the falseness of Korah's demand for liberation from the rule of law was in his claim that Mosaic Law stifles spirit and liberty and his call for the abrogation of the Torah.

Buber compared the religious attitudes of Korah and Moses. The Deity to whom Moses was devoted establishes the goal and points the way. He writes a guide on stone tables, records His instructions to men in order to lead along His way, and commands men to choose often, repeatedly, and well. The greatness of Moses' devotion to God has to do with his encounter with the popular and mystical Lord, who, rather than demand of men that they purify themselves and become sanctified, treats them as though they were already holy. In contrast to Moses, Korah merely called a Baal by God's name, but in doing so in no way altered the Baal's nature.

In Buber's view Judaism was not originally a system of knowledge; it contained neither any definite and consciously formed ideas nor any express statements about God's nature. Rather the Faith of Israel was what Buber called a "life-relation" to God. "The vigor of [such] a faith," Buber claimed, "cannot be gauged from the strength of the firm knowledge that this God exists (His *existence* is a matter for *theology* and of no concern to religious life, which is based on contact with Him) but from the strength of that devotion to Him by which the lives of believers are determined."[24] Buber described Judaism as a system of testimonies or witnessings of a living relationship with God. God's adherents' consciousness of His unity and exclusive nature evolved from their unreserved and total commitment to His rule. God's absolute nature in Judaism stems from His rule, His oneness from His absolute nature.

God's ineffable name in Hebrew Scripture seemed to Buber to express just such a testimony of Life relation with the Deity. In his book written in collaboration with Franz Rosenzweig, Buber observed that the tetragrammaton YHWH (for which Jews substitute *Adonai*, "my Lord," when reading the name, and which is rendered as *Jehovah* in Christian tradition and *Yahweh* in recent transliteration) is an expanded interjection intended as a calling out to God.[25] Factors of assonance and spelling suggested to Buber that the Ineffable Name is a conflation of the words in Hebrew for "oh," "woe" and "alas." The first two letters YH, for example, occur in the Old Testament as an abbreviated form of the tetragrammaton, and when pronounced become the interjection *yah;* in Psalm 94:12 it serves simultaneously as an exclamation and a play on the Ineffable Name, so that the single word is made to stand for "O Lord." Similarly, if the middle letters HW are construed as the word *hw* (pronounced "ho"), they come to mean "woe" or "alas." In addition, Buber hears echoes of demonstrative pronominal forms. When the tetragrammaton appears as the suffix *yhw* in a name and is pronounced "yahu" (compare *Yirmeyahu:* Jeremiah or "Chosen of God") it recalls to Buber the sound of the demonstrative *zehu,* or "that one"; and Buber even stretches a point by also hearing the sound *hw* (pronouned "hu"), normally the personal pronoun "he" but acting in many contexts as an emphatic or demonstrative form. Hence the tetragrammaton is at once a designation for God and a pointing out of Him; but it is also a sigh, a cry of distress, a gasp of awe before calling on God, a release of the breath of wonder in the presence of unnameable divinity.[26]

The question of God's name is brought up by the Old Testament in the episode of the burning bush recounted in the Book of Exodus. Moses' dialogue with God, who spoke out of the bush that burned and was not consumed, was thought of by Buber as another instance of a witnessing, this time of God's umediated presence in His concrete relation with His people. When Moses demands to know by what name to proclaim God to the people, God answers: I AM THAT I AM (Ex. 3:14). God's answer in Hebrew, *eheyeh asher eheyeh,* is couched in the imperfect tense, which in the grammar of biblical Hebrew is ambiguous with reference to time and implies continuous action initiated in the past or undertaken in the future. "I am that I am" not only declines symmetrically as "I was that I was" and "I shall be that I shall be," but also as "I am that I was," "I am that I shall be," "I was that I am," and so on—the permutations of time sense are many, the meaning one: eternal and ever-changing being. That this is the sense of "I am" intended by the text is shown by its being repeated by God once again in the same verse and explicitly elucidated by Him in the next: "Thus shalt thou say unto the children of Israel, I AM hath sent me unto you," ". . . this is my name for ever, and this is my memorial unto all generations." Buber was, therefore, on firm ground when he interpreted God's "I am—*eheye*" as denoting His "being present" and "being at a particular place, but also His ongoing "becoming" and "taking place," with the further implication that God does not manifest Himself under a permanent guise: although ubiquitous in time, He is protean in form. On this last point Buber concluded that God cannot be conjured in any specific shape, nor can the place and time of His appearance be determined by sorcery. In fact, the whole episode was interpreted by Buber as a proclamation of an end to the magical foundations of religion with the advent of GOD THAT IS among his people, who walks with them through all eternity.[27]

Buber's understanding of the Hebrew prophets' role and his understanding of their teachings derive from Buber's conception of the relationship between God and the individual. Buber thought of this relationship as taking place between a speaking deity who addresses someone, and a particular person having a will of his own, who is free either to welcome God's speech or to shut himself off from it. But the mere hearkening to God's speech is not enough: His address demands *response*. The prophet's role is to interpret the Word made manifest in the events of the personal lives of individuals and the histories of a people and the nations of the world. Historical situations are the signs in which God speaks, and the prophet is the appointed translator of divine language. "These situations are way stations," Buber wrote, "and God summons the prophet to announce to the people where they stand at this moment, to proclaim to them the significance of the choice between the way of the One God and the world's countless crooked paths, to explain to them the meaning of *this* station in *this* historical situation, the implications of the eternal choice at *this* time rather than any other."[28] The people must respond by making a choice. But even if they evade making a choice, this too is a kind of response.

After the establishment of the Jewish monarchy, the conduct of political and social affairs passed into the hands of the king and his ministers. At this moment in Jewish history the prophet of Israel became the representative of the Spirit, in whose behalf he demanded that the king and the royal institutions that controlled political, social, and religious life in the country fulfill God's will. At God's behest the prophet censured the state for its intention of depriving God's authority of its actuality in day-to-day civic and political life. The Bible is filled with the testimonies of the Hebrew prophets' vigorous protests against the erosion by the state of God's authority in both the ritual and cosmic spheres. The royal court and the institutions established by it are represented by Buber as forces that diverted the relation with God in the direction of myth and ritual, and so arrogated to themselves the obligations that belong to men individually in their relationship with the Deity. On the other hand, the figure of the biblical prophet was characterized by Buber as the model of the believer whose piety permeates all his relations, and the advocate of the life of total response.[29]

Buber conceived of the Hebrew Bible as the essential statement of Jewish nationhood and, therefore, the source on which the Jewish people must draw for its national existence. The conception was based on Buber's deep conviction that no sacred writings composed outside the sphere of Old Testament influence are so consummate an expression of the dialogue between Heaven and earth as is Jewish Scripture: "It tells of God's calling man and calling him again, and of man's calling God and calling Him again. . . . Such is the teaching whose substance fills the space of Scripture: our lives are a dialogue between the world above and the world below."[30]

Buber believed that this biblical teaching had contemporary validity. But—he argued—both the traditionally pious and the secularists have in their separate ways managed to undermine its relevance to contemporary life. The pious have done this by assuming that Scripture is a literal transcription of God's direct communication in the past to the group of His elect, and that since then Heaven has become silent and the spirit of God has removed its presence from us and left behind written and oral law as the only source of our knowledge of God's will concerning what we must do and desist from doing. The secularist has done this by reducing the dialogical system of the Old Testament to a mythopoeic technique, and regarding the Scriptures as only a corpus of legends irrelevant to contemporary experience. As an alternative to the attitudes of the orthodoxly religious and unbelievers Buber proposed:

> What had been actual to us still is and always will be. And this actuality, present to us, is the sign and token that it has always been. It is a fact, a deed continually renewing itself, each and every day to the end of time; and it is this that the Hebrew Scriptures have given us in the form of a brilliantly painted recollection of Ancient Days: an image wrapped in lambent radiance. In these events and situations—infinite in number and passing in endless train, yet visible and clear to anyone with a discerning eye—the Almighty speaks to our hearts when our being becomes a unity. And we are even given the language in which to respond to Him: the language of our deeds and conduct when we answer Him by taking action or refraining from it. The totality of all of these responses made by us may legitimately, and in its primary significance, be designated man's duty in his world.[31]

It is from the Bible that we learn this fundamental principle of our existence, Buber claimed. And whenever we read it with authentic devotion, we renew and deepen our self-knowledge.

The attitudes of young people to religion sufficiently engrossed Buber for him to have treated the subject at length. In his study Buber set out to establish whether there exists a common ground between the young and religious belief. In this connection, he raises the question of whether we may legitimately impose on any young person, irrespective of his being a believer or not, a "relation of consent" to religion. Such a demand was not only uncongenial to Buber but greatly repelled him when it involved requiring the young to adhere to a particular creed. "Whoever imposes a single religion on youth has closed the shutters on youth to every window—but one—within the circle of a great mansion; has closed off youth's access to every road—but one—that ascends to the ultimate reaches."[32]

A demand of this nature would be justified were religion actually constituted to guide men to encounter God—a condition that Buber did not believe was fulfilled by the established faiths. He argued that the tenets and precepts of religion change, for they are the result of the spiritual labors of an individual trying to understand the Absolute—whose effects he has experienced within himself—with a set of concrete conceptual images that can be conceived in the mind and realized in action. So that the essence of religion is not its dogmas but the meeting of man with God, whence religious tenets derive in the first place. Neither belief in a particular faith, obedience to the articles of a creed, nor fulfillment of specific commandments, Buber insists, will bring about contact with the Absolute. But,

> When anyone lifts up his soul to Him—never mind the name by which he chooses to designate this act—then all things in the world become holy to him and are sanctified; the *Shekinah,* Divine Presence, comes to rest on them when he walks with them, and the world is made ready for Eternal Life.[33]

Buber described the conventional practices of religious education as an imposition of the yoke of dogma on the young. The principal aim of traditional religious education, he thought, is to persuade young people to commit themselves to a fixed number of precepts that they are forced to learn and expected to obey and enact. However, the goal set by Buber for the religious educator was the awakening of the young to the experience of encounter, their spiritual preparation for a personal confrontation with the Absolute. God's word is taught by religious educators from a book and preached by them as doctrine. But the business of religious education should be to nurture the consciousness that all things in the world, without exception, are potential bearers of the word of God. Rather than represent the worship of God as a matter of prescribed rite, religious education must teach that any act is sacral if it results in union. Life is closer to God than precepts, and a religious educator should not exhort his pupils to order their lives according to religious precepts, but assist them "to see and sense that all of the ways in which a person walks in truth and sanctity ascend to God's portals."[34]

Buber cautioned against two kinds of error to which religious thought and education are prone. The first of these is self-contained rationalism, whereby the religious relation is turned into something remote as a result of the exertion of conscious analytical will. The second error is religious sentimentality, in which the relation is treated as an emotional experience and so reduced to a mere state of mind. Each in its own way limits the scope of religious experience.

Buber felt that by existing in a bond with the nation we preserve ourselves from lapsing into religious solipsism that is the result of secluding ourselves within personal experience. In isolation, we draw from no well deeper than our personal experience; we become involved in an absurd contradiction of trying to confine the infinite within the finiteness of private reality. On the other hand, from our connection with the people and its heritage we derive the power by which we create image and form. Buber described the relationship of an individual with his nation as taking place in, so to speak, three spatial realms: facing him, around him, and within him. Facing him are the Scriptures, in which the individual reads the record of the nation's past, represented as divine action taken by the people as a whole. Around him he sees the people as the actually are, corrupted but still carrying within them the spirit of God. Within himself, the individual senses the presence of a profound indwelling memory of the past.

The effect of the Absolute on the soul of an individual was regarded by Buber as equivalent on a small scale to its influence upon the spirit of humanity as a whole. Little wonder, then, that Buber assigned such great importance to the need of an individual to establish an inner bond with the whole of man's spiritual experience, up to and including the moment of his own participation in it. Utter bewilderment and perplexity is the only response that a person unfortified by a bond with a community of his fellow men is capable of when the voice of God finally reaches him. An individual takes form in his connection with his people, and through it acquires the spiritual weight and substance to face squarely the One who calls him.

The purpose of religion is not served by formularies celebrating ideas that men have elevated to a status of divine truth, Buber maintained. Religious experience is too vital and its scope too vast for it to be contained in a litany. It involves our encounter with absolute mystery—irreducible to a formal credo—which may visit us at any turn in our lives. Religious faith fulfills its real purpose for Buber when it throws open the gates of the soul, prepares us in our inmost being actually to live with the mystery once it confronts us. The fact that the mystery reaches us in the guise of personal experience does not make it a familiar spirit with which we can live tranquilly. As often as not we are overwhelmed by the sheer number and variety of the manifestations of the mystery of faith, stunned by the suddenness of its coming, terrified by its aspect. Our experience of the mystery can be made easier if we have maintained a vital tradition that preserves the testimonies of those who have themselves encountered it. And this is especially true when we are sharers with these witnesses in a historical community—when, in other words, they are of our own kind. Then, "They help us by the purity with which they apprehended the Mystery, came forward to face it, consecrated themselves to it. For faith in its deepest essence means consecration."[35] "Now I know," Buber adds, "that the past, transmitted through the cold apparatus of established religion, comes to us drained of vitality. But it can be revivified. And then we have access once more to the words which were first communicated to us as vital utterances spoken in life, . . . We, too, can hear the voice speaking to us from the written word."[36]

Strict adherence to religious precepts was felt by Buber to be justified only in the case of someone who was convinced that there exists no other way in this world to consecrate himself to God. The observance of religious tenets merely because one is coerced into obeying them is really a secular act. But the demand for such obedience is even worse; it is a profanation of piety. Buber's strictures in this matter were especially harsh when he came to deal with Jewish religious educators who equate their pupil's observation of religious law with obedience to the authority of national-religious will.

The relationship to religion and its body of wisdom was conceived by Buber in a way radically different from the conception of piety as a passive acceptance of imposed tradition. Buber spoke of binding ourselves to the "primal forces" (kohhot kedumim), the vital energies that were generated in the past by the vital response to God. "These are eternal forces which prevent the relation to the Absolute from congealing and becoming a thing a person makes his faith of and does his duty to; they are the forces that time and again turn away from religious dogma and the dead letter of precepts towards the freedom that is God."[37] A faith teaches the distinction between the sacred and profane; the primal forces consecrate the secular by making it the sphere of man's relation to God.

Buber described this binding of ourselves to the primal forces as taking place in two stages. We begin by making a wholehearted commitment to the great enterprise of faith and spirit. Once the commitment has been made we can actually return to a life of faith—a return that to Buber meant the lifelong undertaking of each of us, personally, to engage the Absolute in dialogue. But he believed it would take more than the promptings of our inmost feelings for us to achieve a commitment to spirit and follow in the path of the primal forces. Understanding, reverence, and good faith are required as well. These are the very qualities lacked by so many young people in their dealings with religion, and would have to be nurtured by education. The implication of Buber's position for Jews is that they must study their sacred texts not as mere literature but as primary documents recording the spirit of the nation; and not as canonical books but as the permanent font and reservoir of primal forces.

NOTES

1. Martin Buber, "Likui ha-or ha-elohi" [The Eclipse of divine light], in *Penei adam: behinot be-antropologia filosofit* [The face of man: studies in anthropological philosophy] (Jerusalem: Mosad Bialik, 1962), p. 234.

2. Martin Buber, *Des Baal-Schem-Tow Unterweisung im Umgang mit Gott* [The Baal-Shem-Tov's teachings about God] (Hellerau: Jakob Hegner, 1927), p. 127.

3. Buber, "Likui ha-or ha-elohi," p. 231.

4. Ibid., p. 232.

5. Jean-Paul Sartre, *Situations I* (Paris: Gallimard, 1947), p. 153.

6. Jean-Paul Sartre, *L'existentialisme est un humanisme* (Existentialism as humanism) (Paris: Nagel, 1946), p. 93.

7. Buber, "Likui ha-or ha-elohi," p. 271.

8. Ibid., p. 225.

9. Ibid., pp. 225–26.

10. Ibid., p. 226.

11. Martin Buber, "Ani-ata" [I-Thou], in *Be-sod siah: al ha-adam ve-amidato nokhah hahavaya* [Dialogue: man confronting being] (Jerusalem: Mosad Bialik, 1963), p. 80.

12. Martin Buber, "Du siah" [Dialogue], in *Be-sod siah*, p. 124.

13. Buber, "Ani-ata," p. 63.

14. Buber, "Likui ha-or ha-elohi," p. 319.

15. Buber, "Ani-ata," p. 82.

16. Martin Buber, "Ha-sheela she-ha-yahid nishal" [The question of the single one], in *Be-sod siah*, p. 175.

17. Sören Kierkegaard, *Fear and Trembling and the Sickness unto Death,* trans. Walter Lowrie (New York: Doubleday & Co., 1954).

18. Buber, "Ha-sheela she-ha-yahid nishal, p. 176.

19. Buber, "Ani-ata," p. 86.

20. Martin Buber, "Al ha-hitgalut" [Divine advent], in *Olelot* [Gleanings] (Jerusalem: Mosad Bialik, 1967), p. 7.

21. Buber, "Likui ha-or ha-elohi," p. 245.

22. Martin Buber, *Moshe* [Moses] (Jerusalem: Schocken, 1963).

23. Buber, "Al ha-hitgalut," p. 9.

24. Martin Buber, *Torat ha-neviim* [The doctrine of the prophets], 2d. rev. ed., (Jerusalem: Devir for Mosad Bialik, 1950). See also the introduction to the first edition.

25. Martin Buber and Franz Rosenzweig, *Die Schrift und ihre Verdeutschung* [Scripture and its Germanization] (Berlin; 1939), p. 207.

26. Martin Buber, "Elohei ha-avot" [God of the Fathers], in *Torat ha-neviim,* 2d. ed., pp. 76–90.

27. Martin Buber, *Malkhut shamaiim* [The Kingdom of Heaven] (Jerusalem: Mosad Bialik, 1967), p. 93.

28. Buber, *Torat ha-neviim,* 1st ed., Introduction.

29. See Buber's discussion in his essay, "Ha-milhama al ha-hitgalut" [The struggle over God's advent], in *Torat ha-neviim,* 2d. ed., pp. 76–90.

30. Martin Buber, *Be-mashber ha-ruah: Shelosha neumim al ha-yahadut* [The crisis of spirit: Three addresses about Judaism] (Jerusalem: Mosad Bialik, 1953).

31. Ibid.

32. Martin Buber, *Herut: Masa al noar va-dat* [Freedom: Essay on youth and religion], in *Teuda ve-yiud* [Mission and Purpose] 2 vols. (Jerusalem: Hu-Sifria hu-tsionit 1960), vol. 11, p. 117.

33. Ibid.

34. Ibid. p. 120.

35. Martin Buber, "Deotav ha-kedumim shel ha-noar" [Prejudices of youth], in *Teuda ve-yiud* vol. 2, p. 384.

36. Ibid.

37. Buber, *Ḥerut,* p. 131.

5
Bibical Humanism

The rapid advances made by science in the modern era have greatly augmented man's mastery of his physical environment but they have also led to his unquestioning faith in the potentialities of technology and to his blind acceptance of the authority of scientific assertions. In the wake of the sudden and unexpected realization of all that had only recently seemed unattainable, man has become apotheosized in his own mind and wiped God out of his consciousness. Man the Maker, having harnessed the forces of nature and set them to work in his own behalf, has arrogated to himself the role of Creator and Lord of the Universe. This intoxication with science is popularly expressed by a shallow admiration of data and an occult belief in the omnipotence of technology.

In a world in which religion no longer exerts any influence and from which God has been banished, man no longer concerns himself with his purpose and place in the universe. Vaunting his clear-sighted ominscience, man has lost his gift of religious belief and, with it, his serenity. As man's ability to impose his control on the forces of nature has grown so have his sense of isolation and his terror of solitude in an impersonal universe bereft of God.

Surveying the history of human consciousness, Buber observes: "I discern in the history of the Spirit periods in which man is in possession of a home and periods in which he is homeless. In his domestic periods man lives in the world as at his own fireside, and in homeless periods he exist in the world like a vagrant in an open field under the dome of heaven, and at times lacks so much as four stakes on which to pitch his tent."[1] For Buber, "homelessness" is a condition of modern man, who lives a solitary existence in a spiritually fragmented world. Yet this solitariness is regarded by Buber as an opportunity for contemporary man to discover his humanity in the midst of his sufferings:"In the chill wastes of his isolation man's whole identity has become for him an ineluctable question. And for the very reason that this question is so ruthless and unremitting in exacting from man what is hidden in the innermost recesses of his soul, he continues to acquire self-knowledge."[12] A variety of personal, social, and existential answers have been proposed to the anthropological questions that man has begun to ask himself; however, none of these has provided man with a way out of his predicament. The experience of two world wars and the brutal skirmishes of the cold war have exacerbated man's plight. In recent history, both social and existential doctrines have been invalidated and scientific progress, far from mitigating man's anxiety, has deepened it. Technology has gained ascendancy over its creator, who is left irresolutely to ponder the nature and significance of his existence.

The origins of man's predicament are traced by Buber to the separation that has been made in modern times between life and the spirit. Buber maintains that modern philosophy replaced spirit with intellect, through which contemporary man has aspired to autonomy. However, all of the attempts at finding individualistic solutions to the modern quandary have led to a sharpening of man's sense of isolation. In Buber's view, Hegelian and Marxist social theories, according to which society is the natural abode of the individual, have in the last analysis failed to release man from his alienation, for without a transcendental sanction, society is unable to bind man either to itself or to his fellow man. The attempts of the existentialists to justify man's existence purely within the scope of the human have been equally unsuccessful in reviving man's sense of security. The concept of existence with which Heidegger substituted the idea of God was confined to man and was, therefore, finite; modern man, however, suffers because he has no access to existence that is absolute, eternal, and divine.

In *The Myth of Sisyphus* Albert Camus (1913–1960) represented modern man's persistence in living a life without purpose by the image of the legendary hero of the title, who was condemned in Hades forever to roll uphill a stone that always rolled down again. However, in addition to being condemned to a Sisyphean existence, contemporary man lives in terror and uncertainty. Existentialist literature offers an insight into the nature of existence without faith and the awful silence in which man, friendless and alone, fatalistically contemplates his decline. In the absence of a moral pattern to existence, absurdity becomes life's only constant, and ethical and religious values are reduced to the status of illusions. Thus Jean-Paul Sartre regards despair to be the driving force of human action. Life as portrayed in the private journals of Sartre's hero in *Nausea* is grossly absurd and all that exists in the world a prodigal waste, without meaning or purpose. For Meursault in Camus's *Outsider,* absurdity is a way of life. His behavior amounts to little more than a series of discrete physiological responses to passing stimuli; he undertakes each of his actions without trying to understand them as part of a general pattern, and his whole conduct is an expression of his alien condition in a world that he is consciously bent on opposing.

The modern period, which has been marked by the breakdown of traditional values, the rise of political despotism, and the failure of ethics to keep pace with advances in knowledge, is also characterized by the demand for a return to origins and the classical forms of culture. The "classical" fills a special need created by contemporary humanity's circumstances. Such classicism, moreover, need not refer solely to some remote time and place but can have an abiding and universal significance. Biblical humanism represents Martin Buber's attempt to formulate a classical position that would have relevance to contemporary experience in respect of Judaism. An examination of Buber's concept of biblical humanism may reveal to us some guidelines for educating young Israelis, who have been born into a period in which the traditional verities have been eclipsed and dialogue among men and between man and God have been silenced.

Buber is convinced about the need of Israeli youngsters to acquire the values contained in Jewish history. His arguments on behalf of the study of Jewish history are summed up in his assertion: "We Jews are a community of memory. Common memory is what has animated and sustained us as a single entity."[3] Buber is not implying here that the Jewish nation lives by virture of historical recollection. Rather he is calling our attention to the fact that the nation's memory is transmitted from one generation to the next, and that as this memory is handed on, its scope continually expands as it receives the imprint of the destinies of succeeding generations. Buber explains: "It has acted organically; that is, it has not been solely a spiritual motivation, but a force which sustains, nourishes and animates existence itself. And I do not hesitate to claim that this memory has even exerted a biological effect: it is the source on which Jewish being drew in order to restore its youth."[4]

By memory, Buber does not mean *historical consciousness,* which is possessed by all nations and expressed in all languages. Folk memory, according to Buber, is not the record of the concatenation of objective events but is made up of the concatenation of significant relationships to these events. He even goes so far as to argue that it is folk memory which, in fact, produces such significant relationships.

Buber does not advocate a sentimental contemplation of the past. He is speaking rather of the "objective cohesion that exists between generations," by which "sons and grandsons recollect in their bodies and souls what had happened to their fathers and their fathers' fathers."[5] He is, therefore, concerned not with a regressive examination of history nor with consciousness of past events but with the cohesive unity of all generations achieved through their shared remembrance, which is at once a continuity, a bond, and the fruit of a common undertaking. Knowledge of the past certainly plays a part in the process Buber describes, but only if we understand the special meaning that Buber attaches to the word. Buber's concept of knowledge of the past hinges on his interpretation of the meaning of the Hebrew word for knowledge, *yeda,* which in his view differs from similar words in European languages because it primarily refers to the idea of contact and has to do, therefore, with the establishment of relationships. Thus, the Hebrew language itself reveals the authentic encounter arising out of the *I-Thou* relation. Buber claims, moreover, that the cohesion between generations in Jewish history exists by virtue of an "urge of transmission" to which every

Jew must submit and in accordance with which every father hands on to his children both that which has been "recalled" to him and the substance of the experience which he has gathered during his own lifetime.

One of the dangerous developments in modern Judaism is the erosion of shared recollection and of the urge of transmission. The very survival of Jews as a people is threatened by the rebellion of earlier generations, who demanded a fresh start, free of the "legacy of suffering." Yet those Jewish intellectuals who have been urging that Jews regard themselves as the starting point of the history of Israel, who have sought to sever what is Israeli from what is Jewish and rooted in the Jewish past, and who ask that Israelis become like other nations, fail to understand that their demands cannot be met. For the creation of a new Israeli historical continuity is impossible unless the bond of ancestral memory is revived in some new form. Buber makes the point that even the powerful attraction that the land of Israel has had for Jews is a function of organic recollection.[6]

The decline in the urge of transmission and the severance of recent generations from the past have made necessary a revival of the study of the Hebrew language, the Bible, and the history of Israel. Buber contends that only the "urge to study" can replace the lost urge to transmit. Doubtless the rediscovery of the heritage of the past will involve a long and painful process; however, the fostering of this impulse to study must be one of the principal tasks of the educator in our day. And Jewish historical memory is preserved, according to Buber, in the Hebrew language and the Bible.

Buber identifies the underlying concept of humanity at the very beginning of his discussion of biblical humanism. Humanity is "first of all faith in man, the conviction that man *qua* man is not a zoological species but an entity in his own right, a concrete reality in his own right. But he is this only if he is truly a man; that is, if he realizes and makes actual in his own existence this particularity of his, which is to be found nowhere else in the universe."[7] Buber's definition implies that the quality of humanity is absent from many who are biologically classed as belonging to the human species, and that even those who truly deserve being called men are in danger of inadvertently slipping into a state of inhumanity. The same can be said about periods of history: there exist whole eras in which the principle of humanity loses its force and even disintegrates. At such times man must turn to a period in the past in which the human principle was still strong and existed in a pure state.

Buber holds that man's desire to return to and study his origins is fundamental to human nature. However, the nature of this aspiration to return to origins must be carefully examined in order to determine whether the return being contemplated merely involves an external and artificial imitation of obsolete life forms or is meant to bring about a thoroughgoing change in values. Such a change in values, Buber maintains, must be an expression of the transformation of man's inner existence. Buber regards the return to origins to be particularly urgent in our own period, in which the very principles of life are being undermined and the efforts to endow existence with new forms have failed to satisfy man's spiritual and moral needs. He insists, moreover, that the return to ancient forms of existence need not be merely an assimilation of the whole of antiquity as the material of history; turning to the past—in the sense that Buber has in mind—is a critical and intelligent assimilation of those essentials óf the ancient world that are likely to assist us in our return to the primary sources of our origins.

Considering the origins of humanism, Buber concludes that in antiquity the tradition of representing man was, in a special sense, a linquisitic one. He argues that language—indeed the whole linguistic complex of word formations, connections between sentences, and the rhythmic flow of sounds— is determined by the way in which man is described in antiquity.

Buber's preoccupation with biblical humanism stems from his desire to extract from the language of the Bible the raw material out of which the human personality is formed. Buber regards the Hebrew of the Bible to differ in an essential way from any other language. So, for example, the verbal expression of ancient Greece is abstract and shaped into formal images; it is a language that was esthetically fashioned and, because it was determined in the domain of form, bears the unmistakable imprint of art. In contrast to the Greek, the essence of the biblical mode of speech is in its "naturalness." The perfection of biblical utterance would be marred by art, and it retains its expressive power only when its natural state is unimpaired.

Because the language of ancient Greece was an esthetic and conscious creation, it tends to be monological. The Athenian rhetorician prepared and practiced his speeches, which he later delivered with self-possessed calm. The Hebrew prophet spoke spontaneously and in an anxious heat of concern that he shared with his listeners. For this reason the language of the Bible preserves the dialogical character of living reality.

According to Buber, this difference in the languages of ancient Greece and Israel is carried over into the realm of education. Western humanism perceives language as image and is consciously bent on the creation of forms and the perfection of personality. In biblical humanism, on the other hand, language is a reciprocal event, geared to the open rather than to the self-contained personality and aimed at relation rather than form.

Jewish humanism must therefore be traced to the Bible, which contains the image of "Israeli man" in its distilled and ideal form. Moreover, according to Buber, Jewish humanism has four major implications:

1. A return to the linguistic traditions of the Bible. "The return of the contemporary Jew to his primary roots, which exist where he can hear the voice of the Absolute speaking Hebrew."[8]

2. Study of the Bible not for the sake of its literary, historical, or national value but for its normative representation of biblical man.

3. Adoption of the values of the biblical world while keeping in mind the distinction between what is conditioned by history and what is beyond time

and eternal. For the return to biblical values should not be a regression into history for the sake of perpetuating the past but an effort to infuse our perception of the present with abiding values.

4. The image of man that is formed under the influence of such a relationship with the Bible must be held up "as an authority to contemporary life, to its special conditions, functions and potentialities; for it is solely on the basis of the particular characteristics of contemporary existence that what has been received from this image can be realized."[9]

A better understanding of the pedagogical implications of Buber's concept of biblical humanism would be gained by examining its relationship to his philosophy of dialogue. Malcolm Diamond has observed in his book *Martin Buber: Jewish Existentialist* that although Buber may have interpreted the Bible in terms of dialogical philosophy, the Bible itself was the determining influence on the development of that philosophy.[10] The same point is made by Maurice Friedman in *Martin Buber: The Life of Dialogue*. Friedman rejects the claim that Buber injected his philosophy of dialogue into his interpretation of biblical Judaism, and maintains that the Bible was the foundation on which Buber built his philosophical system. Were it not for the effort and years that Buber dedicated to translating and interpreting the Scriptures—Friedman argues—he would never have been able to arrive at a complete statement of his philosophy.[11]

There are those, however, who have challenged Buber's approach to the Bible: for example James Muilenburg, in his profound essay on Buber as an interpreter of the Bible. While conceding that Buber's concept of the Bible as a dialogue between Heaven and Earth has enormously contributed to our understanding of the nature of biblical religious belief, Muilenburg doubts that Buber's approach can be applied to the Bible as a whole.[12]

In his article on monotheism in Buber's philosophy, Benjamin Oppenheimer offers a comprehensive assessment of Buber's interpretation of the Bible and of the nature and limitations of the educational aspect of Buber's approach to the Bible. Oppenheimer contends that Buber did not pursue his study of the Bible in the spirit of a historian intent of discovering objective truth but as a Jewish educator in search of a truth that was personal to himself and valid for his contemporaries. Thus, Buber's interest in the Bible was selective, and his prejudice in favor of a spiritual understanding of the Bible rather than a critical reading of the text can seriously distort the Bible's content.[13] Any attempt to evaluate Buber's contribution to biblical scholarship must take into account Oppenheimer's criticism of Buber's interpretive method. Nevertheless, Buber's approach to the Bible, when considered from the perspective of education, represents a philosophical and intellectual attitude that has considerable relevance to the problems we face in the contemporary world.

Buber describes the relationship between mankind and God as being dialogical. According to Buber, each of us is capable of establishing a dialogical relationship with our fellow man; such interhuman dialogue can even be achieved without speech, so long as it it mutually undertaken and inwardly transacted. But whereas two persons achieve dialogical communion only by consciously bending their wills to establish mutual contact, God's dialogue with mankind is unceasing. God speaks to humanity through the medium of the events of the physical world, the concrete signs of His colloquy with man. "The signs," Buber notes, "are perceived and manifest themselves to us uninterruptedly and at all times. Being called is what life is about, and there is no need for us to be prepared to beckoned—only to hearken."[14] Buber maintains that mankind's real problem is that it dares not listen: we are all of us encased in a carapace, to whose thickness each generation has added, making our armor ever more impenetrable to the sound of God's words. "The other's waves hum incessantly, but for the most part our receivers are switched off."[15]

Buber's attitude toward the Bible is founded on the assumption that the relationship between a person and a place is determined by the dialogical nature of that relationship. "In none of the sacred writings of other nations," he notes, "is the power of the dialogical principle and the uniqueness of the dialogue between the divine and the earthly glorified and its authority recognized to the extent that it is in the Hebrew Scriptures."[16]

In Buber's view the Judaism of the Bible represents a vital relationship with God. He observes that in biblical Judaism "intensity of faith is not measured according to the extent of the knowledge of God's existence (His 'existence' is a subject for *religious thought* and is of no significance to life lived in faith and based on contact with Him), but is judged on the basis of devotion to God, by which the lives of the faithful are determined."[17] Accordingly, the doctrine of faith is a system of testimonies deriving from a living relationship with God, and the principle upon which this faith is founded is neither God's nature nor His character but the relationship between Him and His people, Israel. Buber goes on to explain that in such a relationship a distinction must be made between the manner in which the relationship is expressed, which is the product of passing historical circumstances, and its permanent essential core, which is unaffected by the flow of history. The Bible records a series of interrelated events involving the encounter between persons and places. These events are interpreted by Buber to be moments of God's direct communication with man:

> In the course of such episodes and situations, which are beyond counting and endlessly succeed one another but are nevertheless clear revelations to anyone with eyes to see, the Almighty addresses our hearts at the moment in which our being becomes one. We even possess a language in which to answer Him: it is the language of our actions, behavior and responses, whether active or passive. . . . We learn this fundamental law of our existence from the Scriptures, and so long as we read them sincerely our self-knowledge is perpetually renewed and deepened within us.[18]

From this follows Buber's assertion that "only that person can be a 'Hebrew' who has hearkened to the voice speaking to him from the Hebrew Bible and responded to the call by his own existence."[19] Here we encounter the source of Buber's conviction that a return to the biblical image of man, rather than being a reversion to the past or a continuation of it, should be a self-renewal that takes full account of contemporary reality.

The different ways in which Buber perceives the biblical dialogue between man and God deserve special consideration. This dialogue begins with God and man mutually calling to one another. God reveals His will to man and calls on man to particpate in its fulfillment. Man, however, is no mere tool in this transaction, for he answers according to his own will, and even if he keeps silent, his silence too is a response to the divine call.

Buber stresses that in the Bible, God's call is not directed solely at the individual person but is also intended for the people as a whole. Moreover, the nation is addressed not as a collection of individuals but as a creature in its own right, from which God demands a reckoning in its capacity as a self-sufficient being. Man's responsibility in this dialogue is, therefore, twofold; he is responsible in both his individual and collective capacities. Hence, Buber proposes that there exists an inseparable bond between the individual and the community of individuals, and that this bond is the characteristic feature of authentic civilization. And as in the case of the individual, the people as an entity are required to enact God's will, and so to be sanctified and become—in the language of the Talmud—a "holy assembly." Just as the individual can freely choose whether or not to enact God's will, so is the nation free to affirm or deny its responsibility before God. In the Bible, God addresses the individual as an integral part of the nation. So that each person, when he responds to the divine call by fulfilling one of the Commandments, acts as an individual who consciously incorporates in himself the whole community.

In this connection, Buber sets forth a number of important moral principles. He condemns moral dualism in the lives of individuals and nations. Thus, actions commonly regarded as shameful in relationships between individuals are often thought to be commendable in respect of relationships between national groups. The same double standard is applied to the behavior of individuals, whose moral existence is held to be subject to two separate authorities, each of which possesses its own system of laws. So, for example, deceit is universally thought of as a vice when it is practiced by someone in his private capacity, but is praised when practiced by him in the name of a political party. "This breach," Buber declares, "is intolerable to Biblical faith, for which deceit in any form is an abomination, even if its purpose is to help the cause of justice to triumph. Indeed, such a form of deceit is flagrantly degenerate, for it poisons the good it uses and corrupts it."[20]

Buber asserts that we destroy our own natures when we draw distinctions between realms of action in which deceit is illegitimate and those in which it is valid. Nevertheless, Buber is aware that absolute justice cannot be applied to life as we actually live it; he admits that in the civic domain we are often compelled to make decisions that involve injustices in order to assure collective survival. He insists, however, that in all such cases we should make our decisions in the full awareness of our ultimate responsibility, and exert our consciences in order to determine the requirements of the public good and to set limits on our actions.

Buber attaches particular importance to the idea that no principle should be established on whose basis it would be possible to exempt any particular aspect of existence from the demands of divine commandment. Moreover, when we are compelled by circumstances to act in contradiction to God's command, our actions should awaken in us feelings of anguish of the kind brought on by any painful sacrifice. "It is this trembling of a compass needle," Buber observes, "which nevertheless continues to point in a single direction, that is Biblical humanism."[21] Modern man, according to Buber, is guilty of confining the divine to a small compartment of existence that man has labeled "religion" and of surrendering the remainder of existence to the dominion of economics, society, the party, and the state.

Buber warns us that the rhetoric of patriotism blurs the distinctions between demands imposed by life and the claims of the will to dominate. He cautions us about the perils that are inherent in modern nationalism, in which truth and justice are defined in terms of the public good. Such an attitude, Buber tells us, can only repel anyone who has been brought up on the humanism of the Bible. When circumstances demand of a person educated in biblical humanism to violate the command of God, he does so only to the extent made necessary by those circumstances, and, aware of his guilt, he is prepared to be held accountable for his actions. "He knows that there is a counterpoise to national existence: that there is a pre-existent determination of truth and untruth, justice and injustice. He knows that ultimately his people can benefit only from truth and justice based on that same pre-existent determination."[22]

Biblical humanism is Buber's answer to nationalism that is devoid of any content other than survival, and whose sole purpose is to transform the Jewish people into a nation that is no different than other nations. In Buber's view, Jewish nationalism that makes no supernational demands on the people must inevitably lead to national ruin. He holds that the status of Jews as a "peculiar people" imposes stern and exacting obligations on the nation. God's choice of the Jews is a choice that makes demands, and the whole future of the Jewish people depends on Israel's fulfillment of the conditions of that election. Indeed the uniqueness of the Jews as the elect people of God—Buber maintains—is a major theme that dominates Jewish existence. Among the nations of the world Jews alone have been from the dawn of their history both a national entity and a religious community. The alliance by which the Twelve Tribes became one nation was also a covenant with the God of Israel. Therefore, Buber notes, Israel's election enjoins the Jews to free themselves from the earthbound dominion of biological law and ascend to the sphere of truth and justice. He explains: "It is God's will that man, whom He created, become man in truth; which is to say, man not only as a distinct phenomenon as he exists among all peoples, but as part of the life of the nation. For such is the blueprint of the existence of humanity in the future: a nation composed of all nations. Israel was chosen to become such an authentic nation, and this is what is meant by a People of God."[23] Buber represents the biblical type as one who faces up to his to his having been chosen and comes to terms with his election by deciding either to submit to its demands and internalize the obligations imposed on him, or to reject the claims made on him and struggle to be free of them.

Buber's ideas concerning the election of the Jewish people have educational ramifications of considerable relevance to today's generation of young people. The young live in a world in which personal moral imperatives and the ethical demands on society are illegitimately distinguished—in which injustice, deceit, and brigandage determine the conduct of states toward one another and the relationship between rulers and the ruled. Buber's concept of the indivisible oneness of God's command to both the individual and the nation offers the hope of extricating mankind from the evils of ethical dualism.

Although the majority of young Jewish people are unsympathetic with the idea of Jewish election, Buber feels that the interpretation of the concept as a "choice that makes demands" may make it acceptable to the young. According to Buber's interpretation, Jews will preserve their separate identity as God's chosen people only for so long as there exists a need for them to fulfill their messianic vocation of annulling ethical dualism. He believes that Israel's task will be completed not when the Jews become like other nations, but when all peoples unite to become one "true nation" on the pattern of the True Israel. The example of the perfection of its own national life rather than words must be the means by which Israel will bestow its special character on the peoples of the world. Thus, Israel puts itself at the head of the world's nations not in order to maintain itself apart from other peoples but to draw them forward along its own path.

The concept of biblical humanism brought Buber into conflict with Kierkegaard, whose philosophy had otherwise exerted a formative influence on Buber's thought. The focus of Buber's disagreement with Kierkegaard is the Danish philosopher's rejection of the ethical content of divine commandment. In *Fear and Trembling,* Kierkegaard cites the story in Genesis of the binding of Isaac, and argues that the manner in which Abraham was tested by God demonstrates that a teleological limitation is imposed on the ethical.[24] In Kierkegaard's view, God can suspend the validity and justice of an ethical action according to His will and purpose. Thus, when God commands Abraham to kill his son, the immorality of Abraham's action is canceled; an action that would have otherwise been a crime is cleansed and exalted because it is inspired by divine will and meant to satisfy God's intention. In the encounter with the divine, the generally valid is replaced by something entirely founded on the relationship between an individual and God, and all absolute values become relative. The ethical values and obligations of man are therefore viewed by Kierkegaard as reflections of God's will. God determines good and evil, but he can also annul that distinction with respect to a particular person with whom He exists in a special relationship. Under these circumstances—Kierkegaard stresses—the person ceases being a mere representative of mankind in general and becomes an exceptional individual, one chosen by God as being worthy of submitting to God's testing.

Kierkegaard argues that in the case of Abraham and Isaac, God did not abrogate the absolute in the domain of values. Although the Deity demanded a sacrifice, He did not explain its significance. The task of interpreting the meaning of the sacrifice was left to the one chosen to fulfill God's demand, and the sacrifice was determined by the circumstances in the life of that person at the time that he was called upon to make his offering. Abraham chose to sacrifice what was most dear to him, and in doing so broke his inner bond with his beloved son in order to bind himself to God. Kierkegaard asserts that Abraham's concession to God is an achievement that cannot be appreciated by anyone who does not perceive its profound significance. On this point Buber takes issue with Kierkegaard. He observes: "It is the language of the Scriptures that makes the difference here: 'thine only son Isaac, whom thou lovest.' There is no room here for interpretation. The man listening has been explicitly told what is demanded of him; God speaks in no riddles here."[25]

Kierkegaard contrasts Agamemnon's sacrifice of Iphigenia with Abraham's sacrifice of Isaac. He notes that Agamemnon was called upon to sacrifice his daughter in order to secure the well-being of his subjects; the Greek tragic hero's action was therefore confined to the domain of the ethical, whereas the biblical hero of faith transcended the moral domain. Kierkegaard maintains that an action that oversteps the bounds of the moral, such as the one contemplated by Abraham, must be motivated by profound religious belief, for Abraham's intention to sacrifice would otherwise have been demonic and have led to murder. The decision to sacrifice his son was made by Abraham in utter solitude, and it is Abraham's total solitariness that makes his condition so awesome. He is the knight-errant of faith, who, alone and without counsel or even the hope of being understood by his fellow men, trod the narrow path of piety and devotion.

Kierkegaard states that were he to interpret the story of the binding of Isaac to a lay audience, he would stress more than any other aspect of the tale the uniqueness of the chosen person, who alone was capable of hearing within himself the voice of God. He would describe Abraham's love of Isaac to have been so great as to have amounted to total self-denial for the sake of a son who had become the object and essence of his father's existence. And as to the question of why Abraham was prepared to sacrifice his son rather than himself, Kierkegaard's reply would be that in Abraham's case the sacrifice of his son was immeasurably more painful; by an act of such total commitment to the Absolute the father would have severed his bond with existence and felled the tree of his hopes for all time. For Isaac, the child of Abraham's old age, was the fulfillment of God's promise to grant Abraham a progeny. Yet Abraham's faith remained steadfast; throughout the episode Abraham refrains from questioning God about His promise, "for in Isaac shall thy seed be called," but hearkens with his whole being to God's command.

Buber observes that Kierkegaard regards as self-evident assumptions that are invalid not only in the world in which Abraham lived but in our own world as well. Buber argues that the problem of Abraham's hearkening should be resolved before broaching the question of his decision. Whose voice—Buber asks—did Abraham hear? He observes that in the Bible there exist two contradictory concepts concerning the voice that addresses man: in one of these the voice is God's and in the other it is Satan's. Abraham would certainly not have mistaken the voice commanding him, "Get thee out of thy country," for any voice other than God's. Buber notes that the episode of the binding of Isaac involves a trial. He adds, moreover, that God's testing of Abraham is the result of Abraham's limitless readiness in the depths of his being to make a sacrifice, and that God did no more than to allow Abraham's resolve to grow to the point of the sacrifice taking place. The very moment, however, that no impediment existed between the intention of sacrifice and its fulfillment, God showed himself to be content with the revelation of Abraham's will to sacrifice and prevented the sacrifice itself from actually being carried out. Buber cites a number of instances in which the Bible tells of sinners who believed that the sacrifice of a child could expiate personal guilt. He then quotes the prophet Micah (6:7), who responded to the question, "Shall I give my firstborn for my transgression, the fruit of my body for the sin of my soul?" by asking, "and what doth the Lord require of thee, but to do justly, and to love mercy, and to walk humbly with thy God?" The point the prophet makes is that God requires no more of man than that he uphold the principles of morality.

Buber regards one of the most important questions facing us today to be whether we are responding to God's voice or to the voice of one of God's imitators. Buber describes the contemporary period as an age in which the widespread repression of the ethical makes it difficult to identify the authentic voice of God. God's imitators continually demand men to sacrifice their Isaac, and the false absolutes that rule the human spirit insistently call for the sacrifice of victims to ideals such as equality and liberty: "In the kingdom of Moloch the righteous deceive and the merciful afflict, and they believe in all innocence that fratricide prepares the way for fraternity! It seems to me that there can be no escape from this, the worst form of idolatry."[26] In Buber's view the only solution to this problem is to awaken human consciousness so that man can recognize the false absolutes for what they are, understand their limitations, and in this way avoid being led astray by the voice of Moloch.

There is an educational purpose to Buber's warning against God's imitators; he is asking us to reevaluate the false voices that call to us in the name of the Absolute. Buber's interpretation of God's trial of Abraham can also serve as a didactic example to the teacher of the Bible, who, in dealing with the story of Abraham and Isaac, must somehow resolve the moral issues posed by God's demand for Isaac's sacrifice.

Buber is greatly preoccupied with the problem of the "hiding of face," or God's turning away from man— a concept that derives from Deuteronomy 31:18. According to Buber, the Bible describes two radically different epochs in which the connection between Heaven and Earth is severed. One such period is called by Buber the "Age of Silence in the Universe." In nature—Buber explains—God speaks in the guise of the Creator, whose act of creation is never-ending. However in the universe, the Revealed God speaks, and periods in which the power of God is visible alternate with those in which God withholds His presence and His voice is stilled. In such ages of "universal silence" the dialogue between man and God no longer takes place.

The periods in which God hides His face from man differ altogether from the periods of silence in the Universe. The hiding of face is defined by Buber as a severance from God rather than God's response to mankind's transgressions. At such times God ceases to watch over the world and withdraws his guidance from it, leaving mankind to echo Abraham's plea: "Shall not the Judge of all the earth do right?"

Buber sees the modern period as one in which Abraham's question has terrifying relevance. When contemporaries ask the question, it takes the form: "Can life with God survive in the period of Auschwitz?"[27] The problem of whether it is still possible to call on God may daunt us, but it demands being dealt with both in our personal lives and in respect of education. It is a problem that is constantly in pupils' minds, yet educators are all too prone to avoid answering it. Even when the murder of six million Jews is brought up in the classroom, the teacher is likely to silence discussion by asserting, "But Jews have survived for all that!"[28]

Buber attempts to deal with the problem by recalling the example of Job's complaint to God for His having withdrawn His justice. Although God's response seems to have no bearing on Job's situation, whose sufferings are not transformed by God's words into justice, Job has heard God's voice. In Buber's interpretation, God has answered Job by appearing and speaking to him. Buber observes that like Job, we too call on God. Therefore, the problem faced by us in the modern world is the renewal of our dialogue with God.

Buber's concept of the nature of biblical faith is central to his view of Judaism and its mission to the modern world. He maintains that abstract truth which is unconnected with reality has no place in biblical Judaism. In the Bible, truth is rooted in a demand to man, the community, and the nation, and is fulfilled in its entirety within temporal reality. According to Buber, two conditions must be met for this demand to be fulfilled. In the first place, fulfillment must embrace the whole life of the nation; its spiritual, cultural, economic, and political existence. Second, the fulfillment must embrace the whole life of the individual; his reason and emotions, his actions and perceptions, his private and public life, his religious and civic existence. In view of the daunting nature of these conditions, we need hardly wonder at men's reluctance to undertake the fulfillment of God's demand for truth and justice. For the sake of their convenience men limit their piety to the domain of religion, whereas they allow themselves freedom to maneuver in all of the other areas of their existence. In this they do violence to the integrity of civilization.

Buber's understanding of the idea of repentance deserves special attention. Ordinarily we take repentance to mean a purging from sin. For Buber, however, repentance means a *return*—not in the sense of a reversion to innocence but of a spiritual reorientation by which the soul makes its way back to God.

Many in Israel question the value of teaching the Bible and demand that the time allotted to Bible studies in the curricula of Israeli schools be drastically curtailed. They reject the view so passionately advocated by the pioneer of modern Hebrew poetry, Hayyim Nahman Bialik, who observed:

> Our teachers deserve to be loudly rebuked for failing to understand that a Jew, even if he is master of countless languages and a paragon of wit, remains an ignoramus if he does not know the Pentateuch. . . . Without the Five Books of Moses, he lacks the foundation on which the edifice of Jewish education must be built. . . . *This book of law shall not depart from thy mouth; but thou shalt always meditate therein night and day.* A Jew ought always to return to it—turn his face to the Book in order to judge if he has become estranged from it. In addition, the book grows in substance with the man: it is the measure of a Jew's spiritual growth.[29]

Buber, too, believes that the Bible has abiding relevance. Each period in history—he tells us—has had to come to terms with the Bible, and each generation has inevitably come into conflict with it. Men have been concerned with the Bible in all times and through their concern have borne witness to it. In our own times, however, the relationship to the Bible has taken another direction. Those of our contemporaries to whom matters of the spirit are important take an entirely different attitude to the Bible from the one adopted in the past; their concern is exclusively spiritual. Thus, Buber observes: "Spirit unattended by obligation is a symptom of our age; the privileges of spirit are announced and its laws proclaimed, but these never touch on life and exist nowhere but in books and polemics."[30] Hence, we live in an age that has experienced the severance of spirit from reality.

The Bible integrates spirit and reality. The events and language of the Bible occur in the world, in the nation, and in each generation. No event in the Bible takes place merely within the limits defined by the relationship between God and an individual. Each occurrence serves, rather, as a medium by which the Word reaches the people, and it is they who are destined to hear the Word and enact its command. But the sanctity that is released into the world in no way frees men from their own laws. Biblical law is meant for humanity as it exists in nature. In the Bible, the spiritual and the physical strive to become one in such a way that spirit becomes life and life becomes a distillation of spirit. Buber insists that those who believe the Bible to be a "religious" text and significant only in respect of one aspect of the spirit deceive themselves. For "only he who comprehends the Bible as an imprint of reality, as an embracing of life, rightly comprehends the Book and is comprehended in it."[31]

Part of the tragedy of our times is that we neither heed Scripture nor take issue with it; we have failed to confront the Bible with life. According to Buber, what is needed in our day is not a reversion to the Bible but something altogether different; a return to the life of unity represented in the Bible an acceptance of the responsibility that we owe to our times and which we must undertake with a heart made accessible to faith. Buber is not referring here to a superficial return to the Bible but to an accessibility to the voice that issues from it. He is, therefore, opposed to the attitude taken by those who read the Bible only for the esthetic experience they derive from it. Buber demands that in our encounter with the Bible we pay attention to what the Bible actually says, for he is convinced that the Bible is a rich source from which modern man can draw instruction and guidance.

As he attempts to deal with the problem of teaching the Bible in a secular world, Buber wonders how pupils who lack any experience with religion and for whom the word "God" is merely an entry in the dictionary can be brought into touch with the Bible. Buber believes that an authentic encounter with the Bible can be achieved only if authentic knowledge of it is acquired. He asserts that modern man is capable of responding on his own initiative and with openhearted faith. This can only take place, however, if man approaches the Bible as if for the first time. Man must free himself from the scientific and theological prejudices he acquired in school, "and stand as someone newborn before the renewed book: then no inhibition will put down a barrier between himself and that which may occur in whatever form it may come his way. He has no advanced knowledge of which parable or image will seize his imagination or change his character, or whence the wind will blow that will bring new content to his life."[32] Only after abandoning his antireligious biases and preconceived ideas does a person become totally accessible to the biblical word for then "He reads aloud what is written, hears the words that issue from his own lips—and this is the content that comes to him; nothing exists here whose meaning is predetermined: time flows into him, so that the whole life of that person becomes a receptacle of time."[33]

The Bible, Buber insists, has demanded of every generation that each individual immerse himself in history to find his own past and future in the world's beginning and end: "Creation is the beginning, Redemption the end. Revelation, however, does not lie statically between the two, fixed in its place for our times; the midpoint is not God's revealing himself on Mount Sinai, but the fact that this Revelation can recur and be perpetually re-experienced under a new guise."[34] Man cannot discover the truth of Creation and Redemption unless he confronts Revelation, and this confrontation has only one meaning: To respond to the moment in which it takes place and to assume responsibility. Modern man rejects the Bible because he has failed to confront Revelation and shrinks from having to assume responsibility.

In elucidating the subject of Revelation, Buber considers the significance of the story of God's transmission of the Law to the Jews. The Bible contains a vivid description of God's fiery descent on a smoke-wreathed Mount Sinai to the sound of trumpets. Buber examines three alternative interpretations of the episode. He first considers the possibility that the story is an allegorical treatment of a purely spiritual event, but dismisses such an interpretation on the grounds that it would detract from the story's value as a reflection of an actual occurrence, and so undermine our experience of the Bible's relationship to reality. Another view, according to which the story represents a supernatural event and is, therefore, inaccessible to rational interpretation, is also rejected by Buber for being excessively theological and detached, and misconstruing the innocence of biblical narrative, which is addressed to life as a whole. Finally, Buber proposes that the Bible records an event that took place in the sensory world that all men inhabit, but which was perceived by this particular group of men as God's revelation to them of Himself, and which was later transmitted by them to succeeding generations in the form of a story consciously shaped by enthusiastic recollection. Buber notes that "Revelation takes place when the witness of an event is physically present and himself perceives the essence of the event and hears what the voice issuing from the event wishes to tell him. Just as the voice makes itself heard in the actual occurrence and within the life of the witness, so can contemporary man find access to the Bible's revelation when he acts as one who repents without rejecting reality."[35]

Buber believes that the whole point of teaching the Bible is to have students understand it as it is written. He argues that even in the case of a difficult and obscure passage which seems to defy understanding we should avoid assuming too hastily that the text is corrupt and requires being recast to suit our notions of a correct reading. With the exception of those very rare instances in which the conclusion that the text is unreliable is forced upon us, we must accept the version that exists to be the only one that is satisfactory in conveying the meaning contained by the passage.

In studying the Bible, we cannot speak of a content which, though it is expressed in a particular way, can also be stated differently. For if the language of the Bible were different, the book would express a different order of thought, one that would be unbiblical. As Buber observes:

> Biblical utterance is never a mere "expression" of some matter having to do with the spiritual or the soul, nor of something between the "moral" and the "religious," nor again of some "historical" or "legendary" situation; rather it is something *spoken* at a particular moment in time and subsequently transmitted in its own idiom: it is utterance which in its own time took the form of tidings, law, prophecy, prayer, story, precept, confession, dialogue—and in this way deposited in the keeping of the organic memory of succeeding generations, where it was preserved and perpetuated while being constantly renewed through living speech.[36]

Speech, therefore, is the soul of what is written in the Bible and the medium by which the letter of the Scriptures is constantly being restored to life.

Buber maintains that the language of the Bible cannot be divorced from the situation out of which it arose. To do so would be to deprive biblical speech of its concreteness. The tangibility of biblical language was conceived in particular circumstances and must be preserved in the form in which it has come down to us. Buber insists that the Bible should not be taught as literature, but as a majestic and many-voiced dialogue that begins in the creation and revelation depicted in Genesis, to which it ultimately returns as prayer. Buber's concept of Bible teaching, which assigns to the student the role of an attentive and active partner in a dialogical encounter, contains an important contribution to the field of education as a whole. One of Buber's pedagogical aims is to teach the student to experience the Bible existentially. In this connection, James Muilenburg is off the mark when he asserts that existential encounter, which is the key to Buber's approach to the Bible, is not contingent on historical circumstances.[37] For Buber, existential encounter must be comprehended as an event occurring at a particular historical time and place. Only then does the encounter involve testimony; the witnessing that is part of the dialogue addressed to all men in all times.

Prophecy, the Law, the Psalms, and biblical narrative are all treated by Buber as forms of speech. Prophecy, for Buber, is an oration spoken by a man who has been sent to address a community in a situation that calls for a decision. Biblical narrative reverberates with the voice of a narrator who offers examples to be praised or reproved. And although the psalms are liturgical, their basic tone is that of a personal cry of despair or exaltation. In all of these Buber hears "the voice of a speaker who, at a given time and because he is addressing his private 'self,' serves his community as a coryphaeus, speaking to it in verse of its destiny and deliverance."[38]

Buber considers that each part of the Scriptures can only be understood if it is thought of as belonging to an organic unity. He does not reject modern biblical criticism; he merely reminds scholars that their work is time bound whereas the Bible is timeless. Although he takes into account modern theories that propose that the received version of the Bible is based on earlier sources, Buber denies that the traditional text is merely an artificial collation created by anthologists. He maintains, rather, that the version of the Bible which has come down to us is solid-cast from a mold formed by a cohesive oral tradition.

Buber tries to demonstrate that all of the canonical books of the Scriptures were chosen and arranged with an eye to preserving biblical unity. He notes, for example, that the technique by which this unity is primarily sustained consists of the repetition of what he calls "lead-words" and "phonetic geminations" (milim manhot and tsimdei hagaiim in Hebrew). By his brilliant analysis Buber sharpens our perception of the Bible's unifying purpose, whose origins he traces to a time long before the establishment of the biblical canon, which he believes to have been formed in a process in which the Bible's various parts were gradually fused to form a homogeneous whole.

For Buber all of the books of the Bible represent revelations of a single content that have assumed different forms. He does not gloss over the fact that the Bible contains many contradictions. But his chief concern is with the inner unities that bind the parts of the Bible and account for its homogeneity. It is this unity that endows the Bible with a forceful and demanding voice which calls on men in all times.

> Biblical humanism, unlike Western humanism, cannot lift men above the issues of the hour; its purpose is to teach men to stand their ground and understand them. This night of terror, these emergent voids, this peril of annihilation—thou shalt not seek refuge from them in the universe of Logos or of perfect form. Stand fast—Hearken to the voice that calls out of the storm—Respond! This terrible world is God's world. It summons you. Withstand its test as a man of God![39]

This is the essence of what biblical humanism has to teach modern man.

NOTES

1. Martin Buber, *Pnei adam: Behinot be-antropologia filosofit* [The face of man: Studies in anthropological philosophy] (Jerusalem: Mosad Bialik, 1962), p. 14.

2. Ibid.

3. Martin Buber, "Talmud Torah—al shum ma?" [Why the Talmud Torah?], in *Darko shel mikra* [The way of the Bible] (Jerusalem: Mosad Bialik, 1964), p. 359.

4. Ibid.

5. Ibid., p. 360.

6. Ibid.

7. Martin Buber, "Humaniut ivrit" [Jewish humanism], in *Teuda ve-yiud* [Mission and purpose] (Jerusalem: ha-Sifria ha-Tsionit, 1961), vol. 2, p. 125.

8. Ibid., p. 127.

9. Ibid.

10. Malcolm L. Diamond, *Martin Buber: Jewish Existentialist* (New York: Oxford University Press, 1960), p. 65.

11. Maurice S. Friedman, *Martin Buber: The Life of Dialogue* (London: Routledge and Kegan Paul), p. 257.

12. James Muilenburg, "Buber as an Interpreter of the Bible," in *The Philosophy of Martin Buber,* ed. Paul A. Schilpp and Maurice Friedman, (London: Cambridge University Press, 1967), p. 384.

13. Benjamin Oppenheimer, "Emunat ha-yihud be-mishnato shel M. Buber" [Monotheism in Buber's philosophy], *Molad* [New Moon] 24 (1967–1968); 207.

14. Martin Buber, *Be-sod siah: Al ha-adam ve-amidato nokhah ha-havaya* [Dialogue: Man and his encounter with being] (Jerusalem: Mosad Bialik, 1963), p. 118.

15. Ibid.

16. Ibid., p. xlvii.

17. Martin Buber, *Torat ha-neviim* [The doctrine of the Prophets], 2d rev. ed., (Tel Aviv: Mosad Bialik and Devir, 1960), p. x.

18. Martin Buber, "Ha-du-siah ben ha-elohim la-adam ba-mikra" [The dialogue between God and man], in *Teuda ve-yiud,* Vol. 1, p. 245.

19. Martin Buber, "Humaniut mikrait" [Biblical humanism], in *Darko shel mikra,* p. 37.

20. Buber, "Ha-du-siah ben ha-elohim la-adam ba-mikra," p. 247.

21. Buber, "Humaniut Ivrit," p. 129.

22. Ibid.

23. Ibid, p. 131.

24. Sören Kierkegaard, *Fear and Trembling and the Sickness unto Death,* trans. Walter Lowrie (New York: Doubleday Co., 1954).

25. Martin Buber, "Likui ha-or ha-elohi" [The Eclipse of divine light], in *Pnei adam,* p. 313.

26. Ibid., p. 315.

27. Buber, "Ha-du-siah ben ha-elohim la-adam ba-mikra," p. 251.

28. Leah Adar and Haim Adler, *Hinukh la-arakhim be-vatei-sefer le-yeladim olim* [Value education in schools for new-immigrant children] (Jerusalem: School of Education of the Hebrew University, 1965), p. 56.

29. Hayyim Nahman Bialik, "Limud ha-tanakh be-vet ha-sefer" [The study of the Bible in schools], *Hed ha-hinukh* (1930); 250–53.

30. Martin Buber, Ben-doreinu ve-ha-mikra [Our contemporaries and the Bible], in *Darko shel mikra,* p. 42.

31. Ibid., p. 43.

32. Ibid., p. 44.

33. Ibid.

34. Ibid., p. 45.

35. Ibid., p. 48.

36. Martin Buber, "Tsiunim le-hugei tanakh" [Remarks for Bible study groups], in *Darko shel mikra*, p. 363.

37. Muilenburg, "Buber as an Interpreter of the Bible," p. 382.

38. Buber, "Tsiunim le-hugei tanakh," p. 364.

39. Buber, "Humaniut ivrit," p. 40.

6

Hasidism And Religious Education

In his novel *Ants,* Yitshak Orpaz tells the story of a married couple who try to save their foundering marriage by changing their neighborhood and building a new home.[1] While their new home is being built, however, they become aware that their old home is being destroyed by an invading horde of ants. In an atmosphere charged with tense expectation, frustrated sexuality, and home-destroying instincts, the conflict between the couple gradually assumes the character of a ritual dance, while around them walls crumble and utter physical ruin sets in. The characters of Orpaz's story live a nightmare existence; profoundly alienated, frustrated, caught in a tangle of erotic complexes, isolated and unable to communicate, they find themselves being sucked into a maelstrom of aggressive urges that bring them to the point of contemplating murder. But as destruction rains down on them they also experience the birth of religious yearning in the guise of limitless expectation. Amid the ruins that set the stage for their encounter and self-revelation, together they await *The Voice;* without refuge and immersed in existential despair born of the failure to communicate, Orpaz's characters anticipate total revelation.

The limitless expectation of the characters in Orpaz's novel is prevalent among our contemporaries, many of whom seem incapable of transcending the monologue taking place within the narrow confines of their own egos and attaining a life of dialogue. They share the fate of Astragon and Vladimir in Beckett's *Waiting for Godot,* who stubbornly cling to the hope of experiencing a revelation of whose nature they remain utterly ignorant. Yet by their self-enclosed and private existence they testify to the deceitful foundation upon which such expectation is based. Monological existence, the consciousness that turns exclusively on itself, existence devoid of content and purpose, haunts modern man. Beckett's characters are gripped by a compulsion to talk, because speech is their last remaining existential faculty. For as Matti Megged has so aptly observed in this connection:

In actual fact speech, by its very nature embodies the expectation of a response. Now the speaker may indeed seem always to be speaking to himself alone; he may even choose such a form of narrative dialogue for the very reason that he knows that there is no longer any point in trying to speak with his fellow man. But speech itself also imposes on him another and contrary kind of knowledge that man is incapable of any utterance unless his words contain the indispensable expectation of an answer, of a response.[2]

Buber has grasped the significance of modern man's dialogical will and religious yearnings:

> I mean the transformation that has taken place in the hearts of some of the young, whose numbers grow ever larger; and although this transformation has yet to be crystallized, nevertheless its reality is unmistakable. The signs of this transformation are apparent not only in the world at large but in our own country as well. The young person to whom I am referring no longer feels himself to be at home either in his group or among his fellows; he has ceased feeling at home in the world. He experiences a sense of utter neglect. He feels himself to be an abandoned child. Behind these agonies of the spirit—which for the most part seem to be unmasterable—there exists a yearning to re-establish the dependence of the power of belief on the absolute and on abiding values, in order that man should once again be able to adhere to them. This transformation is not the effect of an external cause, nor is it the result of the activity of educators; it can only be understood as a new stage in the crisis of man's soul. Yet educators who have established a vital relationship with abiding values have it in their power to sanction this transformation, through the medium of their class-room lectures to be sure, but primarily in an existential way, which is the principal means of education. They have it in their power to instill these yearnings in their pupils. They now can assist the young to discover the path leading to renewed affirmation.[3]

The principal duty of an educator who is intent on transmitting such values to his contemporaries is to familiarize himself with his contemporaries' vision of their world and with their perplexities, to recognize the early symptoms by which the process of spiritual transformation and the profound need of renewing contact with the external world make themselves known. The teacher who wishes to bring about the reestablishment of such contact cannot accomplish his purpose through external compulsion, by weighing down the spirit with the ballast of a system of laws and practical precepts. Rather, he must achieve his purpose through consciousness and profound observation; he must follow a course that begins with man in pursuit of God. Solitary man in an unseeing world is the educator's point of departure and awakened consciousness is his goal. For human existence is not solitary existence but an ongoing colloquy between man and God, in which man's day-to-day deeds and thoughts are the response to questions that God addresses to him.

Religious education arises from man's effort to discover God and is the means by which man approaches God. Such education will eschew to-talitarianism and indoctrination, which are the pitfalls of dogmatic religious instruction. Making man's religious experience a point of departure does not mean that God is being made over into man's image; it is rather a liberation of educational methodology from dogma in order to create an awareness of divinity and bring about the dialogical relationship between man and his Maker. Dialogue of this kind can only take place when there is no separation between God and the world of man. Thus, when we attempt to bring about the encounter of man and God and to renew the intimate dialogue between them, we must first address ourselves to the solitary individual—to his sensibilities, his experiences, and his often latent responsiveness to the call of God. These religious longings belong to the sphere of personal experience and are unamenable to the mediations of institutions, priesthoods, and doctrinal systems. Religiosity, in this sense, is fundamentally opposed to any form of coercion, and nothing could be more alien to its nature than dull submission; for it is the product of the liberation of the spirit, and is ardently bent on unmediated communion with the infinite.

Buber conceives of all of history as an ongoing dialogue between God and His creation; one in which man participates as an active agent by the fact that his life, his thoughts, and his actions constitute a response to God's question. For Buber, man's relation to God is at the center of religious belief, and because of its direct and unmediated character, this relationship is classed by him as belonging to the sphere of religiosity that is experienced inwardly rather than being ecclesiastically organized from without. The revelation of the pupil's inherent religious sensibilities and the revival of the dialogue between man and his creator make up, therefore, the pedagogical goal of religious education, a goal that requires a careful investigation of the means by which it may be achieved.

Buber's philosophy of Hasidism is a rich and instructive source of commentary on a varied and complex universe of education having real and vital significance for our times. "Philosophy" seems, moreover, to be the appropriate term to describe Buber's concept of Hasidism, for Buber's writings on the subject are a highly personal elaboration upon the material of Hasidism and not the product of objective scholarship. Buber's approach to Hasidism follows a pattern that is familiar to us from his Old Testament studies in which the idea of dialogue figures so prominently.[4] Buber typically selects those features of Hasidism whose appeal to contemporary man is most immediate, and those aspects that are most clearly relevant to his life and which are most likely to sustain him in his adversity.

Gershom Scholem has justly observed that Buber pulled together facts about Hasidism and assembled quotations from Hasidic sources in order to suit his own purpose, which was to represent Hasidism not as a historical movement but as a spiritual event.[5] Scholem faults Buber for having omitted from his discussion a great quantity of source material that is essential to the understanding of Hasidism as a historical phenomenon. Further, Scholem reproaches Buber for his habit of citing the material that he actually does bring to our attention in a manner so tendentious that we find it difficult to distinguish between the actual sources and Buber's interpretation of them.

There can be little doubt concerning the validity of Scholem's claim that the spiritual message that Buber has read into Hasidic literature is "fundamentally much too dependent on assumptions whose origin is his personal philosophy, on the elements of religious anarchism and existentialism contained therein, and is not rooted in the substance of the sources themselves. His account of Hasidism omits too much, and what he does choose to include in it is laden with a philosophy of an exceedingly personal nature. Now it may well be that this quality of his thinking is sublime, and both fascinating and inspiring to the modern mind. But if it is our wish to understand the phenomenon called Hasidism for what it really is, both in its glory and in its decline (and in how many ways are these conditions interdependent!), then we shall have to retrace our steps and begin again at the beginning."[6]

Yet when we come to consider the problem of religious education in our times, Buber's concept of Hasidism rather than any other, both in its general outlines and in its principles, answers most significantly to our needs. In taking Buber to task for having erred in his understanding of Hasidism by misreading the sources in the light of his private philosophical convictions, we do no more than satisfy the requirements exacted by historical scholarship. Nevertheless, the philosophy of Hasidism that Buber has developed, by virtue of the impressive and methodical consistency with which it orders and selects the materials of its subject, has much to offer to contemporary education. It is in fact Buber's "religious anarchism," much as it may distort the content of Hasidic thought, which appeals to and inspires our contemporaries. Gerschom Scholem puts the case well when he describes Buber's philosophy as one that, although it calls on man to determine the course of his existence and make his choice, is altogether silent about the exact nature of the course he is to follow and the choice he is supposed to make. Indeed, Buber is explicit in denying that either a man's course or his choice can be defined in the context of the *Other,* where the experience of *I-Thou* is inevitably extinguished. In the sphere of living relationships, on the other hand, nothing can be realized through verbal definition; in it there exist neither laws nor moral precepts. The Hasidic movement never adopted such an attitude, if for no other reason than that it saw itself as completely bound to the traditions of Judaism, whose preoccupation is with a doctrine of laws that specify the actions which ought to be taken by men. For all of that, when our concern is with the question of religious education today, it is the religious existential choice advocated by Buber in his writings on Hasidism which holds out the best promise for the reestablishment of dialogue.

Buber holds that since Hasidism is a way of life rather than a doctrine, our knowledge of it must derive first from its legends and only secondarily from its scholarly writings. The scholarship of Hasidism is commentary, whereas its legend is life itself, which is to say—the source. Although the collection of Hasidic stories does not represent a chronicle of the movement, Buber insists that it is for those who know how to read it more authentic than any historical record. The actual course of events in the history of Hasidism cannot be reconstructed from the corpus of Hasidic tales; yet these stories, although they may misrepresent historical reality, do convey Hasidism's vital core, the living context in which events took place and out of which emerged the tales which were told and retold in innocent wonder until those events become legend. The distortions contained in Hasidic stories were not motivated by the intention to deceive. Rather, Buber argues, the narrators of such tales were responding to an inner necessity that was identical with the one that underlies the Hasidic way of life and having to do with the nature of the bond between a Hasidic rabbi and his community. In Buber's view the Hasidic tale is more than the release of mere verbal energy; it is the active medium by which an event is transmitted to future generations. The significance of a Hasidic story does not reside in the fact of its transmission. The story in its own right constitutes an event which, because it preserves the memory of a sacred occurrence, itself takes on the sanctity of action.

Buber conceives of the Hasidic story as a form of anecdotal legend. In it a single event not only illuminates the whole life of an individual but at the same time expresses the very meaning of existence itself. According to Buber, the authority exerted by the Hasidic anecdote is to be understood in the context of the characteristic tendency of Diaspora Judaism to perceive in a heightened fashion the events of both the past and the present. Thus, he observes:

> Events are perceived and told in such a way that they are made to express something; even more than this, the occurrence is ordered and revealed in such a way that it is made to conclude in something which is actually expressed. Indeed, in Hassidism life itself helps to accomplish this: the zaddik, either consciously or unconsciously, expresses a philosophy by actions which have the appearance of being symbolic, and which often pass over into utterance that either consummates them or in some degree clarifies their meaning.[7]

Buber's reliance on Hasidic legends and tales has come under heavy fire from scholars, among them Rivka Schatz and Gershom Scholem, who have pointed out that Hasidic literature, in addition to its ample store of tales, contains an impressive collection of learned writings rich in the thoughts of the great Hasidic minds.[8] In the eyes of his critics, Buber is guilty of having excluded from his considerations Hasidism's intellectual literary tradition. Gershom Scholem, for example, taking issue with Buber's approach, observes: "The identity that Buber has asserted to exist between legend and life is purely imaginary. The fact of the matter is that these legends are obviously no more than a *commentary* on what Buber is pleased to call "life." Life is revealed in legend as it is in doctrine, but the emergence of this Hasidic way of life, it should be stressed, was profoundly influenced and shaped by the ideas contained in its learned literature, whereas it was clearly not influenced in the initial stages of its existence by legend."[9]

Scholem's observations concerning the primacy of learned literature in the formation of the Hasidic movement are undoubtedly valid when considered from the standpoint of historical research. But when we confront the problem of the influences at work on religious revival, then surely legends, stories, proverbs, and maxims carry very great weight. Moreover, the stories and legends of Hasidism are far more suitable subjects for Buber's subjective manner of interpretation than those of its writings that are devoted to a systematic elaboration of a particular line of thought. Then, too, imaginative Hasidic literature is humanly compelling; it is the mirror of existential choice, of action taken in the world, and more. When considered on their own merit as examples of narrative art, Hasidic tales possess the quality that William Wordsworth called "power," or the capacity to activate. They belong to that class of literature by which the spirit of the reader is so aroused and his sensibilities so broadened that his innate though latent love for the infinite is made actual. Wordsworth distinguished between knowledge and power, likening knowledge to movement in earthbound steps along a single plane and power to taking flight into another element. Humanity, Wordsworth tells us, derives its ideals of justice, hope, truth, mercy, and peace through literary creation—and it is only by virtue of the literature of power that these ideals become more than merely abstract categories. According to Wordsworth, the creative forces by which man generates literature are themselves renewed in the process of creation and become agents that activate.[10] Such energies, when they have been unleashed by a tale originating in the life of a charismatic Hasidic teacher, can preserve their animating force for generations.

Buber knew that Hasidism was tainted by no small degree of decadence even during its early history. He is ready to admit that the Hasidic imagination, for all of its innocence and fervor, had a strong superstitious streak whose effects could be pernicious in the extreme. The primitive cult of the zaddik, or the Hasidic rabbi, and the animosity of his followers toward the adherents of his rivals are examples of the unwholesome tendencies of the movement. However, Buber is emphatic in disclaiming any interest in the decadence of historical Hasidism. The role that he sets aside for himself is the discovery of those aspects of Hasidism that made it one of the greatest manifestations of vital and creative piety in the history of religion, and a movement which was eminently suited to the desire of Jews to worship God in the world and to consecrate their day-to-day existence to Him.

The Hasidic movement is generally seen as a rebellion of religious feeling both against the forces of religious rationalism that aggrandize and at the same time congeal the doctrine of divine transcendentalism, and against religious leadership which transforms acts of piety into autonomous rites divested of their deeper significance. In Buber's analysis, however, the underlying cause of the Hasidic rebellion must be grasped in terms other than those of feeling; not as a rebellion of the oppressed spirit but as a growing perception and exaltation of the vision of God and a triumph of man's will of realization.

The revelation of the existence of a single God is not considered by Buber to have been the preeminent contribution of the Jews to the world; rather it was their having taught of the dialogical relation of this God, of the saying of "Thou" to Him and of standing in His presence. Of all peoples only the Jews—Buber asserts—exist as a nation that hearkens to the spoken word and replies to it:

> God as speaker, creation as speech: the call into the void and the response of things at the very moment of their emergence, the language of creation in the life of each created thing, the life of each man as one who asks and answers—it is in order to proclaim this that Israel came into the world. It taught, it revealed: the true God is the God who can be called, for it is to this end that He calls upon his creatures.[11]

The idea that man's activity itself is an encounter with God is central to Buber's attitude. In this encounter the world is not only the meeting place of the human and the divine but the subject, as well, of their concern. God speaks to man through the available reality summoned by Him to appear to man as man makes his way in the world; and man, in his turn, answers by the actions which he carries out upon this available reality. For Buber, the act of worshiping God has meaning only when it is an intended consecration, perpetually renewed, to this meeting with God in the physical world. "Religion" in its accepted sense is regarded by Buber as a threat to such an encounter. In it the forms by which man consecrates the world to God increasingly acquire an independent life of their own, with the result that the forms themselves are hallowed rather than the everyday life which they are meant to represent. Thus, in religion, life in the world and the worship of God coexist but in no necessary relationship to one another; and the "God" that is worshiped in this way is not really God but merely a poor simulacrum that can be fashioned with ease, so that the true partner in the encounter is absent from religion.

It is Buber's contention that Hasidism was able to inspire its followers to take continuous and unabated pleasure in life and the world as they are experienced here and now. And without dulling the individual's moral consciousness or anesthetizing his sense of the distance between human actuality and divine perfection, it was able to set him on the path leading to God. Hasidism dismantled the barrier between the sacred and the profane by teaching of the sanctification of worldly activity. Buber asserts that man's fulfillment of what is required of him at a particular moment in his life is his profession of the unity of God; what is required of man is therefore unity of soul rather than erudition, wisdom, or inspiration, a spirit bent wholly on attaining the divine goal.

> The world in which we live just as it is, it alone grants us contact with God—that contact which redeems, and the divine principle which resides in the world to the extent that it is given over to each of us into our keeping: and each of our natures as it really is, it in particular is our own unique opportunity of access to Him.[12]

Buber notes that Hasidism never went so far as to embrace the idea of pantheism, a doctrine which undermines the supremacy of the principle of reciprocity between the human and the divine as expressed in the *I-Thou* relation between man and his Creator. Instead, it fixed on the existence of the divine emanations harbored by all creatures and things, and taught how these hidden sparks of divinity might be redeemed and made to rejoin their divine source.

The concept of divine sparks, developed by Cabalism in its late period, was transformed by the founder of Hasidism, the Baal-Shem-Tov, into a moral doctrine and, ultimately, into a mission embracing the whole existence of man. According to the doctrine, as it was developed in Hasidism, it is man's duty to redeem the sparks that fell on all the objects of the world when God created the universe, and to raise them to a higher plane. Not only is this redemption by man of the divine sparks supposed to take place in everyday life, but an individual is thought to be able to redeem the sparks by all of his actions, no matter how ordinary they may be. For even the most profane of actions can be sanctified, and it is by hallowing his ordinary acts that man is able to raise the sparks of divinity. Such actions are for Buber decisive in the renewal of the world; only through a genuine encounter with the physical sphere does man attain authentic existence and so participate in the redemption of the world.

Yet it is doubtful that Buber has actually grasped the essential character of Hasidism. The theory of sparks is the basis of Buber's interpretation of Hasidism as a doctrine of total realization of the "Here and Now." Nevertheless, it is difficult to believe that Buber has faithfully represented the real intention of this idea in Hasidism. Gershom Scholem has shown that Hasidism's views concerning the relationship to the concrete were in fact quite different and a good deal more complex than Buber's representation of them. Scholem's arguments turn on the twist given by Hasidic writers to the Cabalistic concept of the raising of divine sparks. In this connection, Scholem observes:

> Man cannot, as Buber believes, arrive at a union with the "Here and Now" by doing everything that he does in a state of total concentration and dedication, but only through what is *hidden* within the outer guise of the "Here and Now"; for by itself this outer guise neither exalts nor casts down. Joy in life and the world as they actually are—as Buber would have

it—seems to me to be quite a modern idea, and Chassidic writings, as I understand them, are written in a wholly different spirit. They do not urge us to enjoy life as it is, but to the contrary, they improve us by advice; or to put the matter more precisely: they demand of us that we extract, distill from "life as it is" the eternal life of God. However this "extracting"—and here we have the crux of the matter—is an act of abstraction. For it is not the ephemeral "Here and Now" which is the object towards which this joy is directed, but transcendent Everlasting Unity and the Eternal Present.[13]

It is just this concept of abstraction that Buber emphatically rejects. The abstract products of detached ratiocination can exert no influence on the modern mind, Buber believes, because they play no part in the reality experienced by contemporary man. What Buber finds especially difficult to accept is the idea that the tangible encounter with the "Here and Now" merely serves man as a point of departure for transcending reality rather than as the occasion of his realizing and fulfilling it. Contained in the Hasidic notion of the redemption of divine sparks is a destructive principle which Buber is unable to appreciate because it is so alien to his own attitudes. Still, whereas Buber's scholarship is open to question at least on this point, there can be little doubt that his interpretation, when examined with respect to the educational challenges faced by contemporary man, is in the highest degree persuasive.

Gog and Magog is at once Buber's most concise and most lively discussion of his view of Hasidism, and could well provide modern religious education with the incentive it so desperately needs. Of all of Buber's works, none bears better witness than *Gog and Magog* to Buber's personal struggle to grasp the essential nature of Hasidism's philosophy of man. Although the theme of the book centers on the manner of the world's redemption, its argument progresses along mankind's path to God, the significance of which Buber examines from the rival perspectives offered in the interpretations of the Hasidic "schools" of Lublin and Pzhysha, with the latter of whose views Buber identifies.

However, before we would undertake to introduce contemporary students to the complexities of *Gog and Magog* and to the concept of Hasidic doctrine concerning mankind's path to God therein contained, we ought first to examine what Buber has to say in *The Way of Man According to the Teaching of Hasidism,* which is a gem among Buber's interpretive philosophical writings.[14] Following Buber's lead, in *The Way of Man,* then, six subjects can be presented to the student that would serve as the major themes to be discussed in relation to observations and illustrative material contained in Buber's collection of Hasidic stories, *The Hidden Light;* these tales would be taken up again later for comparison and analogy when teaching *Gog and Magog.*

The first of the six topics that Buber proposes as a theme for discussion is *Self-Examination,* or man's response to God's question to Adam, "Where art thou?" Buber recommends that the discussion of this subject should center on the man who evades self-examination and persists in hiding from himself. In every generation, the decision made by an individual to take stock of himself marks his first step toward realizing his humanity.

The Many Ways of Worshiping God and the Special Way is the rubric which introduces the next theme proposed by Buber. The ways in which God can be worshiped are manifold and no single pattern of worship should be selected as the one worthy of being described. For each man brings renewal into the world, and any of his acts can become a way to God. The portion of joy in the world that has been set aside for us, if we sanctify it, leads us to joy in God. No man should set himself apart from nature unless he does so in order to renew himself, thereafter returning to it so as to come into hallowed contact with it and find his way to God. Underlying the view expressed here by Buber is an assumption that has profound pedagogic implications: namely that men differ from one another in their natures, and that there exists no need to make men equal nor any advantage in imposing uniformity on them. Homogeneity can only impede man's quest for a unique path. The course of every man's life can give access to God, and it is the very differences among men in respect of their characters, inclinations, and careers that are the hope of humanity. "Indeed it is by virtue of this capacity of every man to approach the Almighty from his own place and from his own nature that humankind, streaming forward from every direction, can reach Him."[15]

Another significant pedagogic principle emerges from Buber's view that man cannot know the path by which he is to reach God unless he acknowledges his own nature and its unique predisposition. "Know thyself" and "act as thine own inner imperatives command thee," are the precepts with which education begins. Only when education is inwardly motivated rather than external and coercive will it also be authentic and its goal be achieved.

Buber calls his third theme *The Ready Heart.* The divine forces latent in man can integrate the fragmented soul. Such spiritual unity should exist before a man undertakes any enterprise which is out of the ordinary. "When a man has become such a unity, his action too is an integrated whole."[16]

He Who Would Improve the World Must Begin with Himself is the premise of Buber's fourth theme. Hasidism, Buber notes, rather than make man a subject of study, calls on him to better himself. Man must first acknowledge that his conflict with his fellows originates in the conflict taking place within himself. Here, too, an important psychopedagogic principle comes into play: no one aspect of the human soul should be set apart from the others and considered in isolation. What should be dealt with, rather, are all of the aspects of the soul as they exist together, bound to one another in a vital relationship. It is from this principle that we deduce the essential truth about social morality contained in the precept: "he who would improve the world must begin with himself."

The fifth of Buber's proposed subjects is announced by the motto *Attend Not to Thyself,* by which Buber means that whereas a man must choose the self as his point of departure, he must take care not to become himself, as it were, grasped within it. He observes:

> No purpose is served by a soul's seeking its own deliverance within itself. True, every soul must know itself. Yet it must not do so for its own sake: not for its portion in this world nor in the world to come, but for the sake of what it must do in God's world. We are commanded to turn our consciousness from ourselves and direct it towards the world.[17]

Here we have Buber's challenge to the tide of egocentricity in modern times, and his prescription for the means by which an individual can assume responsibility toward the whole of creation.

At Thy Side is Buber's sixth and last theme. Our personal sanctity derives from the sanctification of the human principle, which each man can and must make sacred in his own place and condition. Once again Buber has proposed a precept whose pedagogic implications have an important, even necessary, application to the afflictions that plague contemporary man. Modern man ranges far afield in pursuit of remote goals while he neglects what is to hand. "But it is here," Buber protests, "and nowhere else that we can find the treasure. The surroundings which I feel to be my natural abode, the condition which fate has designated as mine, the things made familiar to me in my day-to-day progress through life and which claim me day after day—here and in these things is the fulfillment of existence, whose portals have been made to open wide before me."[18] Buber's words are addressed directly to us; they speak to us of concern and involvement at a particular time and place, and of action whose end is the attainment of the experience of the divine.

To Judge from the stories included by Buber in *Gog and Magog,* Hasidic literature appears to be a "literature of Power," having as its objective the activation of its audience, and the release and realization of its reader's latent religious energies. "The Hasidic tale is more than a mirror," Buber insists: "The divine essence to which it bears witness endures within it. A miracle retold gathers new strength; energy of the past thrives on in living speech and continues its work for generations."[19] The activating energies released by the tale arouse wonder and devotion in the reader. For this reason the student's first contact with the Hasidic story—that is, his emotional encounter with it—reaps a rich harvest, and, with his teacher's guidance, the student can attain a relationship with the tale that very nearly approaches being spontaneous and immediate. Therefore, at this stage of the student's introduction to Buber's philosophy of Hasidism, the teacher should concern himself with the nurture of the student's emotional receptivity, of his devotional experience, and of his dialogic response to the direct speech contained in the tale. Once the student succeeds in achieving an attitude of receptive rapport with his subject, he is prepared for the succeeding stages of his introduction to Bubber's Hasidic philosophy. In these stages, the student's intellectual and critical faculties would be called on for a systematic examination of the underlying principles of Hasidism as they emerge from his analysis of the hidden meanings symbolized in the actions described in the stories.

The stories of *Gog and Magog* offer a potentially rich and varied store of educational possibilities. Two excellent examples illustrating the educational uses of these stories are the tales of Rabbi Yaakov Yitzhak of Pzhysha entitled, "How I Learned from a Blacksmith" and "How I Learned from a Farmer."[20] In both cases the conspicuous role in which an ordinary laborer is cast serves to remove the distinction between the sacred and profane, and to underscore the idea of the sanctity that is latent in worldly activity.

In the first of these stories, Rabbi Yaakov Yitzhak and the blacksmith of the title become involved in a dispute in which the rabbi is exasperated to the point of protesting, "But you, surely, are incapable of understanding what my business is about!"—to which the blacksmith replies, "That's certainly true. But can you understand what mine is about?" The smith's riposte inspires the rabbi to conclude: "And so it was that I came to learn that this, too, must be learned."

The moral that the Rabbi of Pzhysha drew from his controversy with the smith calls to mind Buber's principle of "inclusion," which asks of the teacher simultaneously to place himself at opposite poles of the educational situation, and to experience both his own role as the one who influences and that of his pupil as one who is being influenced—in other words, to sense in his own person the limitations inherent in Otherness and the grace of communion with another. This is how Buber describes the relationship of inclusion:

> The one who is called upon to influence those receptive to being influenced must continually seek to perceive this action as it is experienced by the other party. He must exist on the opposite side as well, but in such a way that the action being taken by his spirit loses none of its force; he must exist within the domain of the other soul, the one to whom he stands in parallel relationship: not some abstract spirit that he conceives in his mind, but always the concrete soul as it is in its totality and as a soul belonging to this unique person who is a sharer in the common situation of "educating" and "being educated"—a situation which in fact forms a unitary system, although one in which this unique person stands at the opposite end. It is not enough for him merely to imagine the personality of this child; nor is it enough for him to have apprehended that personality directly as a spiritual entity and in this way to acknowledge it. Only when he truly perceives himself on the other side, and experiences in his own

person what it feels like to be there and what the other feels like being there, does he recognize the real limit and transform, in reality, his arbitrary will into volition. . . .[21]

In the situation being described by Buber, inclusion is not reciprocal. Whereas the educator is conscious of his pupil's experience, the pupil cannot know of the education of his teacher; the educator participates from both ends of the shared experience, whereas the pupil is doing so merely from one end of it. In the story of Rabbi Yaakov Yitzhak and the blacksmith, the rabbi is shown to be striving to achieve just such an "inclusive" relationship with his interlocutor as Buber describes.[22]

In the tale about Rabbi Yaakov Yitzhak and the farmer we have another instance of narrative art used as a medium to express a pedagogic attitude. During one of the rabbi's walks—so the story goes—he came across a farmer whose hay cart had overturned. The farmer appealed to the rabbi to help him raise his wagon, but the rabbi answered: "I can't." Hearing this, the farmer rebuked the rabbi, saying: "Oh, but you really can. You just don't want to!" The farmer's words stirred the rabbi's conscience, and he took his place at the farmer's side. After they had managed to lift the wagon and right it, the rabbi asked why the farmer had imagined that he had not wanted to raise the wagon. The farmer replied: "Because you said that you can't. How can a man know that he can't do something if he hasn't tried?" The story as told by Buber differs from its original version,[23] so that we once again encounter Buber in his guise as educator, reworking his Hasidic source in order to uncover the lesson it holds for us in active education.[24]

The subject of prayer and religious devotion should occupy a special place in the teaching of *Gog and Magog,* particularly as they are exemplified in the prayers of the Hasidic preacher Reb Israel, the Maggid of Koznitz:

> He did not pray merely at the appointed times but in the same way that he breathed. He prayed with words and prayed without words. When he prayed aloud, he would mix words of ordinary speech into the prescribed text whenever his heart prompted them to rise to his lips. And sometimes he would even call out an endearment in Polish such as the daughters of peasants will use when they stroll at the fair with their lovers and hanker for a ribbon embroidered with colored thread. But the maggid prayed for no gift. And when he talked to people, the chant of prayer could still be heard in his voice. And one of his attendants tells of him: "You need only see the holy maggid asleep to know that he prays even in his dreams."[25]

When discussing this passage with the class, attention should be drawn to the example that the maggid sets of deep involvement in prayer, to his direct and intimate relationship with God expressed in his use of Polish love words, and to the theme of ongoing confrontation with God both in prayer and action. But even more than this, the lesson learned from the sound of prayer reverberating in the maggid's ordinary conversation is that each of his encounters with the physical world is an act of devotion. His relationship with his fellow men is always an *I-Thou* relationship, and his life is a perpetual prayer. From this point, class discussion can turn to the consideration of the subject of the sanctification of existence, an idea that occupies a central position in Buber's interpretation of Hasidism.

The concept of the sanctification of existence is Buber's special contribution to a world that appeared to him to have lost all meaning with respect to the divine covenant by which man was dedicated to God and which he continually renews at each of his "authentic" encounters with the world. In her article on Buber's thesis of man's encounter with God in Hasidism, Rivka Schatz has put her finger on the weakness of Buber's concept as it bears on Hasidic doctrine: "Hasidim never believed that God demands to be worshiped in the world 'because it is here that He wants to receive a response from me'; and it certainly never assumed that 'man responds by acting upon these available objects,' or that 'the significance of any act of worshiping God is none other than an outgoing rededication and reconsecration in this world to the encounter with God.'" Rivka Schatz buttresses her objections with arguments that are profound as they are convincing, and—in the light of purely historical considerations—irrefutable. But if we regard the idea of man's redemption of the world through his sanctification of life to be a tenet in the mission that Buber conceives for education, it becomes broadly and profoundly significant to the needs of modern man, and can be viewed as a potential foundation upon which education can build in order to nurture a way of life whose goal is inwardly determined. Buber's declaration, "This is how the enterprise of renewing the relation of Reality will be achieved: by authentic contact with concrete things and objects man attains *authentic life,* and in this way can he participate in the redemption of the world," confronts man with an immediate goal which is existentially present to him "here and now."[27]

Religious experience taken as the consummation of dialogic encounter deserves special emphasis in our classroom discussions. In this connection, the idea that mystical experience is the basis of religious life could be examined in the light of theories of education that take no account of the personal encounter with divinity. The scope of our inquiry could then be extended and deepened by a consideration of William James's *The Varieties of Religious Experience* and, in particular, of James's discussion of the spontaneity of personal contact with divinity experienced during states of mystical consciousness.[28] The account of Rabbi Yaakov Yitzhak of Pzhysha's mystical revelation as told in *Gog and Magog* is a concrete example of just such an encounter with the divine:

> I now understood that by study alone a man cannot achieve knowledge. . . . and after all of my delving and searching, it was finally revealed to me—not bit by bit but all at once—that freedom is in the hands of God. It

all came to me suddenly—that is during my morning prayers, when I began saying the verse [of the credo], "Hear O Isral, [The Lord is our God, the Lord is one]." The idea of divine freedom permeated the whole of my physical being and set me so to trembling that it seemed to me that all of my teeth were loosening in my mouth and that I could not say the whole verse through to the last, awful word, "one"....[29]

The passage contains more than merely a circumstantial description of Rabbi Yaakov Yitzhak's mental and physical state when he experienced his revelation, and more than his assertion of the doctrine of divine freedom. More profoundly, Rabbi Yaakov Yitzhak's account concerns the idea of liberation from the "coercions" of the physical world through the contemplation of it and the encounter with it. The means by which freedom from the dictates of the physical world is achieved are represented in two stories about personal temptation told in *Gog and Magog* by Rabbi Yaakov Yitzhak of Pzhysha and his teacher, the Seer of Lublin. Rabbi Yaakov Yitzhak tells of a naked woman appearing to him while he was studying late at night, and how in order to save himself from sin he was forced to flee his room through the window. The Seer of Lublin's tale of his conquest of temptation ends rather differently. He tells of how in his youth he had set out for Lizhensk in order to meet Rabbi Elimelech. After nightfall he lost his way and entered a house whose only occupant was a young woman: "The alarm I felt at the sight of her shook my soul to its depths. Until that moment the only fear I knew was fear of the Lord—blessed be his name!—and the only shame was the shame I felt in loving Him. And now, when my soul was seized by panic, this love was ignited and began to blaze. All of my lust was consumed by fire. At that moment I raised my eyes and lo!—woman, house and forest were gone, and I found myself standing on the road leading to Lizhensk."[30] This, then, is what Hasidism has to teach about man's freedom from dependence on the physical world, whose ultimate truth is God. And it was through his discovery of the divine principle in sensual love that the Seer of Lublin was able to encounter the world of the senses and, rather than flee from it, discover in it the road leading to his teacher, Reb Elimelech of Lizhensk.

In discussing Buber's concept of Hasidism with a class, special consideration ought to be given to the character of the zaddik. Under the influence of the prejudices contained in Jewish Enlightenment literature against Hasidic rabbis, students nowadays experience some difficulty in coming to terms with the figure of the Hasidic saint and community leader. Yet the appearance of the zaddik in Judaism was a logical and necessary result of the popular character of the Hasidic movement, with its demand that religious equality be extended to include the common man. It was around the zaddik's person that Hasidic congregants were united, and it was he who taught them the secret of ecstatic joy, who inspired them to convert the urge to do evil into a will to do good, and to find the way to God even through sin. Buber attaches great significance to Hasidic democracy as expressed in Hasidism's goal to set aside the learned and religious aristocracy that dominated Judaism, and in its stead to erect a pious community in which all persons were equally privileged to pursue union with the Absolute. Hasidism reversed the order of religious priorities: no longer did the men who were expert in oral and written law hold sway over religious life; Hasidism gave precedence, rather, to those who were capable of living the laws—something that was often more easily accomplished by those of little religious sophistication than by scholars. Buber holds the Hasidic congregation to be a social embodiment of the principle of free choice, and the zaddik to represent the type of the "autonomous leader."

How then, Buber asks, can man—and particularly the "common man," with whom Hasidism is chiefly preoccupied—acquire the capacity to experience his life in a condition of ardent joy? What is man to do in order to ensure that he will not lose his unity of soul in the face of the countless perils and complexities that hem him about in the world in which he lives? And should man lose his spiritual unity, what can he do to regain it? Buber insists that in these matters men are in need of assistance, and that such assistance must involve more than merely attending to spiritual needs. For all of these issues are to some extent connected with the whole range of problems, great and small, faced by a man living in the concrete world. So that the earthly principle no less than the heavenly must be attended to, and both body and soul are in need of a minister. In Hasidism, the task of such ministration is in the hands of the zaddik, who exerts his authority not because of any ability to enforce his will but purely by virtue of his personality. The zaddik's leadership is based on his capacity to perceive those who apply to him as individuals having cares and anxieties which he must come to know intimately and in detail, and to which he must provide solutions that have individual and personal relevance. The zaddik knows the relationship that binds body and soul, and has the ability to influence both. He teaches men to conduct their lives in a way that makes their spirits free, and to strengthen their spiritual being within themselves, so that they may cope with their own destinies.

Scholarship is not the zaddik's vocation. His real work is—as Buber puts it—"to be merged with God" and "to make contact with human beings." There is no greater praise of a zaddik than for it to be said of him that he himself is a doctrine: that by the whole of his personality and the sum of his actions, even when they are unpremeditated and routine—whether by his gait, or way of dressing, or of tying his shoes—the zaddik expresses that aspect of Judaism which cannot be put into words and can only be transmitted existentially through the example of a person's life. Although the Hasidic rabbi mediated between men and the Deity, his ultimate purpose is to set aside his disciples' need for his mediation and to teach them of the direct relationship with God, for which his own intercessions cannot be made to substitute. And in order to assist his followers to approach God with the whole of their beings rather than only a part of their lives, the zaddik's activity is directed at every feature of their existence, from their need to earn their bread to their spiritual requirements.

What distinguishes the zaddik in his role as educator is that he himself neither tries to solve the problems of those who seek his help nor to act in their behalf; his special gift is knowing how to guide them until they are able to make their own way. This rule applies as well to the zaddik's attitude toward the soul's confrontation with God. The role of the zaddik here, is to pave the way for his disciples' direct encounter with God and not to offer them a surrogate in God's place. In a Hasid's moment of spiritual crisis, the zaddik strengthens his resolve, and rather than impart the truth to his followers, he helps them to acquire it by themselves. The zaddik inspires his Hasidim to search, to experience, and to take action. He will pray for his Hasidim in their hour of need, but he will not allow them to cast their burdens onto his own shoulders nor to depend on him completely. The zaddik makes no compromises respecting a disciple's spiritual journey to God, without which a Hasid's earthly experience would remain unrealized.

Buber regards the example that the life of a zaddik sets for his followers to have important educational implications; the zaddik's effective influence over other men is exerted more through the manner of his life than through his ideas. In referring to the zaddik's life in this context, Buber does not mean his behavior in exceptional circumstances or his existence as a man of the spirit, but to his unexceptional and unpremeditated conduct as a corporeal and whole human being.

Another educational principle that Buber finds in the relationship of the zaddik with his disciples is that of the educator's descent to the level of the student in order to lift the student to a higher plane of enlightenment. Thus, he observes that the zaddik's mere setting of an example is inadequate when it comes to his dealings with the great mass of ordinary people, who are the special object of Hasidism's mission. The zaddik had therefore to state his creed in a way that was accessible to the people by immersing himself in the life of the masses and speaking their language; he had, as it were, to fall from his great height in order to be able to guide the people to spiritual perfection.

Buber describes the relationship between the zaddik and his disciples in the following way:

> The relationship between the zaddik and his students is purely a matter of the most intense concentration. In this relationship, mutuality develops to the point of greatest clarity. The teacher helps his students to find themselves, and at the moment of his descent his students help him to return and rediscover himself. The teacher lights the candles of his students; they, in turn, surround him and light his way. The student asks, and by means of his question he unconsciously causes an answer to take shape in his teacher's mind that would never have seen the light but for that question being asked.[31]

Here we have a clear case of direct dialogue becoming an intimate and fertile encounter in which questions are the midwives of the answers they seek.

The essence of the zaddik's pedagogy therefore resides in the fact that he allows his disciples to participate in his life and thereby learn the secret of action. So taught Rabbi Menahem Mendel of Rymanov, who is supposed to have learned Torah from each of the limbs of his teacher, Rabbi Elimelech of Lizhensk.

Buber points out that the relationship in Hasidism between student and teacher has its parallel in Zen. In both movements the student-teacher relationship occupies a central position. Both value human truth as movement rather than acquisition, and both are chiefly concerned with the transactions that take place between a student and his teacher. In Hasidism, however, the relationship is more inclusive: the Hasidic teacher's transactions are with an entire community. Moreover, although Hasidism and Zen both perceive truth as human existence, they differ in the manner in which this motion from being to being takes place; in Zen such motion is in the nature of a transmission.

Buber repeatedly stresses the profound seriousness with which Hasidism approached teaching and education. The Baal-Shem-Tov's disciple, the Great Maggid Rabbi Dov Baer of Mezritch, for example, would meditate by teaching. It was therefore his role as a teacher that determined his innermost thoughts. Buber cites one of the Great Maggid's favorite parables as a typical expression of his attitude toward education. In Dov Baer's parable, God's relationship with man is compared to a father, who when teaching his young son, accommodates himself to the needs of the child. So too—the Maggid observes—is the world God's way of accommodating himself to His son, man, whom God nurtures lovingly and gently until that child has matured sufficiently in order to reach Him. The Maggid of Mezritch strove to understand the world through God's pedagogy, perceived by him as a loving relationship between a teacher and a pupil. The mutuality between God and man was to him the essential principle of education.

Buber maintains that the importance of education in the life of Rabbi Dov Baer must be appreciated in order for us properly to understand the traditions concerning the Great Maggid's approach to teaching and the intensity with which he occupied himself with the inner natures and the destinies of each of his disciples. Although the Maggid's students attached a variety of interpretations to his teachings, he persistently refused to commit himself to any single interpretation as the one that was correct. For it was Rabbi Dov Baer's belief that any of the seventy faces that the Torah may reveal to a man represents an authentic vision of truth. This was the reason that the Great Maggid never taught with an eye toward systematically revealing the inner relationships of his teachings. Instead, he instructed his disciples by allusions and parables, which his students had then to order into a proper relation. Rabbi Dov Baer's purpose was to awaken the truth that was latent within his disciples' souls, and his didactic method was a spiritual midwifery by which a truth potentially known to his students became actually known to them.

The Baal-Shem-Tov was not, strictly speaking, a teacher. Buber describes him as one who would at once live, act, minister, heal, pray, interpret, and instruct—so that teaching was to him but one among the many routine ways in which his existence was expressed. The Maggid, on the other hand, was primarily a teacher, although he, too, could not be defined as such in any limited sense. He taught no special skill or profession. "Only when the spiritual world is in decline," Buber observes, "does education constitute even on its highest level an actual profession. At those times in which the common existence of the students and the teacher is thriving, they learn in his presence as apprentices studying a craft with a master might learn from him—whether he will or not—a variety of things which have to do with both performance and life."[22] Similarly, the Great Maggid's disciples claimed that they learned from their teacher's humanity, and that his personality exerted an influence over them that was comparable to doctrine.

Having studied the character of the zaddik, the class can turn its attention to the subject of the Hasidic community's cohesion around the zaddik's personality. The relationship of the zaddik and his disciples is one of mutual help toward self-discovery. By their questions, the disciples draw the zaddik's answers, which, taking the form of commentary and story, raise his followers from the level of their quotidian existence to one of religious exaltation. Buber represents the Hasidic congregation as a dynamic unit:

> The zaddik is joined to [the congregation] by prayer and by Scripture. He prays within it not merely as its spokesman but as its energy center, in which the exaltation of the community's soul is joined and from which the ecstasy emerges which is fused with the ecstasy of his own soul. He speaks to his congregation by his interpretation of Holy Writ and divulges the mystery at the third Sabbath meal. The congregation is the energy field of his discourse, an energy field in which his words lead, step by step, to the gradual revelation of the spirit.[33]

Buber regards personal religiosity to be the essence of Hasidism and the force that shapes the Hasidic community. Hasidism does not aim at the establishment of a secret fraternity that retreats from society into a mystery cult, but aspires to the creation of a community of autonomous individuals who are able both to live their own lives and be joined in intimate association with a leader-teacher. Nor does the zaddik live his life in isolation or, for that matter, solely within the circle of his disciples; he exists in and with the world. And this fact constitutes, in Buber's view, the very core of the zaddik's approach to piety. The members of a Hasidic congregation are joined in an ecstatic union made possible only by its existence around the inspirational source provided in the person of their rabbi. An illustration of the zaddik's position within the community of his adherents can be found in the dialogue recorded in *Gog and Magog* between Rabbi Yaakov Yitzhak of Pzhysha and his disciple Rabbi Simha Bunam.[34]

The central theme of *God and Magog* concerns the manner in which redemption is realized. However, there would be little point in involving students in a discussion of the entire range of Hasidic attitudes on this question. We should confine ourselves, rather, to only those aspects of the subject that are likely to engage the interest of young people today. In this context, the ideological conflict about the goal of Hasidism between Rabbi Yaakov Yitzhak of Pzhysha and his teacher, the Seer of Lublin, deserves particular attention.

Rabbi Yaakov Yitzhak had spent much time cloistered in an attic chamber mastering the deeper mysteries of the Torah. But instead of realizing his aspirations of achieving the highest level of piety, he was cast into the despair of religious doubt, which he sought to resolve by freeing himself from his overweening individuality and joining the circle of the Seer of Lublin. At Lublin, however, he found only a partial solution to his problem, and in the end he left the Seer's court to found a rival school of Hasidism in Pzhysha.

Pzhysha Hasidism, in contrast to the exclusive theocentricity of the school at Lublin, was as much concerned with man as it was with God, which accounts for its strong appeal to Buber. The school founded by Rabbi Yaakov Yitzhak opposed the apocalyptic messianism of Lublin and advocated instead a doctrine of man's existence within Creation. Pzhysha Hasidism neither sought to bring the End of Days closer nor lived in passive expectation of the Messiah's advent. At Pzhysha, the whole of life was regarded as a preparation for the Messiah's advent. Action, rather than being thought of as a way of speeding the Messiah's approach, was taken to mean man's intensive and inward common existence with the created universe.

Buber rejects the creed of messianic eschatology of Rabbi Menahem Mendel of Rymanov and the Cabalistic doctrine of mystical meditation. The occult has no appeal for Buber, who advocates, instead, the sanctification of life, and the preparation of the soul through education.

An instructive example of the doctrinal differences among Hasidim on the subject of redemption is furnished in *Gog and Magog* by a dialogue between Menahem Mendel of Rymanov and Yaakov Yitzhak of Pzhysha:[35] The Rabbi of Rymanov cries out—

"Better that the blood of Israel be shed until it is knee-deep from Prystik to Rymanov if it could put an end to our Exile and Bring on our Redemption!" Taken aback by Menahem Mendel's words, Yaakov Yitzhak replies: "And if this fire is solely a fire of destruction? The Holy One, blessed be He, can ignite a flame and extinguish it, and knows what He does. But we?—Who has given us the authority to wish that evil should grow strong? And how should we tell whom we were assisting in this—the Redeemer or Satan?

Rabbi Yaakov Yitzhak then proposes his own doctrine of redemption: "Redemption—only think of the great opportunity we have of doing real good by means of it! Rabbi, behold that tall tree rising from the soil's depths to the sky. Can you see how it is covered by fresh leaves? Each and every leaf a soul of Israel—thousands upon thousands of souls, and each one awaits you, Rabbi, to make it more perfect that the tree may be redeemed!" Yaakov Yitzhak's arguments fail to move his colleague, who responds by taking a pessimistic view of the efficaciousness of action in the present aimed at the small change of existence. He states: "The time for thinking about individual souls is past!"—To this Yaakov Yitzhak replies with the paramount tenet of his philosophy: "The work of mankind will never succeed if we give no thought to helping the soul which is now in our charge, and to the life shared between souls, and to our own lives, which we share with them, and to their lives with one another." In so saying, the Rabbi of Pzhysha offers a doctrine by which the idea of messianic redemption is replaced with a concept of redemption based on the existence that man shares with the physical world.

We would do well at this point to elucidate the four kinds of Exile and Redemption which, according to Buber, coincide in Hasidic philosophy: (1) The Exile and Redemption of the "Divine Sparks"; (2) the Exile of an Individual and the Redemption of All; (3) national Exile and Redemption; and (4) the Exile and Redemption of the *Shekhina* (God's divine presence among men). Buber emphasizes that not only are national exile and redemption interconnected but that connections exist as well between each of the categories of exile and redemption. He explains that the relationship between the exile and redemption that are national and the other categories is at times so strongly stated in Hasidic language that it does not stop short of comparing the exile of the *Shekhina* to the exile of the nation, but also explicitly asserts their redemption to be analogous. The exile of the Jewish people is seen in Hasidism to be ineluctably bound up with the exile of the world, and the redemption of the nation with the redemption of the soul of an individual. National exile and redemption are not thought of in isolation but solely in relation to the fate of the universe and the individual. The redemption of Israel is therefore not a goal to be pursued for its own sake but is dependent on the correction of a flaw that has penetrated to the very source of existence.

These ideas have immediate relevance to our own times and to our own country. We should give serious thought, therefore, to a concept in which the nation is merged with the world and with the soul of the individual and with God. There is much to be said for Buber's insistence that only by such a merging can Zionism be preserved from following the path of modern nationalism, which, by breaking its links with the world at large, annuls both its reason and right to exist.

Living in a civilization that has lost its faith, and deprived of any vital form of piety to a point of anguish that has put existence itself into question, many in the West have begun to look for a way out of their despair by turning to the spiritual traditions of the Orient. Groups of young people have immersed themselves in the study of Zen and actually sought to accommodate some of its tenets to their own needs. These circumstances lend more than a casual educational significance to Buber's analysis of the relationship between Hasidism and Zen Buddhism.

Zen is a form of late Buddhism that in the sixth century made its way from India to China, reached its creative height there in the eighth century, and took root finally in Japan in the twelfth century. The doctrine of Zen asserts that the absolute can be attained only through the medium of actual experience with palpable and concrete reality. According to Zen, each individual must discover the heart of Buddha in his own heart. Zen thinkers stress that it is not by divorcing ourselves from reality but by dedicating our souls and our lives to it that we achieve spiritual perfection. Only when the whole of a man both as body and spirit is engaged in an enterprise and cleaves to the concrete does man grasp the truth, and through his perception attain the most concentrated form of action.

The sanctity spoken of by Zen sages is no detached and transcendent holiness but one that is altogether human. Joseph Schechter cites a story about a meeting between Tao-Hsien, one of the founding personalities of Zen, and the sage Pe-Yung at the latter's retreat in a temple on a mountain-top. So great was the holiness of Pe-Yung that the birds would make pilgrimages to him with offerings of flowers. As Tao-Hsien and Pe-Yung were speaking, they heard the roar of a wild beast and Tao-Hsien jumped up in alarm. Seeing this, Pe-Yung observed to Tao-Hsien: "Aha, so you're still not free from it!" Later, when Pe-Yung went out, Tao-Hsien carved the Chinese sign for Buddha on the rock upon which Pe-Yung was wont to sit, and when Pe-Yung returned and saw the sacred name he avoided taking his habitual seat. And so it was Tao-Hsien's turn to say: "Aha, so you're still not free from it!" Through Tao-Hsien's remark Pe-Yung attained enlightenment, and from that day forward, the birds would no longer bring him flower offerings. His sanctity ceased being detached and became human. Schechter draws an appropriate parallel between this story and a Hasidic reading given by Menahem Mendel of Kotzk to the verse from Exodus 22:31 (English Standard Version), "And ye shall be holy men unto me," which the Kotzker Rabbi interpreted to mean: "They were holy men with human holiness."[36]

Buber maintains that both Hasidism and Zen share the belief that the way to truth is through the activity which is nearest to hand: when a person carries out an act as it ought to be done and its inner sense is fulfilled, then existence, too, is consummated. He argues that in neither Hasidism nor Zen is truth in the world of man merely a content in the mind. Both regard truth to appear to men solely as human existence. Truth is not a thing thought, or said, or heard—it is something to be lived and comes to us in the guise of life. Buber writes:

> The "Poem of the Experience of Existence," written around the year 700 by a Zen teacher begins with the verse: "Hast thou not observed from thine own life, O Man!—that he is truth itself?" The same view is expressed by Chassidism, which interprets the verse, "And this is the Torah of man," to be directed at the person who himself becomes a complete doctrine. In both cases, and almost in the same language, even the most sacred doctrine is rejected if it exists for a man merely as intellectual content.[37]

The main difference between Zen and Hasidism is that Zen departed from its historical roots in Buddhism to become an ahistorical mysticism of the human personality, whereas even the most personal of Hasidic doctrines arises by way of establishing a link with the historical Mosaic creed. Another significant difference between Zen and Hasidism has to do with their attitudes toward reality. The "realism" of Zen is intended ultimately to be annulled; that of Hasidism is messianic and regarded as something to be fulfilled. When Hasidic realism is concerned with revelation it takes account of the past, and when it is concerned with redemption it considers the future. In Zen the detached and autonomous moment is alone thought to have reality, for it is only then that inner enlightenment takes place; the moment of enlightenment is when time ceases to exist. Hasidism, on the other hand, sanctifies time. In it historical time and the moment existing outside of time merge as revelation and inner illumination meet.

The educator who is capable of accepting the religious vocation urged on him by Buber's concept of Hasidism, who can reveal the "power" contained in the stories of *Gog and Magog,* and who can create around his own person a community of students, will have taken a first step in the direction of religious education.

NOTES

1. Yitshak Orpaz, *Nemalim* [Ants] (Tel Aviv: Am Oved, 1968).

2. Matti Megged, *Dostoyevsky, Kafka, Beckett* (in Hebrew) (Tel-Aviv: Ha-Kibbutz Ha-Meuhad, 1967), p. 143.

3. Martin Buber, "Al A. E. Simon ha-mehanekh" [A. E. Simon, the Educator], in *Ha-adam mul arakav* [Man and his values] (Jerusalem: Magnes, 1959).

4. See chapter 5, "Biblical Humanism."

5. Gershom Scholem, "Perusho shel Martin Buber la-hasidut" [Martin Buber's interpretation of Hassidism], *Amot* 1, hoveret 6 (1963); 29–42.

6. Ibid., p. 42.

7. Martin Buber, *Or haganuz* [The hidden light] (Jerusalem and Tel Aviv: Schocken, 1958), pp. 9–70.

8. Scholem, "Perusho shel Martin Buber," 29–70; Rivka Schatz, "Adam nokhah elohim ve-olam be-mishnat Buber al ha-hasidut" [Man's encounter with God and the world in Buber's concept of Hasidism], *Molad* [New Moon] 18, hoveret: 149–150 (1961): 596–609.

9. Scholem, "Perusho shel Martin Buber," p. 33.

10. Leon Roth, "Ha-meshorer Wordsworth ve-erkhei ha-sifrut ve-ha-hinukh" [The poet Wordsworth and literary and educational values], *Mahbarot la-Sifrut,* 2 hoveret 3–4, 47–55.

11. Martin Buber, *Be-fardes ha-hasidut* [In the Hasidic orchard] (Jerusalem and Tel Aviv: Mosad Bialik and Devir, 1963), p. 10.

12. Buber, *Or ha-ganuz,* p. 15.

13. Scholem, "Perusho shel Martin Buber," p. 37.

14. Martin Buber, *Darko shel adam al-pi torat ha-hasidut* (Jerusalem: Mosad Bialik, 1957). Published in English under the title *The Way of Man According to the Teaching of Hasidism* (London: Routledge and Kegan Paul, 1951). All references in this article are to the Hebrew edition.

15. Ibid., p. 17.

16. Ibid., p. 27.

17. Ibid., p. 39.

18. Ibid., pp. 44–45.

19. Buber, *Or ha-ganuz,* p. 7.

20. Martin Buber, *Gog u-Magog* [Gog and Magog] (Jerusalem: Sifrei Tarshish, 1944), pp. 23–24.

21. Martin Buber, *Be-sod siah* [Dialogue], 2d ed. (Jerusalem: Mosad Bialik, 1963), pp. 257–58.

22. See A. E. Simon "Martin Buber ve-emunat Israel" [Martin Buber and Judaism], *Iyun* [Study] 8, hoveret 1 (1958):33.

23. Buber, *Or ha-ganuz,* pp. 397–98.

24. See Simon, "Martin Buber ve-emunat Israel," p. 34.

25. Buber, *Gog u-Magog,* p. 50.

26. Schatz, "Adam nokhah elohim ve-olam," pp. 599–600.

27. Buber, *Be-fardes ha-hasidut,* p. 57.

28. William James, *The Varieties of Religious Experience* (New York: Longmans, 1902).

29. Buber, *Gog u-Magog,* p. 40.

30. Ibid., p. 39.

31. Buber, *Or haganuz,* p. 17.

32. Ibid., p. 24.

33. Ibid., p. 18.

34. Buber, *Gog u-Magog,* pp. 97–98.

35. Ibid., p. 191.

36. Joseph Schechter, *Shvilim be-hinukh ha-dor* [Pathways in contemporary education] (Tel Aviv: Alef, 1963), p. 197.

37. Buber, *Be-fardes ha-hasidut,* pp. 138–39.

7

The Attitude toward the Arabs as the Central Problem of Jewish Education

As a true humanist educator Martin Buber raises the profoundest moral questions pertaining to the interrelations of the Jewish and Arab populations in Israel. These are the central problems that Zionist national education has to confront; they form an essential part of Zionist education and any attempt to treat them as alien and to disregard them only means self-betrayal and the denial of the very goals of Zionism. These problems, with all their complexity, had to be faced by Jewish education in Israel from the very first days of Jewish resettlement in Israel. With the birth of an autonomous State of Israel and the normalization of Jewish national life, these problematic issues seem to have become less acute and much more peripheral while still remaining unsolved. However, in recent years there has been a certain degree of sobering in this respect, and these questions have regained their central place in Zionist political as well as educational thinking. The argument was reopened. It was recognized that the controversy and the need to draw far-reaching conclusions in this important matter were only postponed for a few years and are again of pertinent interest today. Hence there is renewed significance and validity of Buber's discussion of the interrelations of Arabs and Jews in Israel. One can argue against the political solutions Buber proposed and can disagree with his positions concerning the current affairs of his day, but we cannot disregard his treatment of the issue, the many questions that stimulate us to fresh thinking. We cannot reject Buber's penetrating discussion that draws from the truth inherent in his national, social, and humanistic vision.

One of Buber's basic assumptions was that the Jewish-Arab problem involves two vital demands, which are different in source and nature and which cannot be weighed against each other, nor decided about, in terms of their content. The Jewish demand cannot be rejected because what hinges on it is not only the life of the nation of Israel but also the fulfillment of its divine mission. The Arab demand, too, evokes the love of the land and the faith in it. Buber stresses that we must find some compromise between these two demands, for it is unthinkable that such faith and love for the same piece of land will not overcome the differences of opinions existing between Arabs and Jews, tragic as they may seem.

Both the Jews and the Arabs make demands over the land of Israel, but these demands can, in fact, be compromised if they are translated into the actual needs of living people. The danger arises when these demands are exploited by political forces, changed from practical demands into political principles, and presented with all the cruelty of political endeavors. When this happens, all of life is overshadowed by political slogans, and its realities and possibilities vanish together with the desire for truth and peace. Buber writes to Mahatma Gandhi and reminds him of the observations made in his (Buber's) article "Neither Saint Nor Politician" to the effect that we are all caught in the network of political life. We cannot get away from it however hard we try. The effect of political life is neither external nor superficial; it affects the innermost life of the people yearning for success. In Israeli reality this problem is seen in all its glory. It overcomes not only the spirit of the nation but life itself.

In examining Buber's attitude toward the Arab-Jewish problem we note the clarity and soberness of his views, the lack of illusion in his approach, his recognition of the Jews' right for existence and self-defense as a primary fact, and, at the same time, his great moral and human sensitivity. Buber realizes that there is no life without some degree of injustice, that the requirement to defend Jewish existence may involve injustice toward the Arab neighbors, but his main emphasis is on our awareness of this possibility and on the willingness to say: "Let us do no *more* injustice than we absolutely have to in order to preserve our lives." This moral responsibility is not absolute and its scope cannot be determined once and forever. The degree of actual injustice that is unavoidable in every particular case cannot be predetermined, but has to be always reexamined and struggled with. Only a person who can truly assess and minimize the amount of evil he commits either as an individual or as a member of a group can claim to live a fully human life. The same goes for a nation, for a nation's responsibility toward life is no different from that of an individual. Furthermore, a person cannot hope to maintain a high moral standing as an individual while shirking his moral responsibilities as a member of a group or nation.

Buber argues against those who follow the path of violence, who regard his position as a mere "moral demand" that cannot go hand in hand with current political demands. Buber stresses that this is not true. However, the extent to which his vision can be materialized would depend on the will of the people. A person whose only desire is to strengthen the nation will find himself treading a purely nationalistic path—and according to Buber, both the goal and the road leading to the attainment of nationalism are against the very essence of the people of Israel. Such a person is likely to follow short-range policies that do not take into account the possibility of injustice. However, it is unthinkable that the road to the self-fulfillment of the nation of Israel should be marked with injustice from the very start. Buber stresses that the history of the Jewish nation has not conformed to regular historical laws as is indicated by its very survival. This was the result of the moral message it carried for the world that was part of its essence whether or not this was recognized by the Jewish people. Injustice toward the Arabs is not only a moral sin but also a political crime, since it will prevent the Nation of Israel from achieving its true goal.

Buber stresses that one of the most difficult political as well as educational problems is the fact that Jews have never lived in Israel *with* the Arabs but *side by side* with them.

As an educator and philosopher Buber tries to clarify the nature of the Jews' link with the East. He rejects the empty political claim often made by enemies of the new Jewish settlement in Israel whereby the Jew is stranger in the East, a messenger of Western Imperialism and is, therefore, alien in spirit, in nature, and in his very essence, to the East.

One of the most important issues an Israeli educator has to address is the question of the attitude of the Jews to the East, their ability to become part of the cultural life of Asia and to contribute to the reawakening of the East.

Buber makes a distinction between the Eastern and the Western types. He describes the Eastern type as the motor type, and the Western type as the sensory type. The motor type feels by means of his movements. The impression hits one of his senses, spreads to all his senses, and the special sensory features of the senses are numbed by the overall assault. In contradistinction, in the sensory man the senses become separated from each other and from the common ground of their organic source. They are led by the most liberated, the most objective of the senses, the sense of light. The triumph of the Greeks in the creative sphere of pure form and shape is the work of this hegemony. In the motor person the sense of sight is not an autonomous ruler, it only serves as a mediator between a world in motion and the hidden movement of man's body, which may take part in the experience of the world's motion.

The Oriental's world view is determined by his character traits. He senses the world rather than getting to know it intellectually. The world catches hold of him and passes through him, whereas the Western man is confronted by the world. According to Buber, "The Occidental's World-image begins with the objective concreteness of the world, even if from there he proceeds to the highest abstractions, or delves into the deepest mysteries of the soul; the Oriental begins with the inwardness of the world, which he experiences in his own inwardness. . . . The Occidental progresses, step by step, from the world's appearance to its truth, or he penetrates to this truth by a flash of intuition; the Oriental carries this truth in the essence of his being, finding it in the world by giving it to the world."[1]

Buber considers both this giving and this discovery as the religious act of the Oriental. All great Oriental religions and teachings stress that the world is not a gift given unto man but a task. It is up to man to actualize the religious vision of a world of truth. The world needs the human spirit and it looks forward to man to come and unify it. Many roads lead man to action, and they differ in the various Eastern religions, but God's way in the world is one and only one. In all Eastern religions this realization penetrates the whole of life. According to Buber, "To the Orient, the contemplated idea is a project that becomes reality only in the lived idea. This alone, the lived idea *is*."[2]

This basic Eastern principle has been developed in all Eastern nations, but in the nation of Israel, which finds itself at the crossroads of East and West, it has been most completely fulfilled. According to Buber, the Jew is the most conspicuous example of the motor man. He grasps the world less by recognizing its separate and varied elements than by recognizing the interrelations between them.

Buber draws a comparison between the Greek and the Jew, his exact opposite: "The Greek wants to master the world, the Jew, to perfect it. For the Greek the World exists; for the Jew, it becomes. The Greek confronts it; the Jew is involved with it. The Greek apprehends it under the aspect of measure, the Jew as intent. For the Greek the deed is in the world, for the Jew the world is in the deed."[3]

It is the basic view of Judaism that action has an absolute, decisive value. Judaism has handed over to the West with the teachings of the East. The West accepts what the East gives him, adapts its gift to his own forms of thinking and feeling, and thereby also changes and improves upon what it has received, but it "has never managed to construct an entire world overflowing with divine teachings on the basis of an unshakable irrational foundation."

What does the West lack and what are its expectations of the East? Buber stresses that the West has developed the most sophisticated body of general knowledge, but cannot find the meaning of life with its own resources; its discipline and control are strong and effective but it cannot find its way by itself. The West has a rich and free art, yet cannot of itself find the portent; it has man of spiritual genius, but none of them have been able to bring up the mystery from the abyss and put it into the hearts of men. It has faith but cannot by itself find its God.

Even when the Jews were uprooted from their land, exiled and scattered all over the world, and suffered torture and degradation, they never ceased being Orientals. They always retained in their heart of hearts the motor greatness that was at the root of their souls and the primary drive for unification. This Oriental spirit, overt or hidden, provides the basis for Buber's belief in the possibility of a new Jewish spiritual act of creation. A great act of creation of this kind cannot be achieved as long as the Jews are scattered all over the world. It can be achieved only with the renewal of a continuous Jewish existence in Israel, which has in the past given rise to some of the most impressive manifestations of Jewish desire for unity.

Buber analyzes the current situation, notes the political-social-spiritual processes taking place, and points out that we are proceeding toward what he likes to call "the Era of the Asian Crisis." Asian leaders submit to the external pressure of European nations. They do not take care of their holiest possession, their great spiritual tradition; on the contrary, they abandon it. In his words: "Asia is being murdered, and it complies with its own murder."

If the world does not want to lose one of its dearest possessions, it must do all it can to open up a new era in which the West will not hold Asia in submission but will help to develop Asia using its own native powers. In fulfilling this universal-historical mission Europe can make use of the Nation of Israel as an intermediary between East and West, since Israel has acquired the art and learning of the West but has not lost its archaic greatness. This nation is destined to form a link between East and West leading to fruitful interaction and combining the spirits of West and East in a new spiritual endeavor.

With that mission of the Israeli nation in mind we must ensure the renewal of its existence in Israel, the development of friendly relations and cooperation with the Arab neighbors, and the construction of an exemplary social, moral, and spiritual way of life that would radiate to the nations surrounding it.

The nation of Israel returns to the East as the son of the East. It is not a missionary of Western imperialism; it has not come to enforce a Western way of life on the East. Just because it has assimilated a Western way of thought it will be easier for Israel to assist in liberating the forces hidden in the East, in bringing the East back to life so as to enable a fruitful encounter of East and West.

The notion of creating a fruitful encounter between East and West and the role of the Jewish nation in such an endeavor seems to present Jewish education with an important and exciting challenge that has to be acted upon, not only accepted or rejected. The narrow limits of national propaganda are made much broader. The question of the attitude toward the Arab neighbors ceases to be a limited political or humanitarian issue and becomes much more meaningful. It requires active cooperation, calls for a redefinition of our national role, and stimulates our thinking with regard to the nature of our return to the East, our integration into the Asian scene and our place in the renewal of Oriental culture. We can argue against Buber's characterization of the Jew as an Oriental, but we must admit that it is highly stimulating and enables a serious and fruitful educational discussion. Indeed, one of our most pertinent educational tasks is to clarify to ourselves the nature of our place and role in Asia, and our possibilities for integration in the life of the East. Buber shakes our educational thought out of its nationalistic routine, which would turn us into just another small nation instead of the unique nation we are, carrying a unique message to the world at large.

At the center of Buber's philosophy is the view that the Jews are not like all nations, whether they recognize this fact or not. They are a unique, unmatched phenomemon, and they form a society in which national tradition and religious faith are inseparably interlocked. This faith is inseparably linked with the land of Israel, the land to which, according to Buber, "The Lord himself sent the people of Israel to the land of Israel so that each should contribute to the perfection of the other as a first step towards universal redemption."

Buber realizes that this immense mission has not been fulfilled, that for hundreds of years the nation has been cut off from the land; moreover, a great part of the Jewish people has lost its faith. However, Buber stresses that the unconscious power of this faith has remained great enough to navigate the Jewish wanderers back to their ancient land at the great historical hour of their national revival.

The actualization of Zionist ideals is not only in the establishment of a Jewish state as a solution to the immediate problems of Jewish life but must be complemented by the materialization of social, spiritual, and humanistic ideals. As long as we keep this in mind, the main test will not be whether the people of Israel are victorious in their struggle against other peoples; to achieve victory they may indulge in trampling the rights of others, measuring their success according to political criteria, in terms of their external achievements following the practice of nationismal in all nations. According to Buber, the goal of the nation of Israel is not to *attain* but to *mold its own shape,* to redeem its inner, dormant ancient forms.

As early as in his speech "Zion and the Youth" made in German in 1918, Buber draws the attention of the young Zionists to the great responsibility they have undertaken. It depends on them whether Zionism will turn out to be a true fulfillment of a mission or an empty, transient, political achievement. He stresses: "It is up to you, young people, to determine whether Israel will be the center of humanity or a Jewish Albania, the redemption of nations or a ball for the great nations to toy with. Zion will not be established in the world, unless you first establish it in your souls."

In a long series of articles and speeches Buber repeatedly stresses that it is not the ideal of truth, nor the image of truth but the actual practice of truth that is the task of Judaism. The goal of Judaism is neither to construct a philosophical theory nor to produce artistic creation but to shape a new society. A new society cannot be built only by reinforcing it from within while causing destruction and injustice to others, to the neighbors surrounding the newly born Jewish nation in Israel. Indeed, the first and foremost test of this society lies with its attitude toward its neighboring Arab population.

Buber has a bitter argument with the upholders of the nationalist dogma who maintain that it is time that the Israeli nation become master of its own fate, that by developing its own potential it will make the best possible contribution to humanity at large. They reject the demand that Israel should point out new paths, that special missions should be imposed on it and stress that like all other nations it should be allowed to find its own way as an outcome of free competition between the forces at work in it. They maintain that the nation of Israel should not be overburdened with the task of building a new society founded on truth. It should be allowed to live its ordinary national existence as all nations do.

Buber warns against this approach. He stresses that there is no nation in the world that is autonomous; the spirit alone is autonomous. Buber says that the wars and bloodshed in the world prove that as long as the nations refuse to follow the call of the spirit they will devour each other. He says: "We want to follow the call of the spirit, which will through us be materialized and only as long as we submit to the spirit is a grain of truthful life maintained in us; the moment we grow to be like all nations we will cease to be worthy of our existence."[5]

Buber emphasizes that in the messianic dreams of the diaspora, and the movements they gave rise to, there has always been an integration of the national and humanistic perspectives, the longing for the land of Israel and the longing for a society founded on truth. He stresses that if the society in Israel is going to lead a miserable, atheistic existence like many other small countries, there is no hope for Israel.

Buber warns against the attempt to channel the future into schematic patterns. It is not the task of the intellectual or the statesman to provide detailed planning that will determine future directions. The details of the plan have to crystallize out of the conflicts, torments, and trials of the pioneering generations. He also recognizes that the spirit has to set its own limits, beyond which it cannot impose itself on life but wait until it can itself rise out of life. However, within those limits it must manifest its impact.

Buber knows that it is naive to think that social life can be changed by merely abolishing a certain form of government. It is nonsense to assume that by, say, abolishing the autocratic regime in a given country and imposing on it a Communist regime, while people's daily interaction remains unchanged, there will be a social change. In order for a genuine change and genuine renovation of spirit to take place in a society there must first be a real change of spirit in the interaction of its members. Therefore, when a nation leads a normal course of life the chances of reform and renovation are meager. On the other hand, Buber believed that for the Jews who were returning to their homeland after the terrible experience of the Nazi Holocaust the conditions for change were most ripe so that they represented an unprecedented power.

Buber argues against Mahatma Gandhi who claims that the Arabs have a unique right over the land in which they live. Buber asks Gandhi: How did the Arabs acquire this ownership of the land of Israel? They settled the land after conquering it while the Jews started out by buying the land. Does not such peaceful form of acquisition give the Jews some share in the ownership over the land? Buber stresses that it is the right of the nation of Israel, which was driven away from the land by foreign conquerors, to settle the uninhabited regions of Israel without depriving other peoples of their rights, so that it can finally have a land of its own in which it can lead a full national life.

Buber repeatedly makes the point that Zionism asserts the right of the nation of Israel to reestablish its national life in the land of Israel. This right derives from three major sources: one pertains to the historical ties of the people of Israel and the land of their forefathers; the second refers to the fact that after thousands of years in which the land of Israel has been left a desert, the Jews came and turned the places they were allowed to settle into a cultivated, blooming piece of land. The Jewish settlers have acquired their special right over the land by this act of creation.

The third source of the Jews' right over the land is indicative of the future. The great enterprise of building this country has not been undertaken in order to establish yet another small state for yet another small nation; it must mark the beginning of something new, of the fulfillment of a new mission. However, it is for this very reason that the question of the responsibility toward the Arab neighbors, whose fate the Jews must share to a greater or lesser degree, is so acute.

Buber points out that modern Zionism has from the very start contained two bitterly conflicting basic trends. One trend sought to reconstruct the true Israel, so that the spirit and life itself should not be placed side by side but intermingled. Revival does not merely mean safe existence for the nation but a life of spiritual fulfillment. The second trend regarded the notion of revival as a process of normalization. A normal people needs a land, a language, and independence. This has to be attained in any event; the rest will follow by itself. The questions of the quality of life in Israel, and the impact that independence of the Jewish nation may have on the world at large are secondary. Buber considers this latter approach as a betrayal of Zionism.

The national will of the nation of Israel is not directed against any other nation. The people of Israel, who for two thousand years have been a persecuted minority in all countries of the world, must decisively reject any form of national oppression as part of their rightful return to the land of Israel. This return to the homeland must not be at the expense of other people's rights.

Buber mentions three tasks that are necessary conditions for the establishment of Zionism and national revival: (a) Educating the people; (b) working the land (to be accomplished by Jewish labor pioneers); and (c) abolishing external difficulties by diplomatic means.

The task of educating the people comes first both in terms of its temporal order and its importance. The Jewish people have to be educated so that they can prepare themselves for their imminent revival.

Buber is highly critical of the many attempts that had been made toward educating the people. Most of these attempts replaced education with shallow propaganda, resulting in the belittlement of the Zionist ideal. The kind of education that, according to Buber, is required for the accomplishment of Zionist revival has to take the form of great promises involving great demands; promising a life of fulfillment and demanding the whole of the human heart and mind. This cannot be achieved unless everybody invests all of his human potential in the task. Demanding the utmost of others can be legitimate only if one makes similar demands of oneself.

On the other hand, when Buber examines the reality around him, he finds that instead of setting before people profound and far reaching demands related to the whole integrated personality, educators arouse them for transient political objectives. Buber regards this procedure as an apparent, short-term, educational gain and not a long-term accomplishment. His penetrating words should accompany us even today: "A society which demands money of its members will be given alms in return. A society which demands of each of its members the whole of his humanity, will gain his money as well. Purposeless and tasteless concessions made to the people have a boomerang effect in that they turn the original idea into a shallow one."

It seems convenient for education to align itself with superficial goals, to be attracted by external political objectives, and education can easily turn into propaganda. When Buber uses Ahad Ha'am's term "cultivation of hearts," he does not have in mind anything like propaganda, preaching, or indoctrination. Buber requires the whole man, assigns to him a full responsibility, and examines him in the light of his responsiveness to the situation in which he finds himself, the straightforwardness and reciprocity of his relations with others, and his ability to accomplish a genuine dialogue, a relationship of I and Thou, with the Thou preceding the I and constituting a precondition for it. This state of dialogue should hold not only with a close brother but also with a neighbor; it is these relationships that require the whole personality which are a person's real test.

The second task concerns the settlement of the land by way of creative labor, leaving behind a parasitic life dependent on values created by other peoples, thereby accomplishing a genuine return to a full-fledged national life and entering on a new contract with the land.

The third mission—diplomacy—has to provide the necessary conditions for work. In this area Buber points to several failures in Jewish diplomacy:

a. Instead of undertaking to guarantee the conditions required for practical work, it undertook to guarantee the result of this work, which is impossible.

b. It addressed itself almost exclusively to the West and ignored the East, particularly its central problematic issue, the question of the attitude toward the Arabs. This question has not received its proper perspective, and has not been adequately addressed in terms of its long-range ramifications.

According to Buber the first straightforward conclusion that ought to have been to drawn from Balfour's Declaration was the opening up of negotiations with the non-Jewish inhabitants of Palestine. There were two conditions for the successful conclusion of these negotiations:

a. The launching of wide-range, well-planned settlement activities.
b. The preparation of a clear and realistic economic and political program that would form the basis for these negotiations.

There was a great deal of interest in the political statement Buber made at the 12th Zionist Congress held at Karlsbad in 1921. The central features of Buber's statement were as follows:

a. The return to the land of Israel and the revival of national life based on independent labor.
b. This national drive is not directed against any other people.
c. The return to the land of Israel, which will be accomplished through an evergrowing flow of immigration, is not designed to be at the expense of the rights of the Arabs.
d. A rejection of the nationalistic forms of national suppression.
e. A covenant based on justice with the Arab people designed to turn the land of Israel into an economically and culturally blooming piece of earth, whose development will provide each of the people living in it an opportunity for unperturbed self-growth.
f. The purpose of Jewish settlement is not the capitalistic exploitation of a certain piece of land, or of any other imperialistic purposes. It means the creative labor of free people on a commonly shared land.
g. Profound and continuous solidarity will grow between the Jewish and the Arab peoples as a result of their shared true interests, and it will eventually overcome current conflicts.
h. Mutual respect and goodwill will lead to a historical reconvention of the two peoples.

The final resolution of the Congress was much shorter, greatly changed, and hardly reflected the spirit of Buber's words. Buber grieved at the changes and corrections made in his proposal by the wording committee of the Congress, which justified itself by saying that it had to put forth a resolution that would be acceptable to the Congress as a whole. Buber feared that if he refused to agree to these corrections, his proposal would be totally rejected. He wanted to bring about a radical change in the position of the Zionist movement concerning the Arab problem and believed that the very acceptance of his modified proposal would constitute a genuine move toward this change.

Therefore, Buber fought for the acceptance of his own formulation, but gave in each time the acceptance of the proposal hinged on his surrender of various details. Many years later, in 1947, in an open letter addressed to Dr. Judah Magnes, Buber still expresses his pain and disappointment on reading the corrected version of his proposal. He says: "When the wording committee completed its work and the accepted version was brought to my hotel in a neatly typed copy—I saw a series of beautiful and persuasive sentences, but the bone and marrow of my original proposal were not there."

Buber had a serious argument with Gandhi concerning the principle of nonviolence, for which Gandhi devotedly preached. Gandhi had no understanding whatsoever of the severe state of the Jews during the Nazi Holocaust or of the complex relations between the Jews and the Arabs in Israel. When Gandhi writes that the Jews ought to respond to Nazi prosecution by means of civil resistance, stressing that the Jews' "voluntary suffering" would finally overcome the calculated violence of the Nazi regime, his words read as extremely naive, testifying to the extent to which Gandhi was detached from the gruesome reality of Nazi Germany.

Buber assured Gandhi that the people of Israel had no wish to practice violence. This people had not formulated like Jesus or Gandhi himself a whole thesis of nonviolence, because it recognized that every person must sometimes practice violence in defending his own, let alone his children's, existence. On the other hand, the people of Israel had propagated from the very beginnings of its history the teachings of justice and peace. This nation had believed and taught that peace is the goal of the nations and that justice will necessarily lead to it. Therefore, the nation of Israel cannot practice violence out of its own free will.

Gandhi blamed the settlers in Israel for their external nonviolence, calling it empty, the nonviolence of the weak and the helpless. Gandhi despised the nonviolence of the weak, and stressed that genuine and intentional nonviolence could not be a result of external compulsion. Buber stressed that Gandhi's condemnation of the nonviolence of the Jews as based on weakness had no support in reality. He wrote to Gandhi: "You do not know, or do not wish to know, what spiritual strength, what Satyagraha, was required in order to restrain ourselves here in face of the blind violence directed against us, our wives and children, day after day, year after year, and not to respond with counter-violence."

Buber repeatedly emphasizes that he refuses to accept the nonviolence principle as the only principle that is applicable in all situations. It does not accept the prohibition to fight evil where it threatens to overthrow good. Buber does not want violence. Buber's principle will do all it can to avoid having to overthrow evil by violent means but if it has no other way of preventing evil from overthrowing good, it will not hesitate to practice violence.

Buber stresses that if he were asked to formulate his own truth it would be characterized neither by the principle of nonviolence nor that emerging from Indian poetry, but that expressed in the following conception: "There is no better rule for a man than to pursue justice, apart from the pursuit of love. We must fight for justice, but with a measure of love."

This formulation, which combines justice, the fight for justice, and love, carries a more sober, more valid, and more suitable message for the social and political situation in Israel at those times, as well as in our times, than did Gandhi's message. Every educator should present both conceptions— Gandhi's and Buber's—and confront his students with the way of politics— so that they can weigh the moral, humanistic, social, and national consequences of the various approaches. Gandhi wanted to combine religion and politics; Buber considers this possibility and says that there is an inherent difference between the way of politics and the path of religion: a political objective can be successfuly attained whereas a religious goal is forever an unattainable dream, merely pointing the way for humanity to follow. Clearly, education must relate to these different ways and provide a measure for determining which is best.

Buber fought against the limited method of conventional nationalism, which emphasizes that everyone has to treat his own people in absolute terms and all other peoples in relative ones, and to measure his own nation according to its great hours and all other nations according to their hard times.

Buber painfully recognized that the Arabs are despised by many and are considered inferior to the Jews. He stresses that as long as we have not learned to know the inner life of a people, its inner drives and basic principles of conduct, we will tend to interpret differences in life-style as marks of inferiority. In Buber's words: "The inner reality of every nation has a value in its own right, and every way you try to measure it will be nothing but a mistake."

In order to bring out this issue in all its extremity Buber mentions the fact that the people of Israel have been long held inferior by the other nations and are still regarded as inferior and alien. The people of Israel must not do unto others what others have done unto them; they must not let themselves be drawn in to the fallacy of treating the little-known stranger as inferior to them. This is a perversion that goes against all measure of justice and morality.

Buber says that we must possess the ability to envisage the state of mind and being of the stranger, in the form of our own spiritual reality. He realizes with great anxiety the extent to which Jews are ignorant of the Arab as a man. Buber made these statements at the 16th Zionist Congress in Basel in 1929, but they seem to be no less valid today, even with respect to the Israeli Arabs who are citizens of the State of Israel.

Buber calls for a better understanding of Israeli Arabs. He emphasizes that we must not ignore the fact that the Arabs have a vital contact with the land. He says: "They, not we, have something that may rightfully be described as Israeli style; their farmers' huts look as if they have grown out of this earth, while the houses of Tel-Aviv look as if they were placed on top of it; Abraham's deep bows when ushering in his guests can still be observed nowadays, but not among us." From a political and even tactical point of view there is no greater mistake than treating an opponent as if he were cast in one permanent pattern. Accepting such a view amounts to surrendering to the irrational element in our existence. Only by confronting the true substance of our opponent can we pass the test of reality. The people of Israel have often committed this fallacy and at a very high cost.

Buber stressed the need for cooperation between the Arabs and Jews for the purpose of developing the land of Israel in a mutual effort to turn it into an exemplary part of Asia. This cooperation should involve two independent and equal nations, each of which is autonomous in its own society and culture, but both of which are united in the enterprise of developing their common homeland with a federal management of their common interests.

Buber realized that a new and prospering element could not establish itself among the nations of the Middle East if it functioned as a representative of the Western world. He calls for genuine mutual understanding between Arabs and Jews, and not as a mere tactical move. In his words: "We are not concerned with fake solidarity, but with a genuine, comprehensive solidarity based on objective grounds. Only this kind of solidarity can help us confront the many external dangers which may threaten us, and for which we have to be prepared."

At a time when Zionist thought was not prepared to really address the problem of the interrelations between Arabs and Jews, this problem played a central role in Buber's thought. He recognized as early as the 1920s the crucial role the Middle East was to play in world policy and chronology of war, and believed that when the Jews found their place in the Middle East they would play a central role in shaping the face of the universe.

Chaim Arlozorov, who was educated in the light of Buber's teachings, was close in spirit to Buber's approach and considered it a realistic and necessary political thesis. In his article entitled "The Events of May," written after the events that took place in May 1921, when he took an active part in defending the neighborhood of Newe Shalom between Jaffa and Tel-Aviv, Arlozorov was able to suppress his feelings of anger, bitterness, and mourning and bring to bear clear and genuine political considerations. He said that whoever does not wish to carry out an ostrich-type policy, to close an eye to the reality of things, will find that in our situation, in our desire to guarantee for ourselves the freedom to act and to build our national home, we have only one way open to us; the way of peace, and only one national policy: the policy of mutual understanding. In a place where such tremendous forces were pushed into one and the same political framework, where movements and crucial matters come up against each other in one way—only mutual agreement can lead to success. Buber stressed that the contract between the Arabs and Jews was necessary also from the economic point of view. A national, long-standing economy can be built in Israel only if the Jews seriously consider a general, wide-ranging economical system for the land of Israel. Jewish interests will have a firm foundation only if they are commensurate with the interests of the other inhabitants of the land.

Buber was not so naive as to believe that such cooperation could be easily achieved, that the wide gulf separating Arabs and Jews, which was real and not illusory or political, could be easily bridged, but he believed that there was room for a common policy for the whole land. Despite his sobernness, Buber's way of stating this proposition has more than a trifle of naivety in it. He says: "Since both they and we love the land, and wish to see it prosper in the future, and since we love the land and seek its prosperity together, we can work for it together, too." Buber stresses that there is no lack of other beneficial elements for active cooperation between the two peoples in creative and constructive tasks. The historical aspect should not be disregarded concerning their common forefather, Abraham. All these linked up the Jewish and Arab peoples in the first days of the Semitic tribes. According to Buber, it was not accidental that during the long days of exile it was only the Spanish-Arab period that was the time of intellectual blossoming for the Jews.

In order to demonstrate the serious intentions of the Zionist institutions to proceed toward an understanding and a settlement with the Arabs, Buber proposed to the 16th Zionist Congress to call together a permanent committee for the land of Israel, that would form an advisory body to the Jewish Agency in all questions pertaining to the Arabs. This proposal was accepted. After the 1929 events, Chaim Kalvariski, who was known for his good contacts with the Arabs and his favorable attitude toward them, was called back to the political leadership of the Zionist movement and was asked to head the Arab Office, which was supervised by the Jewish Agency and the National Committee. This Arab Committee ceased to operate in October 1931 and some of its employees were later employed by the Jewish Agency.

Buber immigrated to Israel in 1938 and the first article he published in Israel dealt with the problem of the perverse relations between Arabs and Jews in Israel. At the beginning of September 1937 a pan-Arab Congress convened in Syria which worked out a plan for war. At the end of September 1938 there erupted bloody disturbances of Arab terrorists, who attacked remote Jewish settlements, lay in ambush in the fields and along the roads, or planned and carried out concentrated attacks on Jewish centers. The number of Jewish victims of the Arab raids gradually increased.

Some of the active members of the Haganah demanded violent reactions, calling for counterattacks on the Arab terrorists. The Zionist leadership sought to restrain these responses and to take care that the Jewish reactions be limited to direct counterattacks on Arab terrorists. Those who demanded direct and violent responses began to organize themselves in groups and launched into separate military action of their own accord. These actions usually took the form of acts of retaliation, including the throwing of bombs into Arab crowds, and caused a great deal of killing among the Arabs.

Buber was extremely angry at these groups. He warned against the increasing number of voices heard among the Jewish people who called: "If we cannot defend ourselves against the wolves, we'd better turn into wolves as well.—and they forget that the whole purpose of the Jewish enterprise in Israel was to go back to becoming wholesome men."

Buber stresses that nothing can be achieved through blind violence, but that everything can be lost. If violence is allowed to have its own way, the road toward peace with the Arabs may be lost despite the fact that it is the historical destiny of Arabs and Jews to live together and to share in the enterprise of building the land. Buber feared that the Jews' acts of violence would unite all the Arab population in Israel against the Jewish revival and would result in a loss of the approval with which some of the nations of the world approached this national revival. But, however great the external loss would be, the internal loss would be even greater.

Buber does not oppose self-defense, but cries out against hurting the innocent. He calls for self-control, which he considers the true measure of bravery. The same spirit of things can be found in his "Samsons." Buber analyzes the circumstances which have led to the severe deterioration of the relationships with the Arabs. Buber considers the roots of this deterioration to lie in the attitude of the Jewish settlers who acted as if the land were empty of inhabitants, as if the Arab inhabitants did not have to be taken into account. No serious attempt was made to cooperate with this population in seriously allowing it to participate in the constructive enterprise undertaken by the Jewish settlers, both in terms of work and in terms of profits. There was an overreliance on the protection of foreign nations and the League of Nations, and on the promises of one nation or another. Buber makes penetrating comments that are still relevant: "We have not told ourselves that promises of this kind in the political world . . . are valid only as long as the world political situation, which is created by force of promises of this type, is stable, as for the event that it is not we must find some guarantee of another type, to be ready for us instead of a declaration—a reality, just the reality of a common enterprise, of shared interests with our neighbors in the land of Israel."

It is doubtful whether we can find a statement that is as relevant to the present-day situation as in Buber's words. Today, too, Jews in Israel must take care not to rely on the promises of a land or lands, which are valid for a short period of time only, and to seek out practical, long-term solutions.

Buber realized that in those days what was required was a united battle of the whole Jewish population in Israel against the "White Book," but this battle, he maintained, should not be expressed in terms of violence against the Arab neighbors or by cutting all relations with the British, a move that might block the way to further reconciliation with the Arabs.

Buber's battle against violence on the part of various groups among the Jewish population went on for years. In 1948 he published, in collaboration with Magnes and D. W. Senator, a letter to the press, in which they called out against the ever increasing number of innocent victims among Arabs and Jews and the lack of adequate response on the part of both Jewish and Arab institutions in preventing these despicable events. A war psychosis was developing following which every stranger was suspected of being a murderer or a criminal. This is the state of mind that drives people to the murder of innocent passersby. This letter is concluded with the following call: "Let us not destroy the moral foundations of our life and future with our own hands."

Similarly bitter and painful reproaches were voiced by Buber as a response to the destruction of an Arab village in 1958 at which Buber was deeply shaken.

Buber's position concerning the Arab question was not a theoretical one. He was personally involved in attempts to materialize his views about the covenant required between Arabs and Jews that was to be based on mutual understanding, shared interests, and common action. After a long pause in his active political involvement following his disappointment at the way his proposals were modified, even distorted, at the Zionist Congress at Karlsbad in 1921, a disappointment that drove Buber to the conclusion that "from now on I have to give up written resolutions and content myself with oral statements." Buber joined in the activity of The Arab-Jewish Cooperation and the group known by the name of Unity. He considered these two frameworks as appropriate for the fulfillment of his political-social-national and humanistic vision.

The league and Unity associations were preceded by other groups and associations that were guided by the same principles, and a brief survey of their activities is in place. As early as 1925, an Israeli association for the promotion of friendship between Arabs and Jews and for finding a generally accepted solution to the future of Israel was founded. This association was given the name of "Brit Shalom" and grew mainly out of the personal initiative of the German-Jewish Oriental scholar, Joseph Horowitz, who was a professor of Semitic languages at Frankfurt University, attended the opening celebrations of the Hebrew University in Jerusalem, and was a member of its board of trustees. He was particularly concerned with developing peaceful relations between Arabs and Jews in the land of Israel. On his way to the celebrations of the Hebrew University Horowitz visited Cairo and Damascus, met with many Arab leaders, and got the impression that the

Arab National Movement might agree to Jewish settlement in Israel if it were carried out in cooperation with the Arabs.

When he came to Israel, Horowitz met Dr. Arthur Rupin, who headed the Israeli Office of World Zionist Federation and was also the head of the settlement department of the Jewish Agency. Rupin was impressed by Horowitz's views and helped to establish the association of Brit Shalom. Among the founding members of this organization were: Rabbi Benjamin, Prof. S. H. Bergmann, Chaim Kalwariski, Dr. J. Loria, and Dr. J. Tahon. Additional members later joined the organization such as Prof. Gershom Shalom, Dr. Abraham Katsenelson, and Prof. A. A. Simon. In August 1930 a series of proposals was published by the organization concerning possible cooperative projects of Arabs and Jews in the areas of administration, economy, medicine, education, and culture. These proposals were the first to bring up the suggestion that Israel should be a binational state, in which Arabs and Jews would enjoy equal rights, disregarding their relative proportion in the population.

Within the "Brit Shalom" organization there were serious differences of opinion with regards to central issues. One group of members, headed by Dr. Rupin, wished the organization to assume the character of a research association, a forum for social and political discussions, whose conclusions and proposals would be brought before the Zionist institutions. Another group, headed by Rabi Benjamin and Chaim Kalowariski, wished to work out a clear and systematic policy and fight for the actualization of this policy. Another area of disagreement was the question of immigration. Many of the members agreed to a temporary delimitation of Jewish immigration to Israel in order to facilitate the achievement of an agreement with the Arabs, while a minority of them, headed by Rabbi Benjamin, fought against this move, maintaining that any agreement between Arabs and Jews must involve a recognition of extensive Jewish immigration to Israel.

The "Brit Shalom" organization was not wholeheartedly accepted by the various elements of the Jewish population in Israel. It was bitterly attacked by the Revisionists, and its goals were misconstrued by other organizations as well, including the "Hashomer Hatzair" movement. The "Brit Shalom" organization did not become popular with the public at large, and its activities were interrupted in the early 1930s.

In 1936 a new organization comprising part of the former "Brit Shalom" members as well as leaders of the Sephardic Jewish community which included some of oldest Sephardic families, was established. Among its founders were Dr. Yitsak Epstein, Rabbi Meir Berlin, and David Yelin. The organization defined itself as a "nonpolitical organization, whose aim it is to gain a better familiarity with the East and to establish social, cultural and economic links with the states of the East and a proper explanation for the need for Jewish labour in the land of Israel."

This group put out several publications concerning the Arab problem and made propaganda for closer relations between Arabs and Jews for the sake of peace and cooperation. But it did not have a clear ideological line and was not able to offer a substantial political program, and was soon dissolved. In 1939 a third organization was established—The League for Rapprochement and Arab-Jewish Cooperation. This league called for efforts toward finding a solution to the national conflict between Arabs and Jews, toward cooperation in defending themselves from the hazards of the Second World War, and toward establishing long-standing cooperation after the war was over. Buber took part in the activities of this organization and greatly approved of its endeavors and was a member of its subcommittee for education and culture.

In 1942 this league was joined by the kibbutz trend aligned to the "Shomer Tzair" movement, and the "Socialist League" whose members were ideologically close to the former but did not join kibbutzim. Its platform, which was signed, among others, by Buber, included the following points:

a. A recognition of the fact that the growth of Israel as the commonly shared land of the Jewish people returning to its ancient homeland and the Arab people living in Israel has to be based on constant, all-embracing mutual understanding between the two peoples.

b. The principle of the Jews' return to their historical homeland for the purpose of reconstructing their independent national life defines the Jews' unquestionable rights. Similar rights concern the rights of the Arabs to maintain an independent national life on the one hand, and to have meaningful contacts with other parts of the Arab world on the other.

c. A recognition of the Jews' rights to settle in Israel to the extent allowed by the economic capacity of the country, so as to guarantee the growth of full economic, social, cultural, and political life, all in cooperation with the Arab nation.

d. Agreements concerning predefined immigration quotas for a period of a number of years, but the rejection of any inclination to turn the Jewish people into a national minority in the land of Israel.

e. The following are considered by the league as basic principles for any Jewish Arab settlement:

   1. Admitting the Jews' rights to return to their historical homeland and to reconstruct its national life there as well as the Arabs' rights to live an independent national life, while maintaining their contacts with other parts of the Arab world.

   2. Mutual respect for each others' independence.

   3. Binational rule in the land of Israel.

   4. A favorable attitude toward the participation of the land of Israel, as a binational independent unit in a federacy of neighboring nations, after the ground for this has been prepared and the basic rights and vital

interests of the Arab and Jewish nations living in Israel have been secured.

f. The tasks of the league:

1. To fight within the Jewish camp and the Zionist movement for a policy oriented toward cooperation and agreement between Arabs and Jews.
2. To work toward the establishment of an Arab league, similar in character to the Jewish one, which could serve as its ally.
3. To initiate cooperative projects with the Arabs in the area of economics, culture, politics, and social affairs.
4. Research.
5. The training of personnel for activities among the Arabs.

Buber considered this platform as truly reflecting his views and was glad to be one of those who confirmed and signed the platform.

In August 1942, Magnes established in Jerusalem the "Ihud" (Unity) Organization. Magnes was elected president and Buber was a member of its board of directors. The "Ihud" organization adopted the principles of the League for Rapprochement and Arab-Jewish Cooperation and considered itself an active partner in its operations. "Ihud" published a journal under the name *Problems* with Buber as its publisher and A. E. Simon as its editor.

Buber devoted a great deal of effort and spirit in the work of "Ihud." In it he saw the realization of his political dream.

With the dissolution of the League for Rapprochement and Arab-Jewish Cooperation at the establishment of the state of Israel, a small circle comprising of "Ihud" members continued to exist. After the death of Magnes, Rabbi Benjamin was elected president of the organization and also acted as editor of *Ner,* the association's magazine during the 1950s. Buber published articles in *Ner* and took part in the activities of "Ihud." Simon recounts that "even in his advanced old age, after his 85th birthday, Buber presided over meetings of Ihud's Board of Directors which were held at his home."

In discussing the activities of the League for Rapprochement and Arab-Jewish Cooperation it should be stressed that the section in its platform related to the attempt to establish a similar organization on the Arab side was not easy to accomplish. There was hardly any response to the league's call among potential Arab allies. However, there was one favorable sign; a courageous attempt toward Arab-Jewish cooperation did take place, and although many historians tend to view it as a transient and meaningless episode, it seems that from an educational point of view at least it should receive the recognition this tragic episode deserves. It is often stressed—and quite rightly so—that the Arabs have erected an impenetrable wall against which all the calls for peace, for understanding, and for dialogue have struck and come to grief. This example of a break through this thick wall, however temporary it was, presents us with an example of the possibility of real dialogue in the future. Educators need examples of this type; they carry a message, and however tentative this message may be, it is important in discussions concerning the possibility of peace. This token of readiness for cooperation with the Arabs can be found in the chronicle of cooperation and mutual help between the League for Rapprochement and Arab-Jewish Cooperation and the Arab association "Palestine al G'adida" headed by Fawzi el-Husseini. This was an attempt to maintain the unity of the land, while solving the political problem by way of Arab-Jewish agreement on the basis of full cooperation between the two peoples in all areas of life, with political equality between them, Jewish immigration constrained by the economic capacity of the land of Israel, and joining the shared but independent land of Israel in a federacy of neighboring states to be established in the future.

Fawzi el-Husseini was a son of the famous Husseini family, cousin of the Mufti, Haj Amin el-Husseini, who was one of the most violent instigators of hatred and bloodshed of Arabs against Jews. Fawzi himself had been active in terrorist operations against the Jews but reached the conclusion that the only way of fulfilling the hopes of Israeli Arabs was to reach an agreement with the Jews and to cooperate with them in fulfilling the national desires of both sides. Fawzi found political partners and made efforts to fulfill his ideas in an agreement with the League for Rapprochement and Arab-Jewish Cooperation. He made preparations to publish a magazine named *El Icha* (Fraternity) in which the principles of the "Palestine al G'adida" association would be expressed and developed, and he established a club and generally tried hard to disseminate its ideas. The Arab political leadership greatly disapproved of and feared his activities. Gamal el-Husseini, the acting director of the Arab Supreme Committee, sent Fawzi a warning, and having refused to pay any attention to this warning, Fawzi was killed on November 23, 1946, by "unidentified killers." Gamal el Husseini did not admit to have had any part in planning Fawzi's murder, but took overall responsibility for "actions against traitors." Aubry Hodes, who worked for *New Outlook,* a magazine devoted to improving the relations between Arabs and Jews in the Middle East, tells about a conversation he had with Buber concerning Fawzi el-Husseini. Buber described Fawzi as a serious and honest man, who was not afraid to express his opinions and to act in accordance with them. Buber maintained that the times were not yet ripe for a man like Fawzi el Husseini. Arab extremists could not bear his moderate tone and therefore set out to kill him. Buber told Hodes that Fawzi's friends came to him and consulted him about the best way to continue their activities, and after many deliberations Buber suggested that they should each go his own way. Buber realized that if they continued their cooperation with Jews they would be murdered one by one. In his words: "We could not take it upon ourselves."

In a conference of representatives of Jewish Organizations held at the Biltmore Hotel in New York early in May 1942, a number of resolutions were passed, later to be known as the Biltmore Plan which formed the basis for the political activities of the Zionist movement. These resolutions included a demand to open up the gates of Israel for mass Jewish immigration, a decision to transfer all the issues concerning absorption and development to the hands of the Jewish Agency, and particularly a call to establish an independent Jewish community in Israel. Buber rejected the idea of a uninational Jewish State and compared the relations between Arabs and Jews to the story of the Giveonim. The Israelites agreed with the Giveonim that they should be the "wood cutters and water drawers for the whole community." This may turn out to be the fate of the Arabs in Israel, whom the Biltmore plan may turn into second-rate citizens.

Buber believed that for the nation of Israel to be able to renew its life it would require a strong and well-developed autonomy. It would require not only the ability to preserve and develop its new–old Hebrew culture in a free manner but also the opportunity to determine for itself in an unconstrained way its social structure and forms, which are oriented toward social renovation in a spirit of cooperation and friendliness. The Arab people, too, require a strong and well-developed autonomy in Israel. The two nations should not be in each other's way and should not disturb the free growth of each other's spiritual and social values.

According to Buber this need for autonomy does not mean that each of the two nations needs a state in which to rule. The Arab or Jewish populations in Israel do not each need a separate state in which to develop their potentials. Instead, Buber proposes a shared social-political binational framework, in which each nation would run its own internal matters separately, and the two nations would cooperate in working out issues of common interest. Buber believes that a binational framework of this type, with well-divided areas of Arab-Jewish settlement, but maintaining full economic cooperation, preserving the rights of the two partners without paying attention to the changing numerical relations among them, and with a commonly shared autonomy, will give each party all it really needs. If such an arrangement could indeed be achieved, neither nation will have to fear being numerically overruled by the other, and mass Jewish immigration will not seem to the Arabs to be a threat to their existence. Buber goes even further and says that "since the freedom of self-determination and the development potential of the Jewish community will be anchored in the unshakable framework of this bi-national social-political organization, there will be nothing to prevent this organization from joining a federacy of Arab states, and this, in turn, will give the Arab community in Israel further guarantees for its status."

Buber believes that this vision may come true if it is preceded by two large-scale, out-of-the-ordinary moves: a spiritual-social move and an economic-technical one. The spiritual-political activities are designed to prepare the hearts of people in both nations for peaceful cooperation and have the spirit affect the more earthly and technical areas of life with its indefatigable desire for peace between the two nations.

At the heart of the technical-economic operation Buber envisages a large scale enterprise for the development of the country, based on an enormous irrigation project, which, on the one hand, would greatly increase the amount of agriculturally profitable land, and, on the other hand, would provide energy sources for large-scale local industry and thus guarantee to it a central position in the economy of the Middle East. Rather than a heterogeneous stretch of land, made up of a dynamic Jewish element and a largely static Arab element, there would be established a homogeneous area of intensive production. In order for this vision to materialize, the Arab population has to be fully involved in this enterprise, not only in profiting from these developments but in actively contributing to them as well.

Buber analyzes the political situation all over the world and realizes that nations expend their energies on the international scene in wars, conflicts over power, achievements, and possessions. The great nations do not seek to settle the conflicts between the smaller nations, but on the contrary try to sharpen them and make them even more extreme in order to exploit them in their battle over power and world control.

The small nations themselves, which have been permeated by politicization, try, on their part, to use the great nations' drive for world control for their own political ends. In this hopeless vicious circle, international relations become more and more tense. This holds for the interrelationships between Arabs and Jews as well.

Buber dreamed about a genuine international authority, whose task it would be to settle conflicts among nations. Buber says:

> The problem of the land of Israel, the problem of Arab-Jewish relations, is one of the most difficult problems in present-day politics, if not the most difficult of all. Let this problem then be a test to the world. Out of all the nations there have to rise men of spirit who are independent in their thought and who have not fallen prey to the universal war of all against all for the sake of power and possessions. They have to meet together and find a way for both nations to work together towards the correction of this complicated state-of-affairs, but they also have to take care of the future, of things beyond the present moment.

Until the establishment of this binational social-political framework which he was planning could be accomplished, Buber suggested that the running of the common affairs of the two nations be left in the hands of this international circle of impartial great men.

In connection with this issue of binationalism in long-term perspective, A. E. Simon recalls comments made by Buber in the year of his death. Simon brought up the question of binationalism and expressed his doubts at the idea. He said: "If the English and French Canadians in the Quebec province cannot peacefully handle their own affairs, and if nearby Cyprus is going to be divided between Greeks and Turks, and if Catholic and Protestant Irishmen find themselves in a bloody state of war—what will become of us?"[6] Buber's reply, quoted by Simon, clarifies his approach and throws light on his political vision. Buber replies: "The notion of binationalism was for me only a step toward a wider goal: an Arab-Jewish Confederacy in the area, or part of it. Now we may possibly have to first reach a contract between the nations while maintaining a relative geographical separation."[7]

Buber accepted the reality whereby the desire to become an active group within a larger framework of an Asian confederacy had to be replaced by a more limited goal of establishing a small state, which continuously faces the dangers of standing in opposition to its geopolitical environment, and having constantly to invest much of its energy in military preparations rather than in social and cultural enterprises.

In Buber's words, the goal of the renewed Jewish settlement in Israel had to be its participation in the development of a newly flourishing and powerful Middle East. The objective process that could lead to the fulfillment of this goal was the pioneering enterprise of Jewish settlement in Israel.

This enterprise, which by its nature was based on selectivity, was to grow organically out of an agreement with the Arab neighbors and in this way to form a basis of trust, of mutual planning and cooperative efforts of the inhabitants of Israel and the area at large.

Buber stressed that the idea of a full revival of the nation of Israel and its integration in the revival of the Middle East would not succeed in the framework of mass settlement without due preparation, but would require generations of Jews who would labor in Israel to achieve this end. This would require several generations of pioneering in terms of work as well as peace efforts, and a principle of organic and selective development. This could be accomplished by pioneering settlement, settlement of laborers who see their own as well as their children's fate as linked with the growth of this land. The settlers would have to establish a growing community that would deserve its autonomy and would demand independence by force of its right. This community would have to be established on the basis of cooperation with its neighbors, helping them to improve their economy, which would cultivate feelings of solidarity and would thus provide a firm basis for shared efforts of these two nations.

This gradual growth of selective Jewish population was interrupted from without. Instead of a slow, selective flow for the purpose of establishing a firm basis and a radiating center in Israel, a flow of enthusiastic pioneers, of people set on changing their lives and on fulfilling their idealistic goals, there came a tremendous flow of people escaping the Nazi holocaust, homeless, persecuted refugees. This unpredictable state of affairs set the stage for the world's acceptance of the establishment of a state of Israel. As a direct consequence of this the selective center was not established and the gates of the country were opened for the great stream of immigrants. Arab-Jewish solidarity was not established either as a fact or as a mutually accepted plan for cooperation. The Arabs viewed Jewish mass immigration as a threat and considered the Zionist movement as an "agent of imperialism."

Buber points out that the prospects of establishing the Jewish state abolished the prospects of the growth of something greater and more powerful than it. Instead of a nation constructing its life in cooperation with the nations of the Middle East, there emerged, after a difficult and bitter war with all its Arab neighbors, a state that in everybody's eyes was based on robbery. In Buber's words: "The spirit has witnessed the breakdown of a beautiful experiment, which potentially held the blessing of a great future. It was unique of its kind and was swept away by the waves of history."

Buber regarded the division of the land of Israel as a sorry affair, which greatly increased the gap between the Arabs and Jews. Despite this conception, Buber welcomed the existence of a state of Israel and denied anybody the right to question Jewish independence. He stressed that the command to engage in spiritual matters should from now on be fulfilled in Israel. As a first step to its fulfillment Buber considered the attempt to reestablish mutual understanding with the Arabs.

Buber warned that this state of war and constant aggression between Arabs and Jews could not be maintained in the long run. There is a limit to how long one can do constructive work with one hand while holding weapons in the other.

The first necessary step toward peace and understanding—Buber believed—was to make real steps toward a solution of the problem of Arab refugees. This concern for the alleviation of the suffering of the victims of war is important not only as a humanitarian act and as a gesture of friendliness but is of utmost importance for the very morality of the state itself. Israel, which won its war in the battlefield, must indicate its generosity and humanitarianism by returning the spiritual balance between might and right.

Buber also fulfilled an important role in the "Mediterranean Talks" held in Florence. He made friends with its former mayor, Giorgio La Pire and in 1960 Buber made an impressive speech in the framework of these talks, which did not directly relate to the question of Arab-Jewish relations but was mainly devoted to the question of peace. Buber came back to this subject many times, and also referred to it in an essay he read at a seminar held in Jerusalem by the Jewish Theological Seminary of New York and was devoted to the subject "Israel and Its Role in Civilization." In this essay, Buber stressed that most of us are caught in a standard political belief that says that after the cold war, which in itself follows the "hot" war, there is the probability of the establishment of peace. Buber says clearly: "I consider it a great illusion. Peace, which is achieved through the termination of war, cold or hot, is no real peace. Real peace, which is to serve as a real solution, is organic peace. Great peace must involve cooperation and nothing else."

We can argue against Buber's political thought, and we can disagree with one detail or another in his evaluation of current events, but we cannot ignore his thought and his approach to these events. Anybody who has anything to do with Zionist and Nationalist education cannot allow himself to be ignorant of this approach, to which much of Buber's life was devoted. Buber did not seek to impose his own way on others, nor did he believe himself to have developed a clear and obligating plan of action. On the contrary, he rejected any form of compulsion. When asked how that organic peace which he desired could be achieved, Buber answered that it seemed extremely difficult to him to accomplish. He was sure that political means would not be sufficient. Following or accompanying any political action there must be a revolutionary change in the peoples of the Middle East, in the direction of greater openness and mutual understanding and readiness for the opening up of a genuine dialogue.

As a true educator, Buber disliked exhibitionistic actions, propaganda for his views and external publicity. He wanted to prepare the hearts of people for the acceptance of his position, to clarify his views, to stimulate discussion, and, mainly, to realize his vision in actual life. When young people turned to him and asked him not to satisfy himself with expressing his position as a philosopher, intellectual, and educator, but to allow them greater activity, such as street demonstrations, to draw public attention by somewhat exhibitionistic means, Buber replied that he did not object to demonstrations, but his question was whether they would be really effective, and what they could be hoped to achieve. In his words, instead of a demonstration by a hundred people, who would parade in front of the Knesset building, let each one of them make contacts with one Arab family. This way, there will be friendly relations between a hundred Jewish and a hundred Arab families all at once. The establishment of relations of this type is both more courageous and more effective than a passing demonstration or pathetic speeches.

For over a half a century Buber repeatedly raised this crucial question, the question of the attitude toward the Arabs and the possibility of establishing a framework for a shared existence in the land of Israel. He was the great stimulator, who even after the establishment of a state of Israel refused to allow the Israeli's conscience to go to sleep or to become deaf to great social and human problems. Since he was a great educator Buber realized that the question of the Israeli attitude toward its Arab neighbors is the central problem of Jewish education in Israel. The test for Israeli educators will lie in the way they confront this problem as well as in the kinds of solutions adopted.

NOTES

1. Martin Buber, "The Spirit of the Orient and Judaism," in *On Judaism*, ed. Nahum N. Glatzer (New York: Schocken Books, 1972), p. 60.

2. Ibid., p. 62.

3. Ibid., p. 66.

4. Martin Buber: *Der Jude und sein Judentum*, [The Jew and his Judaism] *Gesammelte Aufsätze und Reden* (Köln: Joseph Melzer Verlag, 1963), p. 710.

5. Martin Buber: "The Holy Way," in *On Judaism*, pp. 108–48.

6. A. E. Simon: *The Line of Demarcation*, Arab and Afro-Asian Monograph Series 12, Givat Haviva, 1973.

7. Ibid.

8

Aesthetics and Aesthetic Education

Aesthetics and aesthetic education were not the subjects of exhaustive treatment by Buber in any of his writings. But scattered throughout the corpus of his essays—in his anthropological studies, his examinations of the questions concerning mankind, his reflections on religion—Buber's comments, illuminations, and meditations on aesthetics, art, human creativity, the artistic act, distance and relation in art, and aesthetic education are in generous supply. These thoughts should be collected and put into coherent relation, so that the drift of Buber's thinking about art may be followed and light may be thrown on his concept of aesthetics and the education of aesthetics.

A discussion of Buber's concept of aesthetics should properly begin with the consideration of his book *Daniel; Gespräche von der Verwirklichung (Daniel: Discourses about Realization),* which appeared in 1913.[1] This creative and original work is probably Buber's first mature and fundamental statement of his philosophy. In time, as Buber ripened philosophically, he tended to disassociate himself from this early work; nevertheless, the dialogic basis of his thought is already there, although it is as yet not formulated so solidly as it would be in his later years. The core of the book consists of Buber's meditations on man's union with the world and with himself; Buber's principal thesis is that man has before him the possibility of establishing unity in the world, and that whenever he succeeds in this God is created for man. The motto with which Buber introduces his book is quoted from the words of the medieval mystical philosopher John the Scot (Johannes Scotus Erigena, 815–877), and reads: "God was miraculously created, and in a manner which words cannot express in the created universe." In a letter dated August 8, 1951, written to Maurice Friedman, one of the major scholars and translators of Buber's works, Buber not only rejects many of his formulations in the book but repudiates the motto.[2] Yet despite Buber's repudiation of *Daniel,* there is much to be gained from an examination of Buber's discussion in the book of the two classes of relation that man establishes with his environment, with mankind, and with objects. Buber calls one kind of relation *realization,* and the other *orientation.*

"Orientating" man, according to Buber, is unconcerned about a particular object per se, but is only interested in the benefits that man derives from it, in its context and in the state of advancement to which he can bring it. This is the way science and technology relate to objects. By contrast, "realizing" man is altogether subject to the particular object to which he stands in relation; he experiences it with all his senses, indeed lives it. Realization has to do with those situations of exalted experience in life that arise in moments of intense experience and perception. To realize means to place experience under an obligation to no object other than itself; here we have the source of the creativity and daring of the human spirit. Whereas by orientation man merely sets objects in an order and draws connections between them, realization gives rise to a situation in which the totality of the human personality is engaged in an integrated experience. The faculty of realization is strongest in the creative man, in whom the soul's capacity to realize reaches such a pitch of concentrated energy that he creates reality for everyone.

To explain his idea of realization, Buber cites three examples, the first of which is the poet and his manner of using language. The poet's use of language is unlike that of other men. He raises himself to a plane of language high above that of normal, everyday speach; he employs words in a manner that is richer in significance, more lofty than is the wont. The poet has both the ability and the privilege to endow words with new meaning. In fact, language takes on the usages that are created by the poet through his special spiritual experience of the world. Orientating man makes each experience dependent on another, connects things, and learns about one thing from another, whereas realizing man makes the experience dependent on itself alone so that it, exclusively, saturates the whole of him. In order to suitably express his experience, the poet must shatter the trivial routine of the language in common use, which is incapable of expressing the one-time creative experience, and invent a special universe of language that is entirely new in the relation of its elements and in its structure.

The power of realization is stronger in the child and in primitive man than it is in the adult who lives in the complex, intricate, and diffuse reality of technological civilization, and who is dedicated to the principle of orientation. Both the child and primitive man retain the full power of realization, of making experience actual. In them, orientation has not yet canceled their potentialities to actualize.

Creative man, who is dedicated with his whole being to his creation, is the greatest of realizers. But whoever strives to lead a life of replete realization is driven into a condition of solitariness. Complete realization requires the whole of a man; it calls on him to render up all the energies of his spirit, and even of his body. Although realization cannot operate at *all* times (were this the case, then man would become a god), nevertheless, a life exclusively dedicated to orientating and untouched by realization will end in spiritual vacuity. The life of a man alternates, therefore, between orientating and realizing, and moments of full realization are for him those in which his spirit rejoices and is exalted, and which bring in their wake moments of orientation.

In *Daniel,* Buber speaks extensively of the repression in modern times of the potentiality of realization by the drive toward orientation. This tendency represents man's alienation from himself, his transformation into mere object. Self-realization having been lost to him, man deceives himself instead with illusory substitutes, with external achievement that is not life itself; he escapes from full self-realization requiring concentration to the diversions among which his energies are dispersed. Hugo Bergmann, commenting on Buber's analysis, correctly observes: "Since these words were written, this apparatus of dispersal and diversion has been augmented beyond measure, and has enabled men to spend their lives in perpetual flight from authentic existence, from the summons which calls out to man and says to him: 'Be thou!' "[3] Today a mere handful realizes while multitudes implement, perform, and achieve. These many surrender themselves to the pressures of orientation. They accept goals that they already know how to achieve; they possess knowledge and accomplishments, but because they fail to realize experience wholly, they only exist and do not in fact live. Theirs is a substitute for life, a surface existence in which life's substance is exchanged for its husk, to which they apply the elegant epithets of culture, religion, progress, tradition, and intellectuality. Buber dismisses all of these by exclaiming mockingly: "Alas, a thousand inauthentic masks!"[4]

Education has a valuable lesson to learn from Buber's summons in *Daniel* to enhance realization and to desist from the concealment behind surfaces; to refrain from evading realization and seeking refuge in substitutes; to have the courage to live authentically; to augment the concentration of energies rather than disperse them in the pursuit of diversion.

Dispersal and diversion are instruments of orientation. But orientation can be served as well by science and any number of other systems of perceiving the world. Irrationality opens like a frightening chasm at the feet of man, who can confront this abyss in one of two ways. He may, with the help of his orientative faculty, avoid looking in, or he can gaze directly into it, realize the irrational, and, in the full intensity of the moment, assimilate the experience into his innermost being. The man who leads a life of realization perpetually risks everything. His truth is not fixed, nor does it exist statically, but is emergent. Orientating man desires security, needs to know his goal; he wants the guidance of general truth and requires stable laws that will not betray him. Realizing man, on the other hand, lives the truth that he creates from the depths of his inwardness.

Buber grapples continually in *Daniel* with the problem of creating a unity out of the duality of realization and orientation. In the chapter called "Conversation after the Theater," Buber uses a series of examples taken from the experience of theater in order to illustrate the types of polarity that occur in life, and to describe the dialogics which create unity. The first polarity is that of tragedy, in which unity arises from conflict and choice; the second is love, in which unity is created by identification. But the category of duality that is important to aesthetics is Buber's third, wherein the problem of duality is resolved by metamorphic transformation. When the actor identifies so completely with the character whom he portrays that he seems to surrender his own soul and enter into that of the persona, duality is reconciled by the identity achieved through transformation. This process represents the powerful unifying energy that is contained in art.

These ideas of Buber's call for a brief consideration of the relationship of his aesthetic concepts to the philosophy of Henri Bergson, with some of whose principles Buber is in sympathy, while differing with him on a number of significant issues. Bergson examines the nature of art in order to learn from the artist's intuition about philosophical intuition as a whole. Bergson believes that we arrive at absolute reality not by way of conceptual thought but by a vault taken into the very heart of experience through the exercise of intuitive observation. What can be accomplished through visual contemplation is beyond the powers of mere conceptual thought; whereas analysis estranges us from reality by decomposing and mutilating it, observation immerses us in the homogeneous and perpetually unfolding world of becoming. Observation can achieve that which is withheld from intellectual cognition, because the intellect operates by a system of symbols whereas observation identifies with existence itself. Great painters discern aspects of nature that heretofore had never been properly observed, and they impose their visions on the rest of us. The philosopher therefore, after the fashion of the painter, can also gaze at life directly, and, by doing so, can reveal it.

The flaw in Bergson's conception is his belief that should this visual philosophical approach prove to be successful it would become absolute consciousness and replace the variety of contradictory philosophies by a single philosophical system. Buber holds that such a claim is altogether foreign to art and artistic intuition. Although he accepts the assumption that every painter is a discoverer, Buber maintains that the painter reveals merely one aspect of the world, which is only a single aspect of the world's appearance and which expresses the special manner of some painter's particular visual perception. Unquestionably, this aspect of the world would never be revealed but for its being perceived by this particular painter, yet it has no autonomous existence outside of his unique optical perception of it. The world's aspect discovered by the painter is a reality born of relation, the product of encounter. "The art of painting," Buber remarks, "thrives in the limitless diversity and multiplicity of these aspects, to none of which, nor even to their totality, can we attribute the character of absolute comprehension."[5] Buber, examining the issue from the perspective of his own system, argues that were we to consider all of the arts together, we would find that the decisive act out of which the whole enterprise of art emerges is not the cognition of reality but the vital *encounter* with it, which is always being renewed and with which the senses merely interpenetrate.

When examining the problem of the relationship between the natures of man and art, Buber regards art as something formed by man—as the distinctive "formation"[6] of what is distinctively human. Thus, Buber formulates the problem by stating: "We ask about the connection between what is specific to the nature of man and what is specific to the nature of art."[7] Buber neither investigates the historical origins of art nor speculates about its psychological roots in the human spirit; his statement of the problem is purely anthropological, in the philosophical sense of the term. Indeed, Buber questions the soundness of separating aesthetics from anthropological philosophy, for were any philosophical inquiry able to claim to have created a doctrine of beauty that would embrace nature—were, in other words, aesthetics able to exceed the bounds of human creativity—then aesthetics and anthropological philosophy could be investigated separately. No such attempt having been made, however, aesthetics remains a subject that is integrally part of the study of anthropological philosophy.

Buber stresses that the artist is not nature's slave. Nevetherless, Buber argues that no matter to what degree the artist becomes independent of nature and estranges himself from it, he can only create his art by virtue of what he experiences in the life of the senses, in that domain of sensorily perceived events of primary significance in which the encounter with the world plays some part. In Buber's opinion, we can hope for an anthropological achievement by art only when we take into consideration man's dependence on that which abidingly exists even in man's absence.

Buber devotes much attention to the concept of art proposed by Conrad Fiedler (1841–1895), who was the first to consider the problem of the origins of art in human nature. Although greatly in Fiedler's debt for having raised the anthropological issue in respect of art, Buber is at fundamental odds with him over the principles to which Fiedler's formulation of the problem gives rise. Fiedler insisted that aesthetic philosophy must, first and foremost, address itself to the problem of art's origins in man's *spiritual* makeup. This restriction of the problem to the domain of the spiritual is rejected by Buber. In Buber's view, the question of the origins of art should apply to the whole of man and not merely to his spirituality, for the whole personality as both a corporeal and spiritual entity encounters the world. By augmenting the scope of the definition of personality to include the totality of body and spirit, Buber alters the very nature of the question.

Fiedler accorded special importance to consciousness, which he conceived of as having the power to dictate by decree, as it were, the giving of artistic shape to sensory perceptions. Here, Buber takes issue with Fiedler's attempt to establish an altogether too intimate association between art and the conscious mind, and even to subordinate art to consciousness. Were such the case—Buber argues—then we should find ourselves at a loss for the very essence of art, for what Buber calls the *principle of embodiment*. In Buber's words: "While thought and art consummate each other, they are not to be compared to an interlocking pair of limbs, but to two electrically charged poles between which a spark convulsively struggles to emerge."[8]

Fiedler maintains that the whole substance and vitality of aesthetics is in its visual aspect; further, that only the proximity between the artistic and the natural can guarantee that this decisive principle is not obscured in the work of art. Fiedler tried to demonstrate that in nature the visual value of objects is both insignificant and dispersed, so that it is perceived and concentrated only with difficulty. The task of art is to set the visual in order by such means as sifting, selection, and combination. It follows, therefore, that this principle, upon which naturalism builds its universe, is the product of man's intervention in nature.[9] Fiedler, however, is not referring here to nature as the whole visible world that is accessible to normal sensory perception but to nature's special visual formations which reveal themselves only through aesthetic activity. According to Fiedler, the test of the uniqueness of all authentic art is in the degree to which the artist can give expression to nature in a form unlike the commonplace guise under which it appears to every man's elementary perception and idea of it. Moshe Scwarcz, commenting on Fiedler's concept, observes: "Only by virtue of this two-fold significance of nature can we attribute validity to the naturalistic principle of the rootedness of aesthetic activity in nature as its ultimate origin and source." Quoting Fiedler, Scwarcz continues:

"Art is not nature in so far as art's primary significance is the emancipation from those circumstances in which consciousness is in need of the visible world and of rising above it; nevertheless, art is nature, for it is none other than that very process by which the way is paved for the appearance of nature in the distinctive hues that are its own." Hence, we can infer that the ambivalence of nature within the boundaries that are defined by its esthetic embodiment arises, on the one hand, from the physical and spiritual process which leads to the totality of manifestations of mankind's esthetic activity, and, on the other hand, from the manner in which esthetic activity becomes distinctive in the domain of physical and spiritual embodiments.[10]

Buber considers that Fiedler correctly regards the act of art to be a natural extension of the unfolding of a perceptual event, but he is in complete disagreement with Fiedler's attempt to relate his observation to the doctrine of the "world-creating self." In order to clarify his position, Buber refers to an observation by the German Renaissance painter Albrecht Dürer (1471–1528): "Since, in truth, art is fixed in nature, whoever is able to rip it out of her, he it is to whom art belongs."[11] Buber interprets Dürer's remark after his own fashion and in a manner that is very different from that of Fiedler and other commentators. Buber insists on taking the artist at his word, and assuming that Dürer intended his statement to be taken literally as written, Buber interprets it to mean, "that which is enclosed within another substance, although sometimes amenable to being extracted from it, cannot be withdrawn effortlessly nor gently, but must be vigorously and forcefully 'ripped out' of it,"[12] and this lies within the powers of the artist to do. The knowledge transmitted by the artist-teacher to his pupils is that of the artist's wrenching his art from nature. All that is accumulated in the imagination is disclosed and assumes corporality solely in and from within nature, and this disclosure is achieved by labor and is embodied in a novel work of art. The problem raised in this interpretation concerns what we take the word *nature* to mean. Buber believes that what Dürer called nature is simply the sensorially perceived world, which is grasped as something existent and abiding independently of ourselves. Dürer was fortunate to have accepted the world of the senses as mankind's habitat, the natural world in which man exists and upon which man is dependent.

Today, man is subject to the painful tension of the dichotomy between what is comprehended through sensory perception and exists within the sphere of his relation to ordinary reality and what underlies the material world and can only be grasped by means of physics and mathematics, while remaining altogether inaccessible to man in the reality of his experience. Physicists maintain that as a result of the present state of the science, the verbs "to be" and "to know" have lost their unequivocal meaning. In response to the position taken by physicists, Buber argues that the man who is not a physicist yearns to exist in a universe which can be imagined not merely analogically but in actual fact. Thus, he tells us: "What is impossible for a man to imagine is not the nature of the existence of the universe of time and space in its entirety, nor the nature of the existence of each of its parts, nor any number of like notions which directly contradict his every effort to imagine a universe; that is to say, it is impossible to comprehend them in terms of the universe in which life is actually lived."[13]

Buber observes that although experimentation upholds and confirms the fundamental formulations of mathematics—those symbolic representations whose nature is at once abstract and practical—it is precisely at this moment that the alienation of the world becomes frighteningly palpable, and the overwhelming sense of foreignness and insecurity arises in response to the contradiction between the two universes: one which is perceived by the senses and one which remains unintelligible. It is with this latter world, deprived of its likeness, in which man no longer feels himself to be at home, is intimidated by its strangeness, and suffers from a feeling of alienation, that we must begin if we wish to approach the kind of nature concerning which we should be able to say that art is contained in it and that art may be wrenched free of it.

Buber considers that human conduct is determined by countless connections created by movements toward some end and by perceptions of some thing. "There exists no movement which is unconnected, either directly or indirectly, with perception," Buber declares; "and there exists no perception which is unconnected more or less consciously with movement."[14]

Buber notes that a living organism, as a rule, perceives no more than what circumstances require of it to perceive; it moves entirely within a functional orbit and it is usually altogether ignorant about objects and realities which

are extraneous to its needs. Nature, however, aspires to a state of comple-
tion, yearns to be perceived, and so awaits one whose novel character will
make it possible for him to perceive available reality by maintaining the
distance between it and himself, by separating it from himself and holding it
up for his own inspection. "It is by this one," Buber asserts, "that nature in
fact becomes what it is: a whole likely to become manifest part by part."[15]
Man exists in nature not merely as a kinetic creature, that is to say by virtue
of his vital activity alone, but as a perceptive being as well. Man's sensory
presence within nature, his confronting of nature (or, more accurately, of the
x which animates man, which lacks any of the characteristics that make up
its share in the world of sensations during its encounter with man, and about
which man has no real knowledge) is a natural act in which the union between man and nature takes place.

Buber explains that nature and man come into existential encounter when
nature transmits stimuli to man's senses and there emerge out of this encounter the images which fill man's universe of sensations with a blaze of
color and a profusion of sounds: "It itself—the universe of the senses—
issues forth from the encounter between being and being."[16] The images
which arise from the meeting between man and nature constitute a special
reality which is accorded a symbolic status. Thus, Buber observes: "Opposite to that composite within the x—which is itself without visible form when
it encounters me—there emerges a clear visual analogue, which, from this
moment forward, takes x's place in the capacity of a substantial reality
within nature, and whose existential nature depends on me and my like."[17]
In art, a cooperative though unintentional transaction occurs between man
and nature. Within man's perceptual faculties there takes place an operation
of connecting and demarcation, separation and matching, out of which unity
emerges taking on the substance of form. Buber holds that as the extent of
truth or existential fidelity in the transaction increases, so will this transaction assume visual shape. The visual, according to Buber's definition, "is the
fidelity of the bestowal of form on the unfamiliar, a fidelity which acts in
collaboration with the unfamiliar. This is not fidelity to the phenomenon, but
fidelity to being—a being which is unattainable although we exist in relation
with it."[18]

Something that is embedded in nature is retrieved and brought to light by
human perception; however, it is not art. Buber defines it as "visuality."
Every perception is inclined towards form but only the artist adds to the
primary world's configuration, which is the making of every man *qua* man, a
configuration of a second world. This configuration of the artist is the giving
of consummate form, whose nature is highly personal, and is manifest thus,
in an infinite variety of patterns. Perception extracts out of being the world
of which man has need; it conveys to man's sensorium the data he requires
in order to survive. Yet there also exists a tendency that strives to exceed
the limits of merely filtering the world's stimuli. This tendency is realized in

art: "And the visual, as well as the art which is established by it," Buber observes, "vault beyond the limits of need, and transform the permissible into the necesssary."[19]

Art behaves in a way that is different from manner in which perception operates. The artist does not transform whatever it is that he has before him into something objective but shapes it into a plastic form. A significant act is added to perceptual activity, one that transforms that which is present to the artist into what Buber calls the "formation" or *maatsav*. (*Maatsav* is Buber's own coinage in Hebrew, and signifies "that which is formed"; the word is derived by Buber from the verb *itsev*, meaning to "form, fashion or mold." For an explanation of Buber's preference for the word *formation* over *creation*, see note 6 of this chapter). Buber employs the concept here of "formational power." Formational power transforms the parts of what is perceived into entities complete unto themselves, and creates the freedom within whose sphere objects take on an existence of their own. Keeping this point in mind, we can more clearly understand Buber's meaning when he asserts: "The confrontation of art is enacted between the artist's being—not his perception alone, but his being—and the being of x. In so far as he is an artist, he perceives x as an artistic perception, with the aim, that is, of giving complete form, for the sake of the emergence of the formation [*maatsav*]."[20]

Hence, Buber repeatedly argues that art is revelation and disclosure. The artist's imagination is essentially revelation; as he embodies he also reveals. To illustrate his meaning, Buber tells the story of Beethoven's strolls, during which the composer would walk, pencil and music paper in hand. Stopping now and then as if listening attentively, the composer would raise his eyes and then lower them, and jot down his notations. Having told the story, Buber comments: "And here we have a picture that seems almost mythic, and one that bears witness to the fact of this reality. The artist's imagination is in its very essence a revelation by means of the giving of form."[21]

In all the arts, with the single exception of poetry, the artist's aesthetic confrontation with the world is uniquely determined by a single sense. The artist exists solely within one ambience, which is either optical or acoustical. The source of poetry, however, is not the confrontation with the world by means of a single sense but by means of "the primeval structure of man *qua* man," as Buber defines it; "by the primeval structure whose beginning is in sensory experience and whose outer limits are the heavens of the spirit's power to symbolize—that is, language."[22] Whereas the other arts draw upon the domains of time and space, for the art of poetry, language constitutes a third fundamental principle.

Buber defines dialogue to be the fundamental form in which being is cast. In Buber's system, neither the *I* nor the *Thou* can exist separately; there exists only the *I-Thou* relation, which is prior to both *I* and *Thou*. Man is transfigured into the authentic *I* by entering into a direct and unmediated relationship—which is the *Thou* relation—with the other person. Similarly, neither the *I* nor the *Other* can exist apart, but there exists only an *I-Other* relation, which is a relation of a purely technical nature, reserved for routine affairs and practical ends and in which the character of the *Other* is assumed by the other person. As Buber observes: "The primal I-Thou utterance cannot be expressed except with a man's whole being," whereas "the primal I-Other utterance can never be expressed with a man's whole being."[23] Thus, the *I,* although in its very origin is inherent in man, assumes substance by way of the *Thou*'s encounters and relations; nonetheless, the vitality and immediacy of personal relation risks giving place to an attitude which is devoid of the sense of affinity, and which transforms the world into an object that is comprehended in intellectual categories belonging to the *I-Other* relation. Buber draws a clear distinction between the "relation" of *I-Thou* and "experience" and "knowledge," which have to do with the *Other.* By experience and knowledge, both the *I* and its object are condemned to a condition of cold indifference; the object, when used as a mere instrument, never becomes a part of the unfolding of an event, and the self that uses has no part in the world of the objects it exploits. "Experience is not the transaction of an event taking place between itself and the world. But the *I-Thou* relation exists, so to speak, midway between the *I* and the *Thou,* and constitutes an authentic relation of mutuality."[24]

Artistic creation, according to Buber, represents a bipolar relationship. Buber tells us that art is not a subjective activity taking place within the soul of it maker, but the outcome, rather, of encounter with phenomenon, which appears to the soul and summons it to release the potentiality of action. It is for the artist to enact the *I-Thou* in respect of the manifest image. Creation, in short, is dialogue. While giving form, the maker of art utters "Thou" even if the word is not shaped by the artist's lips. Buber holds that art is entirely the relation between the essence of humanity and the essence of things, and that it constitutes that very dialogic middle region taking on the guise of image. He maintains, moreover, that by the artist's visual contemplation of a particular object presented to him, that image is made accessible to the artist which he informs with shape and out of which he creates his art. The creation itself is present even when it is unobserved by man, but it is also dormant and without actual existence until man releases it from its sleep.[25]

The emergence of form is considered by Buber to be a potentiality that is located within man's being. Thus, Buber meditates on a cup that was fashioned long ago by a Japanese potter, and is amazed how much the cup seems to be the work of nature:

> On the clay one could see the delicate imprint of fingers, and one had the impression that the creative power of nature had merely passed through the man's hand, using it to accomplish its own work. And so it is that from the soul's womb—and not, as it were, from our own seed—that the forms

of art, intelligence and society are begot. At times, the soul was without so much as an initial awareness of this form, but only an imagined shadowy semblance; and now that it is born, so simple and rounded is its shape that we find it dificult to believe that it is the child of our very own soul.[26]

The idea of form already latent in matter, of an image destined to be delivered from the material in which it is impressed and awaiting its realization by the artist, is expressed in the work of a number of sculptors, among whom Michelangelo and Rodin figure most prominently. Ernst Simon, calling attention to these masters, notes that these sculptors leave unworked stone around their figures, which have the appearance of emerging from the raw material as if being born from it.[27]

Buber considers this concept in the light of the French poet Paul Valéry's idea that the order of the universe presents itself to the artist as chaos and matter without form, so that the artist should consummate what has been left incomplete. In response to Valéry, Buber makes the point that the Doric column is no mere supplement to a cosmic order which is already in existence, but arose in the process of labor done according to proportions which had until then remained latent. Proportions, dimensions, and pleasures are ever being revealed anew by art.

"Art is neither a recording of naturalistic objectivity nor a gazing into spiritual subjectivity," Buber tells us. "Art is the undertaking and the product of the relationship between human essence and the essence of objects; it is the intermediary sphere that has taken on an image."[28] Buber makes this observation while analyzing "distance" and "relation," which he conceives of as the twofold origin of the essence of the human. He begins his examination of the subject by considering the relation to objects. Although there exist creatures who will use a branch to reach a distant fruit, or who crack the shells of nuts with the aid of stones, these creatures never preserve the tool that they use nor do they accord it a special place in the world. The tools are temporary and acquire no permanence in the animal's consciousness as instruments possessing special properties that make them useful. Man alone puts objects at a distance, endows them with autonomy, and regards them as tools to which he continually returns in order to make use of them. The tool preserves its recognized and familiar nature as a particular object that is available for use by man. Buber explains his point by observing:

The ape is capable of manipulating a branch as a tool; but man alone can endow this branch with a distinct existence of its own, by which it becomes, now and ever more, "weapon" to be repeatedly made use of. From this point forward, all work carried out on it in order to make it more perfectly the staff it ought to be does not alter its essential nature: *techne* merely realizes what has been separated and distinguished through a primal separation and distinction by the agency, shall we say, of a primal *nomos*.[29]

Here, then, the activity of toolmaking is explained. But what of the making of art? In aesthetic creation, a new dimension is added, for in art we witness an act performed that is without a prior form or image and whose scope exceeds the narrow confines of technical purpose. In Buber's view, man is not satisfied merely to place the objects he makes use of at a distance and to endow them with autonomy. Man has also the wish to enter into direct relation with objects and to stamp them with the seal of his relation to himself, "not for him the mere use of them," Buber says of the relationship between man and objects, "nor does even the strength with which he grasps them ease his mind; he is fulfilled when they become his in another way: when he stamps them with the image and form of his relation to them."[30]

Buber considers that man, unlike other creatures, confronts the world from a distance, and can at all times enter into relation with it. This twofold relationship is nowhere more evident than in language. According to Buber, it is solely man who speaks because he alone has the capacity to address something which is other than himself, and he can do so for the very reason that it is different and confronts him at a distance. When, however, man addresses that other thing, he also enters into a relation with it. "Nevertheless, the creation of language also signifies a new function of distance," Buber argues; "for even the most primitive speech is not an end in itself, as is an outcry or the sounding of an alarm; rather, man extracts the word from himself and deposits it in being. And the word exists and abides, a linguistic presence gathering strength by perpetually being revitalized through true relation—through the spoken nature of the word."[31]

Poetry, Buber maintains, is discourse; it is speech addressed to the *Thou,* which assumes the guise of whoever the partner in discourse may be. In consideration of the status of poetry as speech, Buber raises the question of whether the content of poetry may be tested, as is dialogue, by the standard of truth. Buber's answer is both affirmative and negative: "Every authentic poem is also truth; but this truth exists outside of every relation for the sake of expressing something communicable. We designate by the title "poem" that verbal image which appears only rarely and by which we assimilate a truth which can assume verbal form in no way other than this: by image."[32]

Buber's observations on this point assume importance not only for the understanding of poetry but also for the methods by which poetry is taught. In the first stage of analyzing a poem, teachers customarily lead their pupils in a paraphrase of the poem. In Buber's view, any paraphrase deprives a poem of its truth, because the poem's existence is solely defined by its verbal image. Buber argues, and with considerable justice, that an analysis concerned with understanding something other than the way in which the poem's image is expressed must end by misconstruing the poem: "That conceptualization whose established aim is to elucidate and make familiar something cognizable misconceives the poem's true structure and misconstrues the poem's truth."[33] Teacher's of literature, many of whom are prone to such misconstructions, would do well to take Buber's warning to heart.

In discussing the subject of the creative impulse in respect of the source of the urge and capacity to give form, Buber addresses himself to the significance of the phenomenon of the artist. Buber attempts to resolve the problem of why man is not content to remain passive in his encounter with the *x* and let the sensory world take on form as it will. Why, in other words is man required to set his shaping faculties in motion and to give form in novel ways? To resolve the problem, Buber takes the situation of encounter for his starting point. Man, Buber asserts, desires more than what the senses offer; he wants to plumb the depths of visual form in order to establish form by the work of his own hand.

Buber identifies two interrelated tendencies to which man is prone— namely, the reluctance to be content with the gratification of need, and the desire for consummated relation. Neither the fulfillment of need nor the pursuit, through play, of something beyond need are sufficient to satisfy man. Buber argues that when the quality that marks the private self is aroused in man, so, too, is his reluctance to confine his fulfillment merely to what nature offers him and to the bonus to which he treats himself when he is at play. At such times, there emerges in man the "yearning for consummate relation." Describing this process, Buber observes:

> Relations which are incomplete belong to the substances of the world of utility and to what is acquired or accrues in the course of man's play. But a man who becomes a personality strives to exceed these bounds. He is no longer content to exist within those limits and that stage which are necessary in order to overcome the perpetually raging adversities of existence and in order to take part in the disciplined license of play. A loftier aspiration comes into existence; one in which there is a consciousness of the essence of personality.[34]

In opposition to the world's estrangement from man and man's own alienation, there exists, according to Buber, a tetrad of forces by which man is raised above his natural state and which establishes humanity as an autonomous existential domain. Buber defines these forces as consciousness, love, art, and faith. When considering the subject of art, Buber stresses that the artist yearns to live and to enact a complete relation within the sensory sphere toward which his art is directed. This the artist accomplishes by the giving of visual and plastic form. "He does not copy the form," Buber observes, "nor, for that matter, does he deviate from it, but impels it upwards—without necessarily doing so within the confines of the individual objects, but within the full potentiality of the single sense; as that sense becomes manifest to him, he thrusts it upwards to the limits of its perfection, to its reification in a consummately modeled form, and the whole of the visual or acoustical field is always immersed in a new form."[35]

The faculty of endowing with form is the property of the artist. This faculty, moreover, is confined to a specific sense, such as the visual and acoustic, within which the artist realizes his art. According to Buber, there is no way to pass from one sphere to another; although it is possible to experience the encounter of these domains, this experience will not lead to the complete relation that is achieved by the giving of visual and plastic form. Buber's ideas on this point call to mind those expressed by Paul Valéry in connection with an experience the poet describes in his essay "Poetry and Abstract Thought":

> While strolling, I hummed a tune to a poem, or, more accurately, a tune hummed itself using me as its instrument. This melody became increasingly intricate and complex, and its reasonableness was far in excess of all that I was able to create by means of my normal aptitude for rhythm——
> —in vain had I been graced by the gift that had been granted to me; I was unable to do anything with this gift, which, had it been given to a musician, would doubtless have acquired value, form and continuity. As for myself, these rhythmic forms, conjoining, intertwining and separating within my soul, uselessly offered me the possibility of a creation whose harmonic and intricate form, seen from afar, left me desolate and despairing before my own ignorance. . . . It is here that the profound difference exists between the spontaneous fecundity of the spirit, or more accurately, of the totality of our sensibilities, and the formation of works of art.[36]

In his essay "On education" Buber applies the term "creation" in its original sense—that is, God's divine commandment, by which the world was created out of a void—to man's faculty to give form. The term has acquired currency as a word describing the faculty that exists in all men and which needs only to be nurtured in order to be made actual. Art is the sphere within which the faculty of the production of objects attains its most complete state. Buber believes that all men are favored to varying degrees with some form of this ability. "These potentialities must be developed," Buber tells us, "and the education of the whole personality must be based on them—on this natural activity of the self."[37]

Buber speaks of an autonomous drive, which he calls "the instinct to make things" and which cannot be derived from man's other urges. This instinct, which is already in evidence in the infant, accounts for the desire to witness the emergence of form out of material which to the senses appears to be without form. The child wishes to participate in the process of the formation of things. Buber cautions that this instinct should not be confused with what he calls "the instinct for keeping busy," which he maintains does not exist at all: "What is important is that by one's own action, performed in a state of feeling which is at the height of its intensity, there emerges something which heretofore had not been, which had as yet neither existed nor been created."[38]

Buber is expecially insistent that the instinct to make things cannot alone lead to the establishment of the two requirements of authentic human existence: "partnership" and the "relation of mutuality." Buber elaborately describes the isolation of man in the role of creator. Although creative man is free and master of his deeds, he remains solitary; even when his art is understood and accepted by an enthusiastic public, creative man finds no release from his solitude: "Only when someone grasps his hand, not as 'creator' but as a fellow creature lost in the world, in order to be his companion, friend or lover, can he come to know mutuality and acquire a share in it. Education which is based merely on the development of the instinct to make things is likely to bring down upon mankind a new and most painful solitude."[39]

Buber is aware of the interdependence of art and the whole of man's cultural activity. This interdependence of art and culture is examined by Buber in his essay "On the Nature of Culture." Buber begins his consideration of the subject of culture from the perspective of sociologists who argue that culture, rather than being a homogeneous entity, is made up of two aspects, which they identify as "the process of civilization" and "the dynamics of culture." In the end Buber rejects the distinction between culture and civilization, and even discerns in the fact of this separation both a symptom and an expression of cultural disintegration. Nevertheless, our discussion would perhaps benefit from an examination of the distinction drawn in a number of definitions of civilization and culture, and from a consideration of Buber's antipathy toward the attempt to separate the two realms.

The process of civilization is, according to Buber, "the penetration of the mind into all of the precincts of experience; the refinement of experience by intelligence; the rationalization of experience."[40] This process is constituted by the growing influence of intelligence on the representation of the world and the self; on the rational formation of the scientific, practical, and purposive order of reality; and on the realization of this order by the creation of an apparatus of tools and regimens. The dynamics of culture, on the other hand, are, "the motions by which the soul expresses itself; they are the soul's desire and exertions to acquire its essential form; in contrast to this movement, everything which is contained in available reality is merely the raw material out of which form is fashioned."[41] According to Buber, consciousness is the sum and essence of civilization, whereas spiritual truth stands in the same relation to culture. Civilization has to do with the world already in existence and does no more than reveal that world; culture, however, is engaged in creation. Thus, culture is a one-time occurrence, and civilization is collective and cumulative. Culture cannot be amassed or inherited; each generation in turn must re-create it because it is a direct expression of the human spirit. The objects of civilization are a means to an end—those of culture are significant in themselves.

Buber, arguing on historical grounds, concludes that at no period during which a higher culture has flourished can we observe a significant distinction between culture and civilization. Drawing on the examples of the ancient cultures of Greece, Japan, and China, Buber attempts to demonstrate that this distinction appears in none of them; rather, he argues that each of these cultures contains what he calls a *system of life:* "The system of life of a people who are in the first bloom of their existence is a vital unity of all the components of life and their domains, whether spiritual or material; it is a unity which is based on a sole principle, which is not conceptual but hidden and felt, and whose entirety cannot be grasped by concepts but only intimated by them. This vital principle affects all of life's phenomena and all of the undertakings of a people. . . ."[42] The principle identified by Buber does not exert its influence through the conscious mind; that influence is exerted by a vital force upon the forces of life, by the force of the center upon the forces of the periphery. Around the core of this influence all of life's aspects, all of its domains, phenomena, and enterprises are united. A homogeneous current, as it were, flows through them all, and, despite the changes of hue they undergo, a homogeneous form takes shape. The domains of culture become distinct and acquire autonomy in the course of a culture's development; nevertheless, they maintain their connection with the central principle and with one another. The moment this connection slackens or breaks, however, the culture loses its vitality.

Turning to classical Greece, Buber cites the example of Greek shipwrights who built their ships in the shape of birds, and argues that the difference between them and the sculptor who carved a figure of Apollo was one of degree merely: "He as they has no intention to *give expression to his spirit,* but to make something which is to occupy a certain place and fulfill a certain purpose: its place—the temple, its purpose—ritual."[43] Thus, exposing the aesthetic functionalism in the work of both the craftsman and the artist of ancient Greece, Buber makes the point that it is a mistake to apply esthetic standards to these cultural undertakings and to regard them as "expressions" of culture, when the latter is conceived in terms of the distinction between culture and civilization. "The whole modern idea of expression as the essence of the creation of art becomes insignificant when considered against the enormity of objective reality, which we gauge by the walls of a building much as we gauge antediluvian beasts by their skeletons."[44]

Buber remains faithful to his basic thesis that true culture is the unity of the spirit active in all spheres of experience: in the sphere of the ordering of life and in the sphere of its exaltation; in the domain of overt purposiveness and in the one whose purpose is hidden. Indeed, it is the relation between all of these spheres that testifies to the inner truth of cultures. In this connection, Moshe Scwarcz is entirely correct when he observes: "This view of the fundamentally ordered nature of human culture reveals the core of Buber's esthetic concept, despite the fact that his observations and assumptions concerning the ways in which culture is revealed and made manifest are rooted (in their latter significance) in man's fundamental conscious and behavioral attitude towards his environment. This attitude is, in fact, a mark of the realistic and pragmatic basis of Buber's esthetics."[45]

Buber is aware that it is impossible to understand the homogeneity of culture without grasping the dichotomy that exists in every cultural process. Buber's examination of some of the manifestations of this dichotomy and his discussions of some of the major problems connected with cultural activity have important implications for education. He lays stress, for example, on the two aspects of culture: creation and tradition. According to Buber, culture derives its vitality from constantly renewed creativity; when such renewal is discontinued culture goes into decline. However, no new cultural enterprise can become an integral part of culture unless it participates in a process of transmission and reception and becomes a part of the activity of past and future generations. As Buber asserts: "Culture has two faces: revolution and conservation, that is, initiative and survival. Alone, each of these has great historical value, but they have cultural value only when they exist together."[46] Buber's words have particular relevance to our own age, characterized by unremitting renewal and changing realities, by rebellion against tradition and growing contempt for the accumulated heritage of the past.

Along with his observations concerning the dual nature of cultural activity, Buber sounds a serious note of warning. Culture molds the customs of men and raises the standards by which men form their associations; but at the same time, beyond its connections with life, culture also forms a universe of created objects, each of which exists independently, and all of which taken together constitute the special world of mankind. It is in respect of this latter world that Buber cautions education about its orientation: "That cultural existence which does not take into account the world of creations and does not acquire new meanings from this world faces the peril of being congealed into conventional courtesy, and that creation which has no need of the marking of the passage of time confronts the peril of the isolation of the spirit. Education can become the field in which the two activities are joined in an association of superior merit."[47]

Buber discerns two principles at work in the activities of culture: the growth of creation and the growth of consciousness. He maintains that periods of true cultural unity are those in which there is a union of form and consummating consciousness. In connection with these principles, Buber proposes the concept of "synthetic encounter." This concept appears have profound implications for the fields of literary and art criticism and to be of crucial importance to the teaching of art and literature. Buber's notion of synthetic encounter based on the union of form and consummating consciousness has particular relevance to our own age of scientism in the study of art and letters, when the technicians of criticism conceive the whole of their task to be the dismantling of the objects of their study into constituent parts while their labors yield a profligate accumulation of analyses of works of literature and the plastic arts. Education in our times, too, tends to adopt the methods of scientific analysis, and, as a consequence, is often driven to disown its own nature. Buber comments on the situation in education by observing: "Even in the field of education, the inner form cannot be revealed except by means of the educator's consummating consciousness which reveres the secret of growth. This, then, is what may be termed 'synthetic encounter', whereas detached rational consciousness can do no more than reveal a secret—not the *real* secret of growth but only its apparent secret— by means of false analysis."[48]

The concepts of synthetic encounter have exerted considerable influence on the great students of literature and art who have adopted a synthetic approach to their subjects.[49] The adherents of synthetic criticism assume a philosophical stance that is fundamentally antagonistic to the widespread tendency to treat the field of aesthetics as a thing apart. They reject the concept of creation imprisoned within itself, of the object of consciousness constituting an entirely self-contained entity. The analytic approach holds that the process by which an art object becomes known is one in which the whole is broken down into the various elements that make up its content and form. Literary analytics approaches the work of art as a complete and self-contained reality that is granted to us whole. The units of language, content, and form are regarded by the analysts of literature as evidence of the self-contained wholeness of a literary composition. The synthetic approach starkly contrasts with the method that uses analysis as the exclusive tool by which literature and the visual arts are studied. According to the syntheticists, the pleasure derived from the arts is the fruit of synthetic encounter, by which the scope of significant relations continuously expands and whose core of the union of form and consummating intelligence is increasingly enlarged.

In attempting to grasp the nature of culture, Buber proposes the following definition: "The communal formation of one society, which is conceived in the marriage of communal spirit and communal life—this, then, is culture."[50] Buber's definition raises difficulties, however. What of individual formations? According to Buber's definition, isolated creative undertakings cannot constitute culture. The realities of the poet, painter, and musician are no proof of the reality of a culture; nor, for that matter, can the existence of a vast public accessible to cultural values be taken to indicate the reality of a nation in possession of a culture. For properly speaking, *only the communal formation of society is culture*. If such is the case, how then is communal formation made possible? Buber is well aware that art is the product of individual labor and that only individuals have been great creators of art. Although communal activity takes place in science, technology, and social organization, it is uncharacteristic of either art or metaphysics, about both of which Buber observes: "When we confront some of the great enterprises in these fields, we sometimes have the sense that here is the result of man's utterest isolation."[51]

By analyzing the significance of communal spirit and communal existence, Buber attempts to grapple with the problem raised by his definition of culture. On the basis of his investigations of examples offered by classical Greece and twelfth- and thirteenth-century Italy, Buber concludes that although no communal activity is taking place during the ripe phases of a culture, nevertheless art is, so to speak, an epitome, in the special idiom of the artist, of the communal life and spirit of a particular society. Buber maintains that a profound connection exists between an artist of genius and the people, a relation which Buber illustrates with a quotation from Goethe: "My work is the work of a collective world called Goethe."[52] However, Buber is unable to accept the idea implicit in Goethe's dictum that every work of art is the result of assimilation. Putting things in sharper focus, Buber remarks:

> If you investigate the nature of a novel shape present in any one of the major undertakings carried out in the prime of a period of culture—and most especially of a period which is in ascendancy—if you investigate the nature of the shape of a thought, a poetical rhythm, a line of architecture whose like cannot be discovered in the past and which, though seeming to be self-evident as if it had always been and is even now part of our world, you will find, in fact, that the formal basis of this shape has no personal character but that it has a kind of anonymity, a kind of unintentional objectivity, yet one which is like a part of nature; this is the mute sprouting out of the people's midst, the fruit of the pairing of communal spirit and life, communal formation.[53]

These processes find their expression in the work of the individual person of genius, in whose being the existence of the nation is concentrated.

Buber's concept of the relationship between the artist and the community at large puts into sharper relief his view of the way in which art is apprehended. Buber believes that the cognition of a work of art is nothing other than the encounter between the viewer, hearer, or reader with the art object. The work of art, Buber asserts, longs to be completed in the spectator's soul. The encounter with art is not one in which the work of art offers itself whole for passive reception but is an active encounter in which the spectator or auditor commits himself to finish what is left unsaid by the work of art, to reply to the questions posed by it, to enact a relation with it—in brief, to engage in dialogue. Buber expresses deep anxiety concerning the advent of formalism, by which artists no longer address themselves to general understanding and, instead, turn their art into the exclusive property of dissident groups, professionals, and the adherents of certain movements and schools. Buber's attitude toward formalism accounts for the unsympathetic view he takes of the extreme type of analytical criticism that investigates a work of art as if it were something entirely self-contained and explains Buber's preference for syntheticism, which integrates the encounter of a work of art with the whole complex of universal human experience, binds the person experiencing a work of art with the ages, opens him to the active perception of art, and binds the moment of his experience and enjoyment of art to history. Taking his cue from the teachings of the Baal-Shem-Tov, founder of the Hasidic movement, who believed that every encounter that a man experiences, no matter how small, has a hidden significance, Buber notes: "Even were our soul to attain the most exalted heights of culture, it would still lack the vital sap of creation should we fail to give to those minor daily encounters what they rightly deserve, so that the waters of life might issue out of them and stream into our soul."[54]

Buber's concept of aesthetics in relation to Jewish life and Jewish spiritual creativity are of special interest. Although Buber disagreed sharply with those who are drawn to the Bible merely as a source of aesthetic experience and pleasure, nevertheless, in his many books and essays dedicated to the subject,[55] he has taken great pains to understand the structure of the Bible in both artistic and historical terms.[56] In his interpretation of the Bible, Buber has consistently viewed its unity of content and form from a fundamentally aesthetic perspective:

> Under no circumstances and in no way can one fuse or refine a particular *content* from the unalloyed ore of the Bible unless everything remains in the homogeneous form which does not exist in separation—for a real poem has no existence in separation. Nowhere here can one pursue a given primary *what* which has clothed itself in this *how* and which, at the same time, can assume another *how*; everything in the Bible is an authentic utterance, and every separation of content from form seems to me to be the product of false analysis.[57]

Buber rejects any attempt to separate content from form; he opposes biblical scholarship which concentrates on the descriptive and ornamental aspects of biblical style. For Buber, the biblical text is a homogeneous verbal and aesthetic unity that transmits what it has to say by virtue of the entirety of its being and form; not by means of its vocables, images, similes, and metaphors but by means of its words. What is expressed in the Bible cannot be said in another way without acquiring another meaning; no single expression or word in the Bible can be exchanged for another, because the biblical version is the only verbal form that is appropriate to what is being expressed. Buber believes that there is no place in biblical studies for considering content to be something which may assume a given formal configuration but could just as well assume another pattern. Buber maintains that when the Bible is considered as a unity of content and form, it can be thought of as poetry, which he defines as: "That image, which need not be uncommon, formed by the word which announces the truth to us which cannot be expressed verbally except by this means—by means of this image."[58]

In his capacity as philosopher, interpreter, and translator of the Old Testament, Buber's consistent approach to biblical studies can be described by what Buber's collaborator in the translation of the Bible, Franz Rosenzweig, has called "the non-esthetic and supra-esthetic esthetics of the Bible."[59] In the course of his discussions of biblical "lead-words," for example, Buber discovers that these play a variety of important expressive roles both as aesthetic tools of the author and as the expressive means by which the precise significance of what is said is made emphatic and elucidated.[60]

The subject of aesthetics even makes its way into Buber's studies of Hasidic doctrine, which provide Buber with the opportunity to shed light on the relationship of Jews to aesthetic experience. In "The Hidden Light" Buber cites a parable told by Rabbi Israel of Ruzhin:

> Once, while many sages were gathered around his table, the Ruzhiner asked: "Why do people take issue with Maimonides?" One of the sages answered: "Because he says someplace that Aristotle knew more about the heavenly spheres than did the prophet Ezekiel." The Ruzhiner said: "Maimonides' words are true. Two men came to the King's palace. One had traveled throughout the world and, observing the luxurious furnishings and the treasures with an expert's eye, could not have his fill of seeing them. The second passed through the halls and said merely: "This is the King's house, this his regalia, and in only a little moment I shall see the face of my Lord the King."[61]

The Jew resembles the second man, who speaks only of seeing the face of the king, while paying no heed to the beauty and luxury of the ornaments of the palace. Although Hasidism esteems these ornaments, it is also aware that they have no existence in themselves. This is Hasidism's attitude toward melody, song, and dance, which of themselves are of no importance except as part of dialogue, as part of the discourse with God.[62] The aesthetic intention is weakened here, while beauty is the instrument of divine fulfillment. The Baal-Shem-Tov, interpreting the verse from II Kings 3:15, "And it came to pass, when the minstrel played, that the hand of the Lord came upon him," comments: "The minstrel who plays beautifully has a number of ulterior motives and is proud of the sound of his playing. Not so the instrument which he plays: it is inanimate and has no ulterior motive. This, then, is the interpretation of the minstrel's playing: if the minstrel can play with no ulterior motive, exactly as his instrument, then the hand of the Lord will come upon him."[63] Buber considers that the significance of song and dance in Hasidism is similar to that of painting in Zen Buddhism. Whereas silence is esteemed in the teachings of both Hasidism and Zen, in neither is this the result of the desire to abstain from oral expression, but stems from the wish to relinquish the use of conceptual language in connection with what is inaccessible to concepts. Zen monks are painters, but they never create art for its own sake. Hasidim, do not paint, dance, and make music, but, "All of this—" Buber declares, "song, painting and dance—are directed towards discourse and grasped in discourse."[64]

The Jews, in Buber's view, are spiritually and aesthetically closer in many ways to Orientals than they are to Westerners.[65] Buber classifies Occidental man as a "sensory type" and Oriental man as a "motor type."[66] The visual sense is dominant in sensory man. The victory of Hellenism in the fields of pure form and aesthetic refinements is the outcome of the hegemony of the sense of sight. In the man belonging to the motor type, vision, rather than being dominant, merely acts as an intermediary between the world that exists in a state of motion and the hidden motion of the body; the world reveals itself to him in the form of boundless motion which passes through him. The world takes hold of and penetrates Eastern man, while it merely confronts Europeans. All the characteristics that Buber discovers in Oriental man he explicitly attributes to Jews as well. Jews comprehend the world less from the isolated and distinct existence of its multifarious objects than from the relation between them, from their collective association with one another. Buber maintains that the Jew is in every way the opposite of the Greek, and he summarizes the differences between the two in the following way:

> The Greek says that the world must be conquered, the Jew that it must be consummated. For the Greek the world exists, whereas for the Jew the world is becoming; the Greek stands opposite the world and the Jew cleaves to it; the Greek knows the world from the mirror reflecting dimension, and the Jew knows it from the mirror of inwardness, of significance; for the Greek the act exists in the world, and for the Jew—the world is in the act.[67]

A discussion of Buber's concept of aesthetics and his view of aesthetic education would remain incomplete were we to omit a topic which, though it may appear to be of only marginal significance to our subject, nevertheless helps clarify a number of Buber's attitudes toward the aesthetic experience, the means by which it is achieved, and the use of drugs to stimulate aesthetic and mystical experiences. Buber examines Aldous Huxley's praises of the drug mescaline, whose effects on himself Huxley closely studied and described. Huxley claimed that what he saw under the drug's influence were not only merely hallucinations detached from reality, but his own immediate environment appearing to him in the guise of unexpected colors and the heightened presence of every object in his vicinity. Huxley compared his drug-induced visions to the perceptions revealed in cubist painting.

For Huxley, total aestheticism respecting objects is only the first step toward another kind of vision, which he regards as more sensitive, comprehensive, and exalted than normal perception, and which he characterizes as a "sacramental" vision of reality. In response to Huxley's claim, Buber observes: "In religion the word 'sacrament' signifies the preparation of the whole personality which, by its physical existence, has become worthy of coming into relation with the transcendental. Huxley, however, intends the expression 'sacramental vision' to mean only penetration and absorption into the depths of the sensory world."[68]

Huxley perceives the drug-induced state to be an escape from the personality and the environment. Huxley argues, moreover, that the desire for such a flight exists in all men. In his view, the longing to get outside of oneself is the desire for liberation from the material goals that enmesh the personality, and from the sphere of the personality's existence in a situation of ongoing and unfulfilled orientation. Buber rejects the idea of such flight, and argues that escape into drugs does not lead to a free participation in a shared existence, but rather to an immersion into an utterly private sphere with which the fugitive is united for a mere few hours. What Huxley treats as a chemical release, Buber considers to be "a release not merely from the petty self which is caught in the tangle of its own efforts to satisfy its needs, but also from the personality that participates in the partnership of the logos and the cosmos; a release from the summons—often highly inconvenient—to continue as a personality."[69]

Buber holds that Huxley's notion of release from the environment is actually flight rather than liberation. Buber grants that a man has a right to struggle with and to change his condition and environment, but he denies man's right to escape temporarily from the claims of his situation in order to escape into what Buber describes as the "condition of nullity." Buber maintains that the use of drugs is an escape of this kind.

The experience of total aestheticism induced by drugs, and the artist's desire to experience reality more deeply by means of drugs are subjects that would bear our closer scrutiny. Huxley argues that there are two stages to drug-induced intoxication. In the first stage, we perceive objects inwardly in the way that an artist sees them; both perception and experience assume great intensity, whereas objects take on greater depth and substance, and are illuminated by a rich inner light. In the second stage the subject enjoys, if only to a limited degree, a mystical experience.

Huxley holds that during moments of true creativity, the artist becomes disengaged from the world of commonplace perception and is raised to another visual plane that is unique to himself, thereby achieving the creative experience of the realization of new forms. At such times, the artist falls completely under the influences of his creative urge and creative powers. Huxley understands the process as having to do with a manner of seeing the world with heightened intensity simply because this is the way things are in reality. Buber, however, takes a different view of the matter:

That which we term "reality" always appears only in our personal relation with things whose essential nature is forever closed and sealed to us; but there are also personal relations which are freer and more immediate than others, and by which things are seen in a way which is sharper, fresher and more profound. Both creation and intoxication belong to this class of relations; however, the fundamental difference between these states is revealed in the fact that mescaline intoxication, for example, arbitrarily creates a change in our consciousness, whereas *the goal of the artist places him in a special and unarbitrary relation with available reality.* Hence, by willing that which is appropriate for him to will, he consciously realizes his act as an artist. *Rather than the intrusion of the arbitrary, there is the making of art.*[70] (Italics mine.)

Buber altogether rejects the concept of the escape of the artist. He believes that during the creative process the artist, rather than escape, is overpowered by something whose source is outside of himself. The artist is not immersed in a spiritual condition in which he is visited by his aesthetic vision but assumes the vision himself; rather than take flight, the artist dedicates himself entirely, both his vital personality and his private existence wholly, in order to persist in the task which has been imposed on him. Finally, Buber asserts that the flight from a shared universe to a private sphere when conceived as creative experience is no more than "an escape from the existential claim addressing itself to the personality and demanding to be confirmed and validated in ourselves. This is no more than an escape from the authentic discourse conducted in an idiom within whose domain response is demanded. And this response is the reply of responsibility."[71] Buber's observations concerning authentic dialogue in which response and the reply of responsibility are required constitute a fitting summation of Buber's aesthetic thinking and of the demands he makes on aesthetic education.

NOTES

1. Martin Buber, *Daniel:* Gespräche von der Verwirklichung [*Daniel: Dialogues on Realization*]. (Leipzig: Insel Verlag, 1913).

2. Maurice S. Friedman, *Martin Buber: Life of Dialogue* (London: Routledge and Kegan Paul, 1955), p. 38.

3. Samuel Hugo Bergmann, *Ha-filosofia ha-dialogit mi-kierkegaard ad Buber* [Dialogic philosophy from Kierkegaard to Buber] (Jerusalem: Mosad Bialik, 1973), p. 252.

4. Buber enlarges on this subject, which has important educational and cultural implications, in the chapter, "Von der Wirklichkeit" [About reality], *Daniel*, pp. 29–47.

5. Martin Buber, *"Bergson ve-ha-intuitsia"* [Bergson and Intuition], in *Pnei adam: Beḥinot be-antropolpogia filosofit.* [The Face of Man: Studies in Anthropological philosophy] (Jerusalem: Mosad Bialik, 1962), p. 430.

6. Buber is careful to avoid the word *yetsira* or "creation" in connection with the artist's work, and in its place uses the words *maatsav* or *mabad,* the first of which was coined by him and intended to convey the idea of "the object which is formed" and the second having the meaning of a "deed" or "action." His avoidance of *yetsira* depends on its association in the

Bible and in later Jewish tradition with God's creation of the universe, of man and of all living creatures out of the formless void.

7. Martin Buber, "Ha-adam u-maatsavo" [Man and what he forms], in *Pnei adam,* p. 132.

8. Ibid., p. 135.

9. Conrad Fiedler, "*Über den Ursprung der Künstlerischen Tätigkeit* (About the Origin of the Activity of Art), in *Gesammelte Schriften* (Munich: Piper, 1913), Vol. 1, pp. 137–369.

10. Moshe Scwarcz, *Safa, mitus, omanut* [Language, myth, art] (Jerusalem: Schocken, 1967), p. 312.

11. Buber, "Ha-adam u-maatsavo," p. 135.

12. Ibid., p. 136.

13. Ibid., p. 139.

14. Ibid., p. 140.

15. Ibid., p. 142.

16. Ibid., p. 143.

17. Ibid.

18. Ibid., p. 144.

19. Ibid., p. 145.

20. Ibid.

21. Ibid., p. 146.

22. Ibid., p. 147.

23. Martin Buber, *Be-sod siah: Al ha-adam ve-amidato nokhah ha-havaya* [Dialogue: About man and his confrontation with being] (Jerusalem: Mosad Bialik, 1964); see in addition Samuel Hugo Bergmann's lucid interpretation, "Ha-hashiva ha-du-sihit shel M. M. Buber" [The dialogic thought of Martin Buber], ibid., pp. xi–xlvi.

24. Bergmann, "Ha-hashiva ha-du-sihit shel M. M. Buber," p. xvi.

25. Martin Buber, "Al mahuta shel ha-tarbut" [On the nature of culture], in *Pnei adam,* p. 31.

26. Ibid., p. 384.

27. Ernst Simon, "Martin Buber, the Educator," in *The Philosophy of Martin Buber,* ed. Paul Arthur Schilpp and Maurice Friedman, (London: Cambridge University Press, 1967), p. 559.

28. Martin Buber, "Rahak ve-zika" [Distance and relation], in *Pnei adam,* p. 125.

29. Ibid., p. 124.

30. Ibid., p. 125.

31. Martin Buber, "Ha-mila ha-meduberet" ["The spoken word"], in *Pnei adam,* p. 184.

32. Ibid.

33. Ibid., p. 185.

34. Buber, "Ha-adam u-maatsavo," p. 148.

35. Ibid., p. 150.

36. Paul Valéry, *Poésy et pensée abstracts,* Zaharoff Lecture (Oxford, 1939), pp. 10–11.

37. Martin Buber, "Al ha-maaseh ha-hinukhi," in *Be-sod siah,* p. 239.

38. Ibid., p. 240.

39. Ibid., p. 243.

40. Buber, "Al mahuta shel ha-tarbut," p. 377.

41. Ibid., p. 378.

42. Ibid., p. 379.

43. Ibid., p. 380.

44. Ibid., pp. 380–81.

45. Scwarcz, *Safa, mitus, omanut,* p. 318.

46. Buber, "Al mahuta shel ha-tarbut," p. 383.

47. Ibid., p. 384.

48. Ibid., p. 385.

49. For an incisive discussion of this subject, see: Alexander Barzel, *Ha-siha ha-gdola: Masot al tarbut ve-sifrut* [The great discourse: Essays on culture and literature] (Rehavia and

Tel Aviv: Sifriat Poalim, 1971); also see my article, "Al ha-gisha ha-sintetit la-sifrut" [The synthetic approach to literature], *Moznayim* [Scales] (Kislew-Tebet, 1975):79–80.

50. Buber, "Al mahuta shel ha-tarbut," p. 388.

51. Ibid., p. 389.

52. Ibid., p. 391.

53. Ibid., p. 392.

54. Martin Buber, *Darko shel adam al-pi torat ha-ḥasidut* [Man's way according to the teaching of hasidism] (Jerusalem: Mosad Bialik, 1957), p. 46.

55. See especially, Buber's *Darko shel mikra* [The way of the Old Testament] (Jerusalem: Mosad Bialik, 1964); and *Malkhut ha-shamayim* [The Kingdom of Heaven] (Tel Aviv: Mosad Bialik "Dvir," 1950).

56. See my article, " 'Humanizm mikrai' be-mishnato shel Buber" [Old Testament humanism in Buber's Philosophy], in *Iyunim be-ḥinukh,* ḥoveret 3 (Shebat, 1975: 11–30.

57. Martin Buber, "Leshona shel bsora" [The language of tidings], in *Darko shel mikra,* p. 273.

58. Martin Buber, *Logos: Zwei Reden* [Logos: Two lectures] (Heidelberg: Verlag Lambert Schneider, 1962), p. 23.

59. Martin Buber, "Tirgum ha-mikra: kavanato ve-darkhav" [Translation of the Bible: its direction and its methods] in *Darko shel mikra,* p. 357.

60. See principally, Martin Buber, "Signon ha-mila ha-manḥa be-sifrei ha-tora" [The style of the lead-word in the books of the Pentateuch], and Ha-mila ha-manḥa ve-av-ha-tsura shel ha-neum [The lead-word and the archetype of the oration], in *Darko shel mikra.* pp. 284–307. Also see the introduction of Meier Weiss, "Be-sod siaḥ ha-mikra" [The Dialogue of the Old Testament], ibid. pp. ix–xxxiii; and Yehoshua Amir, "Buber ke-farshan ha-mikra" [Buber as interpreter of the Old Testament], *Amor (criteria),* 19 (1965); 26–29.

61. Martin Buber, *Or ha-ganuz* [The hidden light] (Jerusalem and Tel Aviv: Schocken, 1958), pp. 278–79.

62. See my article, "Torat ha-ḥasidut shel Buber ke-manof le-ḥinukh religiozi" [Buber's doctrine of Hasidism as an incentive to religious education], *Iyunim be-ḥinukh, (Studies in education)* ḥoveret 5 (Kislev, 1975):45–62.

63. Buber, *Or ha-ganuz,* p. 74.

64. Martin Buber, *Be-fardes ha-ḥasidut* [In the Hasidic garden] (Tel Aviv: Mosad Bialik "Dvir," 1965), p. 139.

65. The subject has been commented on by Avraham Klein, "Shlosha prakim be-torato shel Martin Buber" [Three parts of Buber's philosophy], *Iyun, Study* 3, 3 (1952): 136–50.

66. Martin Buber, "Ruaḥ ha-mizraḥ ve-ha-yahadut [The spirit of the east and Judaism], in *Teuda vi-y'ud: Maamarim al inyanei ha-yahadut, [Mission and Purpose, Essays on Judaism]* (Jerusalem: Ha-sifria ha-tsionit, 1960): 55.

67. Ibid., p. 61.

68. Martin Buber, "Raui le-yelekh ahar ha-meshutaf" [For those in pursuit of the shared], in *Pnei adam,* p. 163.

69. Ibid., p. 164.

70. Ibid., p. 166.

71. Ibid., p. 173.

9
Adult Education

Martin Buber was concerned with the practical application of the theory of adult education, a field to which he dedicated much thought and which formed the subject of a number of his published studies. The importance that Buber assigned to the subject can be gauged from the thoroughness with which he investigated the historical roots of adult education, examined the theories of adult education propounded by philosophers and educators, and evaluated the outstanding examples of adult-education programs carried out in various countries. This research formed the basis of Buber's attempt to work out an original approach to the field and to devise a pedagogical system of his own.

Buber observes that it is customary to apply the term *adult education* to a wide range of pedagogical activities whose purpose is the dissemination of a variety of beneficial information for the use and enlightenment of grownups. The assumption underlying these activities is that anyone taking lessons, attending lectures, and participating in study groups will add to his store of knowledge, enlarge the scope of his learning, and, ultimately, attain a higher degree of what we are wont to describe as "culture." Buber holds, however, that the mere addition of knowledge—the acquisition, that is, of a quantifiable sum of disparate items of information—hardly merits being called learning, which can only exist when information is organically integrated in a unified spiritual whole. Such unity cannot be achieved solely by the assimilation of the materials of study. Rather than the increment of knowledge, Buber calls for an activity that is at once critical and synthetic, for spiritual enrichment, for the personal reintegration of discrete facts. Learning, then, is not a rote accumulation and mnemonic hoarding of facts, but the critical and considered examination of information that is converted into "active knowledge" and becomes a constituent of personal behavior.

Buber's antipathy toward the mere accumulation and laying-in of unused information divorced from any significant context calls to mind Alfred North Whitehead's warning against what he termed "inert ideas,"[1] by which he meant ideas that are present in our conscious minds but which we neither examine nor recombine in new patterns and therefore make no actual use of. Similarly, Buber reveals an affinity with Nikolai Grundtvig's distinguished disciple, Kristen Kold, who held that the goal of adult eduction should be the nurturing and resuscitation of the mind's organically integrated activity. Buber demands that instead of having the learner's memory impressed with the greatest quantity possible of the data belonging to various disciplines, he should rather be taught in a way that his knowledge—that is the sum of his information—becomes an organic part of his existence. For such an aim to be achieved, the education of mature persons must be directed toward the education of the whole man.

Buber employs the German term for adult education, *Folksbildung*, which translates as "popular education" and whose second component, *Bildung*, embraces two meanings. One meaning refers to knowledge, learning, and the acquisition of information; a second signification of the word is "formation" in the sense of both "giving shape to" and "endowing with spiritual character." For Buber, education requires the simultaneous realization of both of the senses expressed in the German word. Addressing his Hebrew-speaking audience, Buber cautions against taking literally the Hebrew expression for adult education, *haskalat mevugarim*, in which the word for "education" (haskala) *is formed from the same root as the word for "mind" (sekhel)*. Consequently, the Hebrew term implies an appeal only to the intellect and seems to be directed at the acquisition of data, whereas Buber is concerned with the formation of the whole person.

Buber considers the main task of education to be the development of the active spirit. In the course of his school days an adult acquires a large and varied store of information. Therefore, the supplementation of knowledge is of no concern to adult education, whose principal function should be to teach mature persons to take the information they have acquired at school and their current experiences and to adapt them in an intellectually independent and purposive way so as to be able to form personal opinions that are soundly based on the reality of both their own lives and the life of the group. Buber maintains that the self-assurance of adults is not usually based on adequate grounds and causes them to exercise only an apparent control over the situations with which they are confronted in life. It is because of this circumstance that an ever-widening existential breach is formed between reality and appearance, thereby introducing into the lives of men a severe contradiction with damaging consequences. The function of education, according to Buber, is to undermine this false self-confidence and to awaken a person's spirituality so that he can attain authentic autonomy and learn to realize the life of the self as well as to serve the group of which he is a part.

Buber accepts the views of the philosopher Bernhard Bolzano,[2] who lectured on the subject of popular education at Prague between 1811 and 1871. Bolzano distinguished between two categories of opinion. One category is constituted both by the prejudices developed within society, which seem to exert their influence of themselves on young people, and by the deceptions by which individuals and groups purposely try to mislead the young. To this class of opinion Bolzano opposed those opinions that are arrived at by an individual through his personal confrontation with reality. Buber quotes Bolzano's opinion concerning the need to educate a youngster "by diligently training him to adopt good habits of reasoning so that he himself becomes conscious of the absurdity of the reigning prejudices of his environment and will not be led astray by every charlatan who intends to mislead him, but will intelligently examine what he is being told to see if indeed it is true and worthy of being believed."[3]

Buber notes that although we seem to be faced here by the advocacy of individualism or even anarchy, this is not actually the case. For in his essays on ethics, Bolzano establishes as a major principle the selection from among available courses of action that action which, after careful consideration of all possible effects, proves to be the one most likely to advance furthest some aspect of the common good. Bolzano recognized the importance of social responsibility and did not divorce the individual from humanity at large. Buber, following Bolzano, stresses the importance of the development of the spirit of independence in both the young and adults. Buber is not content to let the matter rest here. This independence of spirit must be realized within a "human community," which can only achieve its own social and cultural form when each and every one of its members possesses independence of vision and thought and joins in the common undertaking to create this form.

Buber observes that the very idea of adult education tends to arouse in us a certain degree of skepticism concerning its validity. Are we in any way justified, Buber asks, in speaking of the education of adult persons? To all appearances the adult is a finished being in whom nothing remains to be developed or altered, and on whom no influence can effectively exercise its power to change, arrest, or advance. Buber takes issue with this view of the adult personality. Although admitting that with the passing of youth a man tends to become less tractable and consequently less amenable to formative influence, Buber argues that this does not mean that a man's capacity to change has been diminished; rather it is the readiness to respond to influence that has deteriorated. The adult believes himself to be sufficiently educated and can see no sense in submitting himself to further education. Although he will readily admit to gaps in his knowledge that he is willing to fill by attending classes and listening to lectures, the adult will altogether resist being reconciled to the idea that educational goals are involved here.

In Buber's view, so long as adult education confines itself to the task of transmitting information and providing supplementary instruction, it can do no more than exert an occasional and haphazard educational influence. The education of adults will fulfill its real purpose only when it helps those in its charge to overcome their resistance to being educated and inspires them to genuine independence both in their perception of reality and in their active relation to it. Buber believes that the only development worthy of consideration is self-development, and that the task of adult education is to provide the student with help and guidance in educating himself.

Doubtless such a goal is exceedingly difficult to achieve. Buber is clear about the need to struggle against adult resistance to being educated. A grown person is never disposed to admit that his education is somehow defective or incomplete and that he must submit himself to a program of reeducation that aims at nothing short of bringing about his total spiritual transformation. The readiness to be reeducated and to undergo a revolution of personal values appears only in times of great crisis when the rush of events breaks through the protective walls of the ego and the self's defenses crumble; when both the private and public worlds are undermined. Such crises in the lives of a person or a society, by forcing the barriers of complacency, make the individual and the community accessible to reeducation. Buber holds that there are situations in the history of nations when a people become more pliant and more amenable to being reshaped, and when goals previously thought to be unattainable suddenly become possible. Such times are considered by Buber to be moments of the spirit's ascendancy—to be seized upon and used to advantage by the educator before the old barriers can be restored.

Times of crisis, however, are never propitious for undertaking a methodical examination of the opportunities for the educator to exert his influence on adults. The adult's resistance to being educated cannot be overcome by efforts to change him from without. "In general," Buber tells us, "the adult will never agree to submit to an alien influence aimed at inducing him to become someone other than what he is at that moment. But he will often be prepared to admit that he must be what he is, only more perfectly, more readily and more faithfully so. He will be prepared to acknowledge that he has it in his power to accomplish this through self-education and that he has need of assistance when he chooses such an approach."[4] Even this acknowledgment is difficult to obtain and for this reason it becomes necessary to administer a rough shock to the adult's self-confidence. The technique of the Socratic question recommends itself here as a possible means by which the adult can be made to abandon his complacent assurance.

The Socratic question, which is intended to plant the seed of doubt in the student's mind and cause him to revert to a condition of self-doubt and awareness of his ignorance, would seem to be important to adult education and to provide a key to determining the adult student's readiness to be taught and to solicit knowledge. Yet Buber entertains doubts concerning the validity of Socrates' teaching method, which not only attacks the student's self-confidence but undermines the certitude of opinions as well. In Buber's view it is no longer possible to teach under the guise of seeming ignorance as did Socrates and hope in this way to bring the student to recognize his own lack of knowledge. Buber doubts that the conceptual lucidity to which Socrates aspired is likely to lead to the truth and thereby to an absolute validation that would even include ethics. Although Buber admits that the Socratic question has its uses as a didactic technique whose purpose is to unsettle the student, he insists that from the moment the shock has been administered the educator must engage his students in a dialogue in which he expresses his own opinions without concealing the real extent of his certitude. At the same time he must refrain from casting doubt on the opinions of his students.

The task of the teacher of adults is to help his students to distinguish between authentic and inauthentic opinions and to encourage them to realize this aim through personal choice, self-criticism, and self-education. According to Buber:

> Authentic opinions are those which arise when a person is accessible to the whole of reality and when his actual existence is in harmony with these opinions. A person's established opinion can be considered as authentic when two preconditions are fulfilled: (1) If in acquiring this opinion he has used his perceptions with great impartiality and if, moreover, he has given more complete scope to his opinion by taking into sufficient account the reliable opinions of others. (2) If to the best of his abilities he realizes within his personal existence and by means of his existence that which he believes to be right and desirable, and if, having joined some group which aims at putting this opinion into practice, he will nevertheless defend the opinion's original intention and content against any distortions to which it has been submitted for tactical advantages.[5]

Here we have a system of principles in which objective perception and judgment are complemented by the experience of one's fellow man; in which personal outlook is neither detached nor alienated, and rather than breaking with the continuity of experience joins it and is nourished by it; in which there is an insistence upon truth, a readiness to struggle for its realization, to defend its original core and to ward off all attempts to conspire against it. Yet all of this takes place not in isolation but within the community of men, and in such a way that the association with a community does not lead to a total immersion in the group so that the personality loses its distinctiveness and truth is renounced. These taken together make up the system of values that adult education seeks to develop.

However, the conditions of our own era make it much easier to motivate an adult to participate in some field of study that is included in existing programs of adult education. In part, this is a consequence of the pressures created in modern society, which is characterized by dynamic and rapid-paced change that compels us constantly to extend and update our knowledge, and even to change our behavior patterns. Such is the rapidity of change in our society that education is no longer able to prepare men in their childhood for their roles as adults. It is precisely this circumstance that provides adult education with the opportunity to play an important role by accompanying a man throughout his life. Indeed, this notion gave rise to a new movement in education which attempted to adjust education to a man's needs at each stage of his existence and adopted a position that education does not come to an end when adulthood is reached and is not to be identified with merely one phase of a man's development.

The mature person who feels himself obliged to cope with accelerated change and must face situations in which his knowledge will prove to be obsolete and his habits of thought and conduct no longer appropriate to the reality of his environment will probably be more open to the influence of adult education. However, it is likely that his interest will tend more toward the accumulation of information rather than education in its larger sense. Yet the adult is also aware of the difficulties he experiences in trying to adjust and of the inadequacies of his personality. If, therefore, he is approached by the educator in a way that is personal and intimate rather than being treated anonymously as part of a collective, he will be compelled to respond to the challenge of adult education. An adult faces the necessity of change and yet fears change because it requires reorganization and review— a readjustment of the relation of his inner existence to the external world. In this confrontation with change, he is likely to draw comfort and encouragement from the approach of those educators who follow Buber by stressing the importance of individuality in adult education.

Buber does not deny the legitimacy of the adult's expectations of acquiring information and supplementing his knowledge. Although he recognizes that the transmission of information and knowledge constitutes one—albeit ancillary—function of adult education, Buber regards the guidance of adults in the ways by which genuine knowledge is achieved to have far greater importance. Buber considers that in pursuit of this aim the student must acquire three capacities in the course of his studies. First, the student must adopt a perspective toward his environment and gain experience of it. Buber especially values personal experience and regards it as the critical basis for attaining a true understanding of any subject. In Buber's view, anyone who is deprived of such experience of his reality and of an unprejudiced perception of it is also deprived of the ability to reach beyond the narrow confines of his own world and to achieve a larger view of things. The ever-widening experience gained by a man through experimentation and an ongoing and critical examination of his environment prepares him to understand his changing world, recognize its structure, predict its development, and alter its nature. Consciousness is the process of acting within life's reality, which is always amenable to being changed. Second, the student must learn in the course of his studies how to adapt and refine the material which comes his way in order to reveal and make active its essential aspects. Finally, he must direct his efforts toward creating a vital and personal unity of his knowledge. In this respect, Buber's views on education are close to the ideas of such pragmatists as James, Dewey, and George Herbert Mead. Buber's affinity with pragmatism can be observed from his ideas on personal experience and the involvement of the self in the discovery of truth, from his stress on action and performance, and from his insistence on the unity of theory and practice. An examination of the thought of George Herbert Mead, for example, reveals many points of convergence between Mead's pragmatism and Buber's religious existentialism,[6] although the two schools are dissimilar and, consequently, very unlike in their approaches to education.

Buber examines the historical underpinnings of adult education in the light of his fundamental thesis concerning the development of the active spirit. His investigation is neither systematic nor exhaustive; nor does Buber enlarge on the evolution of the idea of adult education either in Israel or abroad. Rather, Buber is mainly concerned with the discovery of the early origins of what he calls "personal culture." For Buber, this term signifies a culture that favors the development of the autonomous individual because it is alive to the value of the spontaneous individuality of the spirit and recognizes the importance of the contributions of independent men to society. In Buber's view, the teachings of Confucius and Socrates embody this principle.

Buber is well aware of the different attitudes toward education of these two great personalities—differences that are determined by different cultures, backgrounds, and life histories. Confucius (ca. 551–478 B.C.) thought of himself primarily as a bequeather to future generations of the heritage created by the great men of China's past. Confucius is credited with having edited the most ancient of China's great books, and these together with his own extensive commentaries served as the basic texts of Chinese education until the end of the nineteenth century. Confucius taught by gathering to himself a permanent and intimate circle of students, and it is his relation to his students and his efforts to foster their personal and intellectual independence, rather than Confucius's role as transmitter of tradition, which Buber stresses.

Socrates (ca. 469–399 B.C.) adopted an altogether different attitude toward education. He refused to teach any fixed system of knowledge. He chose his students from among the youths whom he met by chance in the streets, in gymnasia, and in private homes. Rather than transmit tradition or conventional ideas to his charges, Socrates engaged them in a discourse whose purpose was to encourage them to independent thought. Buber calls special attention to Socrates' belief that education acts as a midwife to the soul and assists in the process whereby potential knowledge becomes actual. It was Socrates' conviction that every man possesses knowledge of truth, although this knowledge cannot of itself reach a person's conscious mind. The educator, by addressing his questions to the student, helps the student to retrieve the truth by engaging his own intellectual powers. Buber argues that neither Socrates' ideas concerning the independent discovery of truth nor the importance of the process by which the awareness of truth emerges is given the attention it deserves by the followers of the Socratic method of teaching.

Buber notes that it is important to determine whether what has emerged in the student's consciousness is apparent or true knowledge. Buber concludes, therefore, that the teacher must act as his students' collaborator by guiding them in making the distinction between true and false ideas.

Buber feels greater kinship with Socrates than he does with Confucius, the preserver and transmitter of traditions. Buber prefers the position of Socrates, for whom the greatest contribution that a man can make to society is to preserve it from stasis, and to goad it into change. Since it is man who is the creator of society, his first duty is to preserve his own personality, for the existence, advancement, and value of society depend on the preservation, advancement, and value of the self. Socrates, even at the moment when he stood before his judges and awaited a sentence of death, held firm to his convictions concerning the preservation of the self and to his insistence on truth.

The work of Nikolai Frederik Severin Grundtvig (1783–1872), founder of the Danish folk high school, exerted a strong influence on Buber's ideas about adult education. Grundtvig was a poet, theologian, and educator who made an important contribution to adult education in Denmark. After completing his studies at the University of Copenhagen, Grundtvig dedicated himself to the study of Scandinavian literature, Shakespeare, and the philosophies of Schiller and Fichte. Grundtvig published studies on Norse mythology, wrote about the decline of Scandinavia from its heroic past, and translated the Scandinavian Latin chronicles of the Middle Ages into Danish. He was also the editor of a controversial journal and the author of a *History of the World* and made a significant contribution to the scholarship of the Anglo-Saxon epic *Beowulf*. As a theologist, Grundtvig was severely critical of the position of the Danish church, which tended to take a permissive attitude on religious issues. He was especially devoted to the works of the Church Fathers, in whose writings he discovered an example of the continuity of tradition, by which the oral teachings of Jesus were communicated to his disciples and by them to the early Christian communities, until they were finally transmitted to the modern era. Grundtvig stressed the importance of discourse and oral transmission in education as well, and he believed that verbal intimacy between student and teacher was of greater significance to pedagogy than literary enlightenment.

Grundtvig, although he was much concerned about the question of child education, dedicated himself primarily to the problem of the education of adults. Because of his involvement in Denmark's political and social life, Grundtvig sought for the ways by which the condition of the nation might be improved. Grundtvig became involved in the conflict between Danish and German culture that was taking place in the regions of Denmark bordering on Prussia, and in the education of the Danish rural population in order to prepare it to assume the responsible leadership that was its due so that it would be able to establish an agrarian democracy in a country in which a nationalistic bourgeoisie was dominant.

Grundtvig wished to develop a peasant culture that was nourished by religious and nationalistic traditions, but in which men were brought up to be spiritually independent and individually responsible. He believed freedom to be the basis of community of mind and urged the need for freedom of thought and speech, and respect for the opinions of others. He advocated personal responsibility that is soundly based, and opposed coercive tyranny and enforced uniformity of opinion. The task of education, in Grundtvig's view, was to prepare men better to understand the realities of their lives, and he believed that the principle of teaching resided in the educator's direct appeal to students by engaging them in a dialogue that would foster in them a spirit of independence.

With Prussia's victory in the conflict that turned into a war in 1864, Grundtvig became convinced of the urgency of developing the peasant class of Denmark intellectually, so that it could create a viable society and culture. To this end he conceived the idea of establishing a folk high school, which he called The Free School for Adults. The school's purpose was to develop a style of life that suited the special needs of the Danish people.

Buber, who had made a careful study of Grundtvig's educational activities, was convinced that these continued to be a valid source of inspiration on which our own period draws in order to deal with the problem of adult education. Buber notes that Grundtvig had realized that a national style of life cannot be created out of thin air but has to be discovered in the character of the nation. A national pattern of existence is to be conceived of as the product of historical evolution and must be fostered in accordance with the conditions of the contemporary realities. Grundtvig was aware that no society can create its own life-style and image without preserving its connections with tradition, but he regarded loyalty to the past alone to be an inadequate basis for the accomplishment of this end. A vital society must renew its culture by acting upon its current reality. Thus, Grundtvig made use of Christian doctrine for popular education, and also linked it to those primal creative energies of the nation that had achieved a powerful expression in ancient Norse mythology. From his early youth Grundtvig had been educated within the traditions of his native heritage and was actively engaged in fostering its revival during his adult life. When he turned his attentions to the problems of education he sought to reactivate the primordial creative powers that were dormant in popular imagination. It was Grundtvig's aim to create a spiritual axis around which new principles could form.

For the realization of his aims Grundtvig proposed a program of studies for his Free School for Adults. The core of his program was made up of readings from literary classics, principally the Bible, and works belonging to the literature of ancient Denmark. Grundtvig also reserved a very important place for the examination—undertaken mutually by both students and teacher—of contemporary Danish life. Grundtvig particularly valued live discourse, which he perceived to be the principal source of the influence of education. He believed that such dialogue exerted its influence best when it was based on a mutual examination and analysis of social life, and when each student drew on his own experience in order to make his contribution to the common effort to describe and elucidate reality. The exchanges between teacher and class were complemented by a dialogue in which students exchanged stories about their own lives. These transactions took place in an atmosphere of personal intimacy between the teacher and his students.

In Grundtvig's school a program of studies lasted for several months, during which students and teachers lived communally. This communal life constituted the basis for the intimacy that Grundtvig regarded as essential for the maintenance of the influence of the teacher on his students and the students' influence on one another.

Grundtvig gave much thought to the relationship between scientific developments and his educational program. He was determined that the teaching methods employed in his school should be based on the most recent scientific research and the most advanced systems of knowledge. Nevertheless, Grundtvig's approach to pedagogy was neither an imitation of academic teaching methods nor a popularization of them. Grundtvig's formulation of his concept of the relationship between science and education is cited by Buber with approval: "This institution must be sustained by science and must exist in relation to it so as not to contradict it or be left behind by it; yet the school must also exist in its own right in order not to degenerate into the mere tail or empty shadow of science; for it must be an authentic spiritual force, obedient to the claims made by life and the times—the very claims that the learned are wont to despise."[7]

A number of Grundtvig's ideas about adult education struck a responsive chord in Buber's thinking about the subject. Buber was sympathetic with Grundtvig's belief that adult education must act as a spiritual force which, although it exists in relation to science, must respond in the first place to the demands made by life and the historical moment. In order to generate a source of intellectual and spiritual energy, adult education must, while preserving its connection with tradition, also renew it by responding to the demands of contemporary reality. Finally, that dialogue has an important role in the creation of community between teacher and student.

Buber was also favorably disposed to the ideas developed by some of the followers of Grundtvig, such as Kristen Kold and Richard Livingston. Kold, who of the two was closest in time to Grundtvig, established a school in 1850 for young men between the ages of eighteen and twenty-five who would come from the countryside to study during the winter months. Livingston, a scholar of Greek civilization at Oxford, began in 1941 to make a systematic study of education and pedagogy. He conceived of adult education as more than a means of compensating the deficient education of school dropouts; rather, he argued that continuing education is necessary for adults, because all are deficient in their knowledge, and that this deficiency tends to become more marked as the fund of available knowledge expands together with mankind's ambition to create an improved and more humane society. Livingston insists on the need for every person to take time off from his work for a study holiday that would last for a number of weeks, perhaps even months. He argues that such a study program would not only be useful for employers but would also be socially and nationally beneficial. Livingston remarks that a working adult is usually immersed in the trivial details of his everyday activity. He urges that each man must be given the opportunity to consider more than those aspects of the job with which he is directly concerned and to see it in relation to the complex of functions of which his work forms a part. Each person—Livingston argues—must be made conscious that the individual's activity should be directed by principles whose nature must be submitted to personal review; for otherwise, accumulated habit and routine undermine the mind's creative potential, which can only be preserved by ongoing intellectual activity.[8] Although Buber is aware of the difficulties likely to beset efforts to create a school founded on the principle of intimate community between teacher and student, which would be sustained over a reasonable period of time, he insists that when conditions are favorable every effort must be made by those in a position of leadership to establish such an institution. Like Grundtvig—and more insistently than Livingston—Buber insists that adult education must do more than supplement knowledge and broaden intellectual horizons; the aim of adult education—Buber argues—is spiritual renewal.

Buber is aware that there exists theories of education which hold that education that is unconnected with political goals is both ineffectual and undesirable; that breadth of learning diverts attention from the specific goal, which must always be singular and must, therefore, contradict all other goals. The advocates of this position are adherents of ideological groups. They claim that education must be pursued within the confines of a strictly defined group which remains inaccessible to the public at large. Buber rejects the concept of a closed and inaccessible group as the product of a superficial understanding of the nature of education.

Buber points out that there is a need for a third dimension that would add depth to education. He observes that the person who aspires to a goal must be aware not only of where he is headed but from where he comes. We can determine our goals on the basis of private "world-views" which plot our purposes. However, a rather different function is served by our point of origin: "The place from which it is possible for a man really to emerge—not merely observe himself doing so but actually come from it—is not a point or a place at which he stands, but a true and prior position. This position exists in a prior reality which embraces me while I procede towards my goal and which directs me towards my goal—one which I refrain from mentioning lest I fear it—which sustains me and helps me. This is the reality which made me and is destined to carry, preserve and instruct me if I put myself in its care. To return and open wide the gates which were closed fast to this reality—to the people (whose significance is far greater than conceived of by parties in their ongoing dispute concerning them), to the creative forces contained in the people—or, at the very least, to make myself accessible to these forces— this, then, is the object to which education aspires."[9] The concept of the people is not confined by Buber to the contemporary reality of the nation; Buber's concept of the nation embraces the totality of its experience from its origins at the foot of Mount Sinai to the present day.[10] The forces about which Buber speaks represent the totality of folk energies that fill the field of the nation's language, literature, and history from the days of its desert wanderings, through the period of the holocaust and the establishment of the state, and down to our own times. Buber cautions against substituting a vital reality, throbbing with activity and animated by the will to action, with the reductive formulas of theological abstraction.

Buber strongly opposes defining the concept of adult education in terms of closed groups whose activity is confined within the narrow limits of a single conception of the world. He notes that various concepts of national existence exist which are the subject of an ongoing debate among different groups within the nation. Buber insists, however, that the existence of the nation is primary, and that although all of the concepts of the nation tend toward this national being, it itself cannot be contained by any of them or submitted to their authority. "Education"—Buber observes—"sets about to demonstrate the unity which exists in reality and which the plethora of outlooks tends to obscure."[11] Buber does not make the claim that education sets aside ideology, but he argues that the chief concern of education is "that the building of the personality and—need we add?—the building of that great fraternity out of the association of individuals and the complex of their relationship are entirely dependent on the extent to which the relation to reality impinges on the world with which the world is being interpreted by the various ideologies."[12]

Buber concedes that no one can demonstrate the existence of national being except by the very concepts that he has adopted. He maintains, moreover, that this fact constitutes no disadvantage. Buber believes that it is neither possible nor even desirable to educate without some intellectual frame of reference. The only standard to be applied to teaching and education is one that measures the extent to which this outlook favors or impedes our vital relationship to the world we are examining. To what extent then— Buber asks—is a thorough examination of the world possible, and where are we to locate those aspects of the world that present themselves to us to be examined and distinguished? Buber knows that truth in its pure state is unattainable, but he holds that the believer in such a truth who aspires to reveal its existence also participates in its creation. The ideological component of what each man separately regards to be the truth is inseparable from it. Yet each man must take care that this truth is itself not fragmented into parts that represent political or utilitarian considerations. "The principle of relativism rules over me as does death"—Buber proclaims, adding, "but not in the same way, for I can limit the former by saying: 'Thus far and no further!'"[13] Thus, the kind of education which Buber advocates confronts groups that are divided by conflict with a holistic ideology.

Taking this position for his point of departure, Buber rejects a goal regarded by many to be of central importance to education—namely, tolerance of an ideology other than ours which is required of us but an understanding of the shared origins of that ideology and our own, and of the manner in which it diverges from our convictions. "We are not called upon to be neutral but rather to enter into union, into a life of shared responsibility for one another and reciprocal influence. We are not called upon to blur the boundaries that divide associations, groups and parties but to share in the consciousness of a common reality and pass the test of mutual responsibility."[14]

Buber sounds a warning against sectarianism and the formation of self-contained groups to which the Jewish people, wanting an integrated and organized structure in their national life, have been prone. He holds that adult education must bring together groups of different ideological persuasions and help reveal the common ground that these groups share.

In his effort to come to grips with the fragmentation of Jewish existence into contending parties, movements, and sectarian groupings, each of whom calls on the individual to join it, Buber suggests a test containing two criteria by which the individual can made his choice: (1) he can examine the nature, origins, and relation to reality of the underlying principle of an ideology in order to determine whether this principle is merely a public stance or has real substance; and (2) he can try to determine whether an ideology can lead its adherents to a life of realization. Buber believes that only those who realize life's ultimate purpose will create a new and viable reality.

Buber identifies two tasks which education must carry out in respect to those who adhere to ideologies. According to Buber, education must help such persons to anchor their beliefs in their world and must develop in each of them an ideological conscience that would allow them to submit the innumerable small acts by which they realize their ideology to the rigorous standards of personal obligation. "Whoever adheres to an ideology must also bear the responsibility on his own shoulders; his group has neither the ability nor the authority to remove his burden,"[15] Buber asserts. Education must teach those who hold ideologies to pursue the truth sincerely and to approach their ideological commitments in the full awareness of the gravity of their allegiance. Seriousness of purpose, rigorous analysis, and faithful adherence to the truths, principles, and ultimate aims of one's beliefs, and finally, realization—in Buber's view, would provide the basis for saving the world from being what it is in our times, when "great dreams and lofty hopes of humanity are successively realized in the guise of self-caricatures."[16]

Buber is much absorbed by the problem of the relevance of education to the great crisis that has marked our period since the 1930s. Buber tells of how "in a moment of clear vision he discovered that despite mankind's relentless progress—so he was wont to describe it—he was not marching on any paved highway but was constantly compelled to tread, heel-and-toe, along a narrow ridge spanning an abyss."[17] Such awareness and responsibility can help to overcome crisis, but on the condition that we accurately assess the means that we employ. It is precisely at moments of great crisis that mere consideration of the recent past in order to deal with the riddle of the present becomes inadequate; we derive small benefit from our present existence if the whole of our perception is concentrated on the contemporary. Education, both in its general application and in respect to adults, must keep in view both the goals toward which we strive and our beginnings. Such an attitude does not imply the wish to return to a prior stage of development; rather it is motivated by the desire to understand the entire range of issues contained in mankind's development both at the moments of its highest achievements and in the periods of its decline.

While analyzing the changes that have taken place in a world dominated by technology, Buber observes that the dangers faced by man in his changing relationship to the technological world can be defined in psychological terms. As man increasingly becomes an appendage of the machine, he also loses his sense of active enterprise and of personal relation to his actions and undertakings. In addition, man is faced by a danger arising from his changing relationship to society. A threat to which Buber calls our attention is the loss of individuality by the submersion of the private self in the collective.

One of the symptoms of the crisis of contemporary civilization is the appearance of the man without truth. Buber is not referring here to the liar who misrepresents the truth, but to someone far worse: the person who disbelieves in the very existence of a truth by which reality is measured, tested, and judged. Such a person replaces the concept of truth by its perversions, such as "utility" and "advantage", which appear under the guise of the good of the party, the state, or the government. Buber calls for a return to biblical truth, by which he means that which is trustworthy and abiding; not merely something of which we are conscious and which we acknowledge, but something we enact. "Truth is a matter of existence and life," Buber observes. "It is enacted among things and takes place in the world. And it is well that truth should take place in the world. To return to Biblical truth means to teach. Truth exists above you, and it is one truth for all. But it cannot enter your world unless you act it out—each man his own truth—when you live with things continuously and faithfully. It is then that truth takes place; then that you discover it as your truths, human truth."[18]

Buber argues that in order to be preserved humanity has need of men who are free of the collective and truth which is untainted by politicization. Responsibility to truth—Buber holds—is personal responsibility: "We need the individual who confronts the whole of existence which is present to him: one, let us say, who even confronts the public and is responsible for all of existence which is present to him; he willingly accepts responsibility for the public as well. A true unity and an authentic public will never come into being but to the degree that individuals are continuously formed in their individuality, so that through their responsible existence the public can take on new life."[19]

Buber asks whether any sign of hope exists within this crisis and in what way education can help ease the distress suffered in our period. He speaks of our need of first sensing the perplexities of the times as something shared by all: "Only if the spiritual distress of all those who ask reveals the great distress of this hour will all of the unseen tributaries converge to create one great river upon which the urgent question can be carried forward."[20]

Buber holds, however, that this common sense of shared distress is inadequate to the purpose if our awareness is directed only at externals; we must penetrate to the hidden sources of the problem. Buber describes our existence as one that is fragmented into partisan camps, each of which views only itself as embodying truth and the others as incarnations of falsehood; itself as devoted to ideas and others as the thralls of ideologies. "One-to-one Dialogue, unrestrained and unrestricted, becomes increasingly difficult and rare, and the gulf separating man from man grows even wider through ever increasing cruelty; and the danger grows ever more serious that we shall never again be able to bridge the abyss."[21] Buber believes that man's survival as man depends on the revival of dialogue, and that in order to make this dialogue possible we must conquer our own suspicion toward our neighbor and his toward ourselves.

Buber makes a distinction between the suspicions of the distant past, which were the consequence of circumspection in order not to be taken in by appearances, and suspicion in its modern guise, which threatens to undermine the foundations of existence between man and man. We are prone not to take seriously a man's words as they stand, but demand to know his purpose, his unconscious motivation, or the interest of the party to which he belongs. Buber maintains that the theories of Marx and Freud have helped to introduce this suspicion into the relationship between men. Buber's vision of the future is harsh indeed: "Mutual existential suspicion will become so complete that discourse will be silenced and the idea will become the absence of idea."[22] Existential suspicion deprives us of the belief in existence;

it is a disease that attacks the organism constituted by all of mankind. According to Buber it is one of the formative factors in the creation of man's crisis of being.

Buber thinks of every great civilization as being in some way a culture of dialogue. Civilization—according to Buber—has never been limited to the reality of individual intellectuals but evolves out of the transactions that take place among them: "What we call man's creative spirit was discovered only in the discourse between a man and his fellow, in the theoretical and esthetic expression of one who has taken expression to be his goal; and it is he who expresses his thoughts and feelings to those who are capable and ready to understand them properly. The active force creating this situation is the force of dialogue."[23]

Man has a profound need to have his existential identity confirmed by his fellow man. Moreover, such confirmation is authentic only when it is mutually enacted. When a man exists in a state of alienated and mute suspicion he pursues confirmation in ways that are condemned to failure, for he seeks to discover confirmation in himself alone or in the group to which he belongs. Self-confirmation is never lasting and creates the feeling of utter abandonment. The confirmation of the crowd is illusory; the crowd recognizes no man's existence for its own sake, but only insofar as his existence can be used to advantage and, therefore, offers only false confirmation.

The renewal of the relation of dialogue, which constitutes the first step toward resolving the crisis, greatly depends on adult education. Education must begin with the effort to overcome existential suspicion. Adult education, which takes place in the context of fellowship, can reopen dialogue, which represents neither a system of blind faith nor unworldly idealism but is rather the epitome of sober realism.

Although Buber pins part of his hopes for emerging from our crisis on the renewal of the dialogue between man and man, he sees this as merely a first step in the reestablishment of the connection between man's personality and the source of all being.

Turning his attentions to the problem of Jewish adult-education in our times, Buber conceives popular education to be one of the primary goals of the Zionist movement. Buber observes: "The generation of the national movement which does not join the tradition of teaching and study can leave no tradition behind."[24] Thus the connection between generations is formed by teaching and study. Buber argues that teaching and study cannot remain impermanent and unplanned. He, therefore, advocates the establishment of permanent schools of adult education where the best educators will contribute to the making of a generation.

Buber opposes the use of propaganda and exhortation in adult education. Buber was already aware in the 1930s of a fact which to this day escapes the notice of many of our leaders and adult educationalists: namely, that eloquence and emotive rhetoric can no longer shape the whole man. Although national leadership has tried to refute Buber's ideas by pointing to the enormous financial contributions made by Jews to the State of Israel, Buber's arguments remain valid. "No man"—Buber proclaims—"can refute me through the money which is accumulating in our hands. Yet the feeling often overtakes us that men redeem their soul by money. But it is really preferable that the money they give should not represent the beginning but, rather, the end; that they should first dedicate their souls and only afterwards give their money."[25]

Buber speaks of the need to make future generations participants in the idea that shapes and generates tradition. An active tradition arises only when the continuity of a great enterprise is preserved. The "idea" to which Buber refers is the idea of action; the action of a whole group, of which each successive generation assumes its own role in carrying out a great and ramified undertaking.

Buber proposes the creation of an institution of popular education both in Israel and in the Diaspora. As a model for such centers of education, Buber chooses the type of folk school that was established by Grundtvig in Denmark in the midnineteenth century. Buber makes it clear that the Grundtvigian model cannot be adopted in its entirety by Jews and that it will require a radical reworking in order to suit the distinct character of Judaism. Nevertheless, Buber believes that much can be learned from the Danish folk-school experiment.

In conceiving of his school of popular education, Buber imagined groups of young people between the ages of sixteen and twenty-five spending periods of five months with their teachers in the countryside, where they would pursue their studies and play in common. Buber assigns great importance to the part that common meals and the intimate encounter between teacher and students would play in the educational program that he proposes.

Buber holds teaching, which is concerned mainly with the transmission of study matter and which is conducted only at fixed times, to be of little account. Such an approach can exert only a limited educational and formative influence. Buber stresses the importance of mutuality and intimacy in student-teacher relations; consequently he favors teaching which is unpremeditated rather than teaching which is conducted according to a planned program. For Buber it is the actual presence of the teacher, the full participation of his personality, which releases educational energies. This is not to say that Buber holds in contempt teaching which is intentionally and consciously pursued; he wishes rather to emphasize the importance of encounter to education that patterns itself on life.

This is the pattern that Buber wishes to apply to his institutions of popular education. These institutions would not stress regular and disciplined study. They would not be centers of research or of university learning, nor would these institutions aim at instructing its students in specific knowledge for its own sake. Knowledge as taught in these schools would be transmitted as an integral part of education; the selection of subjects and the choice of methods would emerge from the desire to create a link between spiritual performance and living tradition.

Buber recommends that such schools be established in Israel and abroad. These schools would be dedicated to intensive popular education that would be conducted in many small groups which would become bearers of an active and ongoing tradition. Buber foresees the day when such centers will exert an influence on all aspects of adult education everywhere. In addition, Buber would like to see teachers from these centers travel periodically from community to community, in order to live and teach among people whose work prevents them from taking part in intensive school programs. In this way, these sectors of the population, too, would be integrated into the program of study.

During the period of the Nazi rise to power, while he was still residing in Germany, Buber became the moving spirit of an important undertaking in the field of Jewish adult education. In May 1934 while participating in the activities of the Center for Jewish Adult Education *(Mittelstelle für jüdische Erwachsenenbildug bei der Reichsvertretung der deutschen Juden)*, Buber summoned a conference at Hugo Rosenthal's Jewish Village Education Center at Herlingen near Ulm.[26] Buber invited intellectuals and educators whom he regarded as likely recruits for a program of Jewish adult education. In his address at this gathering, Buber introduced his audience to the educational activities of Nikolai Grundtvig. Grundtvig had confronted a spiritual crisis experienced by Denmark in the wake of a military and political one by creating a popular-education movement. Buber called on Jewish educators in Germany to respond to the contemporary crisis of German Jewry by following Grundtvig's example.

The student body at the center was composed of Jewish men and women who were active in either Jewish public life or education. There were rabbis, leaders of Jewish youth movements, teachers at public elementary and high schools, and staff members of Jewish educational institutions.[27] Ernst Simon, who has described the activities of the center, tells of the broad and varied range of its activities and makes a point of stressing the communal framework of its educational program. Students lived together in a village dormitory. They began their day with a communal jog through the village, after which they took breathing exercises. Before breakfast, the religious members of the staff and student body would pray together. Whenever possible classes would meet outdoors. Meals were taken in common, and each meal was preceded by readings from the Bible or the recitation of a Hasidic tale and concluded with the saying of grace.

In the initial stages of the center's educational program, students carried a heavy work load, but it was soon discovered that participants in the program must be given the opportunity to spend time in one another's company in order to become better acquainted. Evenings were therefore set aside for a variety of social activities such as lectures and communal singing.[28]

Buber played a principal role in the activities of the center, where he taught various subjects, particularly in the field of biblical studies. What Buber's students experienced in his classes were not conventional lessons but spiritual encounters and intellectual adventures whose purpose was the elucidation of the nature of the biblical mission.

The center's classes were held at various locations during different seasons of the year, and each class meeting was marked by a different character that was appropriate to the particular season and place. Here we see a partial realization of Buber's program for a center of popular education.

Buber made a special study of adult education in Israel. He was aware that adult education must always exist in relation to the historical situation of a people, for educational goals are greatly determined by the character and content of a nation's historical circumstances. In order to identify the goals that were generated by the historical situation of the state of Israel during the decades of the 1950s and 1960s, Buber set about to examine the nature of that country's life.

The type of the pioneer who set his stamp on the early settlement movements in Israel has succeeded in establishing a strong national center. "The pioneer, in whom the regenerated type of the Jewish nation has crystallized, is not merely the pioneer who has developed and enriched the Land of Israel, but a pioneer of a new life. The Land has taken shape around him and the nation will be formed around him."[29] Buber understood that the renascence of the Jewish people in its own land cannot truly succeed unless its foundations are built on the principle by which those who laid down those foundations were selected to come to Israel. This principle was active during the early period of immigration. During the second stage of the immigration movement, after the First World War, the principle of conscious selection became part of the work of the settlement of the country. The selection was the product of the intense preparations in the Diaspora for settlement in Palestine. Buber argued that by the very nature of the process in which this principle was formed, the lives and activities of future generations were likely to be created around a solid core that had gradually taken shape as successive pioneer immmigrants arrived from the Diaspora.

With the seizure of power by the Nazis, the selective principle of immigration was shattered. The terrible wave of death and annihilation swept away and annulled this organically conceived program. This program had been designed to foster a new unity among its participants that would overcome the spiritual estrangement between the ethnic community and its society, and would assure the community's homogeneous development in the future. The immigration to the state of Israel by various communities, which differed from one another in language, outlook, and custom, posed the threat of renewed division among the people. "The core became surrounded by a husk. . . . the problem of the core's inner layers became increasingly graver. In some places these problems may reach new pathological proportions . . . if all those who believe in *Zion* do not succeed in re-establishing the solid core's control and authority over the unstable periphery. Success in this matter is a life and death issue."[30]

Just how an authentic national unity can be achieved is a taxing problem. If such unity cannot be achieved by external means, where then can the spiritual means be found? Buber discerns one such spiritual force in adult education.

Buber knows that no man who is not a pioneer by nature can be educated to be one—particularly at this late stage in the development of Zionism, when its pioneer principle has lost much of its power to inspire and attract. These individuals must be educated and encouraged to form an elite group that would pursue its work on a small scale and in a manner similar to the way in which the pioneering elite had once exerted its influence on the Diaspora. The creation of an elite corps whose spirit would radiate outwards and inspire the periphery is the goal of education in Israel.

Buber grasps more clearly than do teachers and educationalists in Israel today that it is no longer possible to instill the pioneering spirit by employing means which were valid in the past. The attempt to preserve the pedagogic methods of the past is doomed to failure. The psychological ambience in which contemporary man exists has undergone great change. Contemporary man is marked by a feeling of despair which he experiences in the presence of his fellow man, of society, and of the entire complex of human values.

> At times this despair may wrap itself in the cloak of a political opinion of one kind or another, or it may seek refuge in some group, but it penetrates to the very marrow of the soul, and even the reality of the Jewish State is powerless to overcome it. Indeed, even the concept of nationhood, despite all that it has accomplished is inadequate to the purpose: for it has now become evident that all of the conflicting national ideas taken together and total war undertaken in the name of national survival may ultimately extinguish human existence.[31]

Buber points out that the motive force behind even the heroic age of pioneering in Israel was not solely nationalistic. Rather the chief motive was messianic, despite the secular guise under which it appeared. *Halutziut*—as the spirit of pioneering is called in Israel—was permeated by national and universal values; by values that were both political and abiding. In Buber's view, values that are merely national and political in nature can be neither permanent nor authentic. Buber calls for a return to abiding values, and conceives the primary role of adult education to be the reawakening of an attachment to eternal values.

In order to realize this goal in adult education, we must first recognize the need for forging a new unity out of the realities represented by humanity at large and Israel in particular. Buber holds that abiding values can become part of a people's permanent heritage only if they are drawn from the values which constitute a nation's traditions and introduced into the contemporary realities of national life.

Taking this assumption for his starting point, Buber arrives at a number of clear-cut conclusions concerning the teaching methods of adult educators and the traits that qualify a teacher for fulfilling a role of such momentous importance in our troubled times. For Buber it is clear that only a person who believes in lasting values can teach them. He argues that only those who have either maintained or reacquired their belief in such values, and whose faith is undogmatic but genuinely animated by the breath of life, are qualified for such a task. In connection with the teaching methods appropriate to Jewish adult education, Buber insists that the existential reality of every field of study must be taught, and in a way that awakens the students' consciousness of the fact that this reality is the key to their knowledge of spiritual truth and its workings in the world.[32]

Buber is insistent that in respect of Jewish national life, adult education cannot merely confine itself to the task of assisting the people in joining the struggle for national liberation and integrating in Israeli social and political realities, but it must also stimulate the reawakening of essential being by encouraging an inner renewal. In this context adult education becomes a spur to the abandonment of a way of life that is fraught with inner contradictions and its replacement by a more complete and homogeneous mode of existence.

Hence the educational goal defined by Buber has a significance that is more than merely national. Buber's ideas concerning Jewish education are derived from the concept of national humanism. According to Buber, the Jewish nation exists in order to fulfill its destiny through the realization of the essence of humane Judaism. Buber warns us that to prejudice national education in favor of nationalism, by which the people are conceived of as being an end in themselves rather than merely one among the many principles informing humanity as a whole, is to invite catastrophe. For as Buber remarks: "National education is the means by which Judaism is fulfilled, whereas nationalistic education is the means by which Judaism is emptied of its content under a Jewish flag. It denies our very essence and purpose. Hence, in our country more than elsewhere, nationalistic education becomes largely anti-national."[33]

Buber examines the attitudes of adult educationalists in Israel toward the role that religious and national festivals play in adult education. He is especially concerned with the use of updated versions of the ceremonies associated with the celebration of holidays such as Passover and Jewish Pentecost (the Festival of the First Fruits). Buber does not dismiss the significance of these holidays, whose observance, he admits, can create a sense of unity among the citizens of the state, bind them to their traditions, and nourish their national consciousness. However, Buber is inclined to doubt their usefulness in the task of resuscitating tradition and creating an authentic relationship with the nation's past. He remains unmoved by the easy appeals of the catchwords of "Jewish consciousness" nor is he lured by the symbols and ceremonies of public worship that are mere gestures toward tradition and have only external significance. Characteristically, Buber's approach to the problem is graver in intent and based on a more profound grasp of the issues. He calls for a thorough investigation of the principles of the relationship with tradition and for the imposition of obligations that are sufficiently rigorous to make a claim on the whole man.

Buber identifies three possible types of relationship between the Jewish national movement and tradition. The first of these constitutes an affirmation deriving from accessibility to tradition, whose elements are assimilated and adapted to the needs of the moment. In this way the forces generated by tradition are made to shape the contemporary world according to the needs of the present. The second type of relationship is one of rejection, by which a barrier is erected to the influence of the past, whose ancient wisdom is perceived as no longer worthy of being credited or used. The third category is described by Buber as representing a false relationship between the national movement and tradition; in this type of relationship the values and achievements of national heritage become the glorified objects of overweening national pride: "They are shown to us much as an antiquary might display his collection, or as the regalia is exhibited in a museum now that no king is alive to wear it. Although tradition may be bragged of, no one has faith in its message; it is taught in schools, but not as something which has any relevance to life. In short, we keep it in a box for safekeeping."[34] Buber laments the fact that the relationship of the national movement in Israel to tradition is largely a synthesis of the last two categories.

Buber can find no advantage in either total or selective acceptance of tradition. In either case, acceptance is the product of external intention merely and must remain sterile. The adoption of religious forms without the content of religion is even dangerous, according to Buber. For in themselves, forms are nothing, and the idea of taking over forms that have been emptied of their original significance and filling them with a new content supposed to be more compatible with the times is vainly and artifically conceived. This, then, represents Buber's attitude toward those "innovations in tradition" that are the pride of educators in Israel who wish to make tradition relevant by treating Pentecost as a farmer's festival of nature, or by celebrating the Passover as a holiday of national liberation. Concerning this "modern" treatment of Passover, Buber remarks: "The Passover meal, when it is celebrated merely in order to commemorate the fact of national self-liberation, will inevitably lose its major significance, which can only be perceived through feeling; for every self-liberation is related—as is rind to kernel—to the redemption of mankind and the universe by a redemptive force."[35] Buber does not question the legitimacy of regarding Pentecost to be an agricultural nature festival. However, he insists that we do not discharge our obligations to traditions through symbols exclusively. He reminds us that we must also recognize and express the fact that nature itself is no more than a symbol. For it is only when we dedicate ourselves to what is hidden from the senses that we live authentically. "The Sabbath," Buber reminds us,

> much as we may honor it, will remain a poor and meager thing if the joy we feel on this social day of rest is not penetrated also by the cosmic mystery of labor and rest which is reflected in this day, and which is the same mystery as the one that finds its expression in the story of Genesis— a mystery more glorious than even the most exalted philosophical idea. For the Creator of Heaven and Earth rests from his labors on this day as does the son of a maidservant. It is thus that we feel our own breath inhaled by the elemental soul of the universe.[36]

Buber devoted much thought to the problem of the education of the teachers of adults. His own investigations into the state of adult education convinced Buber that most teachers who are active in the field of popular education are teachers of elementary and secondary school who are working with adults either on a temporary basis or as part-time employment, which they undertake in addition to their normal duties. Buber concludes: "We have need of people who understand that this is not some lesser trade chosen only because of the pressure of circumstances created by the inability of those who enter it to meet the more rigorous requirements of a more prestigious profession; rather it is a vocation of the very highest order, which is certainly no less, and perhaps even more, demanding than any other calling, because it claims the whole personality."[37]

Buber attempted to realize his ideas concerning the training of adult educators by founding a folk teacher's college in cooperation with the Center for Popular Education of the Hebrew University, the government of the state of Israel, and the Jewish Agency. Under Buber's tutelage, the school was organized to train annually a small group of students coming from different ethnic and educational backgrounds. In each of the subjects offered in the college, students were taught by the most respected authority in the field. Buber insisted on limiting the size of the student body, a policy regarded by him to be essential to the college's purpose, which was to train its students for the very important role that they were to play in education. Moreover, Buber held that a group can be taught successfully only if the teacher establishes a personal relationship with each of his students as individuals. Buber regarded intimate personal contact to be the animating force of education.

Historical reality, as it becomes manifest socially, culturally, and politically, made up the principal content of the school's program. Buber believed that his students should be altogether immersed in such reality, that they must be joined to it personally and existentially: "Adult education is always education which establishes bonds; this holds true especially in our own case. Indeed, the power that binds is subject to neither deception nor fallacy but only to reality itself."[38] Therefore the task that Buber sets for his school is to prepare the folk teacher to perceive and understand his existential reality, which must determine the content of his studies.

The establishment of the relationship with reality is an important prerequisite for teaching adults. Buber cautions us, however, against studies that are pursued in isolation, or substituting the idea of truth with a concept of time-bound and transient actuality, or replacing the essence of nationhood by an isolationist nationalism that is alien to the authentic national character of the Jewish people.

> We can never succeed in creating a true bond between the generation of mass immigration to Israel and our nation's renascence unless we bind these people to the nation's fundamental and vital heritage, which exists in a state of ongoing regeneration and survives by virtue of its self-renewals. Moreover, such a binding cannot be achieved unless we join this heritage with the heritage of the human spirit struggling for lasting values. Living Judaism can be taught only by restoring to those who have lost it the faith in the meaning that is contained by life and the universe.[39]

Buber believed that national education can be valid only so long as it is undertaken with an authentic image of humanity in mind. Adult educators in Israel, because they wish to educate their students to be loyal citizens in a unified national polity, are prone to replace national education with nationalist education. To avoid the pitfalls of nationalist education and to realize, instead, the goal of national humanism, we must educate the student to adopt those values of his national movement that are supranational. Buber sternly warns against educational aspirations of the kind that developed in Germany to create a "pure" national type. Education of this kind becomes the victim of a new kind of nationalist covenant that may well be the most sterile of all.[40]

As opposed to those who speak of the teaching methods of education, Buber holds that the principle of education is to be discovered not in teaching but in the teacher. The good teacher educates through his very being and the immediacy of his contact with his students. He educates both by speaking and by his silences, during periods of study and during recesses.

For Buber, education is first and foremost dialogue. It is a discourse in which questions and answers are mutually exchanged. It is the study of mankind, nature, art, and society mutually pursued through the medium of dialogue whose silences are as significant as speech.

In order to elucidate the concept of real dialogue, Buber undertakes to explain the nature of genuine conversation. He tells us that what we generally call conversation is mere idle chatter; rather than speak with one another, men project their voices into a space surrounding a fictitious realm. In conversations of this kind, each of the participants is preoccupied entirely with himself, so that the barrier between the speakers remains unbreached. For dialogue to take place, each participant must be motivated by a conscious intention to address his actual interlocutor.

Dialogue is never debate, which stems from the conflict of ideas and blurs the distinction between the expression of inner convictions and the art of rhetoric. In debate—Buber explains—there is a tendency to ignore the validity of the opponent's opinion, even if its validity is beyond question. On the other hand, in true dialogue each participant accepts the other and addresses him out of a total and heartfelt consciousness of the other's existence. Although each participant in a dialogue may oppose his interlocutor's ideas with his own, he must do so while making himself accessible to his opponent's existence, to the source of the very ideas whose fallacies he is about to demonstrate. In dialogue, man addresses man and thereby confirms the existence of his fellow man.

In examining the problem of the authentic knowledge of an object or person and the significance of addressing them for what they are, Buber speaks of the need of sensing another person or thing as a complete and wholly palpable entity rather than perceiving them as schematic abstractions. Buber identifies speech as the characteristic that distinguishes man from other creatures and objects contained in the universe. In Buber's view, it is speech that determines man's existence and shapes his personality. Thus, for Buber, true knowledge of a person means, "to perceive a man in his integrity as a whole personality made distinct by the uniqueness of the spirit; it means to perceive the dynamic center which impresses all of his manifest aspects, his actions and his conduct, with the stamp of the singularity by which he apprehends the world."[41] True knowledge of another person, which is unattainable when he is perceived as an object apart, becomes possible only when we enter into a straightforward relationship with him; when, in other words, he becomes an actual presence to us.

In his memoirs, Buber describes his discovery of the idea of authentic dialogue. He tells of a twilight stroll in fields when, rapt in his thoughts, he absently struck a tree trunk with his cane. Buber describes how at that instant he had achieved the double awareness of having made contact with being. Rather than apprehending the experience of accidentally having struck an object with a stick, he perceived himself from two perspectives; that of his own person and that of the tree. Thus, in addition to having stumbled on a tree, he had also discovered himself.[42]

The teacher of adults who is intent on initiating true dialogue must understand that it is an experience in which each speaker is conscious of his partners as individuals whom he realizes and makes actual at the very moment of his addressing them, and that by the very fact of his having addressed them he also confirms them. Yet this confirmation is not the same as agreement. Nevertheless, though disagreement over beliefs and opinions will occur, the educator will have acquired a partner in a dialogic experience that affirms the humanity of another person.

In dialogue, moreover, each participant must be prepared to reveal all of his thoughts without concealing or omitting any of them. The dialogue of which Buber speaks is created and sustained by its trustworthiness, and any attempt to give prominence to the self rather than to what is being said will detract from the validity of the experience.

True dialogue can be experienced not only by two persons but can be a colloquy in which many take part, so long as all of the participants are consciously receptive to the dialogic experience. Such is the dialogue that takes place between the teacher and his pupils. In situations of this kind there is no need for everyone to speak in order for the dialogue to take place. There are moments when those who keep silent make the important contributions to the dialogue. Nevertheless, each member of the group must be prepared to say his piece at the moment that the course of the conversation awakens his inner need to give voice to his thoughts. The dialogic experience is unpremeditated. Although it does proceed within the context established from the very moment of its inception, it cannot be planned, nor can its development be consciously determined. Dialogue unfolds according to the dictates of the spirit.

Buber argues that the teacher of adults cannot speak to his pupils from the position of superiority or advantage. The question he asks of his pupils aught not to be a test, nor should he pose his questions as one who already knows the right answer and intends merely to determine if it is also known to his student. In Buber's judgment, the Socratic question—which is designed to demonstrate the inadequacy of the reply and whose whole intention is to pave the way for further questions that probe the issue—has no relevance to adult education. An adult educator who has formulated his questions conceptually expects more than a straightforward reply. His purpose is to encourage his students to give expression and conscious shape to personal experience that they have never had the opportunity to evaluate intellectually. For the teacher to be successful in his endeavor, he must see to it that his students are made to feel that he perceives them as individuals, and that the transactions that take place among the students themselves are conducted in the spirit of sincere fraternity, so that their private inhibitions and natural diffidence in revealing the details of their private experiences may be overcome.

Buber believes that there now exists a growing desire among people to engage in sincere, direct, and unrhetorical dialogue. In Buber's view, most men have lost the art of dialogue and require guidance in order to reacquire their dialogic skills. The adult educator can help men to engage in dialogue only if he keeps in mind the fact that he teaches others as one who is himself constantly learning.

One of the most important tasks of adult education is to elucidate the meaning of ideas. In an age such as ours, when the chatter of the media of mass communication glut our environment, so that we have become accustomed to hold words cheap and treat ideas frivolously, it becomes the task of adult education to reestablish the contours of the ideas held by the student. The adult educator must stimulate his pupils to determine the extent to which his concepts are true. The examination and elucidation of ideas are a necessary precondition of consciousness, and the teacher of adults must train his students to make the transition from conformity to the conventional patterns of thought to independence of mind, from the perception of merely apparent truth to true knowledge.

Buber assumes that there is a connection between ideas and conduct, and argues that this relationship is one in which concepts are not only the expression of action but also determine the character and direction of action. Ideas, in addition to their being the instruments of analysis and logical definition, are the distillations of a complex of feelings, attitudes, expectations, experiences, and reciprocities of response that characterize human relationships. The elucidation of ideas is of such momentous importance to the activities of education precisely because of the mutuality in the relationship between ideas and conduct.

We have already noted Buber's agreement with Grundtvig that adult education should base itself on the findings of science. Although Buber considers it important for a teacher to keep abreast of the research in his field of specialization, he argues that adult education should aim at more than the mere dissemination of the results of scientific research. Students should be given the opportunity of studying the methods of research, and must be taught to appreciate the problems that arise from the findings of scientific investigation. Buber holds that we can learn a great deal from Grundtvig's followers, whose approach to the teaching of mathematics and science was, at least in part, historical. In this way, Grundtvig's disciples introduced their students to the problems of various historical periods, and were able to lead their class in an examination of the solutions that could have been applied to these problems. Buber claims that in this way "the students are made to free themselves from the generalizations and abstractions of scientific statements in order to acquire an active understanding of the inner workings of science. In addition, they come into direct contact with the sublime and critical stance of the spirit as distinct from its actions—the stance by which it reveals its vitality much more than it does by its actual undertakings."[43]

This approach makes it possible to create a bond between humanism and modern science. It allows us to demonstrate the social function of science to the student, so that he can grasp the relationships of the principles of science and those of other fields of learning. Moreover, an educational approach along these lines can cultivate an awareness of the humanistic mission of science, demonstrate the travails of intellectual search, describe man's struggle with nature, reveal the difficulties that beset the scholar's investigations, and help to evaluate the part which is played by our own age in the ongoing pursuit of knowledge.

In Buber's view, a school of adult education is not a surrogate university nor an extension of elementary and high school. Nor should it propose merely to fill gaps in its students' education. One of its principal objects is to prepare the adult to serve his society at the particular historical moment. Buber is also of the opinion that this should be the intention of universities. However, the university is only able to fulfill such a task secondarily, whereas this goal is the major vocation of a school of adult education and determines both its program of studies and its methods of instruction. "We feel justified in saying that while it is appropriate for university teaching to have an educational character, the very goal of a school of popular education is to educate by means of teaching."[44]

As opposed to the university, which is mainly concerned with training in the methods of research, the school of adult education should be concerned with the development of independence of thought. It should concentrate on nurturing the independent understanding of problems and their solutions, especially of those problems which are posed by life itself; it should awaken the powers of perceiving facts, which may then be compared and analyzed. In Buber's vision of popular education, these activities take place under the active guidance of the teacher, and are ultimately integrated with the goal of rousing man's spiritual self so that he acquires the art of educating himself.

These aims are best accomplished—according to Buber—by the elimination of lectures unaccompanied by dialogue, and by giving preference to those who have been trained as teachers over those who have been narrowly trained in specialized fields of study. These requirements would encourage the development of the personal relationship between teachers and students that is necessary to the success of popular education.

Buber's method of adult education begins with receptivity, follows the path of dialogue, and ends with self-education. The *I-Thou* relation between man and man becomes the relation of *I-Thou* with the absolute, and the isolated self gives way to the synthesis of national heritage with the heritage bequeathed by the spirit of man.

NOTES

1. Alfred North Whitehead, *The Aims of Education* (New York: The New American Library of World Literature, 1949).

2. Bernhard Bolzano (1781–1848) was active in Prague as a philosopher, theologian and mathematician. He held the post of professor of Religious Studies at the University of Prague and was also an ordained priest. In 1820, Bolzano was dismissed from his university post and

relieved of his duties as priest because of his advocacy of socialist ideas in his sermons. Thenceforth, he lived in isolation and dedicated himself wholly to his research. Bolzano made a study of almost all of the branches of philosophy, working as well in the fields of psychology, esthetics, and mathematics. Husserl considered him to be one of the greatest logicians of all times. Bolzano's daring and originality is equally evident in his ideas about education, especially in the area of popular education.

3. Martin Buber, "Hinukh mevugarim" [Adult education] in *Teuda vi-y'ud*, [Mission and Purpose: Essays on Judaism] (Jerusalem: Ha-sifria ha-tsionit, 1961), p. 399.

4. Martin Buber, "Hinukh mevugarim: yesodot," ["Adult education: foundations"] *Entsiklopedia hinukhit* [Educational Encyclopedia] vol. 1; (Jerusalem: Ministry of Education and Mosad Bialik, 1961), p. 503.

5. Martin Buber, *Yesodot ha-hinukh*, pp. 503–4.

6. The following article is of some interest in this connection, although the author tends to stress excessively the points of similarity between the philosophies of G. H. Mead and Buber: Paul E. Pfuetze, "Martin Buber and American Pragmatism," in *The Philosophy of Martin Buber*, ed. P. A. Schilpp and M. Friedman (London: Cambridge University Press, 1967), pp. 511–41.

7. Buber, "Hinukh mevugarim," p. 401.

8. Richard Livingston, *Education for a World Adrift* and *The Future in Education* (London: Cambridge University Press, 1941).

9. Martin Buber, "Hinukh u-vhinat olam," in *Teuda vi-y'ud*, vol. 2, p. 413.

10. See the chapter entitled, " 'Humanizem mikrai' be-mishnato shel Martin Buber," in my book, *Martin Buber on Education* (in Hebrew) (Tel Aviv: Yahdav, 1976), pp. 167–90.

11. Buber, "Hinukh u-vhinat olam," p. 414. [Education and World-view].

12. Ibid.

13. Ibid., p. 415.

14. Ibid., p. 416.

15. Ibid., p. 419.

16. Ibid.

17. Martin Buber, "Al ha-mashber ha-gadol," [On the great crisis] in *Teuda vi-y'ud*, vol. 2, p. 75.

18. Martin Buber, "Ha-mashber ve-ha-emet," [The crisis and the truth] in ibid., p. 75.

19. Martin Buber, "Ha-sheela she-ha-yahid nishal," [The question that the individual is asked] in *Be-sod siah: al ha-adam ve-amidato nokhah ha-havaya* [Dialogue: Man and his encounter with existence]. (Jerusalem: Mosad Bialik, 1963), p. 210.

20. Martin Buber, "Tikva le-shea zo," [Hope for this hour] in *Teuda vi-y'ud*, Vol. 2, p. 82.

21. Ibid., p. 83.

22. Ibid., p. 85.

23. Ibid., p. 86.

24. Martin Buber, "Hinukh ha-am—tafkidenu," [Education of the people is our task] in *Teuda vi-y'ud*, Vol. 2, pp. 362–63.

25. Ibid., p. 361.

26. Hugo Rosenthal established a center for Jewish agricultural education in Herlingen, near the city of Ulm. Rosenthal was active as head of the center for six years until Passover, 1966. See his book, *Hinukh u-masoret* [Education and tradition] (Haifa: Department of Education of Haifa, 1966).

27. Ernst Simon, "Jewish Adult Education in Nazi Germany as Spiritual Resistance," *Leo Baeck Institute Yearbook, 1965* (London: East and West Library, 1965), pp. 68–104.

28. Ibid., p. 86.

29. Martin Buber, *Netivot be-utopia* [Paths in utopia] (Tel Aviv: Am Oved, 1947), p. 172.

30. Ibid., pp. 168–69.

31. Buber, "Hinukh mevugarim," p. 407.

32. Ibid., p. 408.

33. Martin Buber, "Rayonot al ha-ḥinukh ha-leumi ve-ha-ḥalutsi," Thoughts on national and pioneer education] in *Teudu vi-y'ud,* Vol. 2, p. 391.

34. Ibid., p. 394.

35. Ibid., p. 385.

36. Ibid.

37. Buber, "Hinukh mevugarim," p. 409.

38. Ibid., p. 411.

39. Ibid.

40. Buber, "Rayonot al ha-hinukh ha-leumi ve-ha-halutsi," p. 390.

41. Martin Buber, "Yesodotav shel ha-ben-enoshi," [The foundation of the interhuman] in *Be-sod siah,* p. 224.

42. Martin Buber, *Pgishot: zikhronot* [Encounters: Recollections] (Jerusalem: Mosad Bialik, 1965), pp. xxxvi–xxxvii.

43. Buber, "Hinukh mevugarim: yesodot," and *Yesodot ha-hinukh,* p. 510.

44. Buber, "Hinukh mevugarim," p. 403.

Select Bibliography

WORKS BY MARTIN BUBER

In German

Des Baal-Schem-Tow Unterweisung im Umgang mit Gott. Hellerau: Jakob Hegner Verlag, 1927.

Bilder von Gut und Böse. Cologne and Olten: Jakob Hegner Verlag, 1952.

Briefwechsel aus sieben Jahrzehnten. Vol. 1: 1897–1918; Vol. 2: 1918–1938. Heidelberg: Verlag Lambert Schneider, 1972, 1973.

Die Chassidische Botschaft. Heidelberg: Verlag Lambert Schneider, 1952.

Die Chassidischen Bücher: Gesamtausgabe. Hellerau: Jakob Hegner Verlag, 1928.

Daniel: Gespräch von der Verwirklichung. Leipzig: Insel Verlag, 1913.

Deutung des Chassidismus. Berlin: Schocken Verlag, 1935.

Dialogisches Leben: Gesammelte Philosophische und Pädagogische Schriften. Zurich: Gregor Müller Verlag, 1947.

Ekstatische Konfessionen. Jena: Eugen Diedrichs Verlag, 1909.

Ereignisse und Begegnungen. Leipzig: Insel Verlag, 1917.

Die Frage an den Einzelnen. Berlin: Schocken Verlag, 1936.

Die Geschichten des Rabbi Nachman. Cologne: Jakob Hegner Verlag, 1955.

Hinweise, Gesammelte Schriften (1910–53). Zurich: Manesse Verlag, 1953.

Ich und Du. Leipzig: Insel Verlag, 1923.

Der Jude und Sein Judentum: Gesammelte Aufsätze und Reden. Cologne: Joseph Melzer Verlag, 1963.

Kampf um Israel: Reden und Schriften (1921–1932). Berlin: Schocken Verlag, 1933.

Die Legende des Baalschem. Frankfurt am Main: Rütten & Loening, 1908.

Mein Weg zum Chassidismus: Erinnerungen. Frankfurt am Main: Rütten & Loening, 1918.

Der Mensch und sein Gebild. Heidelberg: Verlag Lambert Schneider, 1955.

Nachlese. Heidelberg: Verlag Lambert Schneider, 1964.

Pfade in Utopia. Heidelberg: Verlag Lambert Schneider, 1950.

Das Problem des Menschen. Heidelberg: Verlag Lambert Schneider, 1948.

Reden über das Judentum. Frankfurt am Main: Rütten & Loening, 1923.

Reden über Erziehung. Heidelberg: Verlag Lambert Schneider, 1953.

Die Schriften über das Dialogische Prinzip. Heidelberg: Verlag Lambert Schneider, 1954.

Schuld und Schuldgefühle. Heidelberg: Verlag Lambert Schneider, 1958.

Die Stunde und die Erkenntnis: Reden und Aufsätze, 1933–35. Berlin: Schocken Verlag, 1936.

Urdistanz und Beziehung. Heidelberg: Verlag Lambert Schneider, 1951.

Werke: I Schriften zur Philosophie, 1962; *II Schriften zur Bibel,* 1964; *III Schriften zum Chassidismus,* 1963. Munich, Heidelberg.

Worte an die Jugend. Berlin: Schocken Verlag, 1938.

Worte und die Zeit. Vol. 1: *Grundsätze;* vol. 2: *Gemeinschaft.* München: Dreianderverlag, 1919.

Zion als Ziel und Aufgabe. Berlin: Schocken Verlag, 1936.

Zwischen Gesellschaft und Staat. Heidelberg: Verlag Lambert Schneider, 1952.

In English Translation

At the Turning: Three Addresses on Judaism. New York: Farrar, Straus and Young, 1952.

A Believing Humanism: My Testament, 1902–1965. Translated with an Introduction and Explanatory Comments by Maurice Friedman. New York: Simon and Schuster, 1967.

Between Man and Man. Translated by Ronald Gregor Smith. London: Routledge and Kegan Paul, 1947.

Daniel: Dialogues on Realization. Translated with Introduction by Maurice Friedman. New York: Holt, Rinehart and Winston, 1964.

Eclipse of God: Studies in the Relation between Religion and Philosophy. Translated by Maurice S. Friedman et al. New York: Harper and Brothers, 1952.

For the Sake of Heaven. Translated by L. Lewisohn. Philadelphia: The Jewish Publication Society, 1945.

Good and Evil: Two Interpretations. New York: Charles Scribner's Sons, 1953.

Hasidism. New York: The Philosophical Library, 1948.

Hasidism and Modern Man. Translated and edited by Maurice S. Friedman. New York: Horizon Press, 1958.

I and Thou. Translated by Ronald Gregor Smith. Edinburgh: T. and T. Clark, 1937.

Images of Good and Evil. Translated by Michael Bullock. London: Routledge and Kegan Paul, 1952.

Israel and Palestine: The History of Idea. Translated by Stanley Godman. London: East and West Library, 1952.

Israel and the World: Essays in a Time of Crisis. New York: Schocken Books, 1948.

Kingship of God. Translated by Richard Scheimann. London: Allen and Unwin, 1965.

The Knowledge of Man. Edited with an Introductory Essay by Maurice Friedman. Translated by Maurice Friedman and Ronald Gregor Smith. New York: Harper and Row, 1966.

The Legend of the Baal-Shem. Translated by Maurice S. Friedman. London: East and West Library, 1955.

Mamre: Essays in Religion. Translated by Greta Hort. Melbourne and London: Melbourne University Press and Oxford University Press, 1946.

Moses: The Revelation and the Covenant. New York: Harper Torch Books, 1958.

On Judaism. Edited by Nahum N. Glazer. Translated by Eva Jospe et al. New York: Schocken Books, 1967.

The Origin and Meaning of Hasidism. Translated and edited by Maurice S. Friedman. New York: Horizon Press, 1960.

Paths in Utopia. Translated by R. F. C. Hull. London: Routledge and Kegan Paul, 1949.

Pointing the Way: Collected Essays. Translated by Maurice S. Friedman. London: Routledge and Kegan Paul, 1956.

The Prophetic Faith. Translated by Carlyle Witton-Davies. Nw York: The Macmillan Co., 1949.

Tales of Rabbi Nachman. Translated by Maurice Friedman. Bloomington, Ind.: Indiana University Press, 1962.

Tales of the Hasidim: The Early Masters. Translated by Olga Marx. New York: Schocken Books, 1961.

Tales of the Hasidim: The Later Masters. Translated by Olga Marx. New York: Schocken Books, 1961.

Ten Rungs: Hasidic Sayings. Translated by Olga Marx. New York: Schocken Books, 1962.

The Ways of Man According to the Teaching of Hasidism. London: Routledge and Kegan Paul, 1950.

Two Types of Faith. Translated by Norman P. Goldhawk. London: Routledge and Kegan Paul, 1951.

In Hebrew

Be-fardes ha-hasidut [In the Chassidic orchard]. Jerusalem and Tel-Aviv: Mosad Bialik and Devir, 1963.

Be-mashber ha-ruakh: Shelosha neumim al ha-yahadut [The crisis of spirit: Three addresses about Judaism]. Jerusalem: Mosad bialik, 1953.

Be-sod siah: Al ha-adam ve-amidato nokhah ha-havaya [Dialogue: On man and his encounter with existence]. Jerusalem: Mosad Bialik, 1964.

Darko shel adam al-pi torat ha-hasidut [The way of man according to the teaching of Hasidism]. Jerusalem: Mosad Bialik, 1957.

Darko shel mikra [The way of the Bible]. Jerusalem: Mosad Bialik, 1964.

Gog u-Magog [Gog and Magog]. Jerusalem: Sifrei Tarshish, 1944.

Ha-ruah ve-ha-metsiyut [Spirit and reality]. Tel-Aviv: Mahbarot lesifrut, 1952.

Malkhut shmaiim [The kingdom of heaven]. Jerusalem: Mosad Bialik, 1967.

Moshe [Moses]. Jerusalem: Schocken, 1963.

Netivot be-utopia [Paths in utopia]. Tel-Aviv: Am Oved, 1947.

Olelot [Gleanings]. Jerusalem: Mosad Bialik, 1966.

Or ha-ganuz [The hidden light]. Jerusalem and Tel-Aviv: Schocken, 1958.

Pegishot: zikhronot [Encounters: Recollections]. Jerusalem: Mosad Bialik, 1965.

Pnei-adam: Behinot be-antropologia filosofit [The face of man: Studies in anthropological philosophy]. Jerusalem: Mosad Bialik, 1962.

Teuda ve-yiud [Mission and purpose]. Jerusalem: Ha-sifria ha-Tsionit, 1961.
Torat ha-neviim [The doctrine of the prophets]. Tel-Aviv: Mosad Bialik, 1950.

WORKS ABOUT MARTIN BUBER

Books

Balthasar, Hans Urs von. *Martin Buber and Christianity*. Translated by Alexander Dru. London: Harvill Press, 1961.

Ben-Chorin, Schalom. *Zwiesprach mit Martin Buber*. Ein Erinnerungsbuch. Munich: List Verlag, 1966.

Berkovits, Elieser. *Studies in Torah Judaism: A Jewish Critique of the Philosophy of Martin Buber*. New York: Yeshiva University, 1962.

Berl, Heinrich. *Martin Buber und die Wiedergeburt des Judentums aus dem Geiste der Mystik*. Heidelberg, 1924.

Cohen, Arthur. *Martin Buber*. London: Bowes and Bowes, 1957.

Diamond, Malcolm. *Martin Buber, Jewish Existentialist*. New York: Oxford University Press, 1960.

Friedman, Maurice S. *Martin Buber: The Life of Dialogue*. London: Routledge and Kegan Paul, 1955.

————, ed. *Martin Buber and the Theater*. New York: Funk and Wagnalls, 1969.

Goldstein, Walter. *Begegnung mit Martin Buber*. Jerusalem: Edition Dr. Peter Freund, 1943.

————. *Der Glaube Martin Bubers*. Jerusalem: R. Mass, 1969.

————. *Jean-Paul Sartre and Martin Buber: Eine Vergleichende Betrachtung von Existentialismus und Dialogik*. Jerusalem: R. Mass, 1965.

————. *Martin Buber: Gespräche, Briefe, Worte*. Jerusalem: R. Mass, 1967.

Hodes, Aubrey. *Encounter with Martin Buber*. London: Allen Lane; The Penguin Press, 1972.

Kohn, Hans. *Martin Buber, sein Werk und seine Zeit: Ein Versuch über Religion und Politik*. Hellerau: Jacob Hegner Verlag, 1930.

Martin Buber: An Appreciation of His Life and Thought. New York: American Friends of the Hebrew University, 1965.

Martin Buber: L'homme et le philosophe. Centre National des Hautes Etudes Juives. Brussels: Editions de l'Institut de Sociologie de l'Université Libre de Bruxelles, 1968.

Michel, Wilhelm. *Martin Buber: Sein Gang in die Wirklichkeit*. Frankfurt am Main: Rütten & Loening, 1926.

Moore, Donald J. *Martin Buber, Prophet of Religious Secularism*. Philadelphia: The Jewish Publication Society of America, 1974.

Oldham, Joseph Houldsworth. *Real Life Is Meeting*. New York: The Macmillan Co., 1974.

Oliver, Roy. *The Wanderer and the Way*. (The Hebrew Tradition in the Writings of Martin Buber). London: East and West Library, 1968.

Pfeutze, Paul. *Self, Society, Existence*. New York: Harper and Row, 1961.

————. *The Social Self in the Writings of George Herbert Mead and Martin Buber.* New York: Bookman Associates, 1954.

Schaeder, Grete. *The Hebrew-Humanism of Martin Buber.* Translated by Noah Jacobs. Detroit: Wayne State University Press, 1973.

Schaeder, Grete. *Martin Buber: Hebräischer Humanismus.* Göttingen: Vandenhoek & Ruprecht, 1966.

Schilpp, Paul Arthur, and Friedman, Maurice. *The Philosophy of Martin Buber.* The Library of Living Philosophers. London: Cambridge University Press, 1967.

Simon, Charlie May. *Martin Buber: Wisdom in Our Time.* New York: E. P. Dutton and Co., 1969.

Smith, Ronald Gregor. *Martin Buber.* Richmond, Va.: John Knox Press, 1967.

Streiker, Lowell D. *The Promise of Buber.* Philadelphia: J. P. Lippincott Co., 1969.

Articles

Agus, Jacob. *Modern Philosophies of Judaism.* New York: Behrmans Jewish Book House, 1940. Pp. 213–79.

Allentuck, M. "Martin Buber's Aesthetic Theories: Some Reflections," *Journal of Aesthetics and Art Criticism* 30, 1, Fall 1971.

Ames, V. M. "Buber and Mead." *Antioch Review* 27 (Summer 1967):181–91.

Auerbach, Ch. "Reflections on Martin Buber," *Central Conference of American Rabbis Journal* 14 (New York, 1967):28–64.

Balthasar, Hans Urs von. "Martin Buber and Christianity." In *The Philosophy of Martin Buber,* edited by P. A. Schilpp and M. Friedman, pp. 341–60. London: Cambridge University Press, 1967.

Barrett, William. *Irrational Man: A Study of Existential Philosophy.* New York: Doubleday and Co., 1962. Pp. 3–22, 73–79.

Beerman, R. "Soviet-Jewish Philosophers: Existentialism and Buber." *Bulletin on Soviet Jewish Affairs* 3 (1969):20–24.

Berdyaev, Nicholas. *Solitude and Society.* Translated from the Russian by George Reavey. London: Geoffrey Bles, 1938. Pp. 72, 79–85.

Bergman, Samuel Hugo. "Martin Buber: Life as Dialogue." In *Faith and Reason: An Introduction to Modern Jewish Thought,* pp. 81–97. New York: Schocken Books, 1973.

————. "Martin Buber and Mysticism." In *The Philosophy of Martin Buber,* edited by P. A. Schilpp and M. Friedman, pp. 297–308. London: Cambridge University Press, 1967.

Berkovits, Eliezer. "God's Silence in the Dialogue According to Martin Buber." *Tradition* 2 (1970):17–24.

Birnbaum, R. "Baruch Spinoza, Martin Buber: Dialectic and Dialogue." *Person* 84 (1967):119–28.

Blau, Joseph L. "Martin Buber's Religious Philosophy: A Review Article." *Review of Religion* 13 (1948):48–64.

Borouity, E. B. "Education Is Not I-Thou." *Religious Education* 66 (1971):326–31.

Borowitz, E. B. "Two Modern Approaches to God." *Jewish Heritage,* Fall 1963, pp. 10–16.

Bowman, C. M. "Martin Buber and the Voluntary Turning." *Religion in Life* 30 (Winter 1960):81–91.

Brod, Max. "Judaism and Christianity in the Work of Martin Buber." In *The Philosophy of Martin Buber,* edited by P. A. Schilpp and M. Friedman, pp. 319–40. London: Cambridge University Press, 1967.

Brunner, Emil. "Judaism and Christianity in Buber." In *The Philosophy of Martin Buber,* edited by P. A. Schilpp and M. Friedman, pp. 309–18. London: Cambridge University Press, 1967.

Clarke, Sir Fred. *Freedom in the Educative Society: Educational Issues of Today,* edited by W. K. Niblett, pp. 56–68. London: University of London Press, 1948.

Cohen, Aharon. "Buber's Zionism and the Arabs. *New Outlook,* September 1966.

Cohen, Arthur A. "Revelation and Law: Reflections on Martin Buber's Views on Halakah." *Judaism* 1 (1952):250–56.

Coates, J. B. *The Crisis of the Human Person: Some Personalist Interpretations.* London: Longmans, Green and Co., 1949. Pp 23f. 32–35, 65–81, 240–48.

Dale, John. "Martin Buber's Semantic Puzzle." *Religious Studies* 6 (1970):253–61.

Diamond, Malcolm L. "Dialogue and Theology." In *The Philosophy of Martin Buber,* edited by P. A. Schilpp and M. Friedman, pp. 235–48. London: Cambridge University Press, 1967.

Downing, Christine R. "Guilt and Responsibility in the Thought of Martin Buber." *Judaism* 18 (1969):53–63.

———. "Theology as Translation." *Religion in Life* 37 (1968):401–16.

Etscovitz, L. "Religious Education as Sacred and Profane: An Interpretation of Martin Buber." *Religious Education* 64 (1969):279–86.

Fackenheim, Emil L. "Martin Buber's Concept of Revelation." In *The Philosophy of Martin Buber,* edited by P. A. Schilpp and M. Friedman, pp. 273–96. London: Cambridge University Press, 1967.

———. "Some Recent Works by and on Martin Buber." *Religious Education* 54 (1959):413–17.

Farber, Leslie H. "Martin Buber and Psychotherapy. In *The Philosophy of Martin Buber,* edited by P. A. Schilpp and M. Friedman, pp. 577–602. London: Cambridge University Press, 1967.

Fox, E. "The Buber-Rosenzweig Translation of the Bible." *Response* 5, no. 3 (1971–72):29–42.

Fox, Marvin. "Some Problems in Buber's Moral Philosophy." In *The Philosophy of Martin Buber,* edited by P. A. Schilpp and M. Friedman, pp. 151–70. London: Cambridge University Press, 1967.

Frankenstein, Carl. "Buber's Theory of Dialogue: A Critical Re-examination." *Cross Currents* 18 (1968):229–41.

Friedman, Maurice S. "Martin Buber and Christian Thought." *Review of Religion* 18 (November 1953):31–43.

———. "Martin Buber at Seventy-Five." *Religion in Life* 23, no. 3 (1954):405–17.

———. "Martin Buber's Challenge to Jewish Philosophy." *Judaism* 14 (1965):267–76.

———. "Martin Buber's Concept of Education: A New Approach to College Teaching." *Christian Scholar* 40 (1957):109–16.

———. "Martin Buber's Encounter with Mysticism." *Human Inquiries* 10 (1970):43–80.

———. "Martin Buber's New View of Evil." *Judaism* 2, no. 3 (July 1953):239–46.

———. "Martin Buber, Prophet and Philosopher." *Faith Today* 1, no. 5 (December–January 1954–55):

———. "Martin Buber's Theology and Religious Education." *Religious Education* 54 (1959):5–17.

———. "Martin Buber's Theory of Knowledge." *Review of Metaphysics,* December 1954.

———. "Martin Buber's View of Biblical Faith." *The Journal of Bible and Religion* 22 (1954):3–13.

———. "Revelation and Law in the Thought of Martin Buber." *Judaism* 3 (1954):9–19.

———. "Revelation and Reason in Buber's Philosophy of Religion." *Bucknell Review* 18 (1970):69–77.

———. "Symbol, Myth and History in the Thought of Martin Buber." *Journal of Religion* 34 (1954):1–11.

———. "The Bases of Buber's Ethics." In *The Philosophy of Martin Buber,* edited by P. A. Schilpp and M. Friedman, pp. 171–200. London: Cambridge University Press, 1967.

———. "What Is Common to All," *Review of Metaphysics* 2 (1958):359–79.

Glatzer, Nahum N. "Buber as an Interpreter of the Bible." In *The Philosophy of Martin Buber,* edited by P. A. Schilpp and M. Friedman, pp. 361–80. London: Cambridge University Press, 1967.

Goldberger, E. "Dialogue with Martin Buber." *Congress Bi-Weekly* 30 (1963):10–12.

Golffing, F. C. "Israel's Land: Habitation of God." *Commentary* 12 (1951):345–54.

Gordon, Haim. "Would Martin Buber Endorse the Buber Model?" *Educational Theory* 23, no. 3 (Summer 1973):215–23.

Gutch, Kenneth U., and Rosenblatt, Howard S. "Counselor Education: A Touch of Martin Buber's Philosophy." *Counselor Education and Supervision* 13 (1973):8–13.

Halio, Jay L. "The Life of Dialogue in Education," *The Journal of General Education* 14 (1963):213–19.

Hammer, Louis Z. "The Relevance of Buber's Thought to Aesthetics." *The Philosophy of Martin Buber,* edited by P. A. Schilpp and M. Friedman, pp. 609–28. London: Cambridge University Press, 1967.

Hartshorne, Charles. "Martin Buber's Metaphysics," *The Philosophy of Martin Buber,* edited by P. A. Schilpp and M. Friedman, pp. 49–68. London: Cambridge University Press, 1967.

Heiman, L. "God Is My Telephone Operator: An Interview with Martin Buber on His 85th Birthday." *Jewish Digest* 8 (1963):9–14.

Herberg, Will. *Judaism and Modern Man: An Interpretation of Jewish Religion.* New York: Farrar, Straus and Young, 1951.

Hillard, F. H. "A Re-examination of Buber's Address on Education." *British Journal of Educational Studies* 21 (1973):40–49.

Hodes, Aubrey. "The Arab-Jewish Rapprochement: Buber's Plea for Arab-Jewish Understanding." *The Wiener Library Bulletin* 23 (1968–69):16–23.

Jacob, W. "Inter-Religious." *Jewish Heritage,* Fall 1963, pp. 31–35.

Kaplan, Edward K. "Bachelard and Buber: From Aesthetics to Religion." *Judaism* 19 (1970):465–67.

Kaplan, Mordechai M. "Buber's Evaluation of Philosophy, Thought and Religious Tradition." In *The Philosophy of Martin Buber,* edited by P. A. Schilpp and M. Friedman, pp. 249–72. London: Cambridge University Press, 1967.

———. "Martin Buber, Theologian, Philosopher and Prophet." *The Reconstructionist,* May 2, 1952.

Kaufmann, Fritz. "Martin Buber's Philosophy of Religion." In *The Philosophy of Martin Buber,* edited by P. A. Schilpp and M. Friedman, pp. 201–340. London: Cambridge University Press, 1967.

Kaufman, Walter. "Buber's Religious Significance." In *The Philosophy of Martin Buber,* edited by P. A. Schilpp and M. Friedman, pp. 665–85. London: Cambridge University Press, 1967.

Kegley, Charles W. "Buber's Ethics and the Problem of Norms." *Religious Studies* 5 (1969):181–94.

Kerenyi, Carl. "Martin Buber as Classical Author." In *The Philosophy of Martin Buber,* edited by P. A. Schilpp and M. Friedman, pp. 629–38. London: Cambridge University Press, 1967.

Kiner, Eduard Davis. "Some Problems in a Buber Model for Teaching." *Educational Theory* 19 (1969):369–403.

Kohanski, Alexander S. "Martin Buber's Restructuring of Society into a State of Anocracy." *Jewish Social Studies* 34 (1972):42–57.

Kohn, H."Religious Philosophy of Martin Buber." *Menorah Journal* 26 (1938): 173–85.

Koo, Gladys Y. "The Structure And Process of Self." *Educational Theory 14 (1964): 111.17.*

Kraut, Benny. "The Approach to Jewish Law of Martin Buber and Franz Rosenzweig." Tradition: A Journal of Orthodox Thought 12 (1972): 49–71.

Kuhn, Helmut. "Dialogue in Expectation. In *The Philosophy of Martin Buber* edited by P. A. Schilpp and M. Friedman, pp. 639–64. London: Cambridge University Press, 1967.

Kurzweil, Z. E. *Modern Trends in Jewish Education.* New York: Thomas Yoseloff, 1964. Pp. 220–43.

Levinas, Emmanuel. "Martin Buber and the Theory of Knowledge." In *The Philosophy of Martin Buber,* edited by P. A. Schilpp and M. Friedman, pp. 133–50. London: Cambridge University Press, 1967.

Lewis, H. D. "I and Thou." *Hibbert Journal,* 48 (1950): 380–82.

———. "The Elusive Self and the I-Thou Relation." *Royal Institute of Philosophy Lectures 2 (1969): 168–84.*

Lewis, T. N. "The Kingship of God." Dimensions 2 (Summer 1968): 56.

Lewisohn, L. "Martin Buber." *Menorah Journal* 12 (Fall 1926): 65–70.

Liptzin, Solomon. *Germany's Stepchildren.* Philadelphia: The Jewish Publication Society of America, 1944. Pp. 255–69.

Lyon, J. K. "Paul Celan and Martin Buber: Poetry as Dialogue." *Publications of the Modern Language Association of America* 86 (1971): 110–20.

McDermott, John. "Martin Buber and Hans Urs von Balthasar," *Cross Currents* 13 (1963): 115–21.

McNeill, J. J. "Martin Buber's Biblical Philosophy of History." *International Philosophical Quarterly* 6 (March 1966): 90–100.

Marcel, Gabriel. "I and Thou." In *The Philosophy of Martin Buber*, edited by P. A. Schilpp and M. Friedman, pp. 41–48. London: Cambridge University Press, 1967.

Martin, Bernard. *Great 20th Century Jewish Philosophers* (Shestov, Rosenzweig, Buber). New York: The Macmillan Co., 1970. Pp. 238–334.

———. "Martin Buber and 20th Century Judaism." *Central Conference of American Rabbis*. New York, 1967., Pp. 149–64.

May, H. S. "Martin Buber and Mohammed Iqbal, Two Poets of East and West." *Judaism* 18 (1969): 177–87.

Meter, A. "Buber and Mead." *The Antioch Review* 27 (1967): 181–91.

Misrahi, Robert. "The Dialogue in Practice." *New Outlook,* Octoboer–November 1966

Moran, J. A. "Martin Buber and Taoism." *Judaism* 21 (1972): 98–103.

Mullins, James. "The Problem of the Individual in the Philosophies of Dewey and Buber." *Educational Theory* 17 (1967): 76–82.

Oliver, R. "The Baal Shem's New-Year's Sermon: The Hasidic Source of a Key Phrase in the Writings of Martin Buber." *Jewish Quarterly* 20 (1972): 9–13.

Petras, J. W. "God, Man and Society: The Perspectives of Buber and Kierkegaard." *The Journal of Religious Thought* 27 (Washington, 1966–67): 119–28.

Pfuetze, Paul E. "Martin Buber and American Pragmatism." In *The Philosophy of Martin Buber,* edited by P. A. Schilpp and M. Friedman, pp. 511–42. London: Cambridge University Press, 1967.

———. "Martin Buber and Jewish Mysticism." *Religion in Life* 16 (1947): 553–67.

Potok, Ch. "Martin Buber and the Jews." *Commentary* 41, no. 3 (1966): 43–49.

Ramana, Murti V. V. "Buber's Dialogue and Gandhi's Salgagraha." *Journal of the History of Ideas* 29 (New York, 1968): 605–13.

Read, Herbert. *Education through Art.* London: Faber and Faber, Pp. 279–302.

Reeves, Marjorie. *Growing Up in a Modern Society.* London: University of London Press, 1946. Pp. 9–12, 34–38.

Reiner, J. "Religion in the Secular World: Notes on Martin Buber and Radical Theology." *Response* 2 (1968): 3–17.

Rosenblatt, H. S. "Martin Buber's Concepts Applied to Education." *The Educational Forum* 35 (1971): 215–28.

Rotenstreich, Nathan. "The Right and the Limitations of Buber's Dialogical Thought." In *The Philosophy of Martin Buber,* edited by P. A. Schilpp and M. Friedman, pp. 97–132. London: Cambridge University Press, 1967.

Rudovsky, David. "Martin Buber's Existentialism: Sources, Influences and Interpretations." *Journal of Hebraic Studies* 1 (1969): 41–59.

———. "The Neo-Hasidism of Martin Buber." *Religious Education* 62 (New York, 1967): 235–44.

Santmire, Paul H. "I-Thou, I-It, and I-Es." *Journal of Religion* 48 (1968): 260–73.

Schatz Uffenheimer, Rivkah. "Man's Relation to God and World in Buber's Rendering of the Hasidic Teaching." In *The Philosophy of Martin Buber*, edited by P. A. Schilpp and M. Friedman, pp. 403–34. London: Cambridge University Press, 1967.

Schneider, Herbert W. "The Historical Significance of Buber's Philosophy." In *The Philosophy of Martin Buber*, edited by P. A. Schilpp and M. Friedman, pp. 469–74. London: Cambridge University Press, 1967.

Schreiber, M. "Rav Kuk and M. Buber on Teshuvah." *Central Conference of American Rabbis Journal* 16, no. 3 (1969): 31–35.

Schulweis, H. S. "Buber's Broken Dialogue." *Reconstructionist* 38 (October 1972): 7–12.

Scudder, J. R., Jr. "Freedom with Authority: A Buber Model for Teaching." *Educational Theory*, Spring 1968, pp. 133–42.

Shestov, L. "Martin Buber," *Central Conference of American Rabbis Journal* 15, no. 2 (1968): 44–53.

Simon, Ernst. "Buber or Ben-Gurion?" *New Outlook*, September 1966.

———. "From Dialogue to Peace." *Jerusalem Post*, 18 June 1965.

———. "Jewish Adult Education in Nazi Germany as Spiritual Resistance." In *Leo Baeck Institute Year Book, 1965*, pp. 68–104. London: East and West Library.

———. "Martin Buber and German Jewry." In *Leo Baeck Institute Year Book*, 1958, pp. 3–39. London: East and West Library.

———. "Martin Buber: His Way between Thought and Deed." *Jewish Frontier* 15, no. 2 (February 1948): 25–28.

———. "Martin Buber, the Educator." In *The Philosophy of Martin Buber*, edited by P. A. Schilpp and M. Friedman, pp. 543–76. London: Cambridge University Press, 1967.

Simon, H. A. "Martin Buber and the Law, *Central Conference of American Rabbis Journal* 18, no. 2 (1971): 40–44.

Sloyan, Gerald. "Buber and the Significance of Jesus." *The Bridge* 3 (1958): 209–33.

Slusher, H. S. "Philosophical Foundation for Motivation of Community Health Education." *The Journal of School Health* 33 (1963): 353–60.

Smith, C. I. "Single One and the Other." *Hibbert Journal* 46 (1948): 315–21.

Smith, Ronald Gregor. "Distance and Relations." *Hibbert Journal* 49 (1951): 105–13.

———. "Magic Gnosis and Faith." *Christian Scholar* 48 (Winter 1965): 304–8.

———. "Martin Buber's View of the Inter-human." *The Jewish Journal of Sociology* 8 (London, 1966): 64–80.

———. "Religion of Martin Buber." *Theology Today* 12 (1955): 206–15.

Spear, O. "Martin Buber on Nations and World Peace." *Universita* 13 (1971): 269–76.

Stevenson, W. T. "I-Thou and I-It: An Attempted Clarification of Their Relationship." *Journal of Religion* 43 (1963): 193–209.

Taubes, Jacob. "Buber and Philosophy of History." In *The Philosophy of Martin Buber*, edited by P. A. Schilpp and M. Friedman, pp. 435–50. London: Cambridge University Press, 1967.

Tepfer, John J. "Martin Buber and New-Mysticism." In *Yearbook of the Central Conference of American Rabbis, 1934,* pp. 203–19.

Tillich, P. "Martin Buber and Christian Thought; His Threefold Contribution to Protestantism." *Commentary* 5 (1948): 515–21.

Vermes, Pamela. "Martin Buber, A New Appraisal." *Journal of Jewish Studies* 22 (1971): 78–96.

Vogel, M. "Concept of Responsibility in the Thought of Martin Buber." *The Harvard Theological Review* 63 (1970): 159–82.

Wahl, Jean. "Martin Buber and the Philosophies of Existence." In *The Philosophy of Martin Buber,* edited by P. A. Schilpp and M. Friedman, pp. 475–510. London: Cambridge University Press, 1967.

Weizsacker, Carl F. von. "I-Thou and I-It in the Contemporary Natural Sciences." In *The Philosophy of Martin Buber,* edited by P. A. Schilpp and M. Friedman, pp. 603–8. London: Cambridge University Press, 1967.

Weltsch, Robert. "Buber's Political Philosophy." in *The Philosophy of Martin Buber,* edited by P. A. Schilpp and M. Friedman, pp. 435–50. London: Cambridge University Press, 1967.

Wheelwright, Philip. "Buber's Philosophical Anthropology." In *The Philosophy of Martin Buber,* edited by P. A. Schilpp and M. Friedman, pp. 69–95. London: Cambridge University Press, 1967.

Williams, D. D. "Martin Buber and Christian Thought," *Central Conference of American Rabbis* 76 (New York, 1967): 165–78.

Winetrout, Kenneth. "Buber: Philosopher of the I-Thou Dialogue." *Educational Theory* 13 (1963): 53–57.

Wolf, Ernst M. "Martin Buber and German Jewry, Prophet and Teacher to a Generation in Catastrophe." *Judaism* 1, no. 4 (1952): 346–52.

Zeigler, Leslie. "Personal Existence: A Study of Buber and Kierkegaard." *Journal of Religion* 40 (April 1960): 80–94.

Index

271